P9-CDX-082

RANDOM
HOUSE
LARGE
PRINT

A Year *in the* World

Frances
Mayes
RANDOM HOUSE
LARGE PRINT

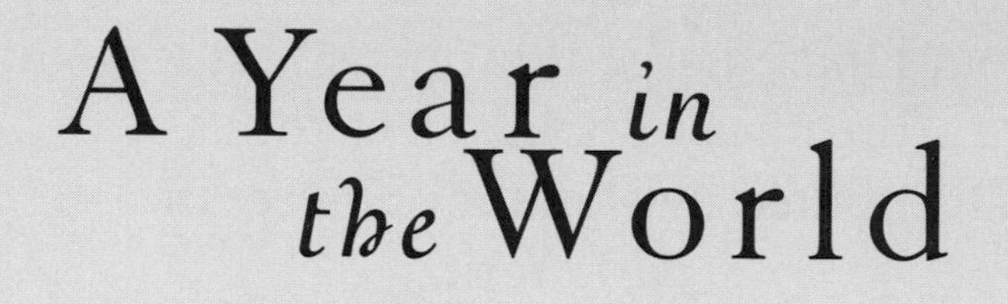

A Year *in the* World

Journeys of a *Passionate* Traveller

Published in the United States of America by
Random House Large Print in association with
Broadway Books, New York.
Distributed by Random House, Inc.,
New York.

Pages 000–000 constitute an extension of
this copyright page.

Title page photograph by Frances Mayes
Endpapers map by Laura Hartman Maestro

**The Library of Congress has established a
Cataloging-in-Publication record for
this title.**

ISBN-13: 978-0-7393-2592-6
ISBN-10: 0-7393-2592-2

www.randomlargeprint.com

FIRST LARGE PRINT EDITION

10 9 8 7 6 5 4 3 2 1

This Large Print edition published in accord
with the standards of the N.A.V.H.

To the couple standing in the middle of the autostrada beside their jackknifed camper.

To the mother and two-year-old boy in seats 42 A and B during the ninth hour of flight.

To the family of six crossing Europe in a Deux Cheveaux singing "Blessed Be the Ties That Bind."

To the small girl screaming on the floor of the trattoria at eleven P.M.

To K.A.T. who said "Good, now I've been and don't have to go again."

To the forgotten new yellow panties and bra left drying on the rim of the hotel bathtub.

To the captain diving into waving algae in search of the dropped scuba mask.

To the suitcase that went to India.

To T.A., who couldn't open the train door and rode on to Castiglion Fiorentino.

To the Southern man limping through Pienza calling to his wife, "I've seen all I want to see."

To the character described by Novalis, who went off to find a blue flower seen in a dream.

To Edward—with you I will go.

Contents

Acknowledgments

We found many friends during these travels and for friendship I am always most grateful. Special thanks to Fulvio, Aurora, and Edoardo Di Rosa, Carlos Lopes, Enver Lucas (Geographic Expeditions), Lori Woods, Susan MacDonald, Cole Dalton, Kate Abbe, Robin and John Heyeck, the Mavromihalis family, Steven Rothfeld, Bernice and Armand Thieblot, Riccardo Bertocci, Maria Ida and Salvatore Avallone of Villa Matilde, Rachid Tabib, Hafid El Amrani, Guvan Demir, and Lina Bartelli. My abiding love to all the writers whose works enriched my travels and stretched my worldview.

Peter Ginsberg of Curtis Brown Ltd., my agent, shares my love of travel, as does Charlie Conrad, my editor at Broadway Books. Both have given me their enthusiasm and expert guidance. I am lucky to work with them, and

with their staffs. My thanks also go to Francesca Liversidge at Transworld; Dave Barbor, for international publications; Terry Karydes, for the design of this book; Laura Maestro, for the map of my travels, and to my publicists, Joanna Pinsker and Rachel Rokicki. Catherine Pollock and Alison Presley brought their ideas and attention to this book. To Steven Barclay of the Steven Barclay Agency, a grand bacione. **May we all toast our travels together soon.**

The wild seed of this book took root long ago, and I offer mille grazie **to my father, who said the family motto should be "Packing and Unpacking," and to my mother, who always said, "Go."**

Preface

Cupolas of Alghero

. . . we are words on a journey
not the inscriptions of settled
people.

—W. S. Merwin

The silhouette of Alghero rises from the Mediterranean. My husband, Ed, and I are walking toward town just after noon, when sunlight slips straight through the clean water, rippling the white bottom of the sea with ribbons of light.

"Limpida," he says, **"chiara."** Limpid, clear, the slow tide pushing light in bright arcs across the sandy floor. Alghero, nominally an Italian town on the western edge of Sardinia, has colorful geometric-tiled cupolas, Catalan street names, Arabic flourishes in the cuisine. I feel a sudden attraction to Spain, to exotic Moorish courtyards, fountains that soothed those desert invaders, to the memory of a Latin man who once whispered to me, "Please, share my darkness in Barcelona." A desire for some fierce, unnameable, dour, and dignified essence of Spain. I imagine walking **there**, along a whitewashed wall, peeling an orange, a book of Lorca's poems in my pocket.

"I'd like to taste the last drop," I say, a non sequitur.

Ed is not bothered by non sequiturs. He just picks up on the word **taste**. "We're going to a trattoria where they specialize in lobster with tomatoes and onions. Sounds delicious—**aragosta all'algherese**—lobster from these waters cooked in the style of Alghero." He consults a piece of paper where he has written an address. "And yes, I know what you mean."

"What if we didn't go home? What if we just kept travelling? The European writers always had their **Wanderjahr**, their year of wandering in their youth. I'd like one of those, even at this late date."

"Probably better now than when you were young. Where do you want to go?"

"How far **are** we from Spain?"

"I must mention that I have a job." He points to a hump of land. "Neptune's Grotto—we'll take a boat out there after lunch. I would like to go to Morocco," he adds.

"Greece was the first foreign place I ever wanted to see and I've never been." A map of the world unscrolls in my mind, the one I looked at when I was ten in a small town in Georgia. Bright flags line the sides of the map, and the countries are saffron, lavender, rose, and mint according to their altitude and geology. Sweden. Poland. The Basque country. India. Then I shift into an explosion of images: I'm threading my way through the spice bazaar in Istanbul, assaulted by hot scents rising from sacks of fenugreek, turmeric, gnarly roots, and dried seeds; we're leaning on the railing of a slow boat when a crocodile splats its tail in the murky green waters of the Nile; Ed is shaking out a picnic cloth as I look into the green dips and curves of a valley punctuated with cromlechs and dolmens; I'm driving past a marsh, russet in autumn light, and I recognize the barrier island off the coast of Georgia, one of the Golden Isles, where I spent summer vacations as a child.

That archipelago was the first place I ever

longed for. During the rainy winter months of my childhood, sometimes mercurial sensations of the island came to me in a rush—humid, salty air catches in my hair, the saw palmettos clatter in the torrid breezes of August, and my hand sweats in our cook Willie Bell's hand as we walk toward a low bridge, where she will lower a crab trap baited with "high" meat into black water. I ached **not** to be in Miss Golf's first-grade classroom, where the floors smelled of pine oil and sawdust and the little letters followed the big letters in colored chalk around the room. I wanted the firm feel of Willie Bell's hand, the horror of rotting raw meat in the crab trap, sunrises on the beach, and the long walk back to the house on the crushed oyster shell path.

At six, that sensation was a tide, a rhythm, a hurt, a joy. This powerful **first** sensation of a place I have come to know well because I've kept it all my life, just as I've kept square thumbnails and insomnia. One of my favorite writers, Freya Stark, acknowledged a similar feeling in **The Valley of the Assassins**: "It shone clearly distinct in the evening light, an impressive sight to the pilgrim. I contemplated it with the feelings due to an object that still has the power to make one travel so far." Her **it** being anything that pulls us hard enough so that we take the passport from the drawer, pack the minimum, and head out the door with an instinct as sure as that of an ancient huntress with quiver and bow.

The urge to travel feels magnetic. Two of my favorite words are linked: **departure time**. And travel whets the emotions, turns upside down the memory bank, and the golden coins scatter. How my mother would have loved the mansard apartment we borrowed from a friend in Paris. Will I be lucky enough to show pieces of the great world to my grandchild? I'm longing to hold his hand when he first steps into a gondola. I've seen his freedom burst upon him on hikes in California. Arms out, he runs forward. I recognize the surge.

Sardinia—the real name: Sardegna. I have wanted to come here since I read D. H. Lawrence's **Sea and Sardinia** years ago in a blank hotel room in Zurich. "It is a small, stony, hen-scratched place of poor people," I read. And "In we roll, into Orosei, a dilapidated, sun-smitten, god-forsaken little town not far from the sea. We descend to the piazza." **We descend to the piazza**. Yes, that's the sentence I liked. I underlined "sun-smitten" in my paperback book, and as I fell asleep, the noise of Zurich traffic below became these waves I see right now lapping the sea wall.

We have a few days. I will look at all the Moorish tiles. Sample the hard pecorino and goat cheeses. Climb around in the prehistoric village. I will not buy one of the million coral necklaces in the shops. We'll look for wild medlar and myrtle, asphodel and capers on the hillsides.

Ed shades his eyes with the guidebook. He points. "The boat can drop us out there—see the white crescent beach—after we see the grotto of fabulous stalactites. Let's eat," he says. **"Andiamo."** Let's go.

Travel pushes my boundaries. Seemingly self-indulgent, travel paradoxically obliterates me-me-me, because very quickly—**prestissimo**—the own-little-self is unlocked from the present and released to move through layers of time. It is not

2006 all over the world. So who are you in a place where 1950 or 1920 is about to arrive? Or where the guide says, "We're not talking about A.D. today. Everything from now on is B.C." I remember the child who came out of a thatched shack deep in the back roads of Nicaragua. She ran to touch the car, her arms thrown up in wonder. She would have looked at the headlights turn on and off all night.

You are released also because you are insignificant to the life of the new place. When you travel, you become invisible, if you want. I do want. I like to be the observer. What makes these people who they are? Could I feel at home here? No one expects you to have the stack of papers back by Tuesday, or to check messages, or to fertilize the geraniums, or to sit full of dread in the waiting room at the proctologist's office. When travelling, you have the delectable possibility of not understanding a word of what is said to you. Language becomes simply a musical background for watching bicycles zoom along a canal, calling for nothing from you. Even better, if you speak the language, you catch nuances and make more contact with people.

Travel releases spontaneity. You become a

godlike creature full of choice, free to visit the stately pleasure domes, make love in the morning, sketch a bell tower, read a history of Byzantium, stare for one hour at the face of Leonardo da Vinci's **Madonna dei fusi**. You open, as in childhood, and—for a time—receive this world. There's the visceral aspect, too—the huntress who is free. Free to go, free to return home bringing memories to lay on the hearth.

A year after those, yes, sun-smitten days in Sardinia, we are going off to Spain; then we have a list of places in the world we would like to call home, at least for a while. At twenty, it's easy to sling on the backpack and take off. Later, you may find the responsibilities that the years layer onto our bodies and souls to be hard-to-impossible to escape. You have to wrench your circumstances to get out from under them. And my home lulls me. The yellow roses on the table, creamy ironed sheets with my mother's monogram, rabbit with fennel baking in the oven, guests about to arrive, my cat Sister purring against my foot, a sunroom full of books. These profound comforts—the joys of **home**. I'm elated when the Yesterday, Today, Tomorrow starts to bloom, when Ed loads the iron table from the consignment shop on top of the car, and when we cook with good friends—Brunswick stew, cornbread, coconut pie.

The thrown-off remark, **I want to taste the last drop**, will go down in my column of the book kept by the heavenly scribe. How did one sentence send me off into an intense five years of boarding planes, buses, trains, ships? The dream of a travel year became compromised by a complicated life. But the trips, arranged by season, become in this book a single year in the world.

A series of events sharpened my sense of **carpe diem**, making me edgy to go. First a friend's heart attack, then my mother's death, then the stunning horror of breast cancer in nine, **nine**, of my closest friends. Two died. Other less drastic forces began to press. Teaching often swamped my writing. I longed for time. Unscheduled time, dream time, quiet time. Not just summers, when it took a month to recover from the exhausting academic year. **Quit**, I thought.

"You could be dead by evening," I read in Proust. Well, I know that. A potato chip truck can flatten you at any given stoplight—this happened to one friend—but knowledge sometimes slides off and sometimes scores a direct hit. The synergy of our decision to travel sent out sine waves. All fall I looked at maps, saying incredulously, "I always meant to go to Scotland." I read **The White Nile**, **Journey into Cyprus**, the poems of Hikmet, **Mornings in Mexico**, and all the Victorian women travellers who crossed Patagonia or Kaffirland and refused to lift their skirts over mudholes in central Africa. From Colette I copied in my yellow notebook, . . . **nothing can equal the savor of that which has been seen, and truly seen**, and also her evocative sentence, **I'm leaving tonight for Limousin.**

In our **carpe diem** state of mind, we decide to take a big risk and live by our wits. Travel will be tied to a bigger word, **freedom.** We resign from our teaching jobs to work as full-time writers and to explore new possibilities. **Are you crazy? Giving up two tenured university jobs in the Bay Area?** Ed turned in his resignation on Valentine's Day and came home with three dozen yellow roses. We're giddy, then scared, then giddy. Imagine—**time**.

• • •

Everything I pick up seems to lure me away. Everything I do in my daily life begins to feel like striking wet matches.

The need to travel is a mysterious force. A desire to **go** runs through me equally with an intense desire to **stay** at home. An equal and opposite thermodynamic principle. When I travel, I think of home and what it means. At home I'm dreaming of catching trains at night in the gray light of Old Europe, or pushing open shutters to see Florence awaken. The balance just slightly tips in the direction of the airport.

I'm looking out my study window at the San Francisco Bay, the blue framed by stands of eucalyptus trees. The wind, I imagine, blew across Asia, then across Hawaii, bringing—if I could smell deeply enough—a trace of plumeria perfume. The western sun makes a grandiose exit in the smeared lavender-pink sky—a Mrs. Gotrocks gold orb sinking behind sacred Mount

Tamalpais. The bay water, running into the ocean! Washing all the miraculous places. With the force of an earthquake, a wild certainty forms in the center of my forehead. Time. To go. Time. Just go.

I asked an impulsive question, **What if we did not go home, what if we kept travelling?** Should you not listen well to the questions you ask out of nowhere? Only in looking back do you find those crumbs you dropped that marked your way forward.

A Year *in the* World

Blood Oranges
Andalucía

Who cut down the moon's
stem?

(Left us roots
Of water.)
How easy to pluck flowers from
This infinite acacia.

—Federico García Lorca

January, old Janus face looking left at the past year and right toward the new. I'm for the new—no mournful backward glance. **Make tracks**, I write one night on the steamed kitchen window.

The year began with a break-in at my house while my husband and I were finishing dinner. Ed had just tipped the last of a **vino nobile** into our glasses. Laughing, we were talking about the turn of the year, with Nina Simone crooning "The Twelfth of Never" to us. We'd cleared the plates, the candles were burning down, and outside the dining room window we saw only our potted lemon trees, swaying snapdragons, and yellow Carolina jasmine, for January in California is a blessed season.

In a flash, everything changed. A man crashed through the living room window, screaming that he wanted to die, then loomed on the middle of the rug, his bundled body in ski jacket, droopy pants, and homeboy hat pulled down around his moony face. Even as I write this, my heart starts to pound.

"Give me a knife," he shouted. "I've never done this before, but I'm doing it now." I thought, not **does he have a gun will we die**, but **he's goofy**. Then terror pumped through every vein in my body. **This can't be happening!** Somehow, we'd stood up. **Run**. My chair tipped over. He lunged into the dining room. I threw my glass of wine in his face, and as he wiped his eyes, we ran out the back door. "I want to die," he shouted to us as we fled into a street darkened by conscientious neighbors in the middle of the latest corruption-engineered energy crisis. Our house was blazing like the **Titanic**; lights flared in every window. Our intruder had been drawn to us like a fluttering moth toward the screen door on a soft southern night.

Ed grabbed a phone on the way out and somehow called 911 as he sprinted across the street. We ran to separate neighbors, hoping to find someone at home on Saturday night. Startled new Chinese neighbors brought me in and handed me the telephone, though they must have thought I was mad, while the intruder followed Ed across the street to our neighbors Arlene and Dan. Interrupted in the middle of a dinner party, they pulled Ed in and slammed the door. Then our intruder broke through their door—just as the police drove up.

That was the beginning. The drugged young man was on the street again in a month. I found his sunglasses in a flower bed. Expensive. I threw them in the trash. The year rolled on and doesn't bear thinking about. Suffice to say the words **surgery, hospitals, deaths**. As the sublime September weather arrived, we all experienced the mind-altering, world-shaking attack on America. Go, bad year. May the stars realign.

Now, Janus, my friend, I am going to Spain

for a winter month in Andalucía. Andalucía, land of the orange and the olive tree. Land of passionate poets and flamenco dancers and late-night dinners with guitar music in jasmine-scented gardens.

Ed flew to Italy a week ago because, as always, we have some complicated building project in progress. En route to Spain, he has detoured to Bramasole, our house in Cortona, to see about the drilling of a well for a nine-hundred-year-old house we have bought in the mountains. We want to accomplish a historic restoration on this stone house built by hermit monks who followed Saint Francis of Assisi. When I last talked to him, the dowser had felt his stick bend in exactly the spot where I did not want a well and had drilled down a hundred meters without finding a drop. We are planning to meet in Madrid.

From San Francisco, I board a flight to Paris and am happy to see my seatmate take out a book instead of a computer. No white aura and tap-tapping for the ten-hour flight. She looks as if she could have been one of my colleagues at the university. Is she going to Europe to research a fresco cycle or to join an archaeological team at a Roman villa excavation? I take out my own book, ready to escape into silence for the duration. She smiles and asks, "What are you reading?"

"A biography of Federico García Lorca—getting ready for Spain. What are you reading?"

"Oh, a book on John three thirteen."

"Three thirteen. I don't know that verse. We used to sing 'John three sixteen, John three sixteen' in rounds at Methodist Sunday school."

The flight attendant comes by with champagne and orange juice. "Just water," my seatmate and I say in unison. We begin to talk about travel and books, chatting easily, though I am, at first, waiting for a chance to retreat. We know nothing of each other and will part when the scramble to exit at Charles de Gaulle begins.

She asks a lot of questions. I tell her I am a former university teacher, now a full-time writer. I tell her about living part of the year in Italy, and that Italy has given me several books, written with joy. She probes. Are my books published? Are they popular? And if so, do I know why? What do I try to accomplish with my writing? How do I feel about people's responses to my books? On and on. I tell her that I'm embarking on the first of many travels and that I hope to write a book about my experiences. Why? What will I be looking for? I am drawn into lengthy explanations. I say I'm interested in the idea and fact of **home**. I'm going to places where I have dreamed of living and will try to settle down in each, read the literature, look at the gardens, shop for what's in season, try to feel **at home**. I'm talking more openly than usual with a stranger. Is she a psychiatrist?

"And you've never felt God's hand on yours?" She looks quizzically at me.

"No. I've felt lucky, though."

"Maybe you are bringing happiness to people through the will of God. Maybe." She smiles.

She answers my own questions evasively. She is holding something back, even in the basic exchanges, such as whether she is on vacation, that simple opening into conversation. Our little equation is out of balance. Finally, I ask bluntly, "What do you do?"

"I . . . I guess you could say I'm a speaker."

"On what subjects?"

Silence. She is gazing out the window. She is a very still person. "I'm part of a foundation.

We try to help in communities with severe problems."

Vague. She sees my questioning look. She frowns. "We're involved in education, and orphanages, and churches."

"Oh, so it's a religious foundation? What religion are you?" I assume she is a Presbyterian or Methodist, a good volunteer for good works, or is involved in Catholic charities.

"I know this is strange, but I have a strong sense about you. I'll just tell you my journey." She then describes the surprise of her conversion, her subsequent adoption of six children from all over the world, her work in Africa and Russia. Her husband, a prominent lawyer, eventually had his own revelation and joins her in her missions. Dinner is served and we talk on.

"You've probably never met anyone like me, anyone who hears the voice of God."

"I think I haven't. You **hear** the voice of God?" **Oh, mamma mia**, I think.

"Yes, he's talking to me right now, all the time."

"What does he sound like?" I wonder if she is speaking metaphorically, living out a grand **as if**.

She laughs. "He's funny sometimes. Sometimes we dance. He's telling me about you, but I don't want you to think I'm a psychic with a neon sign in the window!"

I start to ask sarcastically if he is a good dancer and what kind of dances he leads her in—rhumba? But I don't. As a doubter with strong spiritual interests, I'm tantalized by her big holy spirit visitations. I imagine it feels like a mewling kitten being lifted in the jaws of an enormous mother cat and taken to safety. I'm ready myself but have never felt the slightest inkling that anything out there in the void is the least bit interested in the hairs on my head or the feathers of small sparrows. "If God is talking about me, I'd like to hear what he says because I've never heard from him before tonight." Where's the flight attendant? I'd like a big glass of wine. This is getting surreal. I'm thirty-five thousand feet above terra firma with someone who dances with God.

"Well, I will tell you that He says you have the gift of divine humility. How did you get that? It's so rare."

"Maybe it's a lack of confidence!"

"No, I've seen it in one priest, someone I consulted when I felt the urge to prophesy."

Whoa! Prophesy? "Oh, you're a prophet?" I

toss this off casually, as though it were **Oh, you're from Memphis.**

She looks out the window. Sighs. "I know how it sounds. It's so **simple**." I see her struggling to explain. "I just wait to speak. I wait for God. Sometimes it's just sounds."

"Glossolalia?" She nods. "I've seen that. My friends and I used to peer in the windows at the holy roller and snake-handling churches way down in South Georgia." I don't say that those people fell to the floor writhing and drooling. That we ran away, scared out of our socks. This woman in her Dana Buchman suit and good haircut seems as sane as the United pilot of this plane.

"Have you ever heard of a Charismatic Prophet? That's my calling. I knew I was going to sit beside someone on this flight who would change my life. I always wanted to write. Now I hear how **you** do it and it frees me to try. God put me beside you. Someone, he says, with a holy approach to writing."

Now I'm really fascinated. Someone who not only hears the voice of God but speaks in the tongues of angels and knows what's coming toward us. And I like hearing God's perception that my approach to writing is holy. No one ever has talked to me about the nature of my involvement with words. I've heard plenty about the words themselves but not about the vocation I have. Turbulence starts to shake the overhead compartments. A queasy flyer, I begin to wonder if maybe she is an angel sent to accompany me to the afterlife when the plane spirals down into the Atlantic. But soon the seat belt light flicks off, and the long flight across the waters, black, then leaden, then streaked with sterling light, continues.

As we start our descent into the rainy skies of Paris, she says, "I don't do this. I don't like to debase my gift, but I will tell you something. You are travelling with three angels. One is ministering, one is protecting, and I don't know what the other one is for."

"Oh, no," I say, instantly pessimistic. "Angel of death."

She laughs. "God tells me you are too fatalistic. The third angel is something very good."

Maybe it's the skipping across time zones or the cabin pressure or the lack of sleep, but I willingly close my eyes and try to sense the presence of three angels. Privately, I'm shaken because when I first went to Italy and bought my house, I had a dream that the house held one hundred angels and that I would discover them one by one. Metaphorically, that came true. Starting my travels, I have been given by a stranger three angels to go with me. Without a shred of belief, I can't deny that I am touched.

I give her a list of books I've mentioned and a card with my first name printed on it. I start to write my address but decide that if she wants to reach me, God will direct her.

Madrid. All the connections worked. I find Ed waiting in baggage claim. He looks forlorn—he has arrived with a sinus infection, exacerbated by the changes in pressure while landing. I touch his forehead and find him hot and clammy.

"When I left Bramasole, I was feverish but determined to go. I had to—you'd be waiting. At the ticket counter in Rome, I discovered I'd left my passport at the house. I wanted to climb into a luggage cart and go to sleep. I couldn't face a two-hour drive up to Cortona and two hours back—besides, Giorgio had dropped me at the curb. I asked about the next flight and it was in three hours. I was totally screwed.

Then—I don't know why—the woman handed me a paper to sign. And she said, 'You're going on this flight.' "

"You mean. You flew. Out of Italy. Without a passport?" I'm so shocked I can't utter a whole sentence. This seems impossible, but here he is, his steady eyes smiling at the thought that he slipped freely across international boundaries. We're waiting for my bag, but the remaining ones looping around the claim belt are fewer and fewer.

"Scary, isn't it?"

"After September 11 they let a man on a plane with no papers."

"Maybe it was because I was wearing an Italian suit. Another guy, badly dressed, was trying to get on, and they didn't let him."

My bag has definitely stayed behind in San Francisco or Paris. And I can't find the envelope with the claim check tacked on. Where's my damn ministering angel? I have been travelling twenty hours. We queue with a dozen others. Because I changed carriers in Paris, the pouty-mouthed Air France clerk assures me they have no responsibility for my lost bag, especially since I have no proof that I even checked a bag.

A big Spanish man with a Zapata mustache takes my side, and two Australian boys start chanting "Air Chance, Air Chance." Finally, Miss Cool decides she'll take my hotel number and send out a tracer. As our taxi spins out of the airport on two wheels, Ed says, "Not for nothing is that etymological connection between **travel** and **travail**." The rain looks sooty falling on lead-gray buildings. Suddenly the driver swings around a circle with an enormous fountain; then we're on a tree-lined street along an esplanade lined with one grand building after another. Ah, Madrid. The hotel lights, blurry in the rain, look festive and welcoming. In our room we find a chilled **cava**, Spanish sparkling wine, sent by Lina, a thoughtful Italian friend.

Ed falls into bed after stoking himself with various antihistamines. I pop open the **cava**, pour a glass, empty both little bottles of bubble bath into the tub, and immerse myself. Since dinner is late in Spain, we planned to drift out at ten-thirty, but we're exhausted and instead decide to order room service. Ed feels dizzy. At eleven, the miracle of my suitcase occurs—there it is, wet, dirty, but delivered. I want comfort food. My first meal in Spain: spaghetti with Bolognese sauce. I sink into the down pillows and begin reading **Winter in Majorca**:

> The wind howled down the ravine, the rain lashed our windows, the thunderclaps sounded through our thick walls and interjected a lugubrious note into the children's laughter and games. The eagles and hawks, emboldened by the mist, came down and snatched away our poor sparrows from the pomegranate tree right in front of my very window. The stormy sea kept the boats in the harbor; we felt like prisoners, far away from all intelligent help and any kind of proper friendliness.

George Sand's memoir of a horrid season spent with Frédéric Chopin in Majorca makes me long for California, where the hills are greening with the winter rains and already the daffodils are blowing their yellow trumpets in the new grass. Count this as an inauspicious arrival, Janus. In Scarlet's immortal words, tomorrow is another day.

But as I turn off the light, I invite Madrid to come into my dreams.

• • •

Madrid on a bracing January Thursday. Wind cleared the air. I'm out early, stopping for **churros**, those sweet fritters—a short rope of dough fastened into a circle—just made to dip into hot chocolate on a winter morning. Ed would love them if he weren't in bed with his sinus tightening like a vise, his throat flaming. I circle the Neptune fountain, then head for the Plaza Mayor. A side street looks more intriguing than the big-city business street I'm on, so I turn and soon am rambling among small cafés, bodegas, and food shops. Seven degrees (42° Fahrenheit). The sky **looks** colder than it feels. Or maybe the neighborhood just seems warmer. In the window of the Santeria La Milagrosa I see a black magic altar, little bags of dust, snake skins, geodes, and belts. Wonderful! A ju-ju shop. I go in, breathing in strange aromas of wax, powders, roots. There are tarots, conch shells, coin conjures, little fetish dolls, and special pins for pricking them. I buy soaps that protect one against the evil eye and a wish-fulfillment candle to light for Ed to get well. One of the wish candles is a big pink penis, another a dollar sign.

I find everything I need to attract what I want, repel what I don't, cure what ails me, and destroy gossip, too.

I stop at a café on the splendid Plaza Mayor for a fried pastry, the famous **buñuelos de viento**, puffs of wind, and buy **El País**, a Madrid newspaper, an excellent prop for feeling like a native. With a long-ago summer of study in San Miguel de Allende coming to my aid, I make out that Camilo José Cela, eighty-five, died yesterday. Preparing for this trip I read **Journey to Alcarria** and years ago the novels **The Family of Pascual Duarte, The Hive**, and some stories. The paper lists poetry, drama, many other novels. He was a totally literary animal who dipped into every genre. A man of contradictions, he began as a young Franco soldier; later he became vehemently antifascist. Blunt, prolific, curious, a high-living bon vivant, he turned Spanish writing away from lyric roots toward a dark and brutal realism. His own life was tumultuous. He abandoned his wife of thirty years and took off with a young woman. He was alienated from his only son. Even as he died, he was involved in a lawsuit, the nature of which I can't make out. Odd to think he was dying as we landed. His last words—what consciousness at the end—were to his wife of many years, "Marina, I love you." And then, more astonishingly, he said, "**Viva** Iria Flavia," which is the small town in Galicia where he was born, the town where an Englishman had arrived in 1880 to build a railroad and whose destiny was to become the grandfather of this writer, Don Camilo José Mañuel Juan Ramon Francisco de Jerónimo Cela-Trulock. How jarring, that last tacked-on Anglo-Saxon **Trulock**.

So his last thought turned back to the place of origin, the region where he was shaped. As one formed by black swamp water and red clay and baked in the Georgia sun, I too feel the metabolic correspondence with a taproot. I've never said his name aloud but do now. **Tha lah**, the Ce- undergoing an unlikely transformation.

Ed is up when I return before lunch. He has lurched to the window and looks down at the street with longing. "The Prado," he whispers. "We're in Madrid. I want to go to the Prado." Soon I hear the shower and the buzz of his electric razor. In the black suit that earned him passage **senza passaporta**, he emerges a new man.

Downstairs under the stained-glass dome of the lobby, among the poshly dressed Madrilenians, we have a quick bite. The hard January light through the yellow glass softens and pours in like **vino blanco**, fluid and translucent. In the late morning sun, the wooden supports and buttresses behind the dome are visible through the panels, flowers, and leaves. I wish I hadn't noticed because I'm distracted by the structure. Ed, instead, is staring at his **tortilla de verdura** with garlic sauce. He pushes it toward me, and because I have walked all morning and am starving, I eat his and mine while he sips tepid water.

"Are you sure you want to go out?"

"It's just across the street. Let's **vamos**."

Poor Velázquez. So many portraits of the royals. Those were some plug-ugly people. Wouldn't Velázquez rather have painted crocuses instead of staring into rheumy Hapsburg eyes? Imagine him searching for a shade of puce to plump up lumpy Bourbon faces. I'm sure he did his best to flatter them. I think again of Camilo José Cela, dead yesterday. His serious realistic style was known as **tremendismo**, and in all the literary criticism I've read, his **tremendismo** is posited as a counter to Spanish lyricism. A friend in Cortona, when his son is just too much, says, "Andrea is **tremendo**." Intense, persistent, overwrought, headstrong.

Cela's **The Hive** indicts Franco's fascist rule by depicting characters driven into poverty. Who has more zeal than the convert? Looking at these tortured painters, I think Cela must have taken his instructions from them, the exaggerated realism of El Greco, the dark lonely stares of the Goya portraits, all this black and gray paint. These are Cela characters, a few generations removed. His travel narrative, **Journey to Alcarria**, shows a different strain in his aesthetic. He moves closer to the Don Quixote tradition. His amiable wanderer through the countryside encounters others, picks up and leaves off, unhurriedly observing and moving on. This wanderer exhibits the spirit shown in the quote Cela said he wanted as his epitaph: **Here lies someone who tried to screw his fellow man as little as possible.** The abandoned wife might disagree.

The Prado has nearly nine thousand paintings, though they display only a fraction. **La**

Maja of Goya, the reclining, languorous nude, looks so much like my college roommate that we buy a card to send to her. We find an Annunciation by our friend Fra Angelico, who lived in Cortona for thirteen years, amid a glorious cache of Italian works by Titian, Botticelli, Raphael, Messina, Mantegna. Then we come upon Hieronymus Bosch's **The Garden of Earthly Delights** and so many other world treasures, long familiar but never seen. The Prado's still lifes dazzle. I would like to touch the chocolate-brown background against which Zurbarán painted his four incandescent vessels in shades of ochre and gray. For years I had a poster hanging in my Palo Alto kitchen of his still life of citrus fruits, against the same rich brown, with the lemon trees outside my window echoing the light those fruits can gather into themselves.

Our short time in Madrid passes quickly for me, agonizingly for Ed, who keeps struggling out until he feels weak and must return to bed. Like pilgrims, we go to the restaurant Botin, because it has served everyone under the sun since

1725, including Hemingway, who sat his characters Jake and Lady Brett Ashley there for martinis and solace. We try to imagine Papa digging into the **cochinillo**, the suckling pig, which I choose. Ed orders, then stares at partridge with fava beans, sips half of a glass of wine, and forgoes even a glance at the dessert menu. Later he dreams of crouching in a foxhole while bullets fly. Some page from **The Sun Also Rises** has floated into his sleep.

A visit to a capital city usually proves to be the best introduction to a country. During these first days I'm glad we get to see the Museo Arqueológico Nacional, treasure trove of the Spanish monarchs. As we walk through the Egyptian collection, Ed says, "There's a sheer **quantity** of Egyptian objects in museums around the world. Seems like not a single scarab from that civilization was ever lost."

This museum reminds me of Spain's tentacles reaching out into the Mediterranean world and beyond, and also of Roman roots, the Visigoth era, then the seductive centuries of Arab-Moorish rule, which was firmly established by 756, and the later periods of the Bourbons and Hapsburgs. Layers and layers fuse, as we move from room to room, era to era.

One remnant of Magna Graecia (the South of Italy) is the fabulous statue of the second wife of Augustus, found in Paestum. She's as majestic as the columns of the temples there. I wish I had a full picture of the astronomical, seasonal, and religious mosaic, a Roman survival, and of the Roman well with a relief of the birth of Athena. A stash of intricate, ancient gold jewelry; golden bowls of a Bronze Age solar cult; a small and richly decorated covered jar in **marfil**, ivory, from tenth-century Córdoba—all are exquisite. The Arabic ivory jar was a gift to a caliph's (ruler's) favorite, a woman named Subh, Dawn. Surely she was mightily loved. Cunning carved tiny deer, peacocks, and grapevines cover the surface. A group of eleven Visigoth artifacts surprise me most. I envisioned them as barbarian hordes sweeping down upon Italy, France, and Spain as the Roman Empire eroded. These delicate marvels, crowns and crosses of **oro y pedrería**, gold and semiprecious stone, prove these Germanic people to have been high-caliber artists.

Neolithic, Bronze, all the ages from prehistory onward show the strength of the artistic impulse in the making of knives, vases, gravestones—anything to do with living quotidian life. The impulse to create beauty where you draw water, where you stow your saffron, where you walk, that impulse is intrinsic to life, as it ever has been and will be, and from this place where such remains are gathered, we can only exit with a sense of renewal and joy.

The highlight of Madrid for both of us—easy choice—is our morning at the Museo Thyssen-Bornemisza, one of the primo art experiences of my life, and more so for being unexpected. Three floors of meticulously curated, stupendous work housed in a **palacio**. "Who started this museum?" I ask the taxi driver who has picked us up.

"People with too much money," he answers. But what a gift they gave! There's Piero della Francesca, another local boy from our part of Italy, with a portrait in profile of a blond boy against a dark background. There's Dürer's sublime Adam and Eve, Cranach's very Mediterranean conception of the Madonna, with a palm tree in the background, and her baby about to eat a grape from the bunch in her hand. Is this the only painting where baby Jesus eats solid food? I recall him holding oranges but never in the act of eating. And there's Raphael's stunner, the portrait of a young man who looks as if he might speak to you. Caravaggio, de Hooch, Carpaccio, Memling, Bellini, on and on. Easy to miss because of the small size is **The Virgin of the Dry Tree** by Petrus Christus, a fifteenth-century painter from Bruges. Mary wears blood-of-Jesus red and stands in a tree, completely encircled by bare branches that resemble a crown of thorns. The letter **a** dangles from fifteen branches. We stand before her trying to imagine the mind of the painter. The letters, we read in the museum guide, symbolize Ave Marias. Why fifteen? Why did Christus paint her in a tree, like a wild bird? Her eyes are moon-lidded, her baby is delicate, and she holds him tenderly, the thumb and forefinger of her left hand idly taking the measure of his foot. She poses a rich mystery.

We do not tire, do not flag. Each room shocks me with new energy. We circulate among the paintings as among friends at a party, while meeting strangers we immediately love. Pleased to meet you, Pierfrancesco di Giacomo Foschi, and **gracias** for the portrait of a Florentine lady of the sixteenth century. I like her distracted expression **(I have lost my true love in the bloody conflict**, or—**where did I leave my wretched house keys**?), the noble folds of her puffed salmon-pink sleeves, and her ringed index finger holding open her place in a small book. Also well met: Giovanni Antonio Boltraffio, lucky to have absorbed well the lessons of his teacher, Leonardo da Vinci. His portrait of a lady represents Santa Lucia. So beguiling are her almond-eyed glance and peachy-cream skin that it takes a moment to notice the half-closed eye stuck on a pin, which she holds in the left-hand corner. This attribute reveals her to be Santa Lucia, whose portraits always have beautiful eyes, just to remind the viewer that she was blinded in her martyrdom.

I want to do a few dance steps when I come to Ghirlandaio's **Portrait of Giovanna Tornabuoni**—what a joy. The beauty of the young woman, seated against an unlit background, shines with such luminosity that her body looks lighted from within. She must have seemed so to Domenico Ghirlandaio because painted just behind her is an epigram from the Roman poet Martial that translates: "If you, oh Art, had been able to paint the character and virtue of the sitter, there would not be a more beautiful painting in the world." Her squiggly curls and twisted chignon soften her incised profile, and the cloths of her dress must have been the most sumptuous the Renaissance had to offer. What pure pleasure for Ghirlandaio to have rendered those sheens and designs to glorify La Giovanna's grace. I find equally as compelling Zurbarán's full portrait of Santa Casilda, a dark Spanish beauty with her hair tied in a thin red ribbon. She's resplendent in a jewel-bordered crimson dress, which she lifts in front of her in order to walk, giving the impression that she has paused and half-turned to look directly at someone who has spoken to her. I feel lucky to be that viewer, drawn close by her gaze. She, too, was martyred. When she was caught giving bread to Christians, the bread miraculously transformed into flowers. Was it okay to give flowers but not sustenance? I wonder if the stylized white flowers on her skirt symbolize her martyrdom. The portraits in this museum counter, quite wonderfully, all the Prado's dour faces, their fleshy noses and gray skin.

The landscapes, the superb collection by northern European painters, the still lifes, the Impressionists—three mornings would hardly satisfy me here. Even the twentieth-century group outshines most American museums' collections. Now I must add Madrid to my list of places to visit regularly. We buy the museum's book, even though it weighs about five pounds, because we can't stand the idea of leaving.

Late at night, after a strange seven-to-nine-thirty nap, we venture out to dinner, straggling back to the hotel after midnight, when the Spanish are revved. The famous **cocido madrileño**, a complete meal of soup, chickpeas, and plates of boiled meats, certainly warms the winter night. After the three courses, we tumble back into our Heavenly Beds (available for purchase) at the hotel, Ed cosseted by various pills and me by my biography of Federico García Lorca, his poems, and a stack of history and art books.

We have come to Spain to see Andalucía slowly, as intimately as a foreigner can. For me, this is an ancient quest. When I was thirteen and joined an LP (long-playing) record club, I was sent Ravel's **Bolero** by mistake. As I listened over and over—the first "classical" piece I knew—I imagined myself on an Appaloosa galloping across the Andalucían plains in a flowing cape, hood blown back, my fingers gripping the horse's mane, feeling the gait in my body, the music's switches in tempo like changes in wind patterns. The music forever has attached to the memory of sitting at the dressing table amid my older sister's bottles of perfume and silver brushes and seeing myself as dramatically **other** than the reserved southern child who stared in the mirror. Years later, when my first husband and I lived in graduate student housing at Princeton, a romantic economics student from Nicaragua, Carlos du Bon, used to read Lorca aloud to me under the trees as our small children played with box turtles they'd found in the weeds. Hard to explain such moments. He leaned against a tree in a good Italian suit, tie loosened and his legs crossed. His black, black hair, black as crude oil, his essential Latin nature, his good smell that made me dizzy, his iconographic representation of the foreign, sophisticated, literary possibilities of the world came drifting through to me in the words of Lorca. **Green, green, how much I want you green . . .** I was not-long married. I loved my brilliant and handsome husband, who came from my same southern background. I was transfixed by the white teeth of Carlos, who had studied at the Sorbonne and at El Escorial in

Spain, who spoke Italian and French and German, as well as English and his own Spanish, whose mouth seemed to slide around the words of García Lorca, seemed to lure me toward some wide-open life I did not know. Even now I wonder if his skin simply smelled of the tropics he came from, of mango and salt and lime, or if he doused himself in cologne. I can see his brown fingers holding the book and his intent gaze when he looked up. **Green wind. Green branches . . . how much I want you green . . .**

Tomorrow we go by fast train to Seville.

We are walking across a plaza on our way to sample our first tapas when a genteel-looking older woman, dressed in a blazer and skirt, comes up to us, apologizing for interrupting. What a bad piece of luck she had travelling to Spain and losing her purse on arrival last night for a vacation with friends. The friends have been delayed in Tunisia and won't be back until late tomorrow. "I have the key to their apartment," she said, "but unfortunately, I have no money and no food. My friends have been gone two weeks and left nothing in their place except two oranges. Can you help me? You look like such nice people. I am so embarrassed to ask."

Ed takes out his wallet and gives her ten euros. She thanks us with dignity, and we walk on, talking about how awful it would be to lose your money and credit cards. We're looking for the tapas place whose name we've written on an envelope. Later, we spot the English woman again, but she does not seem to see us.

Just after we arrived at noon, the hotel called their doctor, who came to the room and gave us prescriptions for antibiotics, one for me just in case I caught the infection, one for Ed's sinus pain. At the pharmacy, Ed is given a cup of water with his pills so he can start improving right away. Within hours he begins to feel energy seeping back into his veins. "I'm cured, as of tomorrow," he announces. "Isn't it odd how anything can throw you when you travel, an earache, a lost Visa card, a blister, luggage gone astray. You forget you've arrived in a place you've always wanted to see." By the time we find the tapas bar, he's elated enough to order so many tapas that we never go out to dinner at all. This Spanish rhythm will take some getting used to: the **tapeo** (tapas crawl from bar to bar) in early evening, then dinner never before ten. I like tapas because appetizers on a menu tempt me more than main courses. We try potatoes with a spicy mayonnaise and ham, marinated anchovies, chunky pork loin slices with a green pepper sauce, spinach with bacon and walnuts, and some mixed fried fish, all saucer-sized portions. The white wine tastes like sherry. The waiter tells me that when white wine is aged in **barrique de Jerez**, it picks up the sherry tones. I ask for something not from Jerez barrels, and the Muga, a white Rioja, he brings is light and spicy, great with the white **torta del casar** cheese, which is soft enough to eat with a spoon. Even though we are no longer hungry at all, there's a vague dissatisfaction. Did we have dinner or not? Tonight we're too weary to care.

We fall into the big bed at the Don Alfonso XIII without a thought of when we will awaken and what must be done then. Tired at home, I'm usually overloaded with obligations and the prospect of tomorrow promises more of the same. But **sprung**, out in the world with a small stuffed suitcase and a notebook, tiredness promises big baths and closed draperies to shut out early light, and a telephone in case anything is desired from the kitchen downstairs, and the lovely allure of tomorrow when a foreign city will reveal undreamed pleasures.

We begin early. The harsh two syllables of **Seville**, once here, turn forever into **Sevilla**, because the **-ya** sound of the double **l** seems so natural to this place, the three-note syllables rising and falling like musical fountains in the green and flowering courtyards we glimpsed last night. Next to the hotel is the Royal Tobacco Factory, Prosper Mérimée's imagined locale for **Carmen**. Later Bizet wrote the opera that is now the darling of classical music stations. The formation of cigars by **señoritas** rolling tobacco leaves over their thighs was apparently a major erotic focus of smokers in the nineteenth century. I love the act of art that transfers to a real place an imagined person or event, thereby transforming that place into an aspect of the work of art. Carmen lights this place with her lusty presence. Equally fantastic is the place itself. Who conceived of a factory with arcades and fountained courtyards and chapels and gardens? Oranges grow, not one by one as they do on orange trees at home, but in bunches, like a

grappolo of grapes. I feel right at home as we walk through the arched stone portal. The complex, second largest building in Spain, forms part of the Universidad de Sevilla. Bicycles, gangsta pants, tight T-shirts, unkempt hair, political posters, smoke—I could be in the San Francisco State student union if this building were not so grand. We loop around the building and find the Guadalquiver River. The only line I recall from the letters of the Nicaraguan poet who read Lorca to me comes to mind: **a sky clean with light on the water**. Such a simple line. The whole perspective of town and river looks like an early photograph of itself—the timeless silhouette of the dome, and the cathedral crenelations, the sky in layers of pewter, silver, and pearl, with the Islamic minaret and tower cut out and inserted between water and sky.

On the Isabella bridge, we stop at a **churrería**. Big coils dance in the hot oil. The men turn them with long sticks, then lift out the crisp pastries and hand the **churros** to us in napkins with a paper cup of chocolate for dipping. How does anyone eat a whole one? They're huge. From the middle of the bridge, a good point for surveying Sevilla and indulging in this **churro** tradition, we see many bell towers, fragments of old walls, and boarded-up cafés surrounded by orange trees. Summer must be enchanting along the river, but winter is splendid, too. Sevilla feels much warmer than Madrid, crisp and fresh but not frigid. Soon we are carrying our jackets. The sky has turned cerulean, streaked with broad-brush-stroke clouds.

Over in the Triana section of town the streets turn lively. We crowd into an olive oil stand that sells bulk oil and about fifteen different kinds of olives. Down the block, the owner of a dark shop specializing in the national passion, the local **serrano** and **ibérico** hams, has hung hooved hunks from the ceiling. Little cups attached underneath catch stray drops of fat. The skin looks like an old saddle, but inside the ham resembles the color of a split blood orange. We're given a taste of chewy, streaky, deeply flavorful meat from an **ibérico**, a black pig, then a taste of **serrano**, a white pig. Both taste wild and robust, quite unlike the refined taste of their cousin, Italian prosciutto. The Spanish love their **jamón**, and every province breeds a different variation of this noble Spanish pig. Some are fed only in the wild, others are fed only acorns, some are cross-bred, and some are cured for longer periods—an intricate world of pig. We buy slices to go of an **ibérico de Bellota**. This little pig has gained much of its weight from acorn feasting and is considered the most exquisite taste.

We stumble upon a street of shops full of mantilla combs, fake roses, shawls, coral earrings, castanets, and wild flamenco dresses for all sizes. You can even buy a case for your castanet, should you need one. How brazen that sulfur-yellow dress, form fitting until the kick and swirl of the bottom, all edged with white lace, with the typical strap-over-the-instep flamenco shoes to match. Edged in wide black rickrack, the red polka dot number would fit a girl of five or six. These dresses are from the world of paper dolls—startling that they are real. Shop after shop all devoted to flamenco clothes. There must be balls and fiestas and parades where local women wear these because there are far too many for tourists to buy on a whim.

A knife sharpener on his bicycle passes us, blowing a pipe that sounds like a piccolo. A woman steps out with a knife, and he pushes down the kickstand and reverses the bike seat. He has outfitted the back with two grinding stones. As he pedals, the sharpening stones turn. He sharpens her knife quickly, rotates the seat, and rides off, sounding his plaintive tune. "He's alerting the neighbors to beware of dullness," Ed says. I photograph him but can't capture the tune.

Ed points to a tiled church dome topped with a mustard-colored cupola that looks more like the top of a minaret than a Christian bell tower. I'm already in love with tiles. A baroque blue and white Madonna shrine against an ochre house, an iron balcony with the doorway extravagantly surrounded by a border three tiles deep, and even shiny store numbers encased in elaborate decorative motifs. Houses without tile are still decorated, with pilasters and window surrounds painted in vibrant mustard, the doors green or polished dark wood. On one apartment's roof terrace and balconies, I count 125 pots of geraniums hanging from iron railings. The apartment sports blue awnings, bright-banded doors, and colorful ceramic plates on the walls. How bold! Will we go home and quadruple our potted plants? Order loud bougainvillea vines for every south wall?

Already new words are becoming familiar. **Azulejos**: tiles. Not because azure was the color of most of the early tiles, but because the original Arab word, **az-zulayj**, meant "mosaic bits." You can't stay in Sevilla longer than a day without hearing the word **Mudéjar**. Some of the Muslims who stayed behind when their rulers were routed became Christians or professed as much for safety's sake. Their style, craftsmanship, and artistic achievements identify themselves by this word. Their most intricate work—stare up until your neck aches—you see on their elaborate carved and coffered **artesonado** ceilings. Ed likes the words **celosia**, stone with perforated designs, and **mihrab**, the arch or niche in a mosque that directs the prayers toward Mecca.

And who were these invading Moors who brought their spicy and fragrant foods, their knowledge of algebra, navigation, and irrigation, their love of poetry and music, their passion for the sounds of falling water? In ancient times a Moor was a North African native of Mauritania, now Morocco and Algeria. Later **Moor** came to mean a Berber or a person of mixed Berber and Arab blood. Arab-led Berbers were the conquerors of Spain. Some take the word **Moor** as pejorative and prefer **Arab** or **Saracen**, whose etymological root probably means "easterner, from the place of the rising sun." All these terms are used loosely; any Muslim during the Crusades was known as a Saracen. Others came from the Arabian deserts, often via North Africa because of factional wars among the nomadic tribes. The Berber Almoravids and Almohads, the Abbasids of Baghdad, the Nasrid dynasty, and the powerful Umayyads of Córdoba, who originated in Syria, were the equivalents in Spain of the Medici in Italy. This stew of Muslim people descended onto the native Iberians and began the vast cultural intermingling that made Andalucía a bright torch in the dark ages of Europe.

The red-trimmed café La Tertulia's name is enclosed in a wavy blue and white border. The door is closed today, but I wonder if the café preserves the tradition the name implies. **Tertulias**, gatherings for conversation, began in the eighteenth century. In Madrid I saw listings for literary discussion on Friday afternoons, poetry on weekends, weekly political debates, and meetings for those over eighty. One focuses on talk about "the contemporary fool," which must be an endless discussion. One is held for those **"contra ésto y aquéllo,"** against this and that.

Where to shop in Triana? We ask a woman carrying two huge bags with red chard sticking out the top. She points to a modern building near the bridge. The clean, compact market at first glance appears uninteresting. Much of the food is standard world-market imports—leeks from Holland, plastic-wrapped endive, peppers and fruit with stickers. Then we see vats of brown-striped snails, handfuls of wild asparagus amid the vacuum-wrapped beets, and a tray of wild greens from the fields called **tagarninas del campo**. The conical, chartreuse broccoli that we eat in Italy, known there as **broccolo romano**, here is **rumanescu.**

We wish we could cook, but on this trip we choose an initiation rite in tapas, cheeses, and regional specialties. We pause for lunch at a café where bridge and river meet. The larger plate of tapas, called a **ración**, ration, looks perfect for a light meal. We share codfish with roast peppers and a selection of vegetable croquettes. The thoughtful waiter brings us a **ración** of potatoes with aioli because he thinks we should try his favorite.

Sevilla, a town for the senses, and the air of midday turns balmy and kind. At the Plaza del Altozano, with an old tiled pharmacy and decorative benches under garden walls, many of the houses have **miradores**, literally "viewpoints." When I travelled to Peru, I sketched the mysterious carved wooden enclosures the size of balconies, small upstairs porches from whence you can see but not be seen. I knew they were architectural imports from Spain, but now I see the real Arab origin in the latticed horseshoe arches and the shapes of the wooden cutwork. A **mirador** is known in an Islamic house as a **mashrabiyya**. In Naguib Mahfouz's **Palace Walk**, set in Cairo, a young Muslim girl willfully peers out, almost inviting herself to be seen. Her defiance becomes the crux of her fate. The role of the **mirador** in the lives of generations of Muslim women could occupy years of research. Some miradors are glassed in; some have curtains and plants. The design has survived, probably because the enclosures cut the fierce heat and glare, as well as providing a bit of privacy if you want to nod off over a book or lounge nude with a bowl of cherries. Tile everywhere—even the undersides of the balconies are tiled.

Crossing over the river into the neighborhood called El Arenal, we stop and watch T-shirted kayakers and crew teams zipping along the Guadalquiver. The extraordinary weather holds. I'd like to drop my coat into the water rather than lug it along. Serene as this view is, I'm disconcerted by such an everyday image. After all, the al-wad al-Kabir, the great river, Guadalquiver, are names breathed and repeated in the poems of Lorca: "The open Guadalquiver . . . Ay, Guadalquiver . . . starry Guadalquiver." Ships laden with goods from Spanish exploits in the New World plied this fast-lane interstate highway, sailing up from Cádiz to the city of Sevilla laden with everything they could raid, from silver to sugar: "For the sailboats/Sevilla has a road."

Here Christopher Columbus, né Cristoforo Colombo according to tradition, and later Cristóbal Colón, beseeched King Fernando and Queen Isabella time and again before they yielded and let him sail. When they allowed him to confer with astronomers and mapmakers about his proposed journey, those wise ones sagely concluded: "If the earth is round, you will be compelled to sail up a kind of mountain from Spain, which you cannot do even with the fairest wind, and you could never get back." When Isabella insisted, Fernando finally relented. After all, they had just driven the Arabs out of Granada in that indelible year of 1492, leaving them free to spread the word of God and to rake in the goods. The journal of Christopher Columbus reveals a driven man, one with vision, who kept from his men the true distance the **Niña**, the **Pinta**, and the **Santa María** had sailed, who kept his own counsel, who did step off the edge of the known world.

After weeks at sea came days and days when the sailors smelled land; they spotted floating weeds, a crab, finally a carved stick and a branch with berries. Longing for land, his men on the verge of mutiny, he wrote in his log that the sea was sweet and as calm as the Guadalquiver. Finally, they spotted a coast at night and rode at anchor until morning—what a night! Did anyone sleep? At sunrise they saw naked people gathered on the shore, gazing at them. And the rest is controversy.

"I vividly remember staring at the picture of red-haired Isabella beside Fernando in the fifth-grade history book. Do you?" I ask Ed.

"Yes, the whole story of Columbus—that's

where I first heard of the idea of pushing off from home. Whatever the consequences, he was a seeker. He was after the exciting life, the possibility. I never thought he was motivated just by desire for gold. He was itching to **go**."

"Nobody mentioned that Fernando and Isabella drove out the Jews and sponsored the Inquisition. They just seemed like gods in a fairy kingdom where Columbus built his toy ships and found **us**."

The El Arenal zone seems neighborly with an abundance of tapas bars and small shops. An elegant riding shop near the Plaza de Toros bullring (blessedly closed for the season) reminds us of the great tradition of breeding horses in Spain. Young girls have shopped here for their fine saddles since 1892, saddles upon which one **could** ride with cape flying across the plain of the Guadalquiver to the beat of **Bolero**.

To travel with Ed is to be forever on the quest for the perfect espresso. He rarely encounters the well-made cup, the strong elixir with just the proper layer of **crema**. Nonetheless hope springs at the sight of every machine. Inept packing of the coffee, the wrong grind, the wrong setting—so much to go wrong. Still, he has his nips three or four times a day. I'm annoyed when we must trek from street to street hoping to find the right café after long dinners when I am longing for some heavenly bed. If I bring up this subject, he says, "Well, my love, you have to look at every damn flower in bloom and ascertain the name of it." At an open-air bar, we end our afternoon's meandering with Ed scrutinizing the lack of **crema**, grimacing at the sour brew. Maybe next time.

Ed goes wild for the vibrant tapas scene in Sevilla. So much fish! He loves anything pulled from the waters and tastes the squid, fish, urchins, clams, every little swimmer marinated or grilled or pickled or broiled and served forth on a tapas plate. At a crowded bar with tables spilling out under the orange trees in a plaza, we sample garlic shrimp, grilled baby squid, little cheese toasts, fried salty almonds. Then we move on.

We are able to experience only half the fun. Why didn't I go to Spanish class sophomore year? I recall that I never bought the textbook and even forgot to drop the course by the third week. Later, when I studied in San Miguel de

Allende for a summer, I became friends with the teacher, whose taxi-driver friend took us off road to search for Chichimeca artifacts. We forgot Spanish grammar. He wore small cowboy boots, and he thought my white, white skin was unhealthy looking. He would press my arm with a forefinger like someone testing bread dough. "So too white," he would marvel. "And cat eyes. Bad luck." I have a few pottery shards and a baby skull I picked up in an abandoned cemetery, where boys kicked bones in lieu of a soccer ball. So much for the rigors of learning Spanish. I would love to be able to join in the scene here, even to the limited extent a foreigner might. The tapas ritual is above all about conviviality. Friends meet, share a bite, shift to other friends, then head to another crowded bar where other friends wait. A similar rite, **ombra**, the shadow rounds, takes place in Venice. In early evening neighbors gather at small bars with counters opening to the street for half glasses of wine and saucers of food, then move on, often in groups. The name may have come from the time when gondoliers stood in the shadow of San Marco for a drink. No one really knows, and no one knows the source of tapas either. The word probably comes from **tapar**, "to cover." A plate or a slice of ham resting on top of the wineglass made it easy to carry or, according to some sources, kept the flies out. The name may have come from an official order to eighteenth-century innkeepers to "cover" the stomachs of carriage drivers when they stopped for refreshments. Driving under the influence caused too many tipped carriages. Whatever the source of the name, the custom charms us. Still, I long to ask someone, **How do you do it? All these tastes and then dinner?**

Tonight we are determined to go on from tapas to dinner at eleven. We might have walked ten miles today, but we walk again in the interlude because Sevilla at night becomes **muy simpatica**—the streetlights among the orange trees, the glimpsed courtyards with splashing fountains, the forty horse-drawn carriages—so gallant, unlike the usual tourist conveyances drawn by sad nags—the massive volumes of the cathedral, and the Giralda towering over all. "Isn't it easy to imagine the muezzin's call to prayer falling from the tower over all of us?"

"The guidebook says he rode a donkey up to the top five times a day. The stairs switch back so he wouldn't have to climb."

After several turns, we find ourselves in the

same plaza, and there's the stranded English woman, talking to three tourists. We see the man reach for his wallet. What a scam, and she was so specific (Tunisia, two oranges), so unlikely. She looks like a librarian or teacher on holiday. As she turns from the threesome, she catches sight of us but does not register any recognition. Even after one hour of walking, we should have recognized the two oranges part. Orange trees are everywhere! Reach up and grab one.

La Giralda has become our beacon. At 319 feet high, it's visible from most of Sevilla. A pure minaret, except for the Christian top, La Giralda perfectly encapsulates the harmonious blending of the styles of successive conquerors. When built by the Moorish Almohad rulers in the twelfth century, the minaret was crowned with four golden balls topped by a crescent moon. The spangle of the sun on these spheres was clear to anyone approaching the city. The Torre del Oro on the river once was covered in gold-glazed tiles, also sending a glittering message to boats sailing upstream from Cádiz. Drawings of the minaret from that era show a more delicate structure of graceful proportions. The Christians broadened the entire top third of the tower to incorporate a bell tower—the Christian call to prayer. A figure of Fides, Faith, who defies his name and turns whichever way the wind blows, ornaments the top. Though the earlier structure may be finer, the current one pleases the eye, too. The remodelers retained, in the lower two-thirds, the original decorations, and the horseshoe and multifoil arches on the facade. The horseshoe arch, which seems so quintessentially Moorish, actually came from the Visigoths and inspired the Arabs, becoming, with many variations, their signature arch. You see this kind of marriage of cultures all over the city. The Romans brought Greek principles, the Visigoths took over Roman designs, the Arabs absorbed elements from the Romans and Visigoths, as well as the Greeks, and the Christians venerated the Arab architecture. Vehement as they became about expelling the Arab rule from Spain, the Christians continued to retain, adopt, and adapt from Arab artisans, who had directly shaped the beauty of Andalucía from the eighth until the fifteenth century. The quotes from Arab design continue today. Layers and layers fused, and we have Andalucía.

• • •

The small Plaza de Santa Cruz looks as though actors will emerge any second. Wrought-iron arches suround the plaza planted with orange trees, and vines run from arch to arch. The houses are all dream houses, quintessentially Spanish with their carved doors and iron balconies and proud facades. Through the damask-draped windows we glimpse lighted rooms with baronial furniture, sideboards laden with crystal decanters, and portraits in immense gilt frames. The smell inside must be the same as in my grandfather's house—overripe fruit, wax, cigar smoke, and leather. In one of the mansions, now a restaurant, we dine on sea bass with almond vinaigrette, artichokes with black rice, and fig soufflé. This is grand. I'm turning Spanish. It's late. **Olé!**

At one A.M. we find a taxi and show the driver a Triana address the waiter has written on our bill. In a few minutes we're getting out in front of an unassuming white building that looks like where the Moultrie, Georgia Elks, or Legionnaires hold their pancake breakfasts. Inside, a few people gathered around tables facing a stage chat and visit. I'm surprised to see five or six small children and several elderly people. We find chairs near the front. The flamenco is about to begin.

Afterward, at three-thirty in the morning, no taxi waits outside. We are about to begin the long walk home when the taxi that brought us pulls up. "I thought you might want to drive now." He smiles and opens the back door. "I am sure you have enjoyed your evening." We wanted to kiss him because we are both falling-over tired and overstimulated. The flamenco wrung us out. I have a pounding headache, and Ed is immensely thirsty. We're thrilled straight through by the power of sharp, rhythmic hand clapping, the ear-splitting wailing, and the pained, ecstatic faces of the dancers. At times I felt I should not see the human face in that deep expression of private emotions. I felt the fascination of the voyeur. **Duende** was a word we threw around in graduate school: the summoning of a life-force spirit and the expression of that spirit. I see that we had no idea what it meant. Flamenco lights a brushfire in the blood. All those brightly dressed women twirling and clicking heel-toe, heel-toe, the men in black, thin as whips and vibrantly sexual, the play between them, and the stepping forth for solo dancing. Through the staccato clapping, which times and builds and emphasizes, hands become a musical instrument, powerful punctuation, and raw drive.

"Can you dance flamenco?" I ask the driver.

"Of course. Everyone in Sevilla is born knowing how to dance."

We sit back, looking out the windows. We'd expected a commercialized folkloric experience, all flash and polish. The waiter sent us to the right place. We felt and witnessed a layer of protection stripped away, leaving the dancers and audience, singer and guitarist engaged together in a blood ritual. This is a glimpse into the heart of Andalucía. I wonder if we will reach the core.

Days in Sevilla. Days of sweet air like early spring, sky the same blue as the **azulejos**. I'm drawn to the Convent of San Leandro in Plaza San Idelfonso because the afternoon I happen to visit is Saint Rita's Day, patron saint of lost causes. The church is filled with flowers and praying women, some clutching photographs. "Suffering mothers all," I say to Ed. They kneel and weep and visit and hold each other up. In my life, I have never experienced the comfort of laying down my burden, down at the foot of someone to whom I say **I give up, help me**. And I can only wonder at the succor such an act provides. Do they hear God talking? Do they dance with God? At another door, we place our money on a carved wheel that spins into the convent. Out comes a wooden box of sweets from the cloistered nun on the other side.

In the plaza and along the streets, men in yellow slickers harvest oranges into big burlap sacks. Our shoes on the sidewalks and curbs stick and slide in juice and pulp. I ask a worker if they will make juice concentrate or the famous local marmalade. "Neither," he says, "they're too close to car exhaust. They will go into soaps and perfumes." Oh great, perfume with a hint of toxic fumes. **Azahar**, Arabic for "orange," and then into Spanish, **la naranja**. Here, they drink orange juice like water, sweetening it with a spoon of sugar. In the cathedral orange garden, where the Arabs made their ritual ablutions at the fountain before entering the mosque, the orange trees are intoxicated with birdsong, dripping and heavy on the air. Even the pigeons look holy. There are many in the plazas, but often they're white, not like urban rats aloft but, instead, reminders of the holy spirit honing in on the Annunciation. A young mother in a fitted red jacket calls, **"Venga, caro! Alejandro, venga."** Come here, darling! Alejandro, come. And little Alejandro beams and keeps running away. The children are dressed like children in photographs of the 1940s. Alejandro wears navy short pants buttoned to his crisp white shirt with ruffled collar. His hair is a Byronic toss of ringlets, and his cheeks look like tiny burnished pomegranates. I look carefully at all small children. There is one in our future. My daughter is expecting a baby in March. **Venga, caro**. Perhaps we shall one day be foolish enough to buy him one of the miniature matador's "suits of light" displayed in shops, along with little admiral and sailor suits for small boys.

Sevilla is full of lived life, surprises, and secret loveliness. We locate La Venera, the Venus, a marble scallop shell on a house that once was the center of the city. In steps and in leagues, legal measurements once were made from here.

Two well-fed nuns hoist a stuffed garbage can between them, struggling to keep the can away from their long gray habits. From birdcages perched on balconies or hanging in windows, trills and chirps light the steps of the people below. Ah, Love of God Street. Bells start the dogs barking.

We dip in and out of churches, admiring the little Arab windows, which look as if they're formed by big star-and-moon cookie cutters, and the whitewashed arches in San Marcos, and the plaza behind it laden with oranges. In Santa Catalina we spot an Arab arch behind the Christian arch. The air clouds with the cinnamon smell of incense. By the altar to Santa Lucia, hundreds of pairs of eyes and even sunglasses adorn four panels. I exist visually. If I ever laid down a votive in a church, it would be to Santa Lucia.

To place such a votive, as we see in the archaeological museum, is an ancient instinct. Some of the first found objects shaped in bronze were ex-votos, just as we've observed in the Cortona museum. The Etruscans left thousands of these little animals and figures. Farmers turn them up when they plow. **Please, bless my girl. Please, cure my liver. Thank you for**

tipping me clear of the cart. Please, let me cross the swollen river. Thank you for sparing me when I had fever. The instinct to offer a gift to the gods seems deeply human. The archaeological museum also has a wall of marble squares, each with a footprint. These are exvotos to Isis and Nemesis. The names of the ancient devotees are carved with each footprint. Oddly moving, these surviving gestures toward the holy. They remind me of the thirty-thousand-year-old handprints on the cave wall at Pech Merle. Here, too, we see little heads of bulls thought to have been offered as sacrifice.

The bull! How he charges through Mediterranean history, how he survives as an icon! Spain itself is the shape of a stretched bull hide, Lorca says. Where did the bull symbol start? We've seen them as we've hunched and crawled through prehistoric caves in France. Early painters adorned Altamira's walls with mighty bulls. In the great hall of the bulls at Lascaux, one bull is eighteen feet long, a most potent cultural symbol. Ed tells me that Europa was a Phoenician princess seduced by Zeus while she bathed in the sea with friends. In the form of a bull, he charmed the girls, and when Europa playfully mounted him for a ride, he charged into the sea and swam to Crete. This may be a sun myth, he speculates, since the Semitic origin of **Europa** probably means "west," to which she was brought from the east, the place of sunrise. In almost all the paintings of Europa and the bull, she wears a filmy, flowing dress with at least one breast exposed. The white bull is crowned with flowers as he plows through the waves. At the Villa Giulia in Rome, a 520 B.C. panel shows Europa and the bull accompanied by fish, seabirds, dolphins, and an angel holding rings to clash in each hand. How many artists since have picked up their brushes in the service of this myth: Tintoretto, Raphael, Boucher, Guido Reni, Veronese, Moreau, Picasso, Klee, Ernst, et cetera. On ancient, thumb-worn coins, on Greek vases, and in the paintings, she always holds on to the bull's horns. Since Zeus chose the bull form, obviously the power of this symbol in Crete predated the myth.

How the bull's horns spread throughout Europe as a magical symbol fascinates me. Far into fable and scripture and history, the slaying of a bull, and the trophy of its horn, enabled the warrior to marry the princess or assume the kingship. In Hebrew scripture, the messiah was to accomplish this same feat. In the scriptures, a

reem, a large bull, gives the root to the name **Abraham**. The twists and turns of the bull legend reach from the horned headdresses of Abyssinian Astarte worship, to Minerva, to Mary, standing on a crescent moon, which is also the bull's horn symbol. According to **Plutarch's Lives**, Theseus, spoiling for action, went off to fight a bull in Marathon. He'd then take the conquered live bull to sacrifice at Delphi. Even today a common gesture in our town is the raised two fingers—the **corno**, or horn—showing the sign of a cuckold. Turning the two fingers toward the ground means "Let it not happen here." Newborn babies are given gold bracelets or necklaces with a coral dangle made in the shape of a horn—protection against the evil eye. That legendary half-bull, half-man who lived in the labyrinth at Knossos, and the bull-leaping games acrobats played—these are deep inside our collective Western psyches. I, too, wear an ivory horn and several amulets against the evil eye under my shirt.

In the Plaza Alfalfa (I never thought of this as a Spanish word) the pet market is in full swing when we pass through—green and patterned parrots, exotic shrimp-colored birds, canaries, turquoise and yellow songbirds, and some that look as if they've been netted from the nearest tree. Fish, puppies, kittens, and crowds of people, many of whom are under ten and begging for a hamster. I hate the crush and the smell of feathers and bird lime. Disgusting. We focus on a clutch of nuns, following them out of the mob, their voluminous gray habits moving in front of us like a rain cloud.

The list of tapas we've tasted has grown. In my notebook I've listed in mixed English and Spanish:

- Spinach with bacon and walnuts
- Pork loin with green pepper sauce
- Moussaka with cheese on top
- **Solomillo con ali-oli** (small beef filet with aioli)
- **Bacalao con salmorejo** (cod with dense gazpacho)
- **Pringa casera** (minced meat paté)
- Shrimp croquettes

- **Pan de ajo con carne mechá casera** (garlic bread with larded loin)
- **Chipirón a la plancha** (grilled squid)
- **Empanadas con jamón** (pastry with ham)
- **Empanadas de carne** (with meat)
- Fried anchovies
- Fried tiny fish that look like minnows

We have had late dinners at several of Sevilla's top-rated restaurants, which often are in lovely buildings. Some we found overblown and mincingly formal. Others are rustic, with hams hanging from the ceiling and the grill fired up for fish and steaks. We find that we prefer the adventure of going to three or four tapas bars instead. The restaurants seem more or less like restaurants on other trips, whereas the tapas scene connects us immediately to the rhythm and liveliness of the culture.

We change hotels when our reservation at the Don Alfonso runs out, and suddenly shiny little Czech Skodas are all over the grounds for a convention. We check into a hotel in the Santa Cruz area, where we stay for a couple of days because of the lovely courtyard and the exotic but homey atmosphere. Then we move to another courtyard hotel, where we take two small rooms. On the first day the electricity fizzles out and we go without heat, light, and hot water overnight. No one seems too concerned, so we just walk and walk, come home, light candles in the room, and brush our teeth with bottled water. I'm consoled by all the patterns of tile on the stairways, the trickling fountains, the guitarist who plays in the loggia late in the afternoon, and the desk clerk who loves the history of Sevilla. He greets us, "Did you do a good journey?" The English infinitives **to make, to do** are hell for foreigners in any conjugation and often produce lovely twists. The next day we are moved to a larger room, as a reward, I suppose, for not complaining. I soak in the big blue cement bathtub and think of the poet Antonio Machado, born in one of these palatial houses, where he heard always the sound of water falling. As an adult, he dreamed of a fountain flowing in his heart, dreamed of a hot sun shining in his heart. Such dreams came straight from this place of his childhood and nurtured him throughout his life. Lying in bed, I imagine my heart as a hot sun.

Andalucian towns always have been a source of fantasy. I'm shocked to find that Sevilla has plain-to-ugly surrounds and way too much traffic. Somehow traffic never figures into my travel idylls. It's a heavy spoiler when I arrive somewhere and could be on San Francisco's awful Highway 101. Many European towns have awakened. They've closed off traffic in historic parts of their cities. Florence leads, and I wish all cities would follow suit. We quickly learn where to go in Sevilla's old parts to experience the place's essence and to avoid cars. The horse-drawn carriages manage to feel authentic, lending romance with the sound of hooves and the slow pace.

One of the most civilized aspects of this town is the vast greenness of Parque de María Luisa, which must be a cool green respite when Sevilla turns into the frying pan of Andalucía in summer. We walk the whole morning amid the mimosa and banana plants. The park is full of whimsy—fountains and duck ponds, tile benches, gazebos, and waterfalls. Great tropical trees with roots that seem to pour out at the bottom of the trunk, at home since the explorers returned from New World voyages, make me search for identifying labels, but few have them. One, an **árbol de las lianas**, came from the Amazon. The Swiss Family Robinson could have made their home in the spreading branches. A blind man walks slowly down a path. He knows his way, perhaps by scents and the texture of gravel underfoot. At the monument to the nineteenth-century local poet Gustavo Bécquer, someone has left an extravagant bouquet of bright lilies in the arms of one of the allegorical marble women. Her cool flesh and the hot pink flowers surprise the January morning and make me hope the poet's language was capable of such contrasts. A local history describes him as "an incorrigible Bohemian, who earned a precarious living by translating foreign novels," and who "crooned a weird elfin music." I know him as hopelessly romantic, in the sappy mode, but who occasionally broke through with sharp perceptions such as:

In a brilliant lightning flash we are born
And the brilliance still lasts when we die.
So short is life.

Something about a park is timeless: glimpsing the wild bouquet in the arms of personified love, and the poet up on his pedestal, I think of them standing there all through the blunt and stultifying Franco fascist years, as though love poetry mattered. I resolve to start leaving armfuls of flowers at my holy spots, not just a wildflower or sprig of daphne picked along the way.

We exit the park near the last place where people were burned during that precursor of fascism, that evil twin of Franco's era, the Inquisition, when church and royalty in cahoots went unilaterally crazy, unchecked and blind. Sevilla—here people burned, here marble statues to venerated poets are still visited, here the energy of flamenco could raise the dead, spin them around, and lay them in the ground again.

In no other city have I grasped so quickly the layout of neighborhoods and monuments. A glance at a sixteenth-century map in a book was all it took. The park, the river, the anchor of the

Giralda tower, and that long walk the first day make me feel that I know this place instinctively. We even take shortcuts and land exactly where we want. Getting to know a place on foot connects me to particulars—a green apartment building with a terrace jumbled with banana plants, a grand, peeling turquoise door, the mustard-yellow trimmed bullring with red and black posters of matadors, the tall palms pinwheeling in the sky, the enchanting patio gardens and trickling fountains along Callejón del Agua, Water Street.

I could live here. Is there a Callejón del Sol for me, a Sun Street? With my spotted background in Spanish, and the knowledge I have of Italian, I could cobble together a walking-around Spanish in a few months. I begin to imagine a house with a two-level courtyard and a fountain always singing; tiled rooms, patterned like oriental rugs, are dappled with light from the intricate windows. In the summer I can press my cheek to the tiles for coolness. The gardens are rooms, as the Arabs knew, and the sound of water smooths my sleep. Perhaps I dream of the desert. The shutters of carved wood close on storms that sweep across the plain. The bath is a remnant of a Moorish **ham-**

man, with a deep soaking pool. The vision includes a small blond child playing in the street and calling out his first word in Spanish: **amigo**.

I feel especially at home on Sunday morning in the Plaza del Salvador, where families sit at outdoor cafés sipping orange juice and taking in the sun, while babies climb out of their strollers to chase pigeons. After mass at Iglesia del Salvador, the handsome dark-suited young men with slick hair and the girls in short, short skirts stand under the trees at outdoor tables, as though at a party, drinking beer and eating chips. A cart sells pinwheels. All this under fragrant orange trees in the company of the looming church built on the foundations of a mosque. Rather fantastic children's clothing shops and bridal shops surround the plaza. Probably the impetus for both occasions begins here. We succumb and buy a white outfit for the baby we await in our family: fine cotton smocked a million times in blue, finishes with multiple tucks and dangling ribbons. I wonder who will slide into the pleated arms and pose for a photograph before carrots stain the front.

A taxi ride away we find a wonderful art exhibit in a Carthusian monastery that became a ceramic tile factory, then was restored by the city as a gallery. Even in January some roses and geraniums perk up the courtyards. Vines droop like long hair, blooming with ornamental pink trumpets. The vibrant paintings lead us back into the city to explore the contemporary galleries. At night we try desserts late at various tapas bars: orange rice pudding with cinnamon, quince with cheeses, fig biscuits with walnut sauce. And late, late flamenco. One venue featured a young male dancer full of passion and precision. I was intrigued by his guitarist singer, whose involvement with the dancer seemed almost to make the dance possible. He strained toward the dancer, intently watched, egged him on, pushed his own energy into the dancer. The performance began with a piercing cry, "Aaiiee . . . ," a skull-ringing wail that might have originated with Jewish rituals, for the flamenco weaves the traditions of Gypsies, Muslims, and Jews, bringing their sorrow and passion to indigenous folk music.

I love the moment when the dance suddenly stops and the dancer walks off, as casually as though the light turns and he crosses the street. Snap. The mood is broken. That dramatic shift signifies the difference between the **duende** of the dance and the normal world where we reveal little of what we feel. We like the new phrases we're learning—**toque de palmas**, clapping, **pitos**, finger snapping, **taconeo**, heel stamping. All contribute to the body as instrument. **Castañuelas** comes from **chestnuts**, and perhaps the first castanets were improvised from two dried ones. Ed buys the CD to take home, perhaps to listen to while we cook, so far away from this courtyard open to the stars. "Do you feel that by experiencing flamenco, another room in your mind has opened?" I ask.

"I had a pretty stereotyped impression before. Now we'll be listening to the music, recalling the faces, the passion. Rip-roaring passion."

"Good flamenco tours are sellouts all over the world. Did you know that there are three hundred flamenco schools in Japan? Japan! The center of decorum! What explains the rise in popularity of flamenco, here and everywhere?"

"A yearning. This art touches a yearning we have. The unspoken longings way inside the heart," Ed says.

What man can travel this long road and not fill up his soul with crazy arabesques?

• • •

The day arrives when we are to leave, though we are not going far. We will go to a hacienda in the country where they raise bulls and horses. Sevilla falls away quickly, and we are buzzing in our small rented car toward the **vega**, the plain. Although I never thought so with Las Vegas, the word carries a charge. **Vega**—we begin to experience it as we drive out of Sevilla and the big sky opens over the slightly rolling fields, some with olive trees, some planted with crops, some left to the bulls. My imagined house in Sevilla quickly reabsorbs into a fantasy of a country hacienda, a **cortijo**. We pass them every few miles, stark white, walled, big trees, paradises on their own out in the country.

We check into the Cortijo El Esparragal, three thousand hectares forming a private world with the courtyard as the center of it. A cloister furnished with carved wooden chairs and benches surrounds the arched courtyard with fountain and potted plants. The walls are covered in bull heads and bridles, as in a Florida restaurant where sailfish and marlin hang above the tables. One bull has a bloody tongue and a sword in his back. This is so like the gory religious imagery I found shocking in the Prado. Out in the fields horses play, running from one fence to the opposite. Your heart has to somersault when you see these handsome animals run, turn with a neigh, and race full tilt in the other direction.

We are the only guests, and it's odd—we are in someone's house. All of the family, the girl at the reception tells us, live in Madrid. We settle into our room on a small leafy courtyard. Ed cracks the window so the murmur of the fountain pours in the window. He's soon out the door. The lure of the bull pasture, the long dirt roads to drive in silence, the big shady cork trees, the fragrance of ripe oranges, the private chapel, the miniature bullring—the intact **world** of this hacienda immediately seems compelling to us. I would like a bell tower on my house, and miles of bougainvillea blazing back at the sun. I would like one of these white horses. I would like to paint blue borders and evil eye circles on my house. The stark white haciendas, scattered through the countryside at greater distances than the Tuscan farmhouses, resemble Texas ranches—but of course, those Lazy X ranches descended from the Spanish, as did the tradition of horsemanship.

Having previously traveled only to Barcelona and Majorca in Spain, I did not know how close visually Mexico is to Spain. I attributed characteristics of Mexico to the indigenous population as much as to Spain until we drive through tiny Andalucían towns with their forlorn, weedy parks, their bodegas painted with waist-high bands of aqua or ochre, with human-sized Coca-Cola bottles out front, their dry fountains, and the open doorways where people sit knitting, smoking, or shelling beans. Shops as small as vending machines overflow with ladders, oranges, shoes, paint—all jumbled together. Often in Mexico I have thought, **Where is everybody?** I remember this just as Ed says, "It's quiet as the day after Judgment Day." One lone woman with a bundle of wash poised on her hip sways down the cracked sidewalk. We could be in the Sierra Nevada villages outside San Miguel. But Ed says, "This is limbo. Or this is where you come for a **grande** dose of **duende**."

For lunch, we're alone in the family dining room, presided over by a portrait of the señora who must have decorated these rooms. She's austere in a modest ballgown, no jewelry except for a thin bracelet. Her hair is cropped, her gaze direct, and she is not smiling. She merely looks in charge of her destiny, way back in the 1940s when she sat for this portrait. She chose to hang the walls of her living room with paintings of matadors and famous bulls, probably from this hacienda. Gracious white-gloved women bring us lunch. We don't order; they just bring on the roast pork and platters of potatoes and vegetables. "Are we the only guests?" we ask.

"**Sí**, but the family arrives this afternoon. You see, in this period we are closed." We contemplate this odd reply while we eat. Our reservation must have been a mistake.

Instead of siesta, we settle by the fire with a tiny glass of sherry and read, glancing up at the looming bulls and elegant matadors who have been at home here for so long. When the light drizzle stops, we emerge into the washed afternoon. On our walk, we find wild asparagus, violets, and irises. We startle a jackrabbit in the olive grove, and a troop of seven wild boars startles us. They are so comical looking and seem to take themselves so seriously.

When we come into the living room at the

dinner hour, the family has arrived. They are the early middle-aged daughters and sons of the woman in the portrait, I assume, with their various spouses. No children. They look exactly the way I imagined aristocratic Spaniards in the country would look. They must have been outfitted since infancy in those fancy riding stores in Sevilla with the flat hats, shawls, fine gloves, tooled saddles, and chaps cut in patterns like paper doilies. They sip sherry and talk quietly. Tweed, leather, boots, and big hair. Any one of them certainly could gallop across plains, **Bolero** or not. Not one of them could dance flamenco. They nod to us but say nothing. They're intent on themselves; perhaps they have not been together in a while. On all the tables, framed photographs of them as children and of their ancestors stand guard. We're the interlopers, content to observe. We sink into a sofa and begin talking about the next few days. The family moves into the dining room, where a long table under the eyes of the señora is set with candles and silver. In a few minutes one of the white-gloved maids comes to get us for dinner. We're shown the way, passing the seated family, and not one of them smiles or looks at us. "That would never happen in Italy," I say to Ed.

We're relieved to be taken to a smaller, private dining room, where we dine happily on soup, venison stew, and orange cake.

At breakfast they're nowhere in sight. We're served tortilla-sized pastries wrapped in waxed paper, stamped in red with the name Ines Rosales from nearby Castilleja de la Cuesta. She has made this from wheat, olive oil, essence of anise, and other ingredients the **Oxford Spanish Dictionary** did not see fit to include: **matalahúga** and **ajonjolí**, which I think means "sesame." Nice words to say aloud. The thick coffee ("undrinkable," Ed says) with the aromatic pastry takes me with a Proustian jolt back to Majorca, where my friends Susan and Shera and I rented a house one summer and walked all over the island, with the sea wind stirring the perfumes of shrubs along the coast.

Walking all over Sevilla gave us a sense of intimacy with the city; driving in Andalucía gives us a broader sense of place and of how the larger landscape psychologically imprints those who live here. **Vega**—the wide sky, the home, home on the range, the big sun slipping under the horizon, pulling down a profound darkness. We've found local people cordial but aloof. Is it the xenophobic fear of the stranger on horseback, or a remnant of Franco's cramped society? Vast, vast, endless olive groves carpeted with yellow oxalis puzzle Ed. Where are the houses? The land rolls on, without a dot of human habitation, only those spirits, the majestic, twisted, and sparkling olive trees. Even in January workers are beating the limbs, shaking the trunks with machines, and gathering the fallen drupes from the nets. In the first village we stop to look at Moorish walls and a herd of goats crossing a bridge. The owner of a dusty gift shop tells us that workers commute to the groves and always have. Unlike the Italian system, with a family share-cropping the amount of land they can handle, these seemingly infinite groves are owned by absent landlords but are managed and worked by local teams. Although Spain produces excellent olive oil, much of its exported oil has suffered ruination from bad processing. I've opened some wretched bottles, even when I rented the house on Majorca—thin and tainted with harsh industrial aftertastes. Fine artisan oils exist, if you search. I wish they didn't beat the trees, but if you own a million, something other than the slow human hand will have to get those olives to the mill.

• • •

The open road—almond and plum blossoms are beginning to shake, rattle, and roll. We're heading to Italica, a Roman city settled near the Guadalquiver when the river's course flowed nearer. Hadrian and Trajan were born here. Again, the geography unfolds naturally. A quick orientation, and it is easy to visualize the town flourishing in the second century B.C. on streets wider than Sevilla's. Though only mosaic floors and foundations remain, the reconstructed city rises easily in the imagination, much more so than at all the other hundreds of archaeological sites I've tramped across. We have Italica almost to ourselves, that bonus of travelling in January. The mosaics, mostly in black and white marble, lie intact. Why do we like to walk ancient streets? Curiosity, contemplation, for the surprise of history. These Romans paved their floors with tromp l'oeil squares that become stars. I'm ahead of Ed and call back, "Here's Medusa surrounded by geometric swastikas."

"Too bad Hitler ruined that design forever. Here's a scene for you—The House of the Birds." Bordered squares divide the floor. Each of the thirty-two depicts a different bird. We find Greek key borders, Bacchus, astrological figures, the days of the week mosaic, then the House of Neptune with its reminder of the town's founder, Publius Cornelius Scipio. He's better known to us as Scipio Africanus for his sojourns in Africa, where he defeated Hannibal's Carthaginians and caused Spain to be awarded to the Romans.

Italica, the first Roman town in Iberia, was settled for Scipio's wounded Italian soldiers. There must have been mosaicists among them who fought in the African campaigns. Almost cartoonish squat black warriors with big lips climb palms, ride astride alligators, stand behind shields, and arch, poised to throw arrows. Exotic cranes and ibises intermingle with the border design. In the inside field, fish, seahorses, and mythological sea creatures cavort. The overall effect is muscular, ribald—a pygmy is poked in the rear by a heron, another opens a crocodile's mouth. Perhaps an oral epic was translated into mosaic, if only we could read it.

A workman mops the mosaic floor of one house open to the four winds. He swishes soapy water, then throws down a bucket of clear water. How many thousands of times has someone mopped these sturdy floors! Their makers set each marble chip on a layer of plaster, on top of a layer of lime and earthenware fragments, on top of a layer of lime and stone, on top of a pebble layer. The word **mosaic** comes from the Greek meaning "a patient work worthy of the muses." The first mosaics must have been bits of stone stuck into clay walls to keep them up, to keep them from dripping, to provide a bit of sparkle to a drab room. Then came the incorporation of pieces of lapis lazuli, jasper, onyx, marble, travertine, malachite—pretty colors for making designs and displaying the prosperity of a family. Who can know which is older, rug weaving or mosaics? The designs in mosaics often recall rug patterns and vice versa. As the workman washes, the colors of the stones shine. We take in the blue—fresh as when it was set. So it was always thus; after rain in the uncovered atrium, the family observed how gorgeous their courtyard floor looked when wet.

We have spent the past few hacienda days driving around to small towns where donkeys prove useful. We ate in workers' cafés, searched out

Arab doorways on Christian church grounds, walked in back streets where flowered sheets and orange towels flapped in the breeze and dogs didn't open an eye when we passed. The street life in Carmona reminded me of Cortona's. Babies were admired in the plaza, where boys played ball and clumps of people stood visiting in the sun. A large passing truck stopped, and the driver leaned out to pick a few oranges, then drove on. Like Cortona and all other Tuscan towns, these Andalucían towns have their masterpieces and mysteries. Carmona has many. Sitting in the winter sun, we ordered **tortillitas de bacalao**, cod fritters, and oven-roasted vegetables, and a plate of cheeses as we watched little girls playing with their dolls on a park bench. The cheeses were addictive. We'd known **manchego** in California, though in Spain the taste is saltier, creamier, with a barnyard overtone. The sides are imprinted with a pattern from the grass mold where they're aged. I'm a fan of blue cheeses and have ordered **cabrales** several times. A blend of ewe, goat, and cow milk, the strong flavors are mellowed by the accompanying little dish of quince paste.

The morning seemed to melt seamlessly into an afternoon of exploring the old city. We happened upon the quintessentially Andalucían church of Santa María. Built on the ruins of a mosque, it retains a patio of orange trees, where ritual washing took place. On a column in this peaceful courtyard, we find inscribed a Visigoth calendar of holidays. Again and again these three cultural layers abide, abide.

I'm sure we are not the first to sing "Help, help me Rhonda" as we drive into the fabled white town of Ronda, perched on either side of an impressive abyss. We check into the **parador**, one of the government's chain of inns, usually in historic buildings. Our room lacks charm, but the location can't be matched. Right out the balcony door I look down at the bridge over the canyon and all the small streets and white houses of the old town. The inn's terrace overlooks the gorge and distant mountains. Ronda has all the makings of a bad painting—the whitewashed, geranium-laden, perched tiled-roof town against blue-gray mountains and green fields. The main streets are depressingly jammed with tourists up from the coast on day excursions. Some hefty specimens, scantily clothed, provide their own kind of scenery. Real spring must bring a nightmare of people who in the privacy of their own backyards should never wear shorts but go on tour with their rumps and hams in full view.

Off the main streets we yield to Ronda's beauty. Lanes that once were goat paths wind up and up to quiet and serene residential neighborhoods. These are more appealing to me than **casas colgadas**, the hanging houses so named because they're perched right on the lip of the 525-foot-deep canyon. I'm too insecure to live there. We stop for a lemonade and a look at maps and books. I'm struck, once again, by the strange flattening of a guidebook—town after town, and each one seemingly equal. But the essence of a place, the part of it that picks you up and puts you down somewhere else, cannot be given to the reader through factual description. And maybe not at all. You have to find your own secret images. The slow fall of a coin into the gorge with the sun catching the copper only for a moment, and the fall into nothing says more about a sense of place than three pages of restaurant and hotel descriptions, or dry summations of history that are so compressed they make you dizzy.

I'm tired in Ronda. We both want to retreat for a couple of days and spread out our novels and prop our feet on the low table, or nap, take notes, sip blood orange juice, and partake of the breakfast buffet that features local specialties such as **migas**, a basic country dish of spicy breadcrumbs, chorizo, and garlic, along with platters of fruit and hot **churros**. Breakfast is such a key to the culture. An Italian nipping an espresso, an American chowing down on cereal, eggs, and bacon, the Frenchman grabbing a croissant—breakfast speaks to all the rhythms of the other meals and to the rising and sleeping and working motions. This basic Spanish meal links to people who were heading for hard work and who made do with a bit of meat and leftover bread—whatever was at hand.

The paradors emphasize regional cuisine. So do many local restaurants. Last night we had white almond gazpacho, followed by kid chops and partridge stew. The tapas mania of Sevilla subsides in the country. Hearty food that hunters would like, and plenty of it, seems to be the approach.

The full moon rises out of a pink sky and dangles itself over the gorge—the biggest moon I have seen in my life. I feel the gravity of fullness. So low and enormous, this moon hanging above the canyon. It could plunge into the river below. **Moon**, my daughter's second word. She was a one-year-old pointing to the sky, sensing space and spirit. We lean on the balcony watching the slow trajectory. The Spanish moon has **duende**.

To Marbella and Puerto Banús, just to dip down to the coast. As we drive south, the countryside goes wilder—escarpments and waterfalls, and mountain goats scrambling from rock to rock. "Are they trapped?" I wonder. Peering down from impossible outcrops, they look puzzled as to how they got there. **Help, help me Rhonda.** Hawks transfix in the air over prey. In Italy, this motionless hovering is called Il Santo Spirito because the hawk resembles the holy spirit.

Through a pass, we see the coast and sea. Soon we're zipping by odd developments that look as if they'd landed here by mistake. Wintering English and German tourists pack into these condo and apartment blocks. This is not the ruined western Costa del Sol. The Marbella area is merely overdeveloped, American style. "Are we in Fort Lauderdale?" Ed says. "Look at all that ersatz Tuscan-Mediterranean architecture." But then we find Marbella's lively outdoor cafés around the Plaza de los Naranjos, the nice shops with fine soaps and French sheets, a purely Arab balcony outfitted with a plaster Mary, and again the charm of the air blessed with the scent of orange blossoms. We pass several consignment shops whose windows are filled with Armani and Gucci and Jil Sander. People on vacation must change their minds about what they packed in their suitcases and unload their mistakes rather than take them home. Or maybe they opt to wear less in the lovely sun. In a fancy children's shop, we buy a pair of hand-knitted booties for our Mister X.

Down the road at Puerto Banús, many of the international rich are idling away their January. The yacht harbor, **mamma mia**, is a many-splendored thing. The cool jangles of the rigging and the wavering reflections in the water always give me an adventurous rush, probably that old encoded human desire for quest, for pushing off and heading into the open sea. But these Argonauts seem tightly tethered to land. Boys in crisp shorts polish and buff, flemish ropes, and touch up minute scratches, while portly owners speak into cell phones on the deck. Two women totter in pastel pants and high-heeled sandals across a gangplank. The rings on their fingers are the size of ice cubes. They're **laden** with jewelry. "We're just seeing a stereotype," I tell Ed. "Down below someone is reading Heidegger, and over there on the bow of **Stardust Destiny**, someone is writing a villanelle."

"Dream on. He's working a crossword puzzle, at best. Why tax yourself in this place?" Ferraris slowly cruise the street. We inspect the menus of the seafood restaurants lining the harbor and choose one where the crayfish, crab, and prawns thrash on ice and the fish look bright-eyed. Next to us a German woman orders a Tia Maria on ice after her lunch of grilled fish and white wine. She's tan as a saddle, probably around seventy, with a magenta scarf wound around her neck and hair. Ed asks if she lives here, and yes, she bought a condominium five years ago and has joined book clubs and investment clubs but finds herself bored, hence the second Tia Maria, I assume, and besides the weather (seventy-five degrees today) is frigid but better than the iron-cold of Stuttgart. I fear retirement in places where the climate is the lure.

From Ronda, via Antequera and Archidona, we make our way to Granada, city of García Lorca. Snow tops the surrounding mountains—a Xanadu setting. As we drive closer, we're suddenly lost in dismal sprawl and dirty air. By the time we find our hotel near the Alhambra, we've gone quiet with disappointment. Granada, I'm not falling under your spell. Poetry, roses, nightingales, water gardens, Gypsies—no one's fault but mine that I imagined a fabled city. Or perhaps it is the fault of the Nicaraguan on the lawn at Princeton, leafing through Lorca's poems, stopping at "Ballad of the Three Rivers." The book was worn leather (**cordovan**, I suddenly realize—from Córdoba). **Guadalquiver, high tower/and wind in the orange groves . . ./It carries olives and orange blossoms,/Andalucía, to your seas.** The breeze riffled the pages, tissue thin like an old Bible. Marienoelle, his little daughter, learned her first word that afternoon. **Agua**, she shrieked, **agua**, splashing in the plastic pool. I leaned against a tree, arms folded. From the lips of the Nicaraguan, I learned that Granada has "two rivers, eighty bell towers, four thousand watercourses, fifty fountains." I lost a gold ring that belonged to my husband's family, and I looked in the grass for hours. The poet said nothing about pollution headaches.

We arrive late. From the hotel window, the snowy mountain-ringed city below spreads into endless lights and the wavy slush of traffic noise. To compound our first impression, we face a greasy dinner in the small restaurant highly recommended by the hotel's concierge. Ten o'clock, and the place is empty except for a silent couple having tapas at the bar. The owner nips at a large glass of wine on a sideboard each time he ducks into the room from the kitchen. He seems distraught when we ask for anything. "Must be the concierge's brother," Ed whispers. The uphill route back to the hotel takes us through ominous streets. Federico García Lorca, modest dreamer and son of water, I believe you said **Granada is made for music.** Please forgive me, but your Granada is a disaster. We're relieved to see the hotel looming at the end of the street. Pseudo-Moorish, it is drafty, tiled, and old enough to have character. We chose it because Lorca gave his first poetry reading here. His guitar accompanist was Andrés Segovia. Two young men are getting out of a car. Federico and Andrés? Striding into the lobby, young, full of ideals?

Ed goes upstairs for a bath, and I order a sherry on the glassed-in terrace. The stars are fiery. Hey Federico, I expected horses, moon, jasmine, **duende**, an almond branch against the sky. Doesn't the Arab saying **Paradise is that part of the heavens that is above Granada** have any truth to it? I don't really like sherry, Federico. I'm not even thinking yet of the Alhambra just above us, how that massive presence must have seeped into your brain, must seep into the very canaliculi of every inhabitant of Granada. This nice **fino**—such a warm color—reminds me of my in-laws from my first marriage. Pouring from gallon jugs of cheap sherry into tiny crystal glasses, they tippled from noon on. My husband and I used to count the empties on the back porch and wonder if they were alcoholics. But sitting on a balcony in Granada, that dreary, bleary-eyed old father is the last thing I want to think about, smoking in his chair in the high-ceilinged room, clearing his throat, a weary figure everyone stepped around and tried desperately to glorify or at least explain. I later learned of his sick and evil streak, something I must have known by instinct as a bride. I always shuddered and turned my face away from any welcome or goodbye embrace. Taste is also memory. Maybe he's why sherry burns my mouth with a back taste of medicine and mould.

Better to think of that stellar being, the poet, polar opposite of the downward-dragging former father-in-law. Lorca's meteoric trajectory through life was short—only thirty-nine years. He lived with a powerful exuberance that deserves a lift of the glass anytime. Everything he touched ignited with his creativity. Besides his poetry and plays and lectures, he started a travelling troupe of actors to take drama into the countryside where people did not see plays. He studied flamenco guitar with Gypsies and loved folk music, riddles, and songs. He painted, made puppets, wrote extraordinary letters. He was legendary at the piano, singing with friends until all hours. With other musicians, he organized a local conference in 1922 on **cante jonde**, deep song. "The Gypsy **siguiriya** [a type of deep song] begins with a terrifying outcry," he said in his lecture:

> a scream that divides the landscape into two perfect hemispheres. It is the cry of dead generations, a sharp-edged elegy for lost centuries, the passionate evocation of love under other moons and other winds. Then the melodic phrase gradually reveals the mystery of tones and sets off the jewel-stone sob, a musical tear shed in the river of the voice. No Andalucían hears that cry without a shudder of emotion, nor can other regional songs compare to it in poetic grandeur, and seldom, very seldom, does the human spirit succeed in shaping works of art of such naturalness.

At that conference, local artists awakened to their heritage. Lorca was the brightest bloom of Granada's promise. The Chilean poet Pablo Neruda remembered him as "an effervescent child, the young channel of a powerful river. He squandered his imagination, he spoke with enlightenment . . . He cracked walls with his laughter, he improvised the impossible, and in his hands a prank became a work of art. I have never seen such magnetism and such constructiveness in a human being." I would love to have had him as a close friend. I feel a sharp sting of loss. Wondrous that you can miss someone who died before you were born. **Buenas noches**, Federico. I will try to find **your** Granada.

Fourteen ninety-two resonates in Granada for reasons other than Columbus's New World discovery. That same year this last major city of the Nasrid Arab rulers fell to the forces of our old friends Isabella and Fernando. Prior to their victory, during the 250-year reign of the Nasrids, the fabulous fortress, the Alhambra, symbolized the refinement, play, and range of Moorish art. When Fernando and Isabella took over the keys to the Alhambra, they walked up the hill to claim their new residence, dressed, I'm astounded to read, in Arab clothing. They moved in, these reconquerors, and did their damage to the complex. But they were profoundly acclimated to Moorish design and oddly enough (to the traveller), they were **at home** with the Arab lifestyle.

We're up early—this is the most-visited tourist attraction in the world. We are lucky—few people are here yet—and no tour buses. Only a black cat welcomes us, a reincarnation of our cat, Sister, who lived in feline glory for eighteen years. Here she is, Sister the Moor; she was never put to sleep by a vet named Dr. Blood, never carried away wrapped in a monogrammed green towel I'd had since college.

As we learn about the Alhambra and gardens, what fascinates me most is how art was so closely connected to living. Through the decorative—interior design and landscape design—the entire panoply of Moorish art is displayed. The complex, added on to and improved over two centuries, began with al-Sabikah, a citadel, and eventually included stables, barracks, servants' quarters, and administrative apartments. The exquisite jewel remains the Nasrids' royal palace, their courtyards, baths, and enchanted rooms, along with their gardens, which extend to the Generalife (meaning "the architect's paradise"), their second home (probably bought from the architect) nearby. The Alhambra's gardens recalled the legendary gardens of Damascus. We walk, as they lived, with the sound of water, soothing to us and to the ears of desert people. Green, green—the lush trees and damask roses must have soothed the Nasrids. The intricate stucco carved ceilings, the Mudéjar-tiled walls with epigraphs calligraphed on borders, the horseshoe-arched **mihrabs**, the gold-filigreed walls of complex vegetal and geometric patterns—even with all the splendor, the rooms maintain a human scale. A few rugs, a pile of cushions, a brazier, and we'd be ready to rinse our hands in orange flower water, relax, and settle down for a feast of lamb tagine, stuffed eggplants and cabbages flavored with coriander and cinnamon, preserved lemons, chickpeas with saffron, and a pastry pie of pigeons. The bath, too, reveals an appreciation of life's pleasures. A balcony for poets and musicians rests on top of the tiled soaking pool. The royals could bathe while listening to dulcet music drifting down. The arches, galleries, and entablatures that adorn many rooms are supported by columns. Are the rooms any larger than the grand Berber tents their nomadic ancestors pitched in the sand? Maybe the extensive use of columns comes from an inheritance of tent poles. The 124 columns supporting panels of fretted lattice in the Courtyard of the Lions reminded visitors of palm trees. The central fountain symbolized to them the oasis in the desert. What a marvel, that fountain. The twelve lions—associated with the zodiac—spout water into channels for all the garden. They have a history older than this courtyard. Their mysterious, smooth forms radiate from the flat basin where a jet of water rises in the middle. I've always liked the Latin **hortus conclusus**, "walled garden." In the Old Testament Song of Songs, such a garden is associated with "my sister, my spouse." Later associations of Mary and the walled garden resonated with the purity and beauty of the inviolate body. But earlier, the etymological root of **paradise** reveals the deeply metaphorical workings of the garden in the human psyche. The root of the word **paradise** means "walled garden." The enclosed Islamic gardens profoundly influenced the western medieval gardens. The cruciform designs of the monasteries conveniently paralleled Christian iconography, but the design previously reflected the Islamic concept of paradise, with four rivers flowing out in the cardinal directions from a single source. "Four-chambered heart," Ed muses. "Did they think of that, too?" How did we live so long without knowing what we've learned on this trip?

Many rulers have identified themselves with the sun, but the hubris of the carved stucco inscription in the Hall of the Ambassadors, where the Nasrid rulers greeted their subordinates, must be unsurpassed. Entering this hall, a hard-riding emissary, coming up from the Costa Tropical with a report, might have been stupefied by the deeply coffered ceiling of interlocking marquetry stars, the high windows that shed a line of sunlit arches on the floors, and the miradors with wooden screens carved as finely as lace. But as he waited, he eventually would have focused on the make-no-mistake poem carved in Kufic calligraphy near the throne:

> From me you are welcomed morning and evening by the tongues of blessing, prosperity, happiness, and friendship . . . yet I possess excellence and dignity above all those of my race. Surely we are all parts of the same body; but I am like the heart in the midst of the rest and from the heart springs all energy of soul and life. True, my fellows here may be compared to the signs of the zodiac in the heaven of the dome but I can boast what they are lacking—the honor of a sun, since my lord, the victorious Yusuf, has decorated me with the robes of

> his glory and excellence without disguise, and has made me the throne of his empire. May its eminence be upheld by the Master of Divine Glory and the Celestial Throne.

The rhythmic lettering may be artistic, but the tone says so much: a smooth talker with a welcoming smile and an iron will.

As the emissary exited the Sala de los Embajadores, he could cool off in the Courtyard of the Myrtles, beside a long pool and low stone basin of gurgling water. These fountains and courtyards invite strolling, reading Rumi, sipping jasmine tea. They also bounce their light into the surrounding rooms, glazing the tiles and mottling the walls with wavering shadows. For those who lived their daily lives here, the light, the temperature, even their skin was changed by the wet-watercolor refractions from the fountains and channels. Water is transformative in this architecture. When I look at a floor plan of the Alhambra, I see that water was a building material, with as integral a part in the construction as arches and walls. The Alhambra gardens **are** paradisaical. I easily can imagine this whole place as the afterlife.

In the Alhambra gift shop, we are the only

customers. As we look through the books, I become aware of the piercing sweetness of the background music. "What is that wonderful music?" I ask the girl at the counter.

"Angel Barrios, of course." She looks at me as though I'd asked a totally self-evident question. I've never heard of Angel Barrios. We pick up several books on architecture and the gardens, and two CDs. One, of course, is the haunting music of Angel Barrios wafting about the shop and forever annealing my brain to this day when I finally came to Granada and saw the Alhambra. The other CD is **Noches en los jardines de España**, **Nights in the Gardens of Spain**, by Manuel de Falla, loveliest title and the most tender piano sequences ever to roll off the fingers of any Spanish composer. Back in our room, I listen to both. I'm electrified by Barrios—is he my third angel promised by the prophet who danced with God? I fall into an Alhambra trance. Barrios, I know I will listen to for the rest of my life.

Those who live in the houses scattered below the Alhambra must sip the influence of the palace and gardens with their morning coffee, must always stroll there in their imaginations, as well as on many Sunday afternoons. One of the houses, with a weathered blue, blue door on a lane just below the Alhambra, belonged to Manuel de Falla, a friend of Lorca and also an **appassionato** of Gypsy traditions. With de Falla, Lorca organized the seminal Granada conference on deep song. De Falla, who lived with his sister, could hear faintly from his garden the Alhambra's fountains' spilling notes, a fluid, melancholy sound that entered his compositions. He's long dead in Argentina, his dead-end street completely empty. Lorca lifted that knocker in the shape of a woman's hand. De Falla opened that little window in the door to see who was there. Then the door swung open, and inside they laughed together, and Federico listened to Manuel play and Manuel listened to Federico's latest poem. I imagine them inside, vital and strong, the buzz of their creativity humming in their veins, their hunger a force in the room. A fortunate friendship that ended tragically. I memorize the closed blue door of his whitewashed house.

The Lorcas' **huerta**, small farm, once was a sweet white house in the fields. The family could see the Alhambra and the distant Sierra Nevada mountains. A charming garden surrounded the house. **There is so much jasmine and nightshade in the garden that we all wake up with lyrical headaches.** We can see the ease of the indoor/outdoor life. Now the freeway rims one edge of the property, and ten-story block apartment buildings oppress the other edge. Still, once we are on the grounds, the simple house is profoundly moving. The kitchen's black stove, the small room where Federico slept, the piano, the manuscripts and framed whimsical drawings—the house retains a soul, even given the current institutional status. Outside the grounds a Gypsy woman offers me a bunch of rosemary and I take it because Federico would have.

Today is our Lorca Pilgrimage. We drive across the **vega** to his early childhood home in Fuente Vaqueros (Cowboys' Fountain). The flat landscape, with immense breaks of poplars, feathery in the white, still winter air, feels mysterious, close to Lorca's perception that the **vega** possessed a feeling of immensity and "spiritual density." His synesthetic images must have grown inside him because of his closeness to the earth: "The gray arm of the wind/ wrapped around her waist," and "the sun inside the afternoon/ like the stone in a fruit," and so many others. In the pearly light, the stands of poplars set me dreaming. When the sun burns off the mist, will they be gone? His childhood house, too, is touching—the baby bed, the tile floor, the pump and well in the courtyard, the Mama's boy photographs. Upstairs we see a video of him, grown, with his thespian group, travelling the provinces. His big smile. His vigor. His affection for his fellows breaks out of the film. The family moved again, to Valderrubio, and we go there, too, crossing the big olive country, and finally just peering in the door. Enough. We drive back to Granada, listening to Barrios and de Falla and talking quietly about going home.

Since it's late afternoon when we return, we stop at a Lorca hangout for tapas, then walk down Las Ramblas and through back streets crowded with shoppers. Guitar stores! They're everywhere. In each, someone intently tunes the strings or strums or just gets the feel of holding the instrument. We turn into a shadowy Moroccan area near the university, then end up for dinner in a restaurant where a photo of Lorca hangs above the bar. We are, again, the only ones here. The waiter offers an aged **mahón** cheese from the island of Minorca, which tastes like toasted hazelnuts, and an odd smoky cheese called **idiazabal**. Dinner ends on a grace note.

The fate of Lorca hangs over Granada. Was his death at the hands of the fascists one reason de Falla, who so loved his house under the Alhambra, emigrated to Argentina? Would he have found his beloved city insupportable after he journeyed to government headquarters, attempting to save his friend, only to find out Lorca already had been murdered?

When Carlos introduced me to Lorca's poems, he told me that a rare quetzel bird landed on the roof at his family's farm near León in Nicaragua. The workers were so overcome by the bird's beauty that they did the only thing that came to mind—they shot it dead. Many Spanish birds were shot—the civil war lasted almost three years. From July 1936 until the end of March 1939, that war killed half a million, 130,000 by execution. In Granada around five thousand were executed. At the **huerta** with the flowery garden, Lorca's family must have cried for years.

Lorca was a free spirit but far too intelligent to criticize outright the burgeoning fascist regime. I think he had a sixth sense that he was, nonetheless, in danger. As he boarded a train from Madrid, for what would prove to be his last trip to his family in Granada, he spotted an official from his hometown and raised his forefinger and smallest finger in the air, chanting "Lizard, lizard, lizard" to deflect the evil eye of this member of parliament. His brother-in-law, recently elected mayor of Granada, was murdered eight days before Federico was arrested at the home of the Rosaleses, old friends. Those who took him away, Ruiz Alonso, Juan Luís Trecastro, Luis García Alix, and the name of Governor Valdés, deserve black paint thrown on their graves forever, especially Trecastro, who was overheard the next day saying that the rounds from the fusillade had not killed Lorca; he himself shot "two bullets into his arse for being a queer." Lorca was killed in an olive grove near a spring hallowed to the Moors. They'd called it the Fountain of Tears.

Neruda wrote: "If one had searched diligently, scouring every corner of the land for someone to sacrifice as a symbol, one could not have found in anyone or anything, to the degree it existed in this man who was chosen, the essence of Spain, its vitality and its profundity." Antonio Machado's poem will always remind us that **Granada was the scene of the crime. / Think of it—poor Granada—his Granada.**

One of my favorite quotes from Lorca came from his time in New York. He loved Harlem jazz and connected black music with that of the Gypsies in Andalucía. He said he couldn't understand a world "shameless and cruel enough to divide its people by color when color is in fact the sign of God's artistic genius." Bravo, Federico.

Machado has the last word here:

Friends, carve a monument
out of dream stone
for the poet in the Alhambra
over a fountain where the grieving water

shall say forever
The crime was in Granada, his Granada.

In an antique shop, I buy a marble pomegranate for my desk because **Granada** means "pomegranate." I buy six old blue and white tiles of boar and deer, a small still-life of oranges and lemons, and a bronze-gone-to-verdigris door knocker in the shape of a horse's head, a few small things closely tied to my perceptions of the place. In the back of this crammed shop, the owner and his friend are barely visible amid the chaos. The friend is from Damascus but lives in Granada. He whispers something to the owner; then he opens a small box and gives me a silver hand of Fatima. "For good luck," he says.

"Against evil eye," the friend from Damascus adds. He is dark, with soot-black eyes lighted with little fires. He is missing an incisor, though he smiles broadly. He has much advice about what to see. He runs a falafel shop, speaks six languages. We feel that we are meeting a Moor who came hundreds of years ago, bringing with him cuttings of damask roses, spices, alchemical recipes, and songs. There, Federico, we begin to see.

Someday I will come back to Granada. I loved the tiny Arab bath, the archaeological museum, the unprettified streets of the Albacín area. And the Alhambra charged every neuron in my body. Over the week the geography of the place, the lonely **vega** and the glory of the mountains, began to imprint my senses. But while I was here, I felt restless and agitated. Lorca's ghost walks, uneasy in this city. Some things cannot be forgiven. **The crime was in Granada.**

We like Ubeda immediately. Our **parador** room's balcony overlooks a courtyard, so I'm happy. Like Pienza in Tuscany, Ubeda is a Renaissance town of golden stone that catches the late afternoon light and turns it to warm honey. As we reach the plaza, we see that enormous backhoes have ripped out the entire square. People are routed over wooden sidewalks and away from the construction. We do not get to see the famous statue of the fascist Serro, which locals have peppered with bullets over the years. We walk back toward the **parador** and find St. Paul's Church, which has a mosque shape—square and low. All four sides intrigue me. We find the Renaissance public fountain along one side, carved heads and decorative columns that look almost Venetian on another. What a privilege, to gaze and look at buildings. The church faces a plaza where women are knitting and talking ninety miles an hour. Four boys engage in a fast soccer game. Suddenly the ball hits one of the graceful three-branch wrought-iron streetlights. The lamp shatters, and the plaza comes to a halt for a moment; then the game and the talk resume.

What better relic for a poet/saint than two fingers from the writing hand encased in a silver box on a stand? Spanish tour groups crowd into the rooms where Saint John of the Cross lived and wrote. I first heard of him in college when I read T. S. Eliot, who folded into his poems several quotes from the ascetic Spanish mystic. His philosophical and religious poems are fraught with the suppressed eroticism of mystical love. Lorca saw **duende** in his dark night of the soul, and his constant turning toward deprivation as a way to enlightenment. Much of his writing, however, feels almost homiletic: how to live in this world, self-help for the troubled well, down-home language, and a no-nonsense guide to the sublime. I love best the most poetic poems, where he lets loose his instinct for metaphor and speaks in an intimate voice. Is there a hint of the Arabic poets in his lines?

Now that the bloom uncloses
Catch us the little foxes by the vine,
As we knit cones of roses
Clever as those of pine.
No trespassing about this hill of mine.

Keep north, you winds of death.
Come, southern wind, for lovers. Come and stir
The garden with your breath.

Shake fragrance on the air.
My love will feed among the lilies there.

(From "The Spiritual Canticle,"
translated by
John Frederick Nims)

In his bedroom his hair shirt and the log he used for a pillow are displayed. In other rooms we see paintings of his miracles, one of which seems to have had something to do with asparagus. In his dialogue with Jesus, the painted ribbons of words come out of both mouths.

The Moorish influence in Ubeda is minimal. A door, a gate—we find one arched gate with the characteristic right turn built into it under a double horseshoe. In the shadows we make out a painting of Mary. The faithful have decorated the table below with vases of dusty artificial flowers. Someone has left a doll leg, a red candle, and a pair of eyes painted on metal.

My old habit of looking out for real estate offices and checking "for sale" signs comes back to me here. This is a town I could live in quite comfortably. I imagine the pleasure of anonymity, the spacious days for writing and for reading all of Juan de la Cruz. We could sell all, buy a house on the leafy, angular plaza of Santo Domingo. But tomorrow we press on to Baeza, then on to Córdoba, and then our time in Andalucía will end.

An appealing small town surrounded by olive groves, Baeza is full of cadets from the Guardia Civil academy. They fill the streets in their veridian uniforms, all trim and groomed and young. Many sit in cafés with their girlfriends, enjoying the mild January sun. We meander through the covered market, plazas, and churches. We see the door ajar in a ruined patrician house and slip inside, fantasizing about restoring it to perfection. Across from the **ayuntamiento** (city hall), Ed spots a rose-bordered tile marker on a run-down house with a blue door: AQUI VIVIO EL POETA ANTONIO MACHADO. The poet's house, where his wife of only three years died at twenty, is closed, but we see what he saw as he closed his door every morning and walked to his job teaching languages in the village school. He lived a life of simplicity until he passionately reviled the fascists and had to leave

Spain. He died on his arrival in France in 1939. We drive out into the land of the olives. I read aloud to Ed a few lines of Machado:

Over the olive grove
The owl could be seen
Flying and flying
In its beak it carried
A sprig of green
for holy Mary.
Country around Baeza,
I'll dream of you
When I cannot see you.

A few miles outside town we see a **cortijo** for sale, white walled and serene, with nine thousand olive trees. The price is half what a studio apartment costs in San Francisco. The world cracks open for those willing to take a risk.

A glance at the map of Córdoba makes it clear why we keep getting lost. The Arabs must have had a firm rule—nothing parallel can exist. Streets radiate in star-shaped clusters, following the old labyrinthine **medina** lanes, converging at a church or plaza. Many are too narrow for cars, but we see an intrepid driver, cigarette hanging from his lip, negotiating them anyway. He's pulled his mirrors in and doubtlessly holds his breath as he creeps along with two inches to spare on either side.

We give up trying to figure out where we are and just turn into any old cobbled alley festooned with geraniums. We skirt the Mezquita, the famous mosque, and avoid the river road dense with traffic. Granada, with a major tourist attraction, was surprisingly untouristy. Córdoba has caught on. Shops selling kitschy souvenirs proliferate throughout the whitewashed maze of the old Jewish section. But the area exudes the enchantment of secret courtyards and curly iron gates. I see hardly a street that I don't want to turn down. We keep coming upon very simple and small Gothic churches—an unexpected treat. Some have Arabic touches—a dome, an arch, a window design—showing the continuing Mudéjar influence after the Christian conquest.

Our hotel is across from the Museo Taurino, museum of the bullfight. Oh! Hides and heads, sculptures of gored matadors lying in state. Lorca wondered if **olé** is not related to that moment in Arabic music when the **duende** begins and the crowd cries, **Allah, Allah**. We don't linger. I'm fascinated that the origins of the bullfight root in ritual sacrifice among the Tartessos people, who lived near the delta of the Guadalquivir around 1,000 B.C. This glory eludes me. Perhaps because I come from a culture where death is regarded as something like selling short. Where death is somewhat embarrassing. Again, I turn to Lorca: "Everywhere else . . . death comes, and they draw the curtains. Not in Spain. In Spain they open them. Many Spaniards live indoors until the day they die and are taken out into the sunlight. A dead man in Spain is more alive as a dead man than anyplace else in the world." Yes, with the exception of Mexico. In Guanajuato I passed a coffin-maker's shop. A little girl in pink ruffles played with her dolls inside an open coffin, while her parents attached the lid on another. Life and death are closer companions than we can understand.

We're thrilled to find **churro** stands again. Miguel, who loops dough into hot oil and quickly lifts out the sizzling circle with tongs, tells us how to make them, though we probably miss half the recipe. His are big. He catches on when I say "hula hoop" and gives us an extra with a cup of chocolate. They're best right out of the oil. My capacity for them has increased over the weeks in Spain.

Right across from the Museo de Bellas Artes, Julio Romero de Torres, a local artist who died in 1930, has his own museum. I've never heard of him before today. He was a painter, primarily of women, and he painted some of the loveliest necks imaginable. Some of the many, many paintings slide off into the lugubrious, but enough of them have a quality of transcendental light. His fine small portraits could keep company with the Piero della Francesca, Zurbarán, and Ghirlandaio portraits we saw earlier in the trip in Madrid.

We walk a long way to the Palacio de Viana, a house of many charms. Built in the seventeenth century, the style reveals the moment when Arab domestic architecture formed permanently into what we call Spanish style. Fourteen courtyards make this house a dream. We have to join a group to see the house. The leader speaks in Spanish so we are bored and lost. In a small bedroom a portrait of Franco looms. I would hate to have him looking down on my narrow bed.

We amuse ourselves by imagining that we are buying the place and discuss in whispers what we would plant, how we would rearrange the dreary furniture, and what we'd serve for Sunday lunch in one of the sumptuous courtyards—bitter greens and roast venison, the fried cream with cinnamon ice cream we had last night. Artisan goat cheeses with a glass of **fino** or some little cordial made from ripe cherries. I detour to find a bathroom during the tour, then find myself alone. For fifteen minutes I get the chance to experience the worn tile floors and the views from the windows without the canned litany. Then I am scolded as I turn down a hallway and meet the group. I do love the pattern of days one would live in a house like this, the seamless weaving of inside and outside. "Surely the Spanish devised the most felicitous form of architecture for everyday living," Ed says as we exit and prepare to be lost in the streets of Córdoba again.

"Yes, but think of Pompeii. They had the courtyard concept, too, and way earlier."

"Their courtyard served a practical function—it sloped to a drain. The rainwater funneled into a cistern."

"I like entering a house through a courtyard. Such a cool transition into the private realm from the public. You're in but out."

"Yes, a processional feeling."

We are saving the mosque, one of the great sights of this world, until last. As we walk past a tiny plaza, Ed stops in front of a sculpture of a seated man holding a book. "Maimonides! Of course. I'd forgotten. He was born in Córdoba."

I'm dim on Maimonides but recognize his major work when Ed mentions it, **A Guide for the Perplexed**. "What a contemporary title," I say, "or are we just perpetually perplexed throughout history? I know I am."

"It seems like the right stance in life. Anyone who isn't perplexed is deluded. Let's see—he was a Jew who wrote in Arabic and had to go into exile. No one understands why, but he at some point went to North Africa instead of following the other Jews down into southern Spain. Maybe it was because he felt such strong affinity with Arab culture. Some say he converted to Islam."

We're happy to see him standing his ground

in the small plaza where university students blare their music from open windows all around. He's a good still point of reference for them. Seneca, who became Nero's tutor, also came from Córdoba, and also Averroës, whose commentaries on Aristotle stirred mighty debate in the twelfth century and reawakened discourse all over the continent. While the rest of Europe plodded through the centuries, this city was famous for its immense library of 400,000 books, for lighted streets and houses with hot and cold water, for weavers and ivory carvers, for three hundred baths, fifty hospitals, and seventeen colleges. Mathematicians, philosophers, musicians, and poets were exalted. Even women were writers and musicians. A spirit of tolerance prevailed among the Jews, Muslims, and Christians, creating a munificent climate for the expansion of culture. This **convivencia** (peaceful coexistence) came to a crashing halt in the twelfth century with the rise of the bigoted Almohad rulers, who supplanted the more flexible and intellectual Umayyads. Then in 1236 Fernando III subdued the city and caused the non-Christians to flee.

The Umayyads are the heroes of Córdoba. Their dynasty in Spain began with a fabulous character, Abd ar-Rahman. In 750 he was in his teens when his entire family, the rulers of Syria, was deposed and murdered. Like other pioneers since, he set out for the west, making his way to what he'd heard of as al-Andalus, where he quickly built a loyal following. María Rosa Menocal's **The Ornament of the World** tells how Abd ar-Rahman changed the course of history. She's right. The more I've read about Andalucía, the more I realize that the history I studied in college was a stripped-down version, emphasizing at every turn the joyful triumph of Christianity. Courses often take a path that illustrates certain biases because it's much more vexing to teach contradictions or coexisting truths.

Living in Italy, I began to see more clearly how the Western world was fitted intricately together from all the cultures around **mare nostrum**, our sea, as the Romans intimately called it. Even in Tuscany I began to be aware of the farther influence, the almost-ignored Arab influence. **Saracinesca**, a word we use frequently, reveals the Saracen way with water. They brought west with them elaborate irrigation methods, waterwheels, and evidently a kind of perpendicular faucet that cuts off the flow of water, which is how we use **saracinesca**. On our first trip to Sicily, we had a full exposure to the intermingling of that island's history with the Moors. Now in Andalucía, the depth of the Arab contribution to the Mediterranean cultures almost overwhelms us. There is much to rethink.

The mosque. We've skirted it, looking at the portals that relieve the plain sandstone exterior. Each horseshoe-arch opening, with the door below, reminds me of a schematic human figure, with the radiating design around the arch like a nimbus. Since realistic images were forbidden, I wonder if this design had the hidden purpose of placing the idea of the body within the design. The portal openings are backed by geometric designs of great variety and complexity.

Our big cowboy who took over the town, Abd ar-Rahman, bought a Christian church, which had been built over a Roman temple, and began to enlarge it for a mosque. His heirs continued the work. This is the largest mosque in the world, where you can **feel** how the architecture guides you toward a philosophy of prayer.

The immense, spreading horizontal space keeps you close to the ground, with no sense of hierarchy, no sense of uplifting the spirit toward heaven. It is profoundly unlike the experience of the Gothic but does not feel totally foreign to the experience of the Romanesque. In a mosque, calligraphic inscriptions from the Koran replace the holy images in Christian churches. Wherever you prostrate yourself is holy, as long as you face Mecca; the mosque has no focal-point high altar. Any inspired supplicant can become a prayer leader in his part of the mosque. In the Córdoba mosque, the multiplied columns make it clear to the worshiper that all the space therein is equal space before Allah.

The most often-used word to describe the mosque is **forest**. One writer compared the endless columns topped by arches to a petrified forest. I can support that conceit. There's even a lovely parallel of the inside to the courtyard of trees outside, where the faithful washed before prayer, and—this bends my mind—where scholars sat in appointed spots and discussed recent theories with anyone interested. But walking around the mosque, looking up at the layers of arches, I do not have the sensation of being in a forest. I have a more primitive instinct—

that we are in the mind of Allah. The arches topped with other many-lobed arches form a great brain. The space is intimate, even claustrophobic. At the same time I feel **something is called for here**. I've never had a similar reaction in a building before.

The columns and the sublime cream and terra-cotta colors resemble a paradise, and at the same instant the ludicrous additions later heaped upon the mosque by the Christians are hard to look at. They literally plunked down a large church right in the prayer room of the mosque, a hideous intrusion that disrupts the harmony of the structures. When Charles V finally made it to Córdoba three years after this monstrosity was built, he said, "You have destroyed something that was unique to this world and replaced it with something that can be seen anywhere." Despite his outrage, Charles did nothing to restore the mosque's integrity, so what we have today is this absurd combination, like a camel with a chicken's face. The Christians also walled in many of the arcades, reducing the light inside. Surely this is one of the major architectural atrocities of the world. Luckily, the size makes it possible to ignore the strange church and to dream awhile in the ancient Andalucían manner. In such places, the heart expands and admits the new.

Back in Madrid, we spend the last night at the Ritz in great comfort. The hotel notebook cautions guests not to appear in the lobby in sports attire. If you **must** wear such attire, notify the concierge and he will escort you out another door.

We dress up and have a fine dinner in the hotel restaurant, among all the Spanish families so formally dressed that we feel we've stepped back thirty years. The Gran Reserva Bodegas Muga wine smells like wet violets in spring and the antique rose called Paul Neyron at Bramasole. The cheese, **garrotxa**, tastes like the basket of herbs I pick there when I'm about to prepare a feast. Or maybe I'm homesick. Our neighbor Chiara has sent Ed his **passaporta**. He can leave Spain and enter Italy legally.

It seems like months since we landed, Ed sick, my bag lost. The little jet lifts off for Florence, its motor humming rather oddly, like a paper airplane propelling from an unwinding, twisted rubber band. Ed is sipping water and looking out the window, and I lean over to see Madrid receding into an abstraction. Goodbye to the azure and saffron sky over the **vega**; goodbye to the museum courtyard, where birds drench the air with their song; goodbye to the night when women named Agueda are serenaded; goodbye to the "incorrigible bohemian" now immortalized in marble; goodbye to the Arab inscriptions on the tombs of Isabella and Fernando; goodbye to the sun high over the bullring; goodbye to the turkey thrown from the church tower and the good luck of the catcher; goodbye to the goat marooned on an outcrop; goodbye to the children carrying rosemary wreaths and colored birds in the Virgin's procession; goodbye to the brain of Allah; goodbye to the cold garlic soup of Ronda; goodbye to Machado's words **Beneath the blue of oblivion, the sacred water/ sings nothing—not your name, not mine**; goodbye, Federico García Lorca.

Astrolabe and Cataplana

Portugal

The taxi driver whistles as he leisurely parallels Avenida da Liberdade's long park just coming into leaf. A young March spring with jacaranda and fruit trees at bud break. "Europe, really, really Europe," I say. I'm already under those trees sipping coffee at an art nouveau café, writing new Portuguese words in my notebook. We circle an immense open plaza of fountains, wind up, up, switch-backing into increasingly narrow streets lined with sky-blue and blue-going-to-purple facades and a few of frosted pink with tiled fronts. He stops in front of a dismal funeral parlor with a window full of dead plants warning you of what's inside. Opening my door, he points down what Ed calls a mirror-scraper street. The driver won't enter but motions us to take a right at the end, then a left. Our rented house is **there**, he gestures, turning over his hand three times. We drag our bags over rough cobbles. The area looks seedy but not threatening. The funeral home is tucked in among small restaurants, produce stands with mounds of cabbage, and dim **bottegas**.

"Looks like a real neighborhood." Ed tries to ignore a mongrel snarling from a doorway. Though the dog strains toward Ed, it does not lunge. A sudden shout from inside causes it to go limp and lie down. Mothers are retrieving toddlers from a day care center. A stooped man sets out a plate of food for stray cats just inside an abandoned house. One house looks bombed; several are long gone in decay.

"Everywhere we go will be downhill," I notice. "That means we'll have to climb back up."

"Good," Ed says. **Not good**, I think.

Our block-long street has taken a modest turn toward gentrification. Freshly painted, tiny row houses line both sides, each facade with a window, a door, and a stoop onto the street. And so we arrive at our "home" in Lisbon.

• • •

Our house has been well outfitted as a rental, with yellow walls and practical furnishings. There's even fruit, wine, and a friendly note to welcome us. We inspect the kitchen first, and it is the best room, well equipped for the dinners we expect to cook. We will use the twin bedroom for our baggage and clothes. The double bedroom—oh, so dark—is small but okay as long as the lights are on. We find a large bedroom downstairs, dark as an oubliette. I close the door and won't go downstairs again. The heaters taking the chill off the March afternoon burn paraffin. The oily, medicinal smell makes me woozy probably because I am wary of paraffin. My friend Susan was burned over twenty-five percent of her body when the paraffin she was melting to seal jars of apricot jam caught fire and leaped to her cotton nightgown. Since then I've hardly been able to light a candle. I turn off the heaters and pray for a clement March.

The house was built for servants' quarters adjacent to a looming pink **palácio**, which blocks all light in back. "These row houses must have preceded the **palácio**," I speculate. "If not, why did they bother to build windows that just face walls?"

"Maybe. Or maybe they just wanted the illusion of light, as though you **might** pull open the curtains in the morning and receive a benison of sunlight."

A later owner cut a skylight in the hall. Other than that, light comes in the front window. I lift the lace curtain and look out into the sunny street, packed with cars. "If it were not for cars, the street could be a patio for all the people who've renovated these places."

"Yes, in summer they might catch a breeze."

"They could set tables at the end and dine with the marvelous view of the city. There could be pots of flowers and small trees." Instead, the cars are so closely jammed in that you have to edge through them sideways to reach your door. To exit, they back up. Cars, our boon and freedom, are also the disaster of our time. "Look, the house across the street is for sale."

Ed comes to the window. "Awaiting your cosmetic touch." But I don't think so. I would not be attracted to a one-window house.

• • •

Twilight. We make our way down to the enormous plaza we passed earlier, Praça dos Restauradores. At one end throngs of very black-skinned people congregate. Several of the women, dressed in the brightly patterned cottons of Africa, have tall turban arrangements swaddled around their heads. Ed remembers Portugal's colonies, Cape Verde, Angola, and Mozambique. "Didn't they have Goa, too?" Ed asks. "And Macao? Where is that? They were all over the place."

"All I remember is Brazil. Macao is in the Philippines, no, near Hong Kong." They visit and talk on cell phones, flashing white-white smiles. Others catch the last rays at sidewalk cafés or a stand-up sidewalk bar, taking a nip of **ginjinha**, a favorite drink made from distilled cherries. Everyone is out, as in Tuscany at this hour, picking up bread for dinner, meeting a friend, or stopping for a bunch of flowers at one of the vendors. Lisboans must have the best-kept shoes in Europe—shoe-shine stands are everywhere. In a doorway, a man with elephant man's disease holds out his hat for change. Plum-colored tumors balloon all over his face. He's all tumor, except for one wild eye trained on the world that does not want to see him.

Everyone looks instead at a Gypsy boy playing an accordion, while his little dog, who looks uncannily intelligent, passes a cup for donations. The scene feels oddly out of time and at the same time familiar, as though we've stepped into an archetypal scene that will always be played this way.

Our guidebook mentions a street lined with restaurants jutting off the plaza. The Michelin tasters approve of these restaurants, and we walk down the street hoping instinct will guide us. They look tired. Some have barkers to lure customers. We pick the highest-rated one and have a perfectly nice, if uninspired, dinner of grilled prawns and fried calamari. We don't know what to expect from Portuguese food. We do have wine suggestions from Riccardo, a wine merchant friend in Cortona, so right away we try a Morgada de Santa Catherina, white, silky with a touch of peach.

The climb back somehow doesn't seem as steep as it looks. So much to see along the way—a woman ironing on her balcony, caged birds in open windows, the streets full of boys playing soccer, shop owners sweeping and taking out the trash, a young girl reading at a cash register with overhead neon casting a nimbus around her black hair. From the end of our street, we look out, over the domes and lights and rooftops of the city. How thrilling—an unknown country to explore.

Lusitania, early Portugal, may have been settled by Celts who intermarried with indigenous people. But those first migrants instead may have been from Lusoni, in central Spain, or maybe they were Carthaginian mercenary soldiers. And where were the indigenous people from? We always fall back on Indo-European, a nice catch-all answer. Whoever they were, the first-millennium Lusitani became fiercely bellic when threatened by the Romans. They battled through defeat after defeat before they were once and for all conquered by Augustus. At the Mosteiro dos Jerónimos (Monastery of San Jerome), built to honor Vasco da Gama's passage to India, we have started in the archaeology wing, where we find an exhibit of religious artifacts of the Lusitani people. This is lucky because it starts us at the beginnings of Portuguese history.

We are alone in the cavernous room of recently excavated carved stone and marble altars, gravestones, and sculptures. A young girl's pure face stares back at me from a time when this land was rife with gods, spirits, and protective forces. Labeled a nymph, she may have been a village girl who owned the displayed gold circle earring formed into a tiny hand at its tip. Her first love may have slipped onto her finger the ring engraved with private symbols. Many monuments are dedicated to the strictly local god who protected the region, Endovellicus. I love the gods of the crossroads. Throughout the world people always have recognized the metaphorical significance of the path chosen, the path forsaken. These pagan people worshiped all the usual gods of war, nature, and agriculture, but their religion included much more specialized gods of thermal baths, horses, darts, and the house. Pantheism appeals to me: god in everything. I don't mind if God/gods take many forms. Catholicism channels this deep human need differently; you may pray to the particular saint of parachutists, telecommunications, fertility in mares, hemorrhoids, lost objects, and housework.

Ed leads me to the sculpture of a Janus head on one nape, looking as always toward two different possibilities, but this one looks with male and female faces. The sentiments of the artist spiral outward from one glance at the beautifully modeled faces—the reconciliation of opposites or, it occurs to me, maybe the inevitability of opposite points of view. Imagine excavating marble fragments—fingers, whole hands, unidentifiable bits—then coming upon this head in a heap of rubble. Here's our friend the bull, ever a powerful symbol, this time as a miniature votive statue, then as a larger figure sacrificed to Jupiter, god of divine light and its accompaniment of thunder and lightning. The collection of amulets brings me close to the human hand that held these small jugs, acorns, and fruits, and the inscriptions on funeral markers startle me with poignant voices from such distance in time. One bids farewell to a son who lived only a year and twenty-three days: **Salve, so it is**. Another says: **Italic land begot me, Hispania buried me, I lived five lustra, the sixth winter killed me. In this territory I remained ignored by all and as a guest**. Many bear the inscription: **May the earth be light on you**. The last is an inspiring wish. When I next light a votive candle in a church in memory of my friend Josephine, I will say this for her. The whole exhibit inspires—we see how the land was alive with secret forces.

The monastery complex out in the Belém neighborhood faces the Tejo River, where the watery unknown pulled the explorers out of their safe harbor, their sense of adventure probably as strong as the capitalistic impulse to hunt for black pepper, gold, and spices. The monastery originally was close to the water, but over time the river receded, leaving an expansive space for gardens. Unfortunately, a rail line and a busy highway buzz along in front, seriously disturbing the grandeur of the site. We explore the church and sublime cloister, the refectory with **azulejos** (hand-painted tiles) on the walls. Walking along the three-hundred-meter exterior, we examine the portals. The ornamented doors seem even more precious because they survived the epic earthquake of 1755, which shook down most of the city. The building, started by Manuel I in the heyday of the discoverers' voyages, is considered the apex of the architectural style that flourished under this ruler. Manueline is a hybrid style, Gothic on the way to Renaissance, with a touch of the Moors in its horseshoe arches and rhythmic repetitions. The particularity of the style lies in the details. Doors and windows, built of local stone, are exuberantly carved with anchors, ropes, seahorses, palms, elephants, and even rhinoceroses, all recalling voyages out from the port of Lisbon. Vasco da Gama, buried inside, must rest well in this spot where his accomplishments are celebrated. The site and history intertwine, giving me the impression that each gives light to the other.

Down the street we come to another cause for celebration—this one dedicated to the famous pastry of Lisbon, **pastéis de Belém**. The Antiga Confeitaria de Belém, a crowded bakery-café, lures you from yards away with the toasty scents of the tarts that children must be given from year one. A chaos of mutable lines forms at the counter, where people order sackfuls to take home for Saturday lunch. The delicate layered pastry shell is filled with voluptuous custard, a creamy, irresistible treat. Ed has two. And will, I imagine, every day for the remainder of our trip.

Thus fortified, we walk over to the tower guarding the port entry. It looks like a giant golden chess piece. Every postcard stand features images of this ante-earthquake Manueline

torre, which was the last glimpse of Lisbon the navigators had as they sailed away. It has the unsettling aspect of appearing to be a mediocre watercolor painting of itself.

We return to the monastery for further wonders. Anyone who loves boats should see the Maritime Museum. Also all ten-year-olds and those who remember being ten. Was there ever another craze in the world such as the Portuguese had for sailboats? Every citizen must have had a mad passion for making models; the endless displays attest to this. From palm size to bicycle length, the types, sails, fittings, and furnishings are meticulously worked down to the teeny knots and flemished ropes. Probably thousands more fill the storerooms. Besides the models, the museum fathers also hoarded a vast number of uniforms worn on the discovery ships and their terra-cotta pots and vases for spices. Paintings and ex-votos reveal the peril of shipwreck, fire, and earthquake. In the remains of a "pepper wreck" recently recovered, we see spoons, coins, belt buckles, and blue and white porcelain dishes. Amid all this we come upon Vasco da Gama's portable altar with a statue of San Rafael, which traveled with him to India.

My favorite cases display the instruments of

navigation. There's a travelling set of globes in little round cases. One shows the animals representing the constellations, the other the earth. Someone's pocket sundial in ivory was fitted with a compass. These instruments of beauty performed useful, sometimes life-and-death functions—the inclimator, which takes the angle of heel to port; the gimbled barometer, a gadget fitted with needles that measured azimuths, the horizontal angle between north and the point observed. Armillaries are spheres of circles within circles, usually with a sun positioned in the middle; they show the relative positions of poles, equator, meridians, and the sun. The armillary's value still symbolically reigns: you see one emblazoned on the Portuguese flag.

Most beautiful is the astrolabe. Etymologically the word means "star-taker." It looks like a big magical pocket watch. The metal face, engraved with numbers and zodiacal designs and cursive words, could be something an angel might hold aloft. For me, astrolabes have poetic associations. Chaucer wrote "A Treatise on the Astrolabe," an early (1391) exacting work blending science and art. One of my favorite love stories is that of Héloïse and Abélard. After they chose to live apart in religious orders, she wrote him to announce with "exultation" the birth of their son. She named him Astrolabe.

The instrument came to Europe with the Muslim invasion of Andalucía, though its history goes back to 150 B.C. Hipparchus of Bithynia is most frequently named as the inventor. A pilot today has the control tower; the medieval navigator had the astrolabe. The armillary performs similarly as sort of a three-dimensional astrolabe. The basic astrolabe function was taking longitude and latitude by coordinating celestial points and equatorial lines. A metal disk (the **rete**, "web" or "net") engraved with a star map is superimposed over a larger disk marked with the earth's circumference and markers. A movable ruler that Muslims called the **alidade** calculates relative positions. If you know the location of the sun or a star, your astrolabe can find time and place. The metal ring at the top allows it to be hung, as Chaucer carefully noted, in straight plumb. Though the church considered them instruments of the devil, astrolabes must have been sacred to the captains.

There's more. Actual boats in a drydock warehouse. Slick blue fishing boats with the evil eye protection painted on the prow. Some designs look like Pennsylvania Dutch hex signs. A black rooster decorates a rowboat. We look at the yacht of a king, various types of war boats, and primitive rowboats. We pass on through the carriage museum, which just illustrates that almost everything rescued from history is interesting, if only mildly.

The tram doesn't come. No taxi in sight. We begin the long walk back. Empty plazas seem to be waiting for some military parade to materialize. There's an ease here; the traffic not frenetic. So many pastry shops and cafés. Cat tongues, almond tarts, fruit tarts, citrus tarts. At the blue-and-white-tiled Canecas, the bakers, visible through glass, are flattening rounds of dough, forming a dome, then folding over the edges, leaving a cleft. We buy one of these breads in an oval shape, the opening sprinkled with seeds. We already know the Lisbon bread is especially good.

Ed has learned to order a **bica**, the espresso equivalent. He is thrilled with the coffee. "Better than French. Certainly better than in Spain. It's the old connection with Africa. They must have had good beans early on."

"As good as Italian?"

"Umm, different."

• • •

For the next few days we follow tourist pursuits, interspersing each stop at a museum or castle or church with a visit to a new pastry shop. I become seriously attached to almond tarts. Ed prefers the classic custard tarts and wishes he'd been fed them in childhood. We loiter outside at Café Brasileira, which overlooks a statue of the unruly writer Fernando Pessoa. He might have sat in this chair when he wrote,

> From the terrace of this café I look at life with tremulous eyes. I see just a little of its vast diversity concentrated in this square that's all mine . . . perhaps my greatest ambition is really no more than to keep sitting at this table in this café . . . Ah, the mysteries grazed by ordinary things in our very midst! To think that right here, on the sunlit surface of our complex human life, Time smiles uncertainly on the lips of Mystery! How modern all this sounds! And yet how ancient, how hidden, how full of some other meaning besides the one we see glowing all around us.

Pessoa refused to limit himself to a single persona. His chameleon sensibility gave us many books seemingly written by different authors. **The Book of Disquiet**, one of my favorites, is written in the voice of an insignificant bookkeeper but feels close to autobiography. His translator, Richard Zenith, describes this monumental scrapbook as "anti-literature, a kind of primitive, verbal CAT scan of one man's anguished soul." The book, a wonderful travel companion in Lisbon, consists of small sections, perfect for reading in sips at all the cafés he frequented around town. Pessoa rarely left Lisbon in his adult life, and the city informs, infiltrates, and grounds his writing, no matter how far afield his personas pull his identity. The green sky over the river Tejo, "the potted plants that make each balcony unique," sunset colors turning to gray on buildings, the cry of the lottery ticket seller, the "eternal laundry" drying in the sun—the myriad sensations of the city form the lively background of his pages. I love Sundays in European cities, the sudden quiet of the streets, with the parks full of strollers and children. Pessoa writes:

> I'm writing on a Sunday, the morning far advanced, on a day full of soft light in which,

above the rooftops of the interrupted city, the blue of the always brand-new sky closes the mysterious existence of stars into oblivion.

In me it is also Sunday . . .

My heart is also going to a church, located it doesn't know where. It wears a child's velvet suit, and its face, made rosy by first impressions, smiles without sad eyes above the collar that's too big.

A band of about twelve serious-faced musicians plays in the plaza in front of Pessoa's statue. They seem about to slip into a dirge at any moment.

The funiculars are fun, like rides at a carnival, and with the taxis so plentiful and amazingly cheap, we get all over town with ease, walking one way, riding back the other.

The Fiera da Ladra, the Thief's Fair, has no ship models, no baroque candlesticks, nothing to covet. The thieves must have gone into real estate. Instead I flash on everything I threw away in my whole life—Barbie with one leg, paperbacks missing their covers, sad bathrobes, and old computer keyboards. We leave and meander until we're lost in the Alfama, the labyrinthine historic Arab quarter. You'd need to drop stones to find your way back to where you started. Arm's-width streets twist, climb, double back, drop. Whitewashed houses with flowering pots and crumbling ruins with gaping courtyards open to small plazas with birds competing in the trees for best song of the morning—a soulful neighborhood for spending your days. If I lived in Lisbon, I would choose to live here. Redolent of the souk, the bazaar, the roots of Iberia, the Alfama does not seem just quaint and interesting. At heart, this area remains deeply exotic. Open this door and find the memory of a Muslim mathematician consulting his astrolabe, pass this walled garden and imagine the wives of the house gathered around the fountain under the mimosa. Easily, memory seeks a guitarist playing by moonlight at an upper window, a designer of tiles in a workshop, a child weaving on a doorstep, a sailor packing his duffel. The spirit of the Alfama feels close to the spirit of the artifacts of Lusitania that we saw on the first day. Here's where mystery lingers, where ritual and alchemy and magic take place. This is the center, naturally enough, for **fado**, meaning "fate," the music whose **saudade** rips out of the heart. **Saudade**. We have no equivalent English word. Does that mean we have no equivalent English feeling? A line from Yeats comes close to the meaning: "A pity beyond all telling is hid at the heart of love." But **saudade** connotes, too, a pervasive longing and reaching. It seems to be a lower-voltage force than the Spanish **duende** but springs from the same taproot: we are alone, we will die, life is hard and fleeting—easy realizations but, when experienced from within, profound.

Colors: Islamic turquoise, curry, coral, bone white, the blue layers of the sea. The scents of baking bread, wet stones, and fish frying at outdoor stands. The aromas of coriander and mint and big stews and roast pork emanating from the small neighborhood restaurants, the **tascas**. Menus of today's **prato do dia** are posted in the windows, and we choose a **tasca** with everyone seated together at crowded tables. As we wait, I admire a walnut cake with caramel frosting served to a man across from us. He sees this and reaches over for my fork, handing me back a large bite of his dessert. The waiter brings platters of fish fried in a gossamer, crispy batter, and a spicy eggplant the old Moors would have loved. We are astonished. Here's the real local food. For dessert, old-fashioned baked apples are served to Ed, and to me a flan with cinnamon, a whiff of the Arabs. The bill—twenty euros, a fourth of what the guidebook restaurants cost, and ten times better.

The Alfama slows for afternoon. Music drifts from a window, not **fado**, not fateful, but a whiny Bob Dylan relic inviting a lady to lay across a big brass bed. Instead, a woman hangs her laundry on a balcony, her mouth full of green plastic clothespins. Cheery old trams, red and yellow, ply the main streets. At an antique shop I find blue and white tiles from the 1700s in dusty stacks around the floor. Ed steps outside to call our friend Fulvio in Italy. I see him gesturing to the air like an Italian as I look through a hundred or so tiles and choose four to hang in my California kitchen. **Souvenir**—to come to the aid of memory. I always will like to be reminded of Lisbon. From the castle grounds up top, all of terra-cotta–topped Lisbon spreads out for the viewing, a fortunate city on the water.

Lisbon, like San Francisco, inhabits the edge. The first or last edge? In California along the Pacific coast, I always have the sense that I'm perched on the sharp shoulder of the end of the country—nowhere else to go. On the other side of that cold ocean, waves break on far, adventitious shores. The harsh terrain of the California coast remains a lonely and wild beauty. Geographically, Lisbon feels quite opposite. From here the old navigators ventured south to Africa, around to India, and west, reaching both Newfoundland and Brazil by 1500. Prince Henry the Navigator—I've known his name since fourth grade—charted his sea lanes outward from here, though he never set forth on the waves himself. Magellan, funded by Spain, did. And this was the pin-pricked spot on Vasco da Gama's maps, the home shore. "Bartolomeu Dias," Ed remembers. The names float back from long lost quizzes. **What was the name of Vasco da Gama's ship?** The **San Rafael**, with the **San Gabriel** and the **Berrio** sailing with him. My teachers always were interested in the names of ships and the horses of Confederate generals.

Although the city of Lisbon might remind me also of San Francisco—from the harbor rises a city of hills climbed by picturesque trams, where one lives with the peril of earthquake—it does not. My initial impression dissolves the natural tendency to compare the new to the familiar. This is the first edge of Europe, not the last.

In the Principe Real park we order coffee at a glass café and drink it under an enormous magnolia. A cedar has been trained out over a circular pergola, and men sit under the branches playing cards. The houses around the park speak of the life of the city. Yellow, dark liver-red, pink, they are substantial and not at the peak of perfection but worn to a comfortable patina. A slender girl opens a door and squints up at the sun. Her life inside remains a mystery. Mystery—ah, that word. It appears throughout Pessoa's work, the mystery of the ordinary, the mystery of one life in one place.

The number of bookstores confounds us. Every street! I stop in one to look at cookbooks. We're finding the food good but feel we are missing something. The clerk becomes enthusiastic. She takes down several books, shaking her tight curls and quickly reshelving. She discards the idea of any cookbook other than **Traditional Portuguese Cooking** by Maria de Lourdes Modesto. The first page she shows us features lard water soup. "She does everything right. Look at this recipe for **rissoles**." The pronouncation is something like **ree soysh**. We've seen them in the café display cases. "It's pastry—savory—filled with prawns. Or fish or pork. I have to have **rissoles** every day." She motions at her colleague. "He has to go get them for me," she laughs. "You can tell I like to eat." Her circumference suggests many **rissoles**.

"What are your other favorites?" I take out my notebook. What she likes, we will seek.

"Stuffed spider crab. Baked **bacalhau**, dried cod—oh, **bacalhau** every way. My mother-in-law just puts it in the oven with potatoes and onions and parsley and lemon. We eat cod a thousand ways." As soon as the Atlantic water routes opened, the Portuguese began fishing the Newfoundland seas for cod, drying them like starched white shirts to bring home months later. At every market in Italy and all over the Mediterranean you find piles of stiff cod, but nowhere as often as in Portugal.

"Cabbage," she's saying. "You should come to my house and have my green soup with sausage. You have to slice the cabbage so very fine. The soups of my country! The green bean with mint!" She describes several bread soups with fish or vegetables. We feel more and more famished the longer she talks. I wish she'd send that colleague out for something now. She moves from various preparations of eel to an unlikely-sounding dish, a classic of the region. "And the next time you eat, you must try the **cataplana** of clams and pork."

"What is **cataplana**? A place?"

"My dear, a **cataplana** is what cooks it. The pan with a lid that lifts, the lid pinned together. Like a clam. Every house has one."

"We'll look for that on the menu," Ed promises, as we exit to find one more **sonho**, a fried sugared pastry that lives up to its name, **dream**.

Of the many sights, I'm most awed by the Museu Nacional do Azulejo, housed in the former Convento da Madre de Deus. The history of Portuguese tiles hangs on the walls. The whole city is a wild museum of **azulejos**, but the museum establishes the five-hundred-year context. The history starts with earth-toned Moorish tiles, their colors held separate by ridges, almost like cloisonné. By 1700 Portugal had its own distinctive way with tile, the cool and fresh blue and white. It "wallpapers" churches, banks, entranceways, benches, fountains. All over town blue and white tile pictures announce the pharmacy, butcher, and house number. Art nouveau picked up the tile tradition. We look for those facades with the characteristic curving pinks, yellows, and aquas. Noticing tile patterns and sidewalks of waving stone patterns is part of the joy of walking in Lisbon.

What the fresco is to Italy, the tile panels are to Portugal—elaborate scenes record events and tell stories. Most precious at the museum is the scene of Lisbon created about twenty years before the earthquake ravaged the city. The convent chapel's lower walls depict scenes from the life of Saint Anthony, the shine of the glaze cooling down the heat of the baroque and rococo decorations that cover every square inch of the rest of the chapel. I like all the Moorish geometric and floral designs, so like Persian rugs, which in turn look like gardens. But there's something eternally fresh about the blue and white. We take dozens of pictures, almost all of which turn out to have the glare of flash in the center.

• • •

We're living in a quiet part of Lisbon. At the dining-room table we spread all our books, notebooks, and maps. We play CDs of **fado** while I attempt to read José Saramago's turgid **Journey to Portugal**. Throughout he refers to himself as "the traveller," a stylistic choice I find arch: "Now the traveller is ready to move on from works of art." Delete "the traveller" and "he" and just be straightforward! The writing is studded, however, with bright perceptions and jewel-cut paragraphs that keep me reading. Ed watches an Italian movie with Spanish subtitles, rather an odd activity in Portugal. We have cooked and served our dinner on the coffee table covered by a yellow cloth and set with a glass of freesias to ward off lingering odors of paraffin. Cooking a pan of mixed local sausages and roasted potatoes contributed a few aromas, too. We brought home a box of tarts from the Pasteleria Suica on the plaza. This night offers the pleasure of renting a house—not going out, making a simple meal, and having a few hours with each other and books.

We're getting to know our Calcada de Sant'-Ana neighborhood. The crammed corner grocery, open till midnight, has most everything we need. A sweet park at the top of the hill offers green respite and the sound of a fountain. Nearby the Campo dos Mártires da Pátria, the Field of Martyrs, draws me on my walks because of the clutch of people around the statue of José Thomaz Sousa Martins, a nineteenth-century physician and pharmacist who still wields the hope of cure. Propped around the monument are stacks of marble plaques engraved with thanks, letters of supplication, and wax ex-votos. Notes describe illnesses and ask him for favors. A woman sells bracelets and necklaces with the blue stone for protection against the evil eye. She sells the wax arms, hands, feet, legs, and even eyes that you can buy and then offer at the base of the monument. I buy a few of the ex-votos to take home for my collection and also several of her candles that exorcise bad spirits from the house or promote health. They're primitive, rolled in seeds and grains and herbs. Because of the wind, candles will not stay lighted. People hold them down in a metal drum with fire in the bottom, praying with them for a while, then dropping them into the drum. Sacks of old wax are piled on the side. Sousa Martins's monument is an active spiritual spot. He has been dead 107 years, and how brightly his memory burns. I light a candle in the drum and think hard about the health of those I love. For good measure, I buy two of the evil eye bracelets and slip them on my wrist.

Then we meet Carlos Lopes. That's Carloosh Lope-shs in Portuguese. This language uses many sounds that previously I have heard only from the washing machine. Italian and a smattering of Spanish help—thousands of words are similar—but mostly we are lost.

We drop into the tourist information office in our Rossio neighborhood and ask about cooking schools in town. We're told that none exist, but then the two young women confer and finally come up with an address of a cookware shop in a residential neighborhood where some classes are taught. Also, they tell us, we have to try the owner's chocolate cake, his secret recipe, baked in his nearby shop every day. All the best restaurants serve it. We jump in a taxi immediately and go. At the cookware shop the clerk, a friend of the women at the tourist office, tells us that Carlos is out. We leave our number and ask for directions to the cake shop.

The taxi driver waits while we run in. We

buy the last pieces in the shop, one for each of us and, to his astonishment, one for the taxi driver. The three of us eat in the car. The only sound is slight moans. The light cake is rich, and the quality of the chocolate speaks of tropical earth and rainforests. This is a taste of the heaven that is someday to come to all of us.

When Carlos rings us the next day, we again make our way out to his shop. Even if nothing comes of this, we can eat another piece of his cake. Maybe a whole cake.

Confident, catching us eye to eye with a sherry-brown gaze, Carlos looks as though he could have been one of the navigators. He's a sturdy man, not young, not old. The Portuguese generally look affable, unlike the more chiseled Spanish. He's in a loose cardigan he's had for a long time. I immediately see a person comfortable with himself. Fortunately for us, his English is excellent. After five minutes his wit and irony already shine. We tell him we'd like inside information about the national cuisine, that we're getting whiffs of the real thing but would like to know more. After the first **tasca** lunch, we began to discover the cuisine. Our tome of a cookbook reinforces our instinct that levels and levels of taste exist, beyond the good grilled fish, fried calamari, and crab salads we're ordering each night. He explains that in his classes he teaches local people about sushi, Thai food, Polynesian dishes. "No Portuguese cooking—we all know how to cook that."

"Any chance of a private lesson or two?"

"You come tomorrow to my restaurant in the market building in the Alfama. We will cook a lunch together."

Mercado de Santa Clara, Carlos's restaurant, is on the second floor of the market building, which could be a nineteenth-century train station. It overlooks the Thief's Fair. Lined with windows, the decor is simplicity itself—white tablecloths, little bowls of flowers, and on a serving table one of the chocolate cakes. We meet in the galley kitchen, and Carlos starts to cook. And talk. "The main herbs are coriander, parsley, and oregano. But above all coriander." He chops a large bunch and places it in a bowl beside the stove, at the ready. First he splits each side of a sea bass, filling the cut with the excellent local sea salt, then dips the whole fish in olive oil. He picked up the fish at the market this morning, he tells us as he grills it over a hot, hot flame for five minutes on each side. Done. Then he cooks pork ribs he's marinated since last night in lemon, salt, and the local ready-made pimiento sauce that is essential in every kitchen. I've never seen ribs cooked this way. He melts a dollop of lard in a frying pan, and when it is very hot, he tosses in the ribs. In another pan, he cooks some steamed and chopped rape in a little of the fat from the ribs. He stirs in a couple of handfuls of breadcrumbs.

He's fast. He washes a bowl of clams and adds them to another pan with garlic and olive oil. He squeezes lemon juice over them, then adds a **lot** of coriander and some white wine. Then he puts it all in a copper **cataplana** and cooks it briefly, shaking it as though it were popcorn. What a lunch we are going to have. "This is very simple," he says, breaking eggs into a bowl. "What you have alone at home on Sunday night. It's all in the eggs." And plain to see, the yolks are the wobbly gold of a setting sun. To the eggs he adds diced tomatoes and onion. He scrambles them in a moment. All the while he talks about ingredients, praising the Portuguese mustard, Savora; **piri-piri**, a white-heat sauce made from Angolan peppers; and cumin, which always seasons pork and beef meatballs. When Ed asks if port is used in the kitchen, Carlos laughs. "The Portuguese don't drink port," he claims. He's frying some tiny sole filets, which he first dipped in lemon juice and olive oil, then floured. We ask about restaurants, and he praises the cooking in **tascas**, along with a few other restaurants. He drains the sole on empty egg cartons. "The Portuguese have more restaurants per capita than any other European country," he tells us. I'm sure that's accurate. Every neighborhood is full of **tascas**, and all of them are jammed. "Don't expect salads here. I don't know why, but we never have taken the salad to heart." He sprinkles the sole with parsley and unties his apron.

We eat. Portuguese food is for those who are really hungry. Carlos pours a simple "green wine," Vinho Verde Muralhas de Monção, and then a red Azeitao Periquita Fonseca. The moment for dessert arrives. He has the waiter bring a puff pastry filled with something he describes as a cross between crème brûlée and egg custard, the now-familiar **pastéis de nata**. Which brings me to the famous chocolate cake. When I mention the recipe, he gets a little Mona Lisa smile and asks the waiter to bring over two slices, but he will divulge nothing. I tell him about an almost flourless chocolate cake with ground almonds, a recipe I learned years ago at Simone Beck's cooking school in the South of France, which I have baked at least a hundred times. He brings over tiny glasses of Amarguinha, a dessert **digestivo** made of almonds. As we leave, he will not allow us to pay. I am stunned at this generous man, stunned that he has given his morning to strangers and shared his knowledge and traded life stories over a long, long lunch.

The next morning Carlos calls early. We will meet for dinner, he announces, then go out to hear **fado** in the Alfama. **Fah-do**, he says, like hairdo, not **fah-dough**. We fill the time until then visiting the Ribiera market. Used to Tuscan prices, we're surprised to see good-looking olive oils for four to seven euros a liter. We find goat cheeses wrapped in gauze, and almonds suspended in honey. We take home **massa de pimiento**, the canned spread of puréed pimientos and salt. Since my home state of Georgia is a major producer of the pimiento, I grew up on toasted pimiento-cheese sandwiches, one of the world's great treats. It will be even better with a smear of Portuguese mustard. The stalls, arranged under a vaulted ceiling, display all the vegetables we do not see in restaurants, and sacks of tiny snails and mussels. At the horse butcher's, the meat is oh, so dark—the color of port. In other stands hang sausages in every shade of blood. Most startling are the flowers. Several vendors feature funeral sprays, elaborate horseshoes and fans of chrysanthemums and gladiolus with pastel ribbons and condolences in sequins. En route to mourning, you can pick up an impressive wreath and your carrots at the same time. As Carlos told us, few lettuces but mounds of cabbages. Ed points out the many kinds of oranges. When we have as much as we can carry, we go home.

We meet Carlos at his restaurant in the Alfama and start walking through the maze. After six or so turns, I don't know which direction we face. "Don't walk here alone at night," he tells us.

"Is it dangerous?"

"Well, you would be lost, and sometimes boys snatch bags."

"That's true anywhere on the globe."

"Yes, but you would also be lost."

"That makes sense."

He stops at a closed door with no sign and knocks. We are admitted into a small room with five tables. We are the only guests at this hidden restaurant, which, yes, does have a name: Os Corvos. We're seated at a table next to a wall of wine racks. Without a word, the waiter brings us a Lavradores de Feitoria, from north in the Duoro region, a nice big wine with a plummy almond perfume. Carlos confers, and soon we are eating coriander soup, a variety of pork sausages from the north, some with rice inside, some made from black pig's blood, and some with piquant garlic—true Portuguese tastes, indigenous to this place. Who could expect how the copious use of coriander could add such a fresh dimension? The waiter then brings a salad of dried fava beans, plumped again with oil, garlic, and coriander, then strips of savory roast pork, a mound of ricotta seasoned with oregano, and a bowl of tempura-style green beans. Even though we have feasted long and well, I'm moved to try a butterscotch flan, one of my favorite flavors, and a bite of Ed's frothy soufflé of ground almonds and eggwhites, and just a taste of Carlos's gelato with confit of lemon rind. I'm in love.

After midnight we weave through the Alfama streets again and duck into a low door just as **fado** is about to begin. We have luck: one table is free in the small room, which feels charged with anticipation. Two guitarists step into a clearing, then the **fadista**, who looks as if she knows something about fate herself. She wears the requisite black shawl, and though she is only middle-aged, she looks like an old soul, black eyes reflecting the **saudade** of the world. She does not begin, she erupts. Her voice turns my spine into a live electric wire. I have no idea what the words mean, but her music is preverbal anyway, a direct communication among all of the nerve endings. During intermission Carlos orders Bagaço, much like grappa.

The next singer knocks us off our chairs. He looks so unlikely. The **fadista** fit the role, but Luis Tomar, rigid in his suit, could be selling insurance. Just to prove you can never judge anyone by appearance, his voice, so rife with restrained emotion, sunders the room's atoms. Passion threatens to overwhelm the song at any minute but remains contained, remains pitched to a timbre that corresponds exactly with the synapses of your own private longings and dreams. I wish he would sing forever.

• • •

Now we know how to eat. On our long walks to look at the rhythmic patterned sidewalks and tile-faced buildings—we love coming upon the occasional 1950s tile facade—we stop for lunch at an appealing **tasca**. At night we ignore all the rated restaurants in our guidebooks and follow our noses toward home cooking in our neighborhood. **Tascas** are lively and fun. You are not isolated from others but are in such proximity that an exchange of bites seems normal. Not many tourists, we notice, are among our fellow diners. The plainness of the decor probably puts off the foreign traveller. We go back several times to the Floresta and to the blue-and-white-tiled Minho Verde on our nearby Sant'Ana street for the loud atmosphere, the grilled hunks of pork and big shrimp, duck with rice, green bean soup, and plates of sliced, peeled oranges that are plonked onto the table. Locals are ordering the grilled pork liver and slabs of grilled fish with lemons. The Portuguese breads are simply the best. I could live on bread alone—and the bowls of olives that always appear on the table. At others we try the famous **cataplana** dishes, the lusty stews of pork and clams or of onions, peppers, octopus, and clams. The son shouts orders to Mama in the kitchen. A taffy and white cat slinks around my legs. Ed loves those twelve-euro bills.

"Where do you eat, other than secret places in the Alfama?" Ed asks Carlos. We want to see how new chefs are developing the cuisine. What comes after 365 recipes for dried cod? He gives us names of a few restaurants whose chefs embrace the traditional food but also have fresh ideas of their own, ideas that ultimately enlarge a cuisine. He sends us to Mezzaluna to see what happened to Portuguese food when the Italian Michele Guerrieri came to town.

After all the down-home **tascas**, the cool sophistication of Mezzaluna transports us to Milan or New York. Intimate but not close, the room's mirrors, prints, and gorgeous flowers feel welcoming. We're seated among fashionably dressed Lisboans, women with black upswept hair, big gold jewelry, and fine silk blouses. The men wear dark, important suits. Somehow well-dressed businessmen in Europe look sexy and grand. The couple finishing lunch at the table next to us receives a plate of goat cheeses the size of kumquats. One is wrapped in leaves, another coated with ashes; others are creamy white. Soon we are eating fried and breaded radicchio stuffed with prosciutto. The spinach salad (ah, salad!) is dressed with lemon vinaigrette made with those cunning little local goat cheeses. Michele comes over to the table, and we tell him Carlos sent us. He's a slight, young Italian raised in Naples and in New York, someone who has grown up at home in the world. His smile is wide, and those Neapolitan eyes laugh, too. He brings over a Quinta da Murta, Bucelas, and tells us how much he loves cooking with Portuguese ingredients, especially the seafood, and about his pleasure in bringing those ingredients in contact with Italian pasta. Of course, the whole world has taken to serving pasta with their own ingredients, and his use of local shrimp in a cream sauce with fresh tagliatelle provides easy proof why this is so. He combines pastas with goat, much loved locally and rarely seen on Italian pasta. His localized version of macaroni turns light with the inclusion of arugula, shrimp, and lemon. He has the immigrant zeal. He's opened another restaurant down the street and has started a food magazine, **Gula**. Like an Italian, he visits with his customers, making his way around the room. Star Portuguese products—pimientos, eggs, eggplant, garlic, shellfish, and oranges—

appear in new guises. The platter of oranges comes with a lemon and cider vinaigrette and shredded fennel. I can barely share my rolled eggplant stuffed with tomatoes and goat cheese. And oh yes, this is a fine restaurant: Carlos's chocolate cake wheels by on the dessert cart.

Our time in Lisbon is over. Carlos will come to visit us in Cortona this summer. We are taking off to see some of the interior and north of the country. He has given us names of **tascas** along the way, towns we must detour to see, and wines to try. We will drive inland to Estremoz, then go north to several characteristic towns—Évora, Coimbra, Guimarães, Óbidos—zigzagging where we want, then back south to Sintra, our last stop. We've made reservations at **pousadas**, the inns in historic buildings, and at two villas that have become hotels.

From the car rental office, two turns and we're on the bridge and out of the city. Soon we're in the Alentejo, the pastoral countryside of whitewashed farms with glistening blue doors and waist-high borders painted around the base. Traditional now, the blue border once was believed to ward off the evil eye. Closer to Estremoz, for our first night out, chamomile flowers completely cover the ground under the mutable pewter and silver olive trees. A clump of sheep moves like a huge amoeba among stone walls, where wild pink dog roses clamber.

So many decades passed, and I did not ever see the Alentejo until today, did not enter the double-gated tunnel into Estremoz, or see the plaza and low white houses, did not ever, in all this time passed, discover this shady town with a fountain and a church with tall weeds growing on top of its pediments, white irises, plum trees in bloom, with a market full of caged rabbits, songbirds, chickens, turkeys, stands with swags of rustic sausages, handmade cheeses, bundles of herbs, and stacks of cod, with the scent of orange and lemon in the streets, with houses whose windows and doors have local marble surrounds.

One of those flash epiphanies of travel, the realization that worlds you'd love vibrantly exist outside your ignorance of them. The vitality of many lives you know nothing about. The breeze lifting a blue curtain in a doorway billows just the same whether you are lucky enough to observe it or not. Travel gives such jolts. I could live in this town, so how is it that I've never been here before today?

Partridges! Hams—fat, succulent, leathery, dangling around the tops of stalls. One man with blunt bangs and rosy cheeks sells skins. He holds up a stiff-bristled boar with the toenails still attached. I buy two goatskins because I once stayed at a hotel in Deya, Majorca, where the bedside rugs on brick floors were goatskins. I liked the combination of textures. May they not make the clothes in my suitcase smell gamy. We ask him where to eat, and he motions across the plaza.

Great bread. The texture of pound cake and made with fine cornmeal. We have to wait in the barnlike restaurant because they have dozens of market-day customers and only two people serving. People have the same habit that we observed in Spain—throwing paper on the floor. The floor is littered. Bread and olives and a bottle of water—that's really fine with me, don't even bother to bring us a menu. But the server does, and then she brings around rooster stew with rice and cod with potatoes. Tasty but heavy for midday. We lurch out into the sun and thread our way through the now-deserted streets back uphill to the glorious **pousada**, a castle above the town. Our quarters have a sitting room, fruit with a finger bowl, tall lilies in the bathroom, and a bowl of chrysanthemums between the carved antique twin beds, hard as graves. An ice bucket with a bottle of champagne has been left to chill on a lamp table.

My bed, immaculate in white linen, is slightly wider than a usual twin. The crisp coverlet and soft sheets feel chaste and inviting. Ed half closes the shutters for an afternoon repose. "Don't you like these beds?" I ask. But I hear his breathing fall into the slow motion of dreams. Lying in the laddered light from the shutter, I sink into a very old feeling. I return to my bedroom in Fitzgerald and am again a girl in a white spool bed, an identical empty one beside mine. I can almost touch the scalloped edge of the pink linen bedspread and crisp sheets with my mother's monogram, raised like veins on my grandmother's hand. On the other side of the room stands my revolving bookcase, where I have placed **The Brothers Karamazov** among my Nancy Drew mysteries and only recently outgrown Bobbsey Twins books. My mother has brought home **The Brothers Karamazov** from a shopping trip in Macon when the department store book department (the only place you can buy books within 180 miles of us) had no more Nancy Drews. A thick book, she reasoned, and I went through the Nancys so fast. Accidently, she catapulted me into a new stage of reading, and after that Nancy was over. I always was a reader, but now I first began to be aware of the writer of the book. At the end of Dostoevsky's novel, I felt a surge of exhilaration. I had met something great. That feeling, repeated with each transporting book, has been one of the prime pleasures of living. The blue and black Modern Library edition, heavy among the other flimsy books, became a fact of life. I had taken possession of the skirted dressing table with its silver brushes when my sister went off to college. Her perfume bottles and little tray of orange sticks, emery boards, and tiny scissors in the shape of a crane were my inheritance, too. In the narrow bed I became aware of the word **solitary**. Late at night I listened to Cajun music from a radio station in faraway New Orleans, with ads for hair pomade interspersing the songs. I loved the word **bayou**, loved to hear the phrase **on blue bayou**.

So the twin bed in the Portuguese farmland takes me to the green dial glowing on the radio in the otherwise dark room of the time when I was emerging from childhood. The **pousada** goes completely quiet in the afternoon. The castle seems to fall into a reverie of the sad death of Queen Isabel (perhaps in this room), the royal son who rode out to defeat the Arabs, and Vasco da Gama, who climbed the **azulejo**-lined stairs to meet Manuel and take command of the fleet that opened the passage to India. Because the castle is crowded with so many silent memories, my own past rises, too.

When we veer off road, we're suddenly on a track of crushed marble. Marble yards are littered with enormous Michelangelo-type blocks. We crunch down the road that ends at a cemetery. As in Italy, photographs of the departed decorate the graves. Some have a photo of the whole family. **Eterna saudade** carved on many slabs leaves no doubt as to exactly what **saudade** means. This cemetery in proximity to marble quarries is not quite like others. Laid out like a town with a central monument, the "streets" are lined with houses, like playhouses in elaborate marble, with marble bunk beds for the coffins to rest on. You could reach in beyond the lace curtains and touch the coffins, some of which are covered with silk, like bedspreads. Coffins are marble or wood. Carved saints and ministering angels and even a full-sized soldier at the door of his mausoleum populate this **campo**. The graves of the poor (or those with stingy relatives) are covered with chipped marble or glass. One innovative headstone is actually a cross-section of an oil drum filled with fake flowers and a photo of an old man. Grave number 524 is just a mound of dirt, where someone ended with no further ado when his long day was over.

Down country lanes, simple white churches suddenly appear, their forms as pure as wildflowers. Bulls congregate in the cork groves. Some cousins of Ferdinand the Bull relax in the shade. They gleam like polished copper, and each wears a bell. All the sheep wear bells, too, and when we stop, little symphonies are playing all over the rolling countryside. I hold out my voice recorder so that for the rest of the trip I can listen to this madrigal of the bells. We stop at Glória, where a woman stoops, mopping the marble stones around the outside of a church no larger than my living room. Her own blue-trimmed cottage next door is surrounded by tall daisies and rosemary. She smiles and opens the nave door, welcoming us as if into her home. I smell the clean whitewash, the scrubbed marble floors. She performs her devotion right here. The church possesses a fine beauty. The altar, painted with blue and yellow flowers, and the walls display ex-voto paintings offered by those saved from goring bulls, sinking ships, and tipped-over carts. The spring grasses are luxuriant, bisected, trisected with rivulets and torrents of rushing water. This is joy, to meander on back roads, windows open to sweet-smelling air, stopping to photograph the neat houses draped with yellow Lady Banksia roses, wisteria, gardens blooming with peonies. We pull over at another white church trimmed in heavenly blue, this one surrounded by a meadow of wild blue irises, smaller than the ones at Sea Ranch in California that cover the salty hills above the Pacific. Whitewashed benches in front of the church must invite visiting after services. We rest from our walk through the meadow, listening to the bulls' bells ringing the changes.

• • •

The restaurants in the **pousadas** are committed to preserving local cooking traditions and using the best products of the area. In the baronial dining room we taste a garlic soup with sheep's cheese and bread. Bread soups, called **açordas**, are basic to Portuguese cuisine, just as the famous **ribollita** is to the Tuscan repertoire. I often make another "dry" Tuscan soup of bread and onions. I'm crazy about these soups you can eat with a fork. With such exquisite bread, how could **açordas** be anything other than sumptuous? In Lisbon we tried another with shrimp. We're on the lookout for soups made with pumpkin or chickpeas, both staples in the Alentejo, an area known for delicious soups. Having seen partridges at the market, we are pleased to find them on the menu. Nicely served with bread and sausage stuffing, the partridge is rich and savory. They must have been served to Alfonso, Pedro, and Fernando, the three kings who lived here and to whom we must be indebted for the eventual fate of this **castelo**—a haven for travellers. The cheese course! All those bell-ringing sheep out there in the dark, praise unto you! Is there a saint of cheese? If so, I offer my thanks.

In the maiden bed I dream not a dream, just an image: an iridescent gray pigeon with a blue morning glory blooming on top of its head.

We roam the countryside around Estremoz, looking at the smallest villages' Roman ruins, towers, prehistoric stones scattered across fields, and more of the enchanting white churches left all alone in fields where their beauty attains a sculptural purity. The towns are sometimes so small that we don't realize we've passed them. The whole Alentejo invites walking or bicycling. The sweeping terrain rolls on and on, expansive and empty. In this season the green fields look as though they are underpainted with light. And they are lit also with the music of bells! Oh, for a horse. This province may be Portugal's poorest in income, but the people live in beauty, both their houses and their land, and enjoy the bounty of their own gardens and pigs. They are everywhere welcoming, though our communication, out this far, is almost nil.

Évoramonte is spectacular, a lost-to-the-world white village of church, hermitage, castle, and commanding view. In the cemetery perched on the edge of the steep hill, a life-sized marble angel sits at the head of a grave, looking contemplative. I think I never have seen a seated angel in a cemetery. São Lourenço de Mamporcão, with 558 inhabitants, possesses a little church with such a graceful rounded apse and bell tower that I sit down and try to draw it in my notebook. The organic curve looks as though it were shaped in one sweep by a large hand. Our drive ends in the fortress town of Arriolos, where some houses are trimmed in periwinkle and yellow as well as the familiar blue. Is this town real? A man is **vacuuming** the street—he doesn't miss a butt—with a contraption a bit bigger than our garage vac. The town business is woven rugs, not needlepoint but a larger weave. In the cooperative a woman tells us the entire history of the cottage industry, beginning with the Moor converts, through art nouveau. She says in English, "Now the rugs are made by women who do not want a boss." And who does? In the plaza where the wool dying once took place, a hidden fountain sends random jets of water in various directions, riffs moving at changing speeds and patterns, startling dogs and tourists. What fun to run through in the summer. I am everywhere imagining our new grandson travelling with us in a few years, can almost see him in a blue sunsuit making a dash through the arcs of water. The church, all tiled inside with blue and white scenes of acts of mercy, feels intimate. In response to the white, white town, even the sky seems bluer here. Men in berets play cards at a café, and a few women at looms sit in the doorways for more light. A pillory in the plaza is the only reminder that life was not always so serene in Arriolos.

The next day we move on to the **pousada** at Évora, magnificent Évora. We **have** been deprived in our long lives. What if we never had come? The center of town, the elliptical Praça do Giraldo, surrounded by arcaded sidewalks, outdoor cafés full of people relishing the spring air, and rows of small shops, reminds me of Tuscany—much of life takes place in the navel of the town. Pousada dos Lólos, once a convent, faces the impressive columns of a Roman temple. The arcades are not the only hint of the Moors. A few domes and a ruined gate also remind us, as do the spiderweb streets leading us away and around whatever point on the map we've chosen.

One chosen spot is the Carlos-recommended **tasca** Tasquinha d'Oliveira, small and cheery, with half a dozen tables and walls hung with traditional pottery. The owner immediately starts bringing tapas, so many that we decide to forgo whatever main courses he has cooking. He brings a fantastic red **reserva**, Monte da Penha from Porto Alegre. Here's another divine bread, with a slight hint of rye. Stuffed crab, fried cod fritters, cod and chickpeas, marinated mushrooms with mint, chicken tart, and meat croquettes—all small plates, but the quantity accumulates. We think lunch is over, but he arrives again—a spinach soufflé with shrimp. Then a plate of scrambled eggs with wild asparagus. We come to the bottom of the bottle. Then arrives fresh sheep cheese with pumpkin marmalade and almonds. One spoon of the custard dessert, and my appetite rebounds. This is one of the old convent egg sweets. Bless the nuns who must have entertained themselves in long afternoons by making something good. All these convent recipes feature eggs. Egg appear in soups, too. I don't know another cuisine where eggs are so prominent. Foamy white orbs cover a golden filling. Ed mentions his mother's graham cracker pie. In the background we hear Karen Carpenter singing "on top of the world looking down on creation," poor Karen, an anorexic woman whose voice hovers over a feast.

Outside Évora's walls, the surrounding countryside is littered with dolmens and menhirs. So much prehistoric activity attests to the desirability of this area throughout history. We see a few of the twenty "noteworthy" castles in the nearby villages and the abandoned Tower of the Eagles, but mostly just roam. I would like to come back to Alentejo when the wheat turns the color of molten gold. At evening early spring sunlight falls like a bridal veil over the fields. I start to hum a camp song: "Highlands, thy sunshine is fairest, thy waters are clearest, my summertime home. Bright stars watch over my sleep like the eyes of the angels in heaven's blue dome." Driving through oak forests, we return to our own splendid abode.

We have been given a bedroom and an enormous living room covered on every inch with frescoes. A balcony opens over a courtyard with a grape pergola. Our bed surely was made for a king. The **pousadas'** signature welcome, a bucket with iced champagne, again waits. After such jaunts, what better siesta-time reward than a bath and a bed turned down to linen. Linen promotes good dreams.

Dinner takes place in the convent cloister, where perhaps the nuns served each other the sweets they spent their spare hours devising. The food tastes of ancient rural pleasures, and even the menu's translation gives a hint of rusticity: vinegar and mint soup, black pork lower jaws, sautéed steer, duck chest, crackling scrap fat over asparagus, and pumpakin, which sounds more robust than pumpkin. We eat everything. We're eating our way across Portugal.

In the kingly bed on the pristine linen, I dream that my mother's grave has collapsed and I look in, seeing her red-gold hair, then she seeps out of the grave, wholly herself when young, and says, **I have something to tell you**. But I am horrified, answering, **But you are dead. Dead**. I have the sensation of swelling all over; I am about to rise off the ground and float. Whatever she wants to say, I do not want to hear. I want her back in the ground. Then Ed is shaking me, "You're having a bad dream," and I wake up fully aware of my refusal to listen. If someone comes back from death to tell you something, why not listen? I did not want to.

I slip out early and go downstairs, just as they are setting up the breakfast buffet. The dream disturbs me, and I want to be alone until it recedes. I sit in the cloister with a coffee and a guidebook. When others begin to come in, I walk out into a chill morning. The rows of Roman columns startle me every time I exit. Évora is one of the great small towns of the world. Seignorial in aspect, with parks and mansions, this jewel box is also graced with fountains, parks, museums, and a cathedral of dimensions that inspire awe. I stop in to visit again the serene painted-wood Annunciation angel. The statue leaves Mary to be imagined. It's always easy to imagine Mary. Mothers are like that, no?

By the time I have dispelled my dream, Ed has had the **migas** with bits of pork we loved in Ronda. Fried bread has first "marinated" for several hours in olive oil, usually garlic, and enough hot water to moisten and break apart, and several pastries. "Did you know—you didn't scream—but you gave this weird cry that sounded like a ghost, 'Nooooooo,' like you were falling down a well."

"I think our room must have been the one Queen Isabel died in."

The town is full of restaurants, and this month they all are celebrating local soups. Last month they featured pork, and next month will be lamb. When we see notices on the streets for concerts, dance performances, and art shows, we think of the similar intense cultural life of our adopted home in Cortona. Looking at the menus posted outside each restaurant, I find these soups, all of which I look up in my now-essential Maria Modesto cookbook. The Portuguese range of soups astounds me. Carlos said, "Italians have pasta. We have soup." I'll skip the fava with pig's head in favor of dozens of others. Reading the recipes, I can almost taste these traditional soups that are available all over town this March:

❖ **Sopa de beldroegas**: purslane, which volunteers in my garden. I'll try this soup with the traditional bread base, garlic, and cheese.
❖ **Sopa de poejos**: pennyroyal, which also springs up unasked at Bramasole. This soup, too, is made with soaked bread, with the addition of onion and garlic.

- **Sopa de tomate à Alentejana**, also **Sopa de tomate com toucinho, linguiça e ovos**: tomato soup made with beef stock, sometimes served with sausage and eggs.
- **Açordo de espinafres com queijo fresco, ovos e bacalhau**: "dry" soup of spinach, fresh cheese, eggs, and cod.
- **Sopa de poejos com bacalhau**: pennyroyal with dried cod.
- **Sopa de peixe com hortelã da ribeira**: fish with a strong river mint with the appearance of tarragon.
- **Sopa de cação**: skate with coriander and vinegar, sometimes paprika.
- **Sopa de feijão com mogango**: beans and pumpkin, something the pilgrim families might have made.
- **Sopa alentejana de espargos bravos**: wild asparagus, which is also a Tuscan mania. There the bitter little strings are usually cooked into a frittata.
- **Sopa da panela**: many kinds of meat, bread, and mint.
- **Sopa de alface com queijo fresco e ovos escalfados**: lettuce with fresh sheep's cheese and eggs, which we had at the **pousada** one night. It had a clear broth

with floating ingredients, like a Japanese soup.

- **Sopa de feijão e batata com ossos de porco**: beans, potatoes, and pork bones.
- **Sopa de túberas com linguiça e toucinho**: truffle soup with sausage, fatback, and eggs.
- **Açorda à Alentejana**: bread and garlic.

We reach Óbidos by noon. A walled and white town on a hill crowned by a castle and tower, Óbidos's beauty has earned it a stop on every traveller's itinerary. There are few of us at this time of the year, but all the commercial activity in town is geared toward the tourist trade. Something inevitably goes out of the life of a town when that happens. The houses are appealing, bedecked with flowers and the whitewash often trimmed with sunny yellow borders. The largest wisteria trunk in Christendom travels along the side of a village house. Many sweet churches invite one to stop awhile. After Estremoz and Évora, we're less enchanted here. We could have been the first tourists ever in Estremoz as far as I could tell, and Évora, a

UNESCO World Heritage site like Óbidos, is not at all subsumed by tourism.

Since we're celebrating my birthday today, Ed urges me to find something special. Because Portugal is known for table linens, coverlets, and sheets, I stop at a shop on an upper street. Everything looks enticing. I select creamy white scalloped sheets with hand-embroidered flowers my mother would have wanted.

At the **pousada**, the castle at the top of town, we are given the room in the tall tower. At first, we're thrilled. **Rapunzel, Rapunzel, let down your golden hair**. We cross a battlement with an enormous view to reach the tower. The entrance opens into a lower room with a little place to sit, an armoire, and a bathroom. To reach the bedroom, you essentially climb an almost vertical, ankle-breaker ladder into a dungeon room with a wood-paneled, curtained canopy bed (how did they ever get it up here?) and a small desk on which waits the **pousada**'s chilled champagne. The three windows are slits through which arrows were shot from crossbows. Since hardly any light comes in, we turn on the bedside lamps, both of which have Christmas-light wattage. The room is literally stone cold. Up this high the wind screams around the corners. Do I feel the tower sway? Downstairs is even colder, and our two bags take most of the space. Although it is only late afternoon, we decide to open the champagne and toast my having a birthday in a real medieval tower. How often will that occur? Ed turns on the television, and from under the duvet in the knight-in-armor bed, we watch a hilariously terrible Elvis Presley movie in English with Portuguese subtitles. By the end, we have finished the whole bottle. To add to the surreal, the **pousada** dining room is empty except for one table of extremely large and well-dressed Portuguese who look as if they stepped out of Botero paintings. They hardly speak at all through course after course of an excellent dinner.

What dream will come to me on my birthday high in a tower? Images influenced by the wedding of Afonso V and Isabel, who wed in the peaceful church on the **parque** when the groom was ten, the bride eight. Or maybe a narrative about the famous Josefa de Óbidos, the seventeenth-century local woman artist much revered, though only two of her paintings remain in town. Nothing, I hope, about the pillory outside Santa Maria. But after the champagne, after the red wine with dinner, I sink into the dark, dark bed and sleep with no dreams at all. Ed is dreaming something because he laughs aloud in his sleep. "What's funny?" I ask in the dark.

"You."

We leave early, after a walk around the town walls and castle. Some distance restores the original enchantment of Óbidos. Moorish porches, stone steps up and down passageways, and the moon-white houses in the early morning certainly cast their spell. And anywhere the scent of orange blossom drifts, I'm happy.

The roads bear much more traffic in the north than in the Alentejo. Portuguese drivers seem rather reckless. We're used to Italian roads, where people drive fast but with their minds on their business. They usually have considerable skill at the wheel. We trail a truck loaded with cork for miles as it weaves down the road. At each bump the cork flies in the air. A man sits on top of a hay wagon pulled by a donkey, driving others on the road to rash acts. Two lanes become three—the middle of the road seems totally what the boys in my hometown used to call "guts go." You keep to your far side and venture into the middle to pass, straddling the yellow line. Two wagons full of Gypsies, pulled by horses with other horses attached behind, trot down the highway. Women ride up top, wearing flowered scarves and nursing their babies. Everyone swerves around them. This is crazy. And dangerous. I try to control Ed's urge to pass by frequent screams.

We're looking for our country-villa-turned-hotel near Coimbra. When we find it, finally, we come upon a teensy oasis, a dreamy, dreamy house ringed by industry and apartment blocks: what they don't show you on a Web site. The place itself, Quinta das Lágrimas, is glorious, a sprawling yellow villa with converging stone staircases on the second level. It's a microcosm of the city of Coimbra, a fabulous small city on the Mondego River, with ugliness all around. We walk in from the hotel, past a fantastic park for children. All the architectural styles of Portugal are reproduced in a miniature village. Once again we say to each other what a perfect vacation Portugal offers for a family with children. The interior of the town drops us into the Old World. A woman with a basket of bread balanced on her head makes her way up a flight of stone steps from one street to the other. Another two carry on their heads big baskets of laundry. The university, oldest and most venerable in Portugal, centers on a square surrounded by buildings where students and professors for centuries have studied and learned. The bell tower dates from 1728. One of the bells, known as the **cabra**, the nanny goat bell, keeps the official time of the city. This is a walking city. The café next to the Santa Cruz church has stoked generations of intellectual coffee sippers both inside, in part of the former church, and at tables outside on the **praça**. The church itself, once elaborately carved in the Manueline style, looks as if a big wave came over a drip castle. Inside, the calming blue and white tile. Outside, a playful fountain with some of the worst street musicians in the world perched around it. We follow the patterned sidewalks for a four-hour walk, absorbing the vibrant life of the town.

Carlos has given us the name of a **tasca**. Fortunately, because it's **so** local we might never have ventured inside if we'd simply peered in the door. Half the size of a one-car garage, the **tasca** is lined floor to ceiling with notes and drawings from patrons, on napkins, notebook paper, matchbooks—anything. One flick of a match, and we'd be torched. We're squeezed into chairs at a tiny corner table, and three regional cheeses are quickly brought, along with a basket of bread that could bring tears to your eyes. Then we are served bowls of cabbage soup. The Portuguese man at the next table offers us some of his wild boar. This never has happened to me in any other country in the world. Then the waiter appears with a pewter platter of grilled pork with chunks of garlic, coriander, and olive oil, followed by a terra-cotta oven dish of rice and beans in broth. A table of men gnaw at what looks like a heap of bones, then move on to pork stew and a bowl of spinach steaming with garlic. We don't even know the name of the place. Is it Manuel ze Dos Ossos? Carlos's address, scrawled in Ed's notepad, says Beco do Forno, 12, behind the Astoria hotel. We couldn't find it and asked several people for the **tasca**. All of them, including a policeman, pointed us here. Every bite is delish, and we relish the atmosphere of workers and businesspeople all chowing down on hearty food.

The restaurant of the country villa, Quinta das Lágrimas, is called Agua. Open just two weeks, it's in the modern addition to the villa. For my taste, they've made a mistake with this addition. It feels like an industrial park café. But the young German chef is deft, and I am blessed with salmon in a poppy sesame crust, a game pie with a dark truffle sauce. Ed has spinach lasagne with saffron and figs. Yikes! But he says, "Not bad." And because he loves cod in all its forms, he orders it with mustard and shallots. This is the first meal we have had in Portugal that only tangentially refers to local tradition. Instead the chef takes in the influences of colonial Portugal. Maybe the people of Coimbra will enjoy this fusion of Portuguese ingredients with references to all the discoverers' conquests in the Americas and the East. I don't know about that saffron and figs, though.

Our trip is coming to an end. So much of Portugal we have missed. We've seen only a few towns in the north, and nothing of the lower Alentejo or the Algarve. I would love to go to Madeira and the Azores. To those ancient gods of the crossroads, I acknowledge how little our choices allow us. Will we return, take another month to explore Portugal? I would like to come back every year and see another piece of this rich puzzle. How little I know. The privilege of this kind of trip is the immersion course in history, art, cuisine, and landscape. How fortunate that our last stop in the north becomes our favorite town.

Guimarães, in the Minho area, is absolutely spectacular, an entirely livable town with wooden and iron balconies, and many half-timbered buildings so that you think you've entered a stage set for a Shakespearean play. Is this Amsterdam? England? If so, a sunny England. All around town we come upon shrines with life-size figures, below whom are placed lighted candles and wax ex-votos of heads and limbs. In 1727 these stations of the cross were erected; five remain. In the residential section, among camellia **trees**, we pass houses in total ruin next to normal houses with gardens and cherry trees in bloom. On some, wooden shingles have been painted to look like tile in blue and white, though there is not much real tile.

Difficult to find, the small **pousada** is one of our favorite places we've ever stayed, partly because it opens onto a **praça** of pleasing dimensions and has the same austere comfort and style of the others, but mainly because of the waiter who tells us, when we say how much we love Portugal, "My country is very small but very much." At breakfast I chat with a woman at the buffet, and somehow she recognizes me as an author she had read, which leads her to invite an entire tour of southern women over to say hello. We have friends in common and much to say. The waiters are all amazed at the furor, and later one discreetly asks me, when their bus has pulled away, "Was madame once a film star?"

In Guimarães, a center for cotton and weaving, I buy more sheets, these finer than the ones I found in Óbidos. "Be careful," the woman who owns the shop tells me, "many are embroidered in China." I find a soft throw and a matelassé blanket cover. Ed is dismayed at what this does to our luggage, especially since we already have a goat scent in our sweaters from the skins we bought in Estremoz.

This is a serene town of beauty and "the birthplace of the nation," as is frequently proclaimed. This slogan goes back to the time when the settlement, a far feifdom of Afonso VI, the ruler of Castile and León, was given to his daughter and her husband. Their son, also an Afonso, turned against his mother after his father's death and grabbed power from her. He then drove out the Moors and in 1139 secured for himself the title of King of Portugal. By 1143 the capital shifted to Coimbra, but memory is long here. I hope they record that he was a terrible son.

The Guimarães area had an extensive previous history, as you can see outside town at the Citânia de Briteiros (Celtic City) archaeological site. The remains partly predate the Celts (600–500 B.C.), with some artifacts dating back to Neolithic times. Many of the votives and carved stones are displayed at the archaeological museum in Guimarães, named Martins Sarmento after the local archaeologist who discovered the site.

Before the medieval Afonso asserted himself, a powerful woman with the fantastic name of Mumadona built the castle that dominates the hilltop. Salazar, the dreary twentieth-century dictator of Portugal, used the adjacent palace for a residence. I'm not much on exploring castles anymore—there's a redundancy to the experience—but this one is fun. It anchors one end of the town and opens to a broad view with Mount Penha in the distance.

Although the capital for only a few years, Guimarães still displays a proud public aspect—gardens, castle, esplanade, statues. You easily sense that the residents have pride in themselves and cherish their well-preserved medieval buildings and many monuments. Tight cobbled streets lined with handsome townhouses wind off the plazas. Iron grill works ornament windows curtained inside with linen or lace. The commercial main street, planted with flowers, remains completely nontouristy. We discuss whether we would have settled in Portugal if we'd known it instead of Italy. The country is fantastically varied within its small borders. I certainly would be happy getting to know the cuisine for a decade or two. History, beauty, endless beaches, and jewel towns like this one lead us to conclude that we would love the chance to live here part time. And Guimarães would be a fine choice. I even pass a dilapidated house with Moorish touches and an overgrown garden that I could walk into and start scraping and painting.

We stop for several local pastries. **Toucinho-do-céu**' must be one of those sweets you have to eat from age four to appreciate. Essentially little flans made of many eggs, pumpkin marmalade, and almonds, they taste cloying and goopy. Pumpkin is used in many local desserts. Pig's blood is another unexpected ingredient in sweets. Today I select only the almond cookies, and Ed has one pastry that is a ringer for a plain old chocolate éclair.

As in the other **pousadas**, the dining room is a bastion of local recipes and ingredients. The young goat, roasted on a bed of herbs, tastes meltingly tender and zesty. Ed likes the bountiful stew made with a mixture of meats and sausages. We've only had a brief glimpse of the Minho area. We admire the neat hilly vineyards and smart villages, the quick-to-smile faces, and the love lavished on the place by people who live here. Tomorrow we must leave for Sintra and our last night in Portugal.

The hotel in Sintra had a previous life as a fabulous villa called House of Seven Sighs. I feel like sighing, too, since this trip must end. Portugal has surprised me more than any country I've ever visited. With the **pousadas** waiting each night, the driving became less stressful—we are assured of a destination with character and a kitchen that knows its business. This must be the least expensive country in Europe for travelling. The **pousadas**, such grand treats, are expensive here but would be considered moderate anywhere else. Wine, pastries, even hand-embroidered sheets bear retro prices. This last hotel, Palácio de Seteais, is not a **pousada**, but in the light room with large windows with the sea far behind the formal garden, we find the same hallmark tray with champagne, plus a few silver dishes of dried apricots, dates, figs, and walnuts. On a crystal compote, they've left us sliced fresh fruits. How gracious that hotels routinely welcome guests with such a civilized gesture. Halls and sitting rooms are painted with mythological scenes in soft colors mellowed by a passing century. The floors are covered in the famous Portuguese needlepoint rugs, which we have not seen anywhere else in Portugal.

Only a few hours south of Guimarães, Sintra is worlds away: a hilly green enclave with a small town clustered around the National Palace, formerly a Moorish palace, which shows in the ground-floor arches, the trim around the roofline. Manueline/ Venetian windows on the second floor somehow adhere stylistically. Inside, we find whole rooms in Sevillian and Mudéjar (Muslim converts to Christianity) tiles. One bedroom's walls are covered in biscuit-colored tiles with raised grape leaves. Tile "rugs" imitate Oriental ones. Some of the decor is downright bizarre. One ceiling is painted with 136 magpies, one for each of Queen Filipa's ladies-in-waiting. King João considered them gossips because they reported to the queen that he'd been seen kissing another woman. He maintained that he was kissing her "for the good," whatever that meant, and he painted a banner with that motto, **"Por Bem."** Whether the queen was convinced, we don't know. I suspect not. In another room blue-and-white-tile hunting scenes cover the walls, and the octagonal paneled ceiling is inlaid with seventy-two deer, each holding the arms of a noble family. Having said earlier that I'm not too inclined to tour castles and palaces, I find this one so odd and fascinating. Sintra has several other storybook castles. Someday I will bring my grandson to explore them, if he is interested in arcane knights and legends of buried gold. The Castle of the Moors at the top of the hill would be a great hike if it were not pouring rain. The crenellations slice across the sky, interrupted by merloned towers. Several other exotic palaces lend a fabled aspect to the hills.

I wonder where the English poet lived when

he was here. Lord Byron, who really got around in his day, loved Sintra and penned a few lines about the town that are reproduced endlessly in guides and brochures. As one who likes to write about places, I have noticed how grateful towns are when they have been praised in print. Any little sentence from Goethe, Mark Twain, or Nathaniel Hawthorne, any couplet by Shelley, Keats, or Dante will be surely picked up and taken to heart forever. The Majorcans even revere George Sand, who described them in **Winter in Majorca** as brutish and backward.

It's easy to see why a poet would be drawn to this craggy and forested landscape of palaces, secret gates, views of the sea, and mysterious fog pulled in from the water by the hotter interior. Moisture drips from trees, and the air makes you want to inhale. Not as fashionable as it once was, Sintra still has its share of hidden estates and a few shops for clothes and home decor. Of course it has a good bakery, a perfect place to try the local specialty, **queijadas de Sintra**, cheesecake tarts with a scent of Moorish cinnamon. Ed wonders if we could take a box of mixed pastries home but, remembering the goatskins and bed linens, decides not. We walk back to the hotel, arriving totally drenched.

Time to crack open that chilly bottle floating in melted ice and raise a glass. Because it is hard to imagine not always travelling, the Greek toast comes to mind: **Live forever**.

The plane from Lisbon to Rome is delayed two hours, and we have drawn seats in the rear. I'm squinched in the middle, and Ed is across the aisle in the window seat. A great deal of chaos goes on around us as people take seats wherever they want, ignoring assigned seats. Everyone is speaking Italian. The flight attendants give up. As we take off, several people shout and scream. Ed and I look at each other: **What's going on?** As soon as the plane is aloft, everyone gets up, visiting, queuing for the bathroom, passing fruit around. The seat belt sign comes on, and the plane starts to jounce. More screams, but no one sits down. So much is being handed back and forth. I am given food and photographs and postcards. The airline's processed sandwiches are greeted with loud cries of **"Che schifo!"** What shit! We are right in the dead center of a group of rowdy southern Italians who have been on a pilgrimage to visit the shrine of Fatima. For most of them, this is the first flight. The party is on. I never have heard so much laughter—or any laughter—on a flight. The man next to me sees my amazement. "Signora, a little confusion is good for the heart." Ed collects several business cards and hears life stories. The pilot begins the descent into Fumicino, and the aisles remain jammed. No one can hear the voices on the speaker admonishing everyone to buckle their seat belts and raise their tray tables. Finally, the attendants start to shout and ride herd. The pilgrims remain quiet only for a moment. We're going home to Italy. Let the singing start.

Spaccanapoli

Split Naples

We stop to listen to four musicians who are playing Brazilian music with gusto. Suddenly, a couple steps away from our small crowd and begins to tango in the street. Naples. Where else in the world does someone tango in the street? Where else do you, too, want to break into a tango in the street? Others gather and clap and shout encouragement. We step back into a bar to watch while savoring the best coffee on planet earth. Concentrated and rich, the flavor bursts, then stays in your mouth. We love the local custom of serving a glass of water with coffee. Everyone seems to drink at least half the water. The reason must be to cool you because the coffee is served quite hot. Even the cup is hot to the touch, though the barmen pluck them easily from the racks set in boiling water. I must sip, but I see the Neapolitans step up to the bar, toss down the coffee in a nip, and exit.

A less-expert couple joins the dance. A little girl raises her arms and starts to wiggle. It's a party. Sometimes all of Naples seems like a party.

We first came here fourteen years ago and were impressed with the vibrancy of the city, awed by the archaeological museum, which houses the finds from Pompeii and Herculaneum, and seduced by the balmy weather. Traffic was memorable. Ed got to drive on the sidewalk. About four years ago we came back, and ever since, weekend by weekend, sometimes week by week, we began to explore the city and its environs. To know Napoli—once you've been, you never want to say Naples again—would take two lifetimes. This month we have two weeks. May is the ideal month for a visit because dozens of monuments and churches usually closed are open in the mornings. May is also the month for walking along the fabled bay. Those ancient Romans didn't miss an aspect of hill or curve of coast. They knew exactly where to site their country villas.

What you read about Naples, you have read over and over. Don't cross into this area, avoid that street, wear a money belt, leave your jewelry at home. Thieves, indolence, corruption, chaos, grime, and murder by the Mafia. Actually the Mafia is not interested in visitors, and the murder rate is considerably higher in most American cities than here. We're supposed to be afraid? We live in the Bay Area. I want to ask those writers who admonish you to beware of Naples: **Heard of Oakland?**

Writers repeat other writers, not noticing that Naples goes around all 360 degrees and that their impressions travel only about ten percent of the way. Travellers, those who've never been there and those who stayed one night en route to Amalfi or Pompeii, also repeat the well-worn words.

This began long ago. The seventeenth- and eighteenth-century travel writers scorched Naples with their prose. "Naples is a paradise inhabited by devils," goes an adage from back in the fourteenth century. The hot sun was blamed for eighteenth-century travellers' impressions of laziness. Is Naples hotter than the Côte d'Azur in August? All the writers could agree that Naples was the golden city, situated most fortunately of all cities on a luxurious sweep of calm blue bay, with Vesuvius and the long arm of the Amalfi coast to balance the composition. The volcano smoked, too, smoked most picturesquely, as the thousands of paintings of the bay attest. (It smoked until 1944, when an eruption sealed the opening.) For those leisurely Europeans on Grand Tour, Vesuvius added the dimension of primitive nature at work just at the edge of the seascape. The harbor view includes the felicitous isles of Procida, Capri, and from certain points Ischia. For the ancient people, the spot was first among the many choice locations in the Mediterranean world. For travellers during the Enlightenment, Naples both allured and revolted. The writers considered the poor of Naples to be mindlessly happy and/or extremely lazy. In an essay in **Voyages and Visions: Towards a Cultural History of Travel**, Melissa Calaresu has written well about these mostly French visitors in her essay "Looking for Virgil's Tomb." "One can say that idleness is the trait truly characteristic of the Neapolitan Nation," she quotes from Richard de Saint-Non. And she finds in Joseph-Jérôme Lefrançais de

Lalande's writing that the Neapolitan appears as "wicked, indolent, and especially inconstant." Calaresu describes the Neapolitan writers who fought back in print, accusing the French of pederasty, buffoonery, plagiarism, and ignorance, but the stereotypes of the eighteenth-century writers, especially Lalande and Saint-Non, endure to this day.

Often Italians also look down on the South, especially Naples. "Africa begins south of Rome," we've heard one time too many.

When I exclaimed over the gorgeous Raoul Bova, who starred in the movie of my book **Under the Tuscan Sun**, our friend Amalia shrugged. "He is not pleasing to me. Perhaps it is because he sounds like a Neapolitan."

As we left for this trip, Beppe, who tends our olives and vegetable garden, arrived with his weed-whacker. "We'll be back on the twentieth—we're going to Naples."

He set down his machine. **"Napoli. Ehhhh. Son' tutti cattivi. Tutti."** They are all bad. All.

A friend gave us a ride to the train. **"Caos. Ladri."** Chaos. Thieves. She held out her hand. "Leave that necklace with me."

"It's not even real—who's going to snatch it off my neck?" I kept the necklace.

• • •

The tango ends. We walk back to the funicular and ride up, straight up, to Piazza Vanvitelli in the new (nineteenth-century) Vomero district, where you lose entirely the raucous energy of Naples. Here you could be in Paris or Verona or any sophisticated city with leafy pedestrian streets lined with cafés, pastry shops, and small businesses of all kinds. The clothing shops are particular to the owner—no look-alike chains here. A group in the street plays—what?—marimbas near a fountain in the abstracted shape of Vesuvius. Water flows instead of lava. In an antique shop we begin to chat with the two owners, Fidele and Roberto, who operate the shop on weekends as a hobby. Their day jobs are internist and lawyer. We buy a small silver cup, and Roberto's wife wraps it as though it were an important gift. They are about to close for lunch, so we walk out with them, and they take us on a little tour of the area, including their own houses down a quiet street with views of the distant bay. We talk restaurants, opera, how Naples is changing. They invite us in for lunch, but we don't want to intrude if they are only being polite. Instead, we exchange numbers and plan on dinner another time.

We stroll on—vegetable shops where each asparagus looks squeaky clean and each lettuce like a spring hat. We pass **friggitorie**, the fried-food stores with tempting **arancini** (crisp rice balls stuffed with cheese or meat sauce), fried pizza, and during this season fried artichokes—so very delicious. I smell the heaps of potato croquettes, and **mozzarella in carrozza**, mozzarella put in a "carriage" of milk-soaked bread and deep fried. The famous Tuscan **crostini**, rounds of bread for many delicious toppings, here are deep-fried disks of pizza dough, which are then spread or piled with whatever the cook fancies.

Vocabulary:
pizzaiolo: a most important occupation, the pizza maker.
mozzarella di bufala: languorous water buffalo in the Campania countryside produce the milk for the cheese loved most in Napoli.

On this first day, we want pizza. The restaurant we choose says Dal 1914. If they've been making pizza that long, they must know how. The cook shoves them inside the wood oven as fast as he can roll the dough and throw on the tomatoes. Someone else brings them out with a long iron spatula. In the restaurant crowded with local families having Saturday lunch, we are the only tourists. I order the classic Margherita, and Ed has his favorite Napolitana, with anchovies and capers.

Neapolitan pizza Margherita is a thing unto itself: not too thin, not too thick; not confused with a lot of different ingredients; the just-right crust, a flaky bite yielding to a softer interior; the vesuviana tomatoes, the freshest **mozzarella di bufala**, and the hint of basil, bringing another touch of Mediterranean essence. The Margherita is a well-written ode to simplicity of ingredients in perfect balance of taste and texture. Often pizza restaurants offer only Margherita and Marinara, but usually you find pizza with escarole, which has been chopped and mixed with raisins, garlic, capers, and sometimes anchovies.

The walkway through the fecund and shadowy garden of Vomero's Villa Floridiana curves enough to make you feel you are in a vast park. The twists ensure that you come all of a sudden upon the elegant white neoclassical villa. In the forecourt, families with babies lie on blankets, and the lawn is a riot of toddlers running, colliding, and being scooped up by their mamas. The eternal soccer game has begun, and the wonk of the ball and the shouts do not disturb a young couple practically making love on the grass nearby. The house is lovelier from the south side, with its long staircase and views across the gulf. This was a pleasure palace for Francesco I di Borbone and his wife, Lucia, Duchess of Floridia. They hired the Tuscan architect Antonio Niccolini, who designed an incarnation of the fabulous San Carlo opera house. He redesigned an existing villa and built in their gardens a private zoo, theatre, round temple, chapel, and fountains. When all the pomp reduced to circumstance, the state acquired the property, which became the home of the Duke of Martina's collections.

The guard and ticket seller seem happy that someone finally has come to view the villa's ceramic museum. I want to see the majolica and porcelain, both such strong local traditional arts. This collection, mainly from the eighteenth century, is idiosyncratic. A case of early forks with two sharp tines. A copper reliquary for the relics of Santa Valeria shows her being decapitated on the lid and on the bottom she hands her own head to a saint while the executioner prances away. So many fine items a collector would be thrilled to discover—just as the Duke of Martina did—at an antique market: Napoleon painted on parchment, dinner ware from the eighteenth-century Royal Porcelain Works of Naples, ivory and coral carvings, a tortoiseshell lorgnette—all contribute to a sense of luxury and refinement that existed during the French Bourbon ascendancy in Naples.

Six thousand plates, vases, statuettes, urns, inkstands, snuffboxes later, we emerge and seek a particularly fragrant pastry shop we passed earlier. We need sustenance before we return to the hotel for a few hours of reading and looking out from the terrace at the magical gulf.

The **dolci** of Naples deserve a book of their own. The French and Spanish heritages, combined with Italian culinary traditions, result in delectable trays of tasty morsels in thousands of shops and bars all over town. We limit ourselves to one in the morning and one in the afternoon, and only split a dessert at night. A little wisp of crunchy **cannolo** pastry slipped around almond cream, another **cannolo** stuffed with chocolate ricotta—what's the harm in that? Especially with another paradigm coffee—barely a spoonful, with a **crema** to coat the lips. Ed is fascinated to see that the espresso machines are, one and all, the pump kind. In Tuscany these have been replaced with push-the-button models. "Oh, no, no," the **barista** tells him, "this way you can really tamp the coffee, and the lever pushes the water through it with more pressure." He points to a gauge and pulls down the lever. He throws up both hands, **What can you do?** "In Tuscany they drink brown water."

When we return to our room, the management has sent us a plate of **sfogliatelle** and a half-bottle of Villa Matilde wine. A **sfogliatella** resembles a clamshell half opened. The pastry, like **millefleurs**, is tender and layered. You bite into dense, sweet ricotta filling. This is one of the great pastries of the world. To prop oneself in a big bed with linen sheets, the windows open to the Briar Rose view of castle, volcano, gulf; to sip a little wine in the late afternoon and pick up one of these irresistibles—this is sybaritic. The Roman hedonists couldn't have enjoyed it more. We spread our maps, cross-reference restaurants in various guides, and make a list of all the treasures in Napoli that we want to see.

By the time we go upstairs to dinner, it's almost ten. But that's early in Naples, and others are arriving also. Since the evening feels too chilly for the terrace, we sit close to the windows so we can see the bobbing lights on fishing boats moving out into the gulf, and the pavé of lights along the water's edge below. Vesuvius looms only as a dark presence in the distance. "Vesuvius," I say. "Just the knowledge of it must influence the minds of people who live here."

"Like San Francisco. At any given moment, all hell could break loose." I know Ed is reliving the 1989 earthquake, when we fled from our house, which felt like a mouse being shaken in the mouth of a cat.

"At least here you could see it coming."

"But they died at Pompeii from the fumes and ashes. That must have happened as fast as an earthquake."

"I think there's something good, though."

"Well, yes, the tomatoes that grow on the slopes. And the grapes."

"Something else. Remember Blake talked about those who learned to walk on frozen toes?

Neapolitani must get some energy, some heat for life from the earth. The caloric strength from underground enters their feet as they learn to walk, giving them more passion and life force."

"It's a theory." Ed smiles. The waiter pours our second Villa Matilde wine of the day, and we toast the shadowy outline of Vesuvius.

Spaccanapoli—the street that splits Naples—symbolizes to me the many split aspects of the city: the sublime and the ugly, the ancient layers of time and the ordinary hustle of the present, the several cultures that shaped the local character (Italian, French, Spanish, and through them a touch of the Moors), the kindness of the climate and the fearful proximity of the volcano, the incredible luxuriant architecture and art and the crumbling, tumbled buildings, the fabulous sophisticated decorative tradition and the folk art religious figures and nativity scenes sold everywhere. This place splits and splits again. The careless beauty of Naples is impossible to contain in a book. The voltage of the city resembles New York's, but the American version is a commercial energy, a drive into the future, while Naples' electricity feels connected to largesse, zest for living, a sexual, grounded force—and timelessness. To grow up here must make the rest of the world seem pallid.

Vocabulary:

decumano: the Latin word for a major street. Spaccanapoli, an arrow-straight street piercing the heart of old Naples, was an important thoroughfare, the **decumano inferiore**, on the Roman town plan. Via Tribunali, parallel and close, was the **decumano maggiore**, and Via Anticaglia was the **decumano superiore**.

presepio: crèche. The **presepio** tradition goes back centuries, and the antique clothed, terra-cotta figures, with expressive faces and the range of Neapolitan gestures, are searched for by aficionados of the tradition. Every citizen must have an ongoing collection. On the side street along the church, San Giorgio Armeno, I find a bevy of delicately painted pastel angels and buy a dozen for Christmas gifts.

scavo: archaeological excavation.

Paleochristian: earliest Christian remains.

corno: horn-shaped object carried, displayed, and worn as protection against the **malocchio**, the evil eye.

Enter Spaccanapoli, and you step onto the ancient Roman grid. The forum, the center of town, was uncovered in this area. Off Spaccanapoli are the narrowest streets on earth, lined with closet-sized artisan shops and little **bottege** whose entire stock you could fit inside two suitcases. The air above the street is alive with the flapping of laundry. I often stop at the top of a street because the dim light looks sinister. Via Tribunali and Via Anticaglia (which becomes Via S.S. Apostoli) are similar in feel to Spaccanapoli—scrunched and lined with palaces, dingy shops, and so many churches I can't keep them separate. Our route goes from Piazza Bellini over to Via Anticaglia, back along to Via Tribunali to the duomo, then cuts over to Spaccanapoli, where we will walk the length to Piazza Gesù. With meandering in between. We're focusing on these streets because along them, and jogging off here and there, are the

monumenti, usually closed, now open on May mornings.

We get dropped off by the taxi at a piazza so Old World it makes you ache. Piazza Bellini seems to be dozing in another century. Decadent terra-cotta, ochre, mustard, and oxblood apartments and cafés circle an excavated Greek ruin, a man napping on a bench, a street lined with bookstores. We hear music here, there, everywhere—someone playing a time-warped violin in the morning, and from another window, a sad sax. We free-fall into a special ambiance we did not know existed but which seems so oddly familiar, so right. Old ladies stare from upper windows as though at something we can't see. Men are raising the **saracinesche** (the folding gates that close Italian shops retain the Saracen name of those who brought them to Italy) and opening the doors to their musical instrument and sheet music shops.

Map in hand, we find courtyards with open staircases zigzagging up four floors, lone palms, old-fashioned nuns in heavy black with crosses, priests in long robes, buildings faded and peeling, abandoned palazzos, a derelict yellow baroque church overtaken by pigeons. An extravaganza of tile covers benches, fountains, paths at the sublime cloister of Santa Chiara. The streets gyrate with daily commerce. And we find open churches! All week we will wander this route among arcaded markets with vegetables spilling out of boxes, fish in blue plastic tubs, cheap shoes, and **presepio** shops. Many of these sell handmade crèche figures. Elaborate scenes involve not just the holy family, wise men, and angels—the whole context of a village is included. Small children are shopping with their parents. I see them buy miniature roof tiles, bread ovens, sections of buildings, artificial fires, tiny fruits in baskets. I collected for my dollhouse like that when I was a child. And everywhere the **corno** is for sale. Jewelry stores sell this protective symbol in coral, turquoise, and gold. The **presepio** shops sell them in terracotta and brass. "Do local people still believe that the **corno** keeps away the evil eye?" I ask in one shop.

The young man, who makes his own **presepio** figures, points to the tiny gold one on a chain around his neck. "We don't believe—but we wear. If you get a new car, a new motorcycle, anything new, you hang a **corno**. You hang a **corno** especially if you don't believe."

Ah, split Naples: Spaccanapoli.

San Lorenzo Maggiore, right in the heart of Naples, must be one of those inexplicable places where magnetic forces beneath the earth converge and pull you toward an invisible crux. It pulled Petrarch, who ran into the church from the rain—such an odd little bit of memory to survive. It pulled Boccaccio inside where he met his Maria, who became Fiametta in his writing. It pulls us away from the fatally picturesque piazza, framed by an arch over the street where the skill of the ten-year-old soccer players enables them to avoid hitting the crowded stands of **corno**, **pulcinella**, and **presepio** wares.

Lorenzo, patron saint of cooks, is one of my favorites. He is always shown holding a rack, on which he was roasted by his persecutors. He is said to have cried out, "Turn me over, I'm done on this side"; I don't doubt it. His restrained Gothic and very masculine church interests me primarily because it's the last layer of a series of previous embodiments. Excavations have shown that the Greek agora lies underneath, and the Roman forum was located nearby. The present church, a baby in historical terms, was built over the Paleochristian church on the same site. Some later baroque overlay has been removed, restoring the architecture to its unadorned simplicity. The Gothic is not common in Tuscany, so the architecture seems foreign, except for the marble columns and **pietra dura** inlay. Inside the door one of the memorialized dead carved in marble looks as if he's taking a siesta after lunch; another props up on his side, as if reading a mystery in bed. In the adjacent cloister and underground lie the remains of the Roman market. Then down a long flight of stairs, and you're suddenly walking along a whole section of Roman street. How spooky Neapolitans must have felt during the air raids of World War II, when they hid from bombs here. Cool, dank, dim—this is a cross-section of the past, with perfectly delineated shops. Like the ones still thriving above, they had one room for sales and a smaller one in back for storage, siesta, and eating. The paved street is about as wide as those that cut between the **decumani**. A section of arcades, too, mirrors the markets above ground. A bread oven, a cistern, a little pass-through window, a stone wash tub—these homey details recall daily life.

After all these marvels, my favorite part of San Lorenzo turns out to be in a wing of the convent, where I find two small rooms of medieval sarcophagi and marble tombstones carved with figures of the deceased. They are all men, probably much taller in death than in life. Each body rests his feet on two dogs like little cushions. The figures rest their heads on marble pillows, indented as though soft. Their hands are crossed in knightly poses, but one man's hands are together in prayer. The beauty of the carved marble invites the hand. When I rub mine over one face, I get a chill, as though the marble man could feel my touch. Long gone to dust, the idealized form remains.

Santa Maria del Purgatorio faces one of the arcaded markets. Grim bronze skulls and crossbones on stone pedestals mark the front entrance. You can see into a dim crypt below, decorated with olive oil cans full of plastic flowers. Standing across the street day after day, selling your produce and chatting with friends, you don't, I suppose, notice the grinning skulls staring at your radicchio.

Santa Maria di Costantinopoli must be the liveliest church in Napoli this morning. As part of the May openings, we are greeted politely by a boy from the convent school, who offers to show us the church. His teacher says **buon giorno**, too, and stands a few feet away to listen to her student practice his English. Soon we're joined by three girls. Is there anything lovelier than eleven- or twelve-year-old girls? Tossing cascades of black hair, flashing brilliant smiles, almost jumping with excitement, they all talk at once, telling us the church was built as a thank-you to Maria for stopping an attack of plague. But, one shouts, the church was supposed to have been built on promises given during an earlier plague, and the people forgot. That's why the plague came back; Maria wanted the church she'd been promised. They propel us to the convent garden where their classmates perform traditional music and dances with great enthusiasm. They refuse to believe that we understand Italian. "Nonstop music. You will listen." Songs involve cartwheels in the dirt, great work on the tambourines, and that quintessential local instrument, the **triccaballacca**, which rings bells and clacks at the same time. Pre-sexy girls go all out to interpret romantic songs.

Hands on hips, eyes rolling, lots of swaying—little innocent Carmens. "Which girl do you like?" I ask the boy. He turns his serious, deep Byzantine eyes to me and smiles. "Not one of these, but there are too many beautiful girls in my school."

The girls pull our sleeves, pointing out the sparse and dusty laurel, bitter orange, mimosa, and mandarin trees, the tiled cupola of the church, and their school, which they so clearly love, abutting a desolate courtyard with broken chairs and trash. "**Abbandonata**," one shrugs.

They offer to show us the church again. When we thank them and say goodbye, each one politely shakes hands, then they're off.

"Pizza pause," Ed says as we leave. We stop in at Campagnola, the plainest of plain places, jammed with locals. The sign proclaims: **Qui si mangia bene e si spende poco**, here one eats well and spends little. This is down home; no guidebooks will point you here. Mama is cooking, and there's no pizza at all, but instead we are tempted by marinated sardines, grilled fish, marinated zucchini, and **peperoni ripieni**. Four tourists look in and recoil. But this many locals can't be wrong. Soon more crowd inside. The husband keeps grabbing folding tables and finding space for them. No one minds because Napoli has the densest population in Italy; they're used to close quarters. When Mama comes by our table, I ask how she made the delicious peppers, which are not really stuffed but rather layered. "Roast the peppers and cut them in strips. Put them in a baking pan and sprinkle them with breadcrumbs, parsley, pine nuts, raisins, and a few pieces of butter, then do that again."

"No olive oil?"

"Of course olive oil. Swim in olive oil. Then you bake."

"That's all? Wasn't there some meat?"

"Sí, come no? E forse un po' di formaggio." Yes, why not? And maybe a little cheese.

We start the long walk back to the hotel. We pass so many Santa Maria churches. Some are named for location: Maria of the arch, the portico, the column, the vista; some are named for memory: Monteoliveto, Jerusalem, a rare snow in summer. But by far most of Mary's churches' names reveal her deepest function to the faithful. She has her churches of miracles, pregnancy, help, concession, faith, patience, purity, health, victory, knowledge, hope, thanks, grace, every good, seven sorrows, and chains—dozens and dozens and dozens of places to appeal to Mary for what ordinary life requires. Her shrines in the street offer a spot to pin a note or a photo so that she will look down with mercy. We stop at all of them. She is outlined in three layers of neon. She is gazing all the way through you. She has a secret smile. One moving Jesus shrine has carved above its niche ADOREMVS in Roman letters. Jesus is crowned with thorns, **ecce homo**, behold the man. His pain is completely surrounded by flowers. "Napoli overwhelms me," I say to Ed. "It's the full-fledged, all-out, big-hearted Mediterranean city."

"In fifteen years it will be the best city in the world to live in. It's got everything. Clean it up, yes. But I hope they leave the ruins, let it continue to run wild, too."

"As much as I love Rome, something about Napoli gets closer to me. I'd love to have been born here. More than anywhere else."

• • •

In the dim siesta light, with the shutters pulled almost closed, I read pages from **The Gallery** by John Horne Burns, a young American soldier stationed here during World War II. I pick up this book as I do Colette's **Earthly Paradise**, because it deeply refreshes. Besides being a clear imagistic writer, who seemed to write with blood instead of ink, Burns understood Italy. Even during war and occupation, even though he was very young, he connected at a cellular level. Having just walked through the glass-vaulted Galleria Umberto I, where his novel is set, I go back to him because of the tremendous love he brought to his writing. He **recognized** Napoli, and the city gave him an opening into understanding how those in tragic circumstances live and even find joy. His method is portraiture. In his pages we meet many American soldiers and many Neapolitans, all caught in stupidity and madness, all given the opportunity to reveal their souls. The ugliness and grace of human character stains and lights every page. On page 347 this description:

> Moe loved the city of Naples . . . Those corners that gave onto nowhere, the sunlight

slanting on a pile of rubble, those faces looking out laughing or weeping at him—all reminded him that his heart was a hinge not a valve. And most of all he loved the titter or hum or roar of Naples, saying to him things older than 1944, things that reached back into a time when men were more united in their chaos, willing to be put against a wall for something they believed. It seemed to Moe that in Naples there had somehow survived the passion and coherence of an old faith. All this he only felt, but the city of Naples comforted him. There was a poultice in its dirt, a natural humanity in its screaming.

Sunday. The city closes. Traffic abates. Families flock to Villa Reale park, where they visit with friends and leisurely walk along the water. The children ride long-maned ponies that are saddled or attached to little carts. Older children rush toward the bumper cars. "They're practicing for adulthood," Ed says. And yes, the children drive with aggression and exuberance. A concert is in progress on the bandstand. We don't go in the aquarium, stocked with fish from the bay, but I love the story of the feast prepared for American generals when the city was liberated during World War II. The larders were bare all over the city, so a seafood dinner was prepared—from the aquarium.

A low-key antique market strings along the edge of the park on the second and fourth Sundays of the month. Vendors seem mainly to visit with other vendors. I pick up a silver saltcellar, and a florid-faced man with eyebrows as big as bird wings calls out, "Oh, lady, that was used by all the Borbone kings, and by Napoleon also." I pick up another. "Where are you from?"

"We live in Tuscany," Ed says.

"You are not Tuscan."

"No, **americani**."

"But you love Tuscany. You are very smart but not too smart. Tuscany is calm, but here"—his gesture takes in the bay—"here it more beautiful."

"Were you born in Napoli?" I ask.

"**Signora**, where else would I be born?" We buy two saltcellars after a little stint of bargaining that feels obligatory on both sides but useless because he hardly budges and the price was low anyway.

The **centro** closes to traffic today, giving us a

taste of what a paradise Napoli would be if only cars could be brought under control.

Sunday is best. On **domenica** you don't feel obliged to go, go, go. A café will do, facing the Castel d'Ovo, the Egg Castle, with blinding light from the bay glancing on our faces. Behind sunglasses we linger over espresso, talking about pizza as an art form, the geekiness of people's travel clothes, Shirley Hazzard's novel **Bay of Noon**, set in Naples, fried **maccheroni** cakes, and courtyards with marble busts and palms.

The day seems to last a week. A soft rain begins. We walk toward the archaeological museum as rain pelts down harder. Ah, Napoli—a city where not only is love king but you can find a taxi in the rain. The museum, what a gift, is almost empty. We linger in all the Pompeii rooms. A few years ago you had to have an appointment to see the so-called "pornographic" paintings from the brothel at Pompeii. Now the door stands open. Pornography is supposed to be titillating; these paintings are simply funny. Someone's gigantic penis must be carried on a tray before the man. There's a little bestiality, not too convincing. We move on to the silver rooms. Wine cups with the grapes in repoussé and handles shaped like beaks of birds, bowls and cups with floral motifs, porridge dishes with short handles just adapted to the hand. These are decorated with hunting scenes, vines, and the head of Medusa. The cooking equipment could work in my kitchen today. Someone's square baking dish and sauté pan lack only the nonstick coating. I wonder what was cooked in the muffin tin with a handle. Maybe the vegetable timbals (**sformati**) we like so much in Tuscany are a precursor of the rich macaroni in pastry **timballi** from the local repertoire. As we always do when we are at this museum, we visit the famous mosaics from the courtyards and garden walls of Pompeii and Herculaneum. Then we see from the window that the rain has stopped.

Walking "home," we stop at the large Feltrinelli bookstore. Inside we hardly can move for all the people. I would like a Neapolitan cookbook. Ed veers off to find a CD of the traditional music of the area. We lose each other for a half hour because he moves on to poetry, and I start looking in the gardening section. This long gentle day with no push to see as much as possible must be similar to living here.

The light on the water looks clean and silvery. Savory smells of roast pork drifting from windows clouded with pasta steam make me long for an invitation to dinner. I imagine living in an apartment with high ceilings and a geranium balcony opening to the view of islands and water. The bright colors inside are those of Matisse's Mediterranean room paintings. In the kitchen, small but with thick marble counters, Ed makes ravioli filled with borage and ricotta, while a **pomorola** (ultimate tomato sauce) simmers. We'll play some Villa-Lobos because it goes with the light Neapolitan air. A Sunday evening at home, when I will bake some olives with fennel seeds and lemon peel, fry a rabbit, and set the table near the balcony's open doors so that when Fidele and Roberto come over with their wives to eat, we can see the last moment of the sunset—perhaps even the green flash. I almost see the frosted glass cups of almond and melon gelato and taste the **zeppole**, those crisp fried cookies. But so far the only reality of this meal is the silver saltcellars I bought this morning, now wrapped in tissue in my bag.

We're content, after all, with a late dinner at a trattoria. Grilled artichokes, pappardelle, cut wider than usual, with roasted peppers, a mixed grill, and the local bread that is like firm cake. I think I can taste the freshness of the wheat. "Put the basket over there. I don't want it in my reach—what a disaster to love bread so much." Every night we are exclaiming over the food. "How can it be so tasty?" And the restaurants are lively with talk and music, for in Naples inevitably someone comes in to sing. Eating out becomes the occasion it was meant to be.

Our days fall into a rhythm. The churches begin to blur. The street food—how fantastic. We try all the ices, the fried macaroni pies and fried pizza, everything but the pigs' feet. We walk until the soles of my feet wear off. **"Che palle!"** a man yells at two boys on a Vespa going full throttle the wrong way down Spaccanapoli. What balls! I notice that the local people give coins and talk to the Gypsies who beg. There are not many—my hometown, San Francisco, beats Naples a thousand times in the number of street people. The Gypsy women sometimes sit in groups with children, sometimes alone. We have been startled at the beauty of most of them, and their clothes don't look bad, either.

They're not ignored; another hint of the beating heart of this city. Same with the Africans selling tissues and CDs and fake designer bags, and the Gypsy men who come through the restaurants selling flowers. They're doing a job, and they're treated politely. Ed always buys the flowers.

The streets—what madness! But after a few days here we realize that our perspective is definitely a foreign one. After a few taxi rides across town, Ed begins to notice that the other driver **expects** to be cut off and will not barrel into the side of the taxi. He watches the maneuvers with admiration. "Are they **good**!" he says, and keeps congratulating the driver: "Bravo, bravo." The U-turns in the middle of streets, which make me clutch Ed's arm, are calculated. If there are four seconds or so before oncoming traffic reaches the driver, he will turn, knowing the approaching cars will brake for him. If there are only two seconds, he will wait. There's choreography to traffic flow. Finally I relax, even when we swerve by a woman with her groceries, baby, and toddler balanced on a Vespa, then an ancient couple on canes, even the traffic cop. About half the time we are overcharged in taxis, but not much, and the detours are interesting. All the drivers like to talk, and we initiate conversations in order to hear the fast, clipped dialect. At tight, tight turns—there are many—everyone gets in on the act. Shop workers emerge to give directions, someone assumes the role of director of the scene, passengers get out of backed-up cars to see what's happening, ten people are gesturing with abandon, and inch by inch, with shouts from everyone, the car turns the corner without scraping the BMW left in the way.

The long afternoons are for our room. I write a little, read, take baths. Late, we walk out again, go to Capodimonte Museum, a castle, or San Martino for the splendid view and a look at the vast **presepio** collection in elaborate presentations. Whole villages are re-created, with the nativity one activity of many. When we leave there, all the faces we meet look like the **presepio** figures we've just seen. The walk down from San Martino must be one of the world's longest flights of stone steps—building them rivals the Pyramids. Every night we get to eat! In Napoli! We're never home before twelve or one, when we fall into deep sleeps packed with dreams.

• • •

While I'm packing to leave, the maid comes in. Ed slipped out early to take a last turn around the neighborhood. I am in the web of a dream—I'm steering a boat, almost flying over the bay, and a ginger cat sits on my shoulder. I have my sights on—where?

I don't want to leave. When I ask the maid if Naples causes you to dream, she says, "No, signora, you must have eaten pepper."

The Sun on Its Throne

Taormina

Europe can be divided into two categories—countries with riotous balconies of geraniums and bougainvillea, and countries without. Italy falls into category one, and nowhere more so than in Taormina. Like Capri, Taormina is where the gods tumped over their baskets of blessings. The earth has not formed, nor can I imagine, a place more captivating. Taormina's wavering coast below the town, a limpid sea, the perfectly positioned Greco-Roman theatre, and craggy Monte Tauro (here's our bull again) rising above the village would be stupendous enough, but that basket of blessings also deposited Mount Etna, often disappearing in mist and suddenly reappearing like a mirage in the distance. In winter, from a sunny window, you see the cone frosted with snow. Today the volcano is clear-cut in the blue air, and I easily imagine lava beginning to ooze down the slopes.

I walk before breakfast, savoring the architectural details along Corso Umberto Primo, greet shop owners who are sprinkling the street from a bottle of **acqua minerale** before sweeping around their thresholds, and explore the intriguing **vicoli** that ascend or descend on either side of the street. A stepped street, appropriately called Vicolo Stretto, must be eighteen inches wide; someone could get stuck. I like being out early before the tour buses arrive. Taormina's magnetism has pulled travellers for centuries. Early, then again by evening, the coast clears. One of my favorite things about Taormina: very few pigeons.

There's a reason we congregate in these hot spots—to worship beauty and to feel its effects light up the electrolytes in the bloodstream. I am here for another reason as well. I am reading and rereading the Sicilian writers, Leonardo Sciascia and Giuseppe di Lampedusa. A few months ago I came across a telling line in Sciascia's **The Wine-Dark Sea**. After a funny, ironic exchange on the shortcomings of Sicilians, a character "brightens up at the sight of the sea off Taormina. 'What a sea! Where else would you see anything like this?' " I suddenly thought I would like to read these native Sicilian writers **in situ** and try to see how the island affects their work, how their works are shaped by the place. I would like to know Sicily; what better way than through the insights of passionate writers?

I missed Taormina on my first trip to Sicily. Then two springs ago I was on a boat that let us off here briefly for a tantalizing glimpse of town and a quick tour of the Greek theatre with a stupefying view of the coast and looming Mount Etna. Always a fool for beauty, I said to Ed, "How soon can we come back?"

Sicily, with the possible exception of Napoli, seems to me the most complex place in Italy, and yet most of us arrive burdened by so many Mafia stereotypes that we hardly see the real place. What if I would like to write a novel set here? I hope my stack of books on the bedside table will give me clues to approaching Sicily as a traveller and as a writer. I am a Californian by persuasion, a southerner by genetic stamp. But in the fifteen years since I have forsaken my native land and adopted Tuscany as a new home and way of life, my ingrained sense-of-place ideas have been forced to adapt. Because Sicily seems so profoundly itself, I am curious to know if writers reflect that.

Writing **Under the Tuscan Sun** and **Bella Tuscany** made me realize the depth of my interest in the mysterious intertwining of character and place. The southerner, especially the southern writer, knows instinctively that those swirling tornadoes, the smoking vat of barbecue sauce that could scour your throat, a suffocating scent of magnolia, the snake handlers, kudzu creeping over the windowsill, the throb of cicadas—all have as much to do with their personal stories and written narratives as any character or action at play in the imagination.

From what point, I wonder, does the Sicilian who feels the desire to write begin? How would the intense sense of place I—a foreigner—feel work out if I had learned to walk on stony streets, had been given sips of wine as a one-year-old, had been doted on by an entire village, as babies are in these parts? Or what if I'd had to eke a living from the parched land where the feudal world only recently ended? Art and refinement belonged to few indeed. I assume I would seek in my writing epiphany, illumination, revelation, memory, and the joy of seeing, glimpsing a moment, satisfying a passion for texture, form, or (more elusively) color. But that's what I do now. I need to know more about the writers' intertwinings with this big greenhouse floating in the sea.

I tended to think of the South as the landscape that formed me and informed my writing, that the influence was fixed. As I lived in Italy and began to write memoirs, I was changing, and my writing was changing as well. I don't remember which writer said that his home was his subject matter. I resist that idea but may someday accept the truth in it. My feelings bolted their arbor and started scrambling up the subject of a house in a foreign country.

The scene reenacts every morning in thousands of piazzas all over Italy. We are drinking coffee under an awning, looking at the facade of the duomo. A man in a crisp blue shirt is engrossed in a Nadine Gordimer paperback. Two French tourists order **caffè americano**. A girl tossing her strawberry-blond hair breaks the fast with Coca-Cola and a cigarette. Across from me, Ed in a yellow shirt, my own ray of sun, is intent on **La Repubblica**. The Italians, of course, rarely linger. They take their espresso as though they're having a shot at a clinic. One motion, gone. But one signora sits outside with cappuccino reading **Venerdi**. The waiter notices my bookmark, a metal flower on a red ribbon. **"Carina,"** he says, adorable. Very original, he continues. His delight in something so insignificant delights me.

As I leave, I take the bookmark to him. **"Un regalo piccolo,"** a little gift. You would think I'd given him a Rolex. His shouts of **grazie, grazie** follow us across the piazza, and I wonder for the thousandth time—why go anywhere, ever, other than Italy.

In most of Italy, art feels as innate as breath. Natural as this is for the Italians, a frontal confrontation with art causes major shock to the traveller, especially the one who comes here to work on books, paintings, music, or photographs. Suddenly one's passion for making a creative work becomes a natural act. This is profoundly stirring. An unknown sense for most Americans over the age of ten.

I wonder sometimes if the strongest drive throughout the history of the Italian peninsula has been the impulse toward art. Around Cortona archaeologists still are discovering thousand-year-old Etruscan tombs, digging out of the muck a gold necklace fashioned so delicately that it stops your heart, a bronze animal votive so cunningly wrought that you want to grab the tiny bull and run. The reach of the artist is long, long, long as time. Across Italian history this has been so, and who knows why. "Cortona is a spiritual center; there's a magnetism in the earth you can feel," the owner of the bookstore tells me. "Go stand on the steps of San Francesco—it is especially strong there."

Although I am not inclined toward the mystical, I never doubted her for a minute because when I went to Italy, I began to write spontaneously, with pleasure, with focus, with ease. My form changed. The fatalistic, elegiac, and dark motion of my poetry turned toward the Italian light as easily as the local giant sunflowers swivel toward the sun. The people I have come to know in Cortona are genuine, direct, courteous, expansive, with a few rotten characters thrown in the mix. I get so accustomed to the constant kissing that when I return to the United States I find myself kissing people who do not expect that. The more I heard the laughter in the piazza, the more laughter I found inside my daily life. Could these qualities shape a writing style?

A place never can be neutral; wherever you put yourself, the filings are magnetized and begin their alignments. That lover of the Mediterranean world Lawrence Durrell believed that "you could exterminate the French at a blow and resettle the country with Tartars, and within two generations discover, to your astonishment, that the national characteristics were back at norm." All landscapes, he says, pose the same question to the traveller: "I am watching you—are you watching yourself in me?"

Both Lampedusa and Sciascia are skilled liberators of the revealing image, what T. S. Eliot called the objective correlative. What they "set free," as Michelangelo freed his images from marble, is what may enable me to grasp a Sicily that is probably otherwise unavailable. Images, when they arise from the place, turn emblematic, transcending mere sensory detail. Through the **giusto**, just, image, we are time travellers.

Proust wrote in "On Art and Literature": "What intellect restores to us under the name of the past is not the past. In reality as soon as each hour of one's life has died, it embodies itself in some material object . . . and hides there. There it remains captive, captive forever, unless we should happen on the object, recognize what lies within, call it by its name, and so set it free." There—Proust recognizes the **liberation** of the image, as Michelangelo recognized his figures wanting to be freed from the blocks of marble he carved, just as Lampedusa and Sciascia chose images so truly that they shine as icons.

In my "walking notebook": tile rooftops, a handmade ladder propped in a fig tree, olive trees beside a stone wall, a man outlined in a doorway—these images are contemporary or medieval or Roman and so partake of the timeless. A stone wall glinting in the wet light—what stone does to light speaks emblematically to a sense of time that floats from one era to the next. In a nimbus of gold, a little dirt-colored donkey stands against a whitewashed wall, a stony path winds into a smoky aura of light; a man with a birthmark covering half his face tips his chair against the wall under the arbor and laughs; a distant tower seems to exist through a long telescope into time.

I travel for images. I read for images, too, because the choice cumulatively creates the style of an author. Why does Lampedusa lavish words over what food was served at a ball? Because he is showing us what the people expect and how they perceive. The powerful imagistic language of Lampedusa and Sciascia conveys more in a few pages than chapters and chapters of history. I must admit to a gratitude because histories of Sicily are hopelessly dense. This island has been tossed and criss-crossed and stomped on and razed beyond counting. That these two writers take on Sicily's daunting history and subsume it within the lives of their characters gives you, finally, a grasp of the sequence of takeovers and makeovers. And more.

• • •

Giuseppe di Lampedusa, the older of the two, was born in 1896 into one of the oldest aristocratic Sicilian families. He was Duke of Palma and, eventually, Prince of Lampedusa. The tiny boy was named Giuseppe Maria Fabrizio Salvatore Stefano Vittorio Tomasi di Lampedusa. He was very attached to his mother, had a playboy youth, studied law, and then was folded into World War I, where he fought and was captured in Hungary. He walked back to Italy and suffered a breakdown. During the fascist years he travelled, lived abroad a great deal, and married a Latvian baroness.

During his life he published nothing except three articles on French literature in a small periodical. His grand family palazzo on via Lampedusa, 17, in Palermo was bombed in 1943. **Il Gattopardo**, **The Leopard**, which he labored over for years, was rejected for publication, but in one of those cruel twists of fate, the year after his death in 1957 from lung cancer the book was published and became an international megasuccess. E. M. Forster called it "one of the great lonely books." Visconti made an ambitious, sensuous movie version starring Burt Lancaster in 1963. Posthumously, a book of stories and two volumes of essays were published.

The Leopard rose from his intimate knowledge of the Sicilian aristocracy. Family members inspired some of the characters, and we can be sure they were not pleased. The book begins in 1860 and ends in 1910, the formative years when the Italian nation went from a squabbling group of duchies, papal states, and foreign possessions to a unified (more or less) country. The book starts during the years of Garibaldi's foray into Sicily—a torch to the Sicilian time warp. Lampedusa shows the rings of effects on the family of the Prince of Salina, Don Fabrizio.

First and last, we have the influence of the brutal, munificent Mediterranean sun. The narrator says, early in the book: "The sun, which was still far from its blazing zenith on that morning of the thirteenth of May, showed itself to be the true ruler of Sicily; the crude, brash sun, the drugging sun, which annulled every will, kept all things in servile immobility, cradled in violence as arbitrary as dreams."

Lampedusa associates the sun with the annulling of the will, with immobility, and random violence. These characteristics also flow relentlessly through the lives of his characters. The sun over Sicily never is passive in **The Leopard**. Here the family is about to have lunch outside: "All around quivered the funereal countryside, yellow with stubble, black with burned patches, the lament of cicadas filled the sky. It was like a death rattle of parched Sicily at the end of August vainly awaiting rain."

Even in October, the sun reigns: "The rains had come, the rains had gone, and the sun was back on its throne like an absolute monarch . . . The heat braced without burning, the light domineered but let colors live; from the soil cautiously sprouted clover and mint, and on faces appeared diffident hopes."

Near the end of the book, the sun is described again: "It was midday on a Monday at the end of July, and away in front of him spread the sea of Palermo, compact, oily, inert, improbably motionless, crouching like a dog trying to make itself invisible at its master's threats; but up there the static perpendicular sun was straddling it and lashing at it pitilessly. The silence was absolute."

The sun is god and mirror. And still is. I'm reading outside on a chaise longue beside the hotel pool. The sun has driven me to the shade of the hedge, and every half hour I have to move because it has invaded again. A small, finely made Sicilian man near me is reading, I'm shocked to see, Sciascia's **The Wine-Dark Sea**. Three screaming and crying French children with a nanny should be taken to their naps. Waiters dressed in dinner jackets circulate with pitchers of lemonade. And there's the pride of the EU, a bronzed couple with impeccable bodies; he toned and slender, his wavy black hair slicked back, his sensual molded lips almost pouting, and she a nymph in pink thong, breasts the shape of oranges popping from the inadequate-to-the-task triangles that almost cover her nipples. I cover my face with **The Leopard** and doze.

The prince is a fabulous, unforgettable character. He's very tall. The leopard insignia, appearing on pillows and in crumbling stone above doorways, symbolizes his noble family—and it becomes him. His big hand is often called a paw. He's like a lethargic leopard, who may turn predator at any moment. He has rapacious appetites toward women and goes out stalking at night, but toward morning, back in the marriage bed, he can still make his wife cry out to Mary and the saints. He rules his properties with bored attention. We see him as the last of his type. The feudal expanse of his properties will be lost in a generation. But something larger is at stake; the whole way of life, decadent and beautiful (and of course, hideously unfair), is disappearing. His own numerous children are too much under his influence to remark on this, but his favorite nephew, the impudent and fun Tancredi, has joined the forces of Garibaldi. The nephew throws his energy into the life of the prince, who is smart enough to see the changes coming but too long enervated by the centuries of other victors to join in or to try to stop them.

The prince's daughter, Concetta, loves Tancredi, but he falls hard for Angelica, a juicy daughter of the new-money, crude, Snopes-type character, Don Calogero, who is a rising force in the new order. Already Don Calogero owns more land than the prince. Now, through this marriage of Angelica to Tancredi, he is about to be absorbed into the family. He's a boor but a smart one. The prince is humiliated when, wearing afternoon dress himself, he has to greet Don Calogero in evening clothes at dinner. He is consoled somewhat to observe that the tailoring on Don Calogero's tails is a disastrous failure, the tails pointing up, the cut appalling, the buttoned shoes. Each of these characters comes to represent an historical quality at work in the fabric of society.

Lampedusa reveals the accommodations of the prince to inevitable change through his own thoughts and actions, rarely through the overvoice of the narrator. As he meets Don Calogero frequently over the marriage contract of Angelica and Tancredi, he finds an admiration growing on him:

> He became used to the ill-shaven cheeks, the plebeian accent, the odd clothes, and the persistent odor of stale sweat, and he began to realize the man's rare intelligence. Many problems that had seemed insoluble to the Prince were resolved in a trice by Don Calogero; free as he was from the shackles imposed on many other men by honesty, decency, and plain good manners, he moved through the jungle of life with the confidence of an elephant which advances in a straight line, rooting up trees and

> trampling down lairs, without even noticing scratches of thorns and moans of the crushed.

Like other big cats, the prince toys with his prey.

Fortunately, Lampedusa is such a powerful writer that I never feel I am reading a historical novel; by the end of the book not only have I read a magnificent piece of imaginative writing but I understand the scaffolding holding up contemporary Sicily. When the prince is approached about becoming a senator in the new Italy, I get the impression that he doesn't know whether to laugh or cry. In his long **no**, the Prince gives Chevalley, the representative of the Turin government, an earful. And the reader absorbs the deep background of the Sicilian character.

> In Sicily it doesn't matter whether things are done well or done badly; the sin which we Sicilians never forgive is simply that of "doing" at all. We are old, Chevalley, very old. For more than twenty-five centuries we've been bearing the weight of a superb and heterogeneous civilization, all from outside, none made by ourselves, none that we could call our own.

We're as white as you are, Chevalley, and as the Queen of England; and yet for two thousand and five hundred years we've been a colony. I don't say that in complaint; it's our fault. But even so we're worn out and exhausted.

For the prince, Garibaldi's changes come way too late. He sees Sicily in its new role as:

a centenarian being dragged in a Bath chair around the Great Exhibition in London, understanding nothing and caring about nothing . . . Sleep, my dear Chevalley, sleep, that is what Sicilians want, and they will always hate anyone who tries to wake them, even in order to bring them the most wonderful of gifts; and I must say, between ourselves, I have strong doubts whether the new Kingdom will have many gifts for us in its luggage.

Then he downshifts to first gear:

All Sicilian expression, even the most violent, is really wish-fulfillment; our sensuality is a hankering for oblivion, our shooting and knifing a hankering for death; our laziness, our spiced and drugged sherbets, a hankering for

> voluptuous immobility, that is, for death again; our meditative air is that of a void wanting to scrutinize the enigmas of nirvana . . . novelties attract us only when they are dead, incapable of arousing vital currents; that is what gives rise to the extraordinary phenomenon of the constant formation of myths which would be venerable if they were really ancient, but which are really nothing but sinister attempts to plunge us back into a past that attracts us only because it is dead.

Chevalley does not understand all this but rises to the occasion and speaks idealistically of Sicily's future. But the prince continues in his voice-of-the-ages mode:

> Sicilians never want to improve for the simple reason that they think themselves perfect; their vanity is stronger than their misery; every invasion by outsiders . . . upsets their illusion of achieved perfection, risks disturbing their satisfied waiting for nothing; having been trampled on by a dozen different peoples, they consider they have an imperial past which gives them a right to a grand funeral.

Lampedusa's knife-twist comes at the end of the meeting, when the prince recommends, instead of himself, the badly dressed upstart Calogero as just the man for the new order. This bell-tolling is not only the witty and deeply exhausted voice of the many-times-conquered aristocrat, who has made accommodations all along the bumpy road of history; it's a breathtaking, dark cultural analysis of Sicily at the historical juncture of unification. The indictment and the finesse of Lampedusa's prose sends me out into the streets—perhaps for one of those spiced sherbets he mentioned, or his favorite rum jelly.

Pasticceria Minotauro displays no rum jellies, but the prince might indulge in a finger-size **cannolo** filled with chocolate cream and dipped in chopped pistachios. Or one of the pastry boats mounded with cream and strawberries. Ed and I split a **cannolo**, then make our way down the street for cups of hazelnut and melon gelato.

What is that fragrance? A white datura, most

decadent of flowers, seems to drip its narcotizing perfume over a stone wall. To walk through Taormina is to traverse layers of scents—oleander and roses, the nutmeg spiciness of creamy stock, weedy nasturtiums, all these mixed with the wafting aromas of good sauces cooking. A blue Cinque Cento filled with flats of red geraniums parks beside a stand selling blood orange juice. Moonvine and morning glories sprawl over hibiscus hedges and twine around satellite dishes and electrical wires. A delivery truck has run over a flowerpot. People emerge from shops and houses. Much discussion ensues. A loudspeaker announces another truck laden with tomatoes and onions. He runs over the remains of the pot, and the crowd's interest shifts to the gorgeous ripe tomatoes grown on the fertile slopes of Etna.

We stop to gaze at a window arranged with trays of candied fruits, gleaming like jewels. The prince perhaps partook of **cedro candito**, those huge gnarly lemons, almost all peel, as well as the whole candied oranges and lemons, and the array of marzipan fruits, and piles of **torrone bianco con fighi secchi**, white candy with nuts and dried figs.

Even inside the duomo, lilies drench the gray

air with their sweet deathly scent. They're enlivened by glass jars of pagan birds of paradise on several altars, and arrangements of white and yellow roses and lemons. Those praying inhale these sanctious odors of flowers, along with the final whiffs of incense left behind by the priests.

It is enlightening to read, right after **The Leopard**, the works of Leonardo Sciascia.

He was born in 1921 in the small town of Racalmuto, a quarter of a century after Lampedusa and at the opposite end of the class spectrum. His father worked in the sulfur mines. He was a bookish boy and rose above his beginnings to become a schoolteacher. In the prince's time he probably would have been a priest. Also a late starter, he did not publish his first book until the age of forty. Astonishingly, **The Leopard**, which seems from another century, had been published only three years previously.

These two writers, so disparate in birth circumstances, are nevertheless brothers. Sciascia, like Lampedusa, is funny and deeply fatalistic—two intrinsically Sicilian qualities that emerge from both writers' characters. Sciascia sometimes reminds me of Pirandello, the writer from Agrigento, but then I remember that they both wrote out of a similar aptitude for taking core samples from the layers of reality. The literature of the South, my American South too, always verges on the absurd. Sciascia, who grew up under fascism, was the first to write directly about the Cosa Nostra. He later became a member of the European Parliament, abandoning fiction for pamphlets, essays, and speeches. Lampedusa and Sciascia both wrote about the mindset of Sicilians. Although Sciascia's subject is often the Mafia, his fiction delves more into the perspective of the national character that makes the Mafia possible rather than into the surface reality of the mob. As one reviewer noted, the Mafia was "both the cancer eating away at his society and a spark of rebellion kept alive in the hearts of a conquered people."

Conquered. That word again. A key. "I don't have a great creative imagination," Sciascia remarked to an interviewer. "All my books are the story of a series of historical delusions seen in the light of the present." **Sicilian Uncles**, four long short stories, shows a different uncle-type character at four points of hope: in and after World War II, during the rise of Communism, during the Garibaldi years, and during the Spanish Civil War. Always there's that sun, "scorching down enough to flay you alive."

At each crux, the hope turns to disillusionment. "This is a country," a character says, "where the left hand doesn't trust the right hand, even if they both belong to the same man." The soldier fighting in Spain gradually realizes he's fighting against the poor, his own kind. The feudal empires of the Spanish rich are as frightening as those in Sicily. The worshiper of Stalin begins to hear that he's not the idealist he thought but instead is a horrid lout. The so-called "little man" will always be duped by the powerful. On a train a man meets a man who works in oil. He doesn't even believe there is oil in Sicily, but the man assures him that there is. "Oil?" the character Micciché says:

> "They'll soon grab it . . . One long pipe-line from Gela to Milan and they can just drain it off. The devotees, those who have the interests of Sicily at heart, will be left wringing their hands . . . I'd rather not talk about it."
>
> "But if this happens . . . won't Sicilians, too, be to blame?"
>
> "Certainly: it's a Sicilian failing to stand

around and wait for the ripe fruit to fall off the tree straight into our mouths."

"We're not like that," chimed in the girl. "The fact is, that we like to make others believe the worst about us, like people who imagine that they are suffering from every illness under the sun."

That's where Micciché agrees, brightens up at the sight of the sea off Taormina, and says, "What a sea! Where else would you see anything like this?"

Sicily and the sea, two in one, impossible to separate. In "The Long Crossing" a boatload of Sicilians sets off from a deserted beach. They are immigrating to America. They listen to the sea, which to them sounds like "the wild-animal breath of the world itself," gasping and dying. They are the typical "huddled masses." After eleven days of squalid living, they're dumped on the shore, they think near Trenton, New Jersey. They disperse and soon hear singing. Must be Italians living nearby. Then a Fiat passes, then another. They have landed in Sicily. Duped again.

And thus the mindset that secretly approves of those bold ones who take the law into their own hands. Before the Mafia, many admired the bandits who demanded protection fees from towns and robbed and pillaged Sicily for generations. What have the little people ever gotten from the law? The South is only changing now, slowly, slowly. Any benefit that's ever come their way has been taken by someone.

Sciascia is wildly but subtly comic at every turn in these stories, especially in **The Wine-Dark Sea**. You have to love the characters in these stories.

Fatalism this deep is often comic—the absurd is only the other side of the mirror. In Lampedusa, the prince suffers from existential loneliness. Sciascia's characters have more heat. They're involved in love and honor and idealism and craftiness and cynicism. They're closer to the complex Sicilians of today. Both writers force the reader to unravel the stereotypes forever.

When I first went to Sicily, I wrote innocently, "It is easy to see why all those conquering hordes wanted this island. The landscape is everywhere various or dramatic. Anytime the perfume of orange and lemon groves wafts in the window, the human body has to feel suffused with a languorous well-being." Already the spirit of the place was beginning to imbue my mind. The sun can break stones, Pirandello wrote. Place **will** have its way with us. I'm fascinated to the core to learn how fundamentally different Sicily is, to learn that the world is not small, is not reduced to phrases such as **global economy** or **global village** or **one world**. These ancient people are not like us. I am so thankful for that.

My favorite place to read is the public garden. When I leave the hotel, I tell Ed, "I'm going out to drink a cup of beauty." He's on the terrace with his notebook.

A bench above the sea, that endless vista, and a good book. An olive tree was planted for each soldier killed in World War I; the names are still nailed onto the trees, and I notice that four of them commemorate boys from the Cacopardos family. Such a sacrifice from one family. The garden with many eccentric follies was built by Florence Trevelyan Cacciola, a Scottish woman who escaped to Taormina in 1889 after a scandalous affair with Edward VII. She settled down to the calmer pastimes of bird-watching and gardening and married a local professor. The family donated the garden to the city in the 1920s. Someone should write a book about the Mediterranean gardens designed and preserved by expatriates. This one steps down in long terraces, offering many places to read or embrace your true love. Behind my bench, a circle of orange trees. Beyond where the eye can see lies Gela, where Aeschylus died when a tortoise carried by an eagle dropped on his head—a fate both my writers would understand. The sun seems to pass through my body. I angle the brim of my hat, find my place, and fall into the world of the book.

Tasting the South

Italy

> Oh, for a beaker full of the
> warm South . . .
>
> —John Keats

Dear Steven,

Yes, we are still travelling in the South. Put Sperlonga on your list. A white village with houses like sugar cubes above the sea, arm-wide cobbled streets running under Moorish arches, and outrageous flowers swagging off balconies like bright skirts of ballgowns. To Ravello tomorrow, one of my favorite perches. When I go to Ravello, I'm always on a honeymoon.

You asked what's great to eat when you and your friend venture south of Rome next month. You know my philosophy—ask well-fed, happy-looking people on the street for a restaurant suggestion. At hotels, the staff sometimes directs you to touristy places, but if you ask specifically, "Where would **you** eat on your anniversary?" you get a different answer. You are going to love the food.

I lived in Italy for years before I understood pasta. The first sentence uttered by Italian **bambini** must be **Pasta, mama, per favore, pasta.** Not only a food, pasta symbolizes home, friends, family, all the good things, and down South this holds even more strongly than other areas that may have their moments with polenta and rice.

When our friend Roberto from Cortona drove to Scandinavia for a vacation, he took a dozen large **pelati**, cans of tomatoes, in his trunk, along with boxes of dried pasta. Only we, the foreigners, were surprised. Italians **fear** finding themselves without pasta. I have friends who have eaten pasta at least once a day their entire lives. Do we have an equivalent in our culture? I don't think so. The Mexicans have the tortilla.

Pasta seems eternal but isn't. Only since the eleventh century have Italian housewives wielded the rolling pin, turning out fettuccine, tagliatelle, spaghetti, and hundreds of other shapes—shells, ears, wheels, butterflies, even little radiators. Remember the big pasta seashells stuffed with cheeses and shrimp that I made for you? Down here those shells come in several sizes. In the South—pasta, pasta, pasta, big portions, served more al dente than in the North. The texture is toothsome, even chewy. Along with olive oil, it's **the** keystone of home cooking.

You've heard, I'm sure, that Marco Polo brought pasta back from China. He didn't. He brought back some breadfruit concoction, decidedly inferior to a mound of steaming macaroni. Maybe the Etruscans invented it, maybe the Romans, or Arabs. No one recorded the moment when the first plate of lasagne plonked down on the table. I like to think the creator was a Neapolitan **nonna**, with a house full of grandchildren, who said to herself, **Let's just see what happens if I pinch this dough into pieces and throw them in boiling water instead of baking the same old griddlecake in the ashes.**

From visiting us, you know pasta in Tuscany. The pasta down South ups the ante. We use red pepper flakes decorously in

Tuscany. Here, they tip the jar. Almost everything is served **all'arrabbiata**, angry. A famous dish in Puglia, **spaghetti alla zappatora**, ditch digger's pasta, has a tomato sauce with red-hot peppers and lots of garlic. In Sicily there's a **rigatoni alla carrettiere**, cart driver's rigatoni, a basic but spicy tomato sauce, this time on chewy rigatoni. The origins are not aristocratic, but the aristocrats eat these dishes, too. Italian cooking crosses classes smoothly—there is no codified, developed haut bourgeois cuisine. In the grandest palazzos they're serving pasta with chopped tomatoes and basil. Nothing beats an old-fashioned **maccheroni al forno**, macaroni cooked in the oven with **mozzarella di bufala**, spicy sausage, and tomato and meat sauce. Macaroni with ricotta equals soul food. You meet many oven pastas here; they're not common in Tuscany. Hard **ricotta salata**, similar in taste to feta, often is tossed with cinnamon, sugar, and milk, certainly a throwback to the Arabs. Often the ricotta is combined with ground almonds and pistachios, also a bow to the Arabs, but a good use of what lies at hand.

Around Naples a favorite spaghetti is **alla**

puttanesca, in the style of the whore. Maybe they'd worked up an appetite! The lively sauce combines anchovies, tomatoes, capers, olives, chile peppers, and lots of olive oil. How basic can it get? Mary Taylor Simeti, in her Sicilian memoir **On Persephone's Island**, describes **lasagne cacate**, so delicious sounding with its layers of meat sauce, sausage, onion, ricotta, and pecorino. Delicious until you learn the translation for **lasagne cacate**—shitty lasagna. Sicilian humor—don't be deterred from trying this lusty pasta.

Bring along Clifford Wright's **A Mediterranean Feast**. A copy lives on the backseat of our car when we travel. His detailed history of pasta, plus his grasp of the interrelationships of the various Mediterranean cuisines, makes for exciting reading aloud as Ed swerves along the coastal roads. My other read-aloud companion is the classic **The Food of Italy** by Waverley Root. Some information seems dated, but still fresh is his fine grasp of the food within its culture.

Delicate nuanced food, as in the French cuisine you love so, with its ephemeral sauces, its airy soufflés, does exist, but 99.9 percent of what appears on the plate is of the hearty plow-the-fields and fish-the-sea persuasion. **La cucina casalinga**, home cooking. As you hop about in Italy, the variety from place to place is absolutely astonishing, especially given that most food springs from **la cucina povera**—the poor kitchen, the make-do kitchen. Wild greens, nuts, fish, game, fruit—all the things free for the gathering—appear in every area but in different guises. The South, I've read, is always different, no matter what country, no matter what topic.

Sicily was my introduction to the food of the southern Mediterranean. Everything we tasted seemed revelatory. Street vendors sold tasty **panelli**, chickpea fritters. We stopped in tiny shops for a slice of **sfincione**, pizza topped with large breadcrumbs. Because we were in Palermo on San Giuseppe's day, all the pastry shops offered **sfince**, rice fritters made with ricotta, cinnamon, and candied fruit. All of Palermo seemed like a picnic.

In **Bella Tuscany**, I described the first dinner on that trip. **N'grasciata**, which means "dirty," was suggested by the concierge after we prodded him for an authentic restaurant. The name did not inspire confidence, but we took his word that "the name is just a way of speaking. They have their own fishing boat. I will tell them to expect you." The place was clean and bare, filled with Sicilian families and groups bent over their plates. Most had napkins tucked into their dresses or shirts. There we first met **pomorola**, the South's intense, reduced tomato sauce that makes all others seem sissy. They served a **tris** of pastas: bucatini with sardines, currants, and fennel, orecchiette with bitter greens, and plain spaghetti revved up with the **pomorola**. Then the carts began to roll out of the kitchen—baby octopus, fried **frutti di mare**, whole grilled fish, every little swimmer arrived at our table, along with grilled eggplant, roasted potatoes, and salad. When I could eat no more, the waiter grew concerned. "Signora, you must." He took a bite of squid to show me there was no cause for alarm. When I smiled and shook my head, he gently grabbed a handful of my hair, pulled back my head, and held the fork to my lips. I ate.

We were used to Italian markets, but the Sicilian ones were the most vibrant we'd seen. I wrote in my notebook:

"Lines of lambs, gutted and dripping, eyeballs bulging, hang by their feet. Their little hooves and tails look so sad. Their little guts so horrifying. The rainbows of shining fish on ice, the mounds of shrimp still wiggling their antennae, painted carts of lemons, jewel-colored candied fruits, bins of olives, nuts, seeds—everything is presided over by dealers who shout, sing, cajole, joke, curse, barter, badger . . . A vendor holds out a basket of eels that squirm like live sterling silver. He gyrates his hips to emphasize their movement . . . I wish for a kitchen so I could gather some of the lustrous eggplants and clumps of field greens. My stomach is growling so loud it sounds like a tiny horse neighing. Cooks here are in paradise. I'll never eat lamb again."

So, my friend, get ready. That one day in Palermo rocked my culinary world.

Since then, we've returned to Sicily twice and have taken several trips to Basilicata, Puglia, Naples, Amalfi area, Capri, and Ischia. Like you, Ed enjoys an adventurous palate. He will taste anything and likes some of the most impossible things. When I'm curious but disinclined to order something, he launches right in. Fried newborn fish. Various kidneys. Head cheese. For Easter, Giuseppina served a platter of braised hearts, livers, and lungs—the thought makes my knees weak. Our neighbor stewed a porcupine who had been bothering his chickens. He roasts tiny songbirds. Ed holds out his plate for more while I'm still staring at mine. In the South, anything pulled out of the sea, he's ready to meet with fork aloft.

The cooking traditions along the southern outline of the Italian coast, and on the islands, go back so far in time that they blur. Ovid mentions the "sweet mullet and tender eel" of Taormina's waters. Pliny the Elder was sipping Sicilian wines with pleasure in the first century. The Mediterranean coasts have been won and lost, won again, occupied and fought over. Greeks, Romans, Normans, Phoenicians, Arabs, Angevins—who were they—Carthaginians, Spanish, and on and on—don't make me take the history exam! (American history is so much easier! One course, and you have a good grasp of it.)

How all these invasions blend on the table makes the cuisine of the South so spectacular. The Arabs and Greeks left their fingerprints on every platter—but oddly enough, a main heritage comes from the Americas, the potato, corn, peanut, chocolate, turkey, string bean, pumpkin, and many other exotics those marauding explorers brought home. Once there was no tomato! Italy without the tomato! Imagine. No lemon either, until the Arabs brought them, along with lime, coconut, watermelon, artichoke, cinnamon, eggplant, bitter orange, and mango. What were they eating before? Legumes and fish? The Arabs even brought basic crops—sorghum, sugarcane, and hard wheat. While most of Europe dreamed through the Dark Ages, wherever the Arabs settled there was plenty of light. Waverley Root says, "You could draw a map of the limits of the Moslem invasion by plotting the places where . . . their flaky pastry became established." They loved water and channeled it in quadrants through their gardens to symbolize the cardinal directions in the Garden of Paradise, so frequently mentioned in the Koran. They taught the locals advanced agricultural techniques such as irrigation, from waterwheels and buckets on pulleys to sophisticated connections of wells that linked to underground aquifers. By breaking up the immense holdings of landowners, they initiated a small farm system. Agricultural production burgeoned.

Indigenous people are hardly mentioned in culinary histories. We learn what the invaders brought but not what the locals already were eating. Surely those living in the South had discovered their own big fish stews, though the Greeks get the credit for introducing, via Marseilles, the bouillabaisse equivalent. Today the fish soups of Lecce are famous. I hope you go there—one of those towns you can imagine you could have been born in—and feast your eyes on the fanciful baroque architecture. You can visit the workshops where craftspeople make exquisite papier-mâché crèche figures. I hand-carried an angel with billowing sea-green skirts home to California for the top of my Christmas tree.

Back to food—who knows who **first** threw a mess of fish into a cauldron? I know you like to trace origins, but separating influences way back before the Arabs becomes dicey. Certainly the Romans, as well as the Greeks, introduced many things to eat. Certainly the locals were stomping on their grapes all on their own and making some form of bread/pizza. But it is interesting to realize how many of the defining ingredients were either brought or popularized by the Arabs. All over the South, you find sublime gelato. The Arab touch is in the flavors, the pistachio of Lecce, the jasmine, myrtle, almond, watermelon, lemon, and orange. Sometimes in Sicily you can find rosewater gelato. What a gift.

I can see you out early, walking and gazing, then pausing in a bar for espresso and some glorious little pastry. Ed swears that coffee in the South of Italy is the eighth wonder of the world. I'll never forget his expression when we first landed in the airport in Sicily. I was already eating an **arancino**, a fried rice ball with creamy melted cheese or **ragù** hidden inside. He stared into the cup—I thought he'd seen a bug inside—then lifted his eyes, and I saw that it was, instead, a religious experience he was having.

As far back as Homer, I've found mention of a strong black drink with mysterious properties. Again, the Arabs' trade routes were influential in bringing coffee to Italy from Africa, but navigators from all over were plying the Mediterranean. The sea must have been like Los Angeles freeways. Coffee first arrived in Venice around 1570, where it soon became available in chemists' shops. A coffee bar opened in Venice in 1640; by 1763 there were 218 in the city. Today there must be a thousand. Not everyone was pleased. Some fanatics considered coffee the drink of the devil and asked the pope to ban it. After one sip the pope is said to have exclaimed, "This drink is so delicious that it would be a sin to let only misbelievers drink it! Let's defeat Satan by blessing the drink, which contains nothing objectionable to a Christian." Little did he know he was sanctioning a sacred rite. The Caffè Florian in the Piazza San Marco, where we spent a late afternoon together and you snapped the picture of the couple kissing, still pours forth.

But the coffee of Venice ranks only as semidivine. In Sicily and Naples, through the **barista**'s rituals of preparing the grounds, tamping them just so, and favoring true pump espresso makers (not automatic), coffee achieves an unparalleled concentration and complexity of flavor.

• • •

I know you love artichokes. Wait till you try them here. Freshness makes a difference, as does knowing when to pick. They grow mainly around Bari and Brindisi and beautifully on Sardinia. Artichoke's first cousin, cardoon, is a native, probably from Sicily. We plant these at Bramasole and struggle in the kitchen to release them from their stringy exterior. Poached in broth then treated to a few dabs of béchamel and **parmigiano**, they're not just artichoke's poor relation. Possibly the Arabs or North Africans evolved these thistles into their present states. Southern farmers drive trucks up to our markets in Tuscany with bundles of cardoons and five or six varieties of artichoke, still attached to the stalk. We are lucky enough to buy sackfuls of those prized, small purple-tinged ones. Ed makes a tomato sauce, adding garlic and onions, then stirs in a couple of dozen of these well-trimmed, barely steamed little princes—such a simple process, such a taste. **Carciofi fritti**, fried artichokes, taste better than French fries. A sprinking of coarse salt renders them addictive. I like to fry them in sunflower oil. Often a trattoria will have them, even if the menu does not say so. Ask!

In Puglia, cooks like layers. In high-sided pie plates, called **tielle**, they stack seafood, potatoes, and vegetables, or they use rice, leading some to connect the **tiella** with paella. In method, it's a kind of lasagna without the pasta. One fabulous recipe I found in Nancy Harmon Jenkins's **Flavors of Puglia** is Artichoke Parmesan. Sliced hearts of artichoke are dipped in a batter and fried in olive oil. You then layer the crisp slices with mozzarella and a little **parmigiano.** Fresh tomato sauce is spooned sparingly over the top; then the dish runs into the oven for half an hour.

The fact and fate of the South remains the sea. There are so many tiny places on the water where the fish is delicately fried—**fritto di pesce**—and the ambiance is enlivened by musicians who stroll in and out. At the Trattoria Dora in Naples, I ate a mound of **cicale**, plump crustaceans that resemble their namesake, cicadas. One of the waitresses burst out singing as she served the next table. The restaurant fell silent, and she held forth for fifteen minutes, then scooped up the pasta plates and swept, like the diva she is, into the kitchen while we applauded. Dining in the

South goes like that. Fun. You must eat at Dora. Be sure to make a reservation.

At the crowded pizza places, you sit at a table with other people and try to absorb the noise level. Pizza, which was "bread with a relish" in Roman times, is now so simple—I saw most Neapolitans ordering the basic Margherita over and over. The quality of the mozzarella, made from the milk of water buffalo—imported into Italy from India for some reason around A.D. 600—makes all the difference. They would croak to see how we pile twelve ingredients on pizza in America. Other than mozzarella, the main cheese of the South is pecorino, sheep's milk cheese. **Pecorino fresco** is new and soft; **semistagionato**, somewhat aged, hardens and sharpens in taste; and **stagionata**, aged, is harder even than Parmesan. The **canestrati**, artisan pecorini, bear the mark of the basket (**canestro**) where they were formed. At home in Tuscany the cheeses often are coated with ashes or wrapped in oil-soaked grape or hazelnut leaves. Old baskets for forming ricotta are collectibles, long since replaced by plastic. Pecorino marries well to figs, to sliced pears and apples, and also to dense quince paste. The sacred spring rite requires you to eat pecorino with new fava beans. If you don't like this combination, don't tell anyone. Try also the adorable bulbous **scamorza** from the Abruzzi. This yellow cow's milk cheese is usually roasted in the fireplace—just like marshmallows on a stick—and eaten with bread. The hardened outside gets toasty and the interior turns creamy. We met this on a mountain road in early June. Ten minutes earlier we'd been enjoying the red swaths of poppies across the meadows; then a freakish storm sent flying slush at the windshield. We couldn't see the edge of the road. We pulled over at a trattoria where people were gathered around a bonfire feasting on great hunks of rough bread with melted **scamorza**.

Bread—oh, so good. In Pompeii on the day of the eruption, a bakery had turned out eighty-one round loaves of bread made from wheat and barley flours. There are so many touching details at Pompeii. It's almost as though someone from that era lays a hand on your shoulder when you learn that the loaves were gashed in eight sections so that they could be broken apart easily.

Bread in Naples is cakier than the rough Tuscan bread we're used to. They usually use semolina flour in the South, giving the bread a golden tint and a more briochelike consistency. In English, this is durum wheat flour. I know you don't like the unsalted Tuscan bread, so you'll be happy here. Before the oceans became polluted, bakers often used seawater in making bread. I guess you'd gag if someone did that now. When we're driving, we start out the day at the best **forno** and buy a loaf to take in the car, along with whatever else looks good. I like the ring-shaped, small, herb-scented twists of bread with coarse salt called **taralli**. They're the Pugliese equivalent to pretzels. If they're not fresh, they can crack a tooth. The famous big old **pugliese** loaves are simply the bread of Puglia. They can weigh twenty pounds in some areas. Naturally, as with all bread, you can buy a quarter of a loaf or a half. And buy it, of course, every morning.

A day proceeds like this.

Breakfast: always pastry. **Sfogliatella**, a fan-shaped flaky pastry stuffed with some delectable creamy ricotta filling, with a cappuccino, fuels you for endless sightseeing days. Pastries in Tuscany tend toward dryness.

I always know when I'm truly acclimated there because the pastries start to taste good to me. Then I come South and taste heavenly **cannoli**, that impossibly divine combination of tastes and textures—fried tubular pastry filled with sugared ricotta delicately scented with orange flower water. Often their ends are dipped in chopped nuts. Oh, Lord. I'm not a fool for desserts, but thank you for allowing me back into the pastry shops twice a day. Pastry in Sicily is an art form. I saw a whole Noah's ark made from marzipan.

Lunch: pasta, fish. Maybe I am given to excesses. In Sardinia every day I ate lobster for lunch—then sometimes for dinner. All over that area you meet various types of lobster that don't even look kin to the Maine lobster. Waverley Root says that in Sardinia they eat like Stone Age men. Staring into the eyes of one of these lobsters, you have to agree. It doesn't look like something you'd put in your mouth. Once you do, you want to weep! So tender and sweet. Besides all the get-up-and-plow pastas of the South, one I took to immediately in Sardinia was new to me: fregola. It looks like breadcrumbs, slightly colored by saffron, and is served with salty ricotta. One difference from the usual pastas is that it's cooked in stock. The whiff of lost Araby comes from the saffron and from the mysterious town of Alghero itself, where we stayed in a former villa, turned small hotel, with two friends. We wandered the medinalike streets for a few days, hardly getting in the car at all, pointing to brightly colored tiled cupolas, stopping for strawberry gelato, drinking in the warm May air. Isn't the experience of food too intricately woven into your surroundings for you to know exactly what a taste is? The clear waters, with the sun spangling the floor of the sea, the young man bicycling with his baby on his shoulders, the slow slosh of the tide, the smell of fish scales, salt, iodine, and roses, the sun cutting down a narrow street—all these mix with the memory of the taste of lobster, the taste of a crisp cucumber salad, the taste of an icy amber beer. Maybe that's why when we go home and try a recipe, following all the instructions, it never quite tastes the same as we remembered it from the high terrace over the sea when the water was striated from lavender to gray and a little piece of music hit you right in the breastbone. The food seemed, then, so alive, so perfect and clean there, when the waiter lifted out the whole spine of the fish in one swift movement.

Dinner: a mussel soup with **crostini**, rounds of bread soaked in the broth. Next, a hare with pappardelle, rabbit with fennel, something hearty, or a simple grilled fish. They know to leave a fish alone. Elaborate preparations mask the elemental taste. No nut crusts, no breading, no thick sauces. Just a squeeze of lemon, a sprinkling of parsley and mint. Sardines are loved all over the Mediterranean. Quickly grilled or dipped in vinegar and fried—they convey the essence of the sea.

To extend a summer night down south, end your dinner with a tiny glass of strega, which translates as "witch" but seems instead closer to the angels with its airy floral perfume, or a bracing limoncello, the very tart breath of the citrus groves. By the way, limoncello is very easy to make at home. In a cool place, you steep peels from eight organic lemons in a covered quart of ninety percent proof alcohol for four days, shaking it now and then. On the fifth day, prepare a syrup of fourteen ounces of sugar and a quart of bottled still water. Don't let it boil, just simmer five minutes or so. Strain the lemon mixture and mix it into the syrup. Throw away the peels. Pour into bottles, and cork.

A friend uses the same method to make a laurel elixir, which he serves icy cold. I've had **basilicocello**, too. Even in Tuscany we seek out Moscato Passito di Pantelleria, the dessert wine from the windy Italian island of Pantelleria, way down close to Tunisia. Will you go there? I haven't been but would love to. The wine is lush and smooth and fragrant. You almost want it for a body spray. Stromboli, too, I've missed, maybe because of that dreary movie with Ingrid Bergman.

The southerners are fond of their **amari**, like all Italians. These bitters aid digestion. I don't feel the need for such an aid and don't respond to their cough-syrupy flavors. The South's walnut liqueur makes my tongue raspy, and I fear it will cause my brain to curdle. Ed, however, likes them all, even the artichoke-flavored one, but especially Averna, made from thirty-something herbs. Maybe you and Ed have shared a few late-night nips of this.

The wonder of Italy—it's hard to find a bad

meal. Hard also to have a bad time. **Buon viaggio, amico mio.**

Con affetto,
Francesca

Dear Steven, soon to be Stefano,

Continuing my long love letter to food. I wanted to give you a brief intro to the wine of the South. We're now in Gaeta, another coastal town, with an immense **passeggiata** on Sunday night. Here the bay at dusk looks like lapis lazuli. Everyone strolls. A fabulous tower, made out of stones from all eras, looks just randomly stuck together so that you see traces of Arabs, Greeks, Romans, and latter-day Italians. I wonder how many gelatos I've had in the past three days.

You heard that the South is the "new Tuscany" for wine. That's right. Growers are changing from mass producers of indifferent-to-good everyday wine to more specialized and careful vintages. It's time. The even climate of much of the South, the sun-facing slopes of mineral-rich rocky terrain, and a new awareness—all conspire to change the philosophy of wine making.

Finding good wine is easy. This afternoon before we left Sperlonga, we went into the wine store, and the owner helped us select a half dozen of the area's best bottles to pack into our trunk. The surprise is the price. These wines are still affordable.

We reach constantly to the backseat of our book-mobile car for the yearly edition of the **Gambero Rosso** wine guide. Wines from every region are ranked, with **tre bicchieri**, three glasses, as the optimal wine. Even a one-glass rating is good; only select wines get in. Aside from all the sophisticated ranking, however, in many restaurants they're pouring Uncle's special up to the brim of the glass. Everyone makes wine, or has a cousin who does. Uncle might make the most delicious wine in town.

Within the South, I'd say Sicily is **the** hot spot for wine—especially reds. As the Tuscan and northern Italian wines soar toward the prices of California wines, suddenly the hearty wines of the South look more appealing. Just when I thought I had a handle on the types of grapes in Tuscany, I find that in the South it's all different. Puglia's primary grape variety is the **negroamaro**, meaning "black bitter."

Primitivo grows all around. The American version of that is zinfandel. Grenache, so appreciated by the French, is known as **cannonau** in Sardinia. **Zibibbo** (what a fine name for a cat) grapes are muscat, good for wine and also luscious to eat. The list goes on. Perhaps the most characteristic Sicilian grape is the native **nero d'avola**. We can see how history is always at work in this area. The name of the prized red **aglianico** probably derives from Italian for "Hellenic."

As you drive around the island, order these when they appear on the wine list: Donnafugata—recognize the name from **The Leopard**?—whites and red, also the range of Planeta wines. Even their least expensive ones are good. We drink several Planeta wines in Tuscany. Feudo Principi di Butera makes a big cabernet. Ed is partial to Abbazia Santa Anastasia Litra and Morgante Don Antonio. Cantina Sociale di Trapani also brings out a cabernet you'll enjoy.

But you will make your own discoveries. Just buy the wine guide, and tear out pages for the areas where you travel. If they're out of the wine you ask for, whip out the page and ask for something just as good. I stress again, though, your waiter Massimo's daddy may be an unknown master winemaker. Even if the local wine is rough and ready, you get a taste of the soil and sun of a particular farm. Some names to memorize for the rest of the South: Paternostra, for their **aglianico** wines from Basilicata; Agricola Eubea and Cantina Fiforma Fondiaria di Venosa, also Basilicata producers. Two from Lecce: Cantele Amativo and Agricole Vallone Graticciaia. That's a start.

Villa Matilde epitomizes the zesty spirit of contemporary wines from the South. Odd that this should be so, since their vines come from stock older than the Romans. Our close friend Riccardo Bertocci (remember we had the Slow Food **lardo** dinner with him) represents several of the most distinctive wine producers in Italy. Villa Matilde is one of his favorites. He asked us to rendezvous for lunch at Villa Matilde to meet Maria Ida and Salvatore Avallone, the Neapolitan sister and brother who preside over the vineyards started by their father. We often stay at the Avallone family's hotel in Naples, the Parker, for Old World ambiance, the dining terrace overlooking the Bay, and their scrumptious pastry table at breakfast.

Since we were in nearby Sperlonga, exploring the coast, we settled on Wednesday and drove down to Cellole. I hope you'll go there on your trip. Despite the fireworks around wine produced in the South, there still are very few vineyards where you can visit and taste. You also can stay overnight; the old estate house now serves as a small inn. Maria Ida and Salvatore showed us around. Their father, Francesco Paolo Avallone, practices law in Naples, and the children have taken over the vineyard. They're young and hip and devoted to the wines their father developed after World War II. During his law studies he read Virgil, Horace, Pliny the Elder, Catullus, and other classical authors—does this happen in American law schools?—where he came across references to **falerno**, one of the prime grapes of the Romans. The vines over time had succumbed to disease and neglect. Avallone studied the characteristics mentioned by the authors and set out to find lost stock of this grape in the original location where it had flourished, the Massico area. He and his associates found five **falanghina** vines and so secured a route back to the production of white **falerno**. They found five **piedirosso** (red feet), which with **aglianico** (the "Hellenic" remnant) could combine to make red **falerno**. Many graftings, propagations, and lullabies later, the Villa Matilde slopes again thrive with the ancient heritage grapes of the area. The Avallones still keep the precious vines their father found when he reached far back into history.

At **pranzo** in their restaurant, we were served pumpkin ravioli, veal roast, and a plum **crostata**. Salvatore would eat only a salad after the pasta. He was telling us about the remains of a Roman wine cellar just adjacent to their property, and the other hectares he and Maria Ida have acquired and planted with **coda di volpe** (fox tail), **abbuoto**, and **primitivo** grapes. We liked all the wines he poured, especially the Falerno del Massico Vigna Camarato and the delicate, golden Eleusi Passito, which arrived with the **crostata**. The **passito**'s grapes dry on the vines, concentrating the sweetness until late fall, then age in barriques. Catullus would write an ode.

You'll be singing praises, too, when you arrive in Naples for your month of roaming. Let me know exactly when you're coming. I know a place in Gallipoli where the squid caught last night hang on a clothesline outside the kitchen, waiting to be pounded and dressed in tomatoes and good oil. We could meet in Matera, strangest of cities, and eat vegetable lasagne made with big slabs of pasta, and slow-roasted lamb shanks.

Think of me as you pour a splash of Greco di Tufa in your glass, or think back to the Greeks who brought the vine, or just think of your friend across the table and the night ahead.

Get **The Blue Guide to Southern Italy**. Don't miss Siracusa and the cathedrals in Bitonto and Trani. You'll see many of Italy's one million vineyards, most the size of your backyard. With the olive and wheat, vines make the ancient trinity. You may see remnants of the old style of planting, with the wheat among the olive trees, and the field bordered by vines. If so, take a picture. The trinity is disappearing fast. The bread, the wine, the oil. Life is possible from those. Mark on your map all of Frederick II's castles. You'll be lost a hundred times. Endless, Italy is endless.

Ci vediamo subito,
Frances

Inside the Color Spectrum

Fez

The art of departure I may never master. A smooth departure includes time to pack and think and anticipate. The suitcase, all shoes on the bottom, holds clothes in two basic colors with several tops in lively patterns. Everything fits neatly, and I have room to bring home a couple of souvenirs. The houseplants are watered, newspaper stopped, and two lights set on timers. Dinner will be simple, a salad and soufflé. We will sleep without nightmares, wake with the excitement of the voyage pulsing in our veins, and leave the house with plenty of time. We do not confuse flight times or leave passports behind or forget to turn off the espresso machine.

But usually I would like to be taken to the airport on a stretcher and rolled into the back of the plane where attendants will draw curtains around me, because any departure inevitably brings out the mischief in the gods. The day before you start a long-desired trip, they want you to pass certain tests.

This morning I searched the house for the tickets to Morocco, then finally Ed noticed and said he still had to pick up the tickets. Bramasole's elaborate watering system, which involves two cisterns and the old well, developed an air vacuum hitch. We spent two hours crawling around tanks and shouting "Is it coming?" and finally the water arrived in spurts and jerks. A tube detached, spraying us both. A strange rumbling noise as we took our plates outside for lunch gathered to an unmistakable crash. What a disaster—the important lateral stone wall under the linden trees tumbled down the hill. We dashed to see the last of a rock avalanche landing on the road below. Lucky we were that no one passing by on a morning stroll or bike ride met their dismal fate in our driveway. And so we hauled stone off the road, and Ed went in search of a **muratore** who will repair the damage before another section falls. I canceled my much-needed haircut appointment. I did not pick up the dry cleaning.

Early today in town I said to a friend, "We're leaving tomorrow for Fez." The words seemed miraculous. Fez. I've never put my foot on the continent of Africa before. As I pull my bag from under the bed, I hear a scuffling noise—unmistakable. **Un topo**, a mouse. Fortunately Giusi is downstairs. She's my cooking friend who also looks after Bramasole when we are gone.

"I had a mouse in my **armadio** last year," she says, sprinting up the stairs and shutting the door of the bedroom, closing us in with the mouse. She's armed with rubber gloves and a broom. We pull out the bed. Nothing. Open the **armadio**, where I have hung my summer clothes. Nothing. But in the top drawer of my chest, we find droppings. The mouse has eaten a bead from an African necklace. Resolutely, Giusi opens the drawer at the bottom of the **armadio** and lifts up a folded yellow sweater. Three almost-new mice fall out. I swallow a shriek. Giusi dons the gloves, picks them up, and drops them in a plastic bag. They are unformed and not cute. Their pawing motions and pin-prick eyes make my stomach flip. God's creatures. Under a poncho she finds three more. I hold the bag at arm's length. She pulls out the drawer all the way, and we see the mama, not so small, not a Beatrix Potter–style mouse at all, hiding behind the foot of the **armadio**. The chase is on. Giusi corners her, and she runs between Giusi's legs, under the bed, then back to the **armadio**. I'm afraid she will bite Giusi's ankle. Giusi wields the broom, and I cower in the corner feeling inept. The mouse leaps into the fireplace and disappears up the chimney. We leave a poison dinner for her return. Giusi insists that all my folded clothes must be washed now, since mouse feet have run over them. Visions of black plague victims reel through my head.

And so I pack what I can from the hanging clothes. Late in the afternoon we drive to Rome and spend the night at the airport hotel. Our flight to Casablanca leaves early tomorrow.

We are let out of the taxi at Bab Boujeloud, an entrance into the Fez medina. Hafid El Amrani, the young manager of the house where we are staying, has rescued us in Meknes, an hour away. The car we hired to drive us from the Casablanca airport to Fez finally died outside Meknes, after sputtering and overheating for seven hours. Normally the trip takes three to four hours. The thirty-year-old Mercedes slowed on every slight hill, and when the gauge hit the top of the dial, the driver pulled over and waited for someone to stop and pour a bottle of water into the radiator. Twice the stops involved him scrambling down into a gully to fill a bottle with muddy water. We were in the backseat, temperature outside 104 degrees. The driver was an optimist; each time the radiator was filled, he thought the problem was solved. "Thermostat," Ed said repeatedly. When the car finally refused to go on, we reached a place with enough telephone signal to call Hafid in Fez. Then we had only a couple of hours to wait before he pulled up in an ancient taxi. Is this trip jinxed?

Now he loads our bags into a handcart pushed by a boy. Immediately I see that when we walk through this Blue Gate, we will enter a different world. Laden donkeys with muzzles made from plastic water bottles stand passively under loads of barrels and stuffed sacks. The acrid odor of live wool burns the air. A few red "petite taxis" dart in and out of the square in random patterns, weaving among men in **djellabas** and pointy open-backed yellow shoes. In Tuscany donkeys are gone. I used to see one occasionally fifteen years ago. By now they've been replaced by the charming three-wheel miniature pickups called **Ape**, bees. Here the donkey reigns.

Hafid is handsome, with large eyes straight from a Roman mosaic, eyes the same true black as his hair. He's dressed in jeans, moving agilely through the gate and into the jammed lanes of the medina. Cars would be impossible. Not only are the streets narrow, but the minute kiosk-shops have goods piled outside their doors. People crouch along the edges selling CDs, socks, potatoes, lighters, and tissues. Ed points out that among the things for sale are squares of chocolate from a candy bar, single disposable diapers, and single cigarettes. Every few feet in the cobbled street holes deeper than graves impede progress. Men with picks chop around ancient water pipes in search of a leak or blockage. Odors dating back to the Romans rise from the depths. They look like an illustration for an engraving entitled "A Sisyphean Task." Dirt mounds around the holes must be climbed over. No one seems to have the concept of waiting to pass; everyone plunges onward from both directions—a chaotic traffic jam of people and donkeys, a melting pot with everyone melting. Somehow no one falls in. Hafid and the boy carry the handcart over their heads. Every few minutes someone calls out **"Balak,"** which I quickly learn to translate: donkey about to thunder by.

We would need Ariadne's thread through the labyrinth to find our way out of the medina. Hafid darts and branches down dozens of streets, often, it seems, doubling back. I would like to see a topographical map. "The streets are like those rubber insides of golf balls," I say to Ed.

"More like the intestinal tract of Muhammad. It's visceral."

"Time made a detour around Fez."

"Yes, cross through that gate, and you've stepped into the twilight zone."

Balak, balak.

We arrive at a scruffy door and climb dark, cramped stairs, stumble at a landing where six small children are hovering outside their own door. Hafid opens the door of the **masseria**, the restored guesthouse we'll call home for a few days.

After the squalor of the streets, the thread-bare, sad donkeys, the odors of their manure, the heaped garbage, the mess, we step into a serene and poetic small house with intricately carved four-hundred-year-old plaster walls, delicately colored, with bands of Kufic calligraphy, an arranged marriage of art and geometry. High windows, far above our heads, let in panels of blond light. A few Berber rugs, a shower with seats and copper pails for washing in the style of the **hammam**, a tiled fountain, and low banquette sofas covered in rough hand-woven cloth—everything feels seamless. The roof terrace overlooks the entire medina, a vast warren of sand-colored cubes, all crowned with satellite dishes. The buildings are rough as barnacles. I'm unprepared for the size of the Fez medina.

The medina **is** old Fez. The other two areas of the city are completely separated, three distinct towns. In the distance Hafid points out castles and a tomb on the hill, all the same earth color. Inside, peace seems to emanate from the walls. We are in a secret house in the heart of a mysterious medieval enclave.

When we emerge after quick showers, dark has invaded the medina. Donkeys have been herded inside stables or have headed home to the hills. Although the streets are still crowded, I at least don't fear being shoved into the fetid ditches. I lose count of the turns we make. If we dropped stones or bread to find our way back, we'd never spot them again. Hafid guides us to a small restaurant with dining on a roof terrace and leaves us. Little plates of roasted peppers, carrots seasoned with cumin and vinegar, a version of eggplant caponata, and olives with preserved lemons precede a traditional couscous with seven vegetables. I have loved Moroccan food ever since I went to a cooking demonstration by Paula Wolfert thirty years ago, then cooked my way through her **Couscous and Other Good Food**

from Morocco. I always keep jars of preserved lemons in my fridge. "How can **carrots** taste so good?" Ed reaches again for the tomato and cucumber salad, a twin to the California salsa we make at home. Couscous offers the same opportunities that pasta and tortillas offer Italians and Mexicans. You can improvise. Unlike the instant couscous I often resort to when I'm in a hurry, freshly prepared couscous is fluffy and tender, never glumpy. Tonight the seven vegetables are eggplant, kidney beans, tomatoes, onions, carrots, pumpkin, and cabbage—who would imagine the combination? These are added to the steamed couscous, along with potatoes and **khlii**, a beef confit that is a staple in every kitchen.

"The guidebook said not to eat unpeeled vegetables," I remember. We overlook the Blue Gate where we entered earlier, and without the commerce the scene has turned to slow motion—strollers and beggars, and shop people heading back to the new town. In the medina restaurants do not serve wine because of the many mosques, so cup after cup of mint tea arrives after a meal. Hafid returns for us. Like children, we're led home.

• • •

When mysterious gifts come your way, they must be accepted and understood. As we planned this trip, I looked on the Internet for a place to rent. Rather than making quick stops in several towns, I decided to concentrate on one city. Fez is quintessential Morocco, "the most complete Islamic medieval city in the world," according to my Cadogan guidebook. I'd read so much about Marrakech that Fez seemed more of an adventure. I wanted to see Fez from the inside, not from the vantage of a hotel. Searching for a house, I located a site with an appealing description. The photographs showed the kinds of details that made me smile—a section of ceiling, a doorway. I could tell this was a loving restoration of an authentic old house. I filled in the availability questionnaire and sent an e-mail.

The next morning a long letter awaited me. Lori, the owner of the Fez house, told me that she once met Ed briefly when he was judging a poetry contest that she was administering. He'd shown her and the other poet some photographs of Bramasole as a ruin, just as we embarked on the restoration. The letter said that Ed's photographs and description galvanized her to quit her job and go to Fez to study

Arabic. Remembering Bramasole, she bought the medina house. Along the way, she'd read my books, which also, she said, bolstered her project. She married Hafid's best friend. Her life completely changed. And so, she wrote, she wanted us to stay as her guests. As I read her e-mail, I felt the looping of long strands and read it over and over, marveling at how the motions of give and take remain mysterious, how one never can grasp causality. We accepted. We began a flurry of correspondence. We invited her and her husband to Bramasole.

Now I lie in her bed, happy to hear that birds sing in the medina. That ivory silk **djellaba** hanging on an iron rack belongs to the life Lori made for herself here.

Hafid appears with breakfast. Dense semolina cakes, a fried crepe, coffee made in a Moka pot, and fresh orange juice. We have slept away the obstacle course we traversed to get to this roof open to the white sky.

Hafid takes us to see a five-hundred-year-old house that has been partially restored. Architecture speaks a clear language, translatable by all.

This medina house says: privacy is paramount. Doors and windows face the inner courtyard, not the street. Inside the house you are not to be seen. The three-story interior lavishes ideas of coolness, tranquillity, and meditation on anyone who steps inside the one door. The intact carved plaster panels look like enormous lace handkerchiefs. The courtyard gives a view—look up—of the outside and lights the rooms, though you can always step back into an alcove of shadows. Desert people must always love shadows as much as the sound of running water. I would like to see the house when rain instead of sunlight falls to the blue-and-white-tile ground floor. Within the house, I feel a flow and a sense of connection. Back stairs and twisted passageways lead to catwalks around the courtyard. Off the catwalk are fiercely decorated rooms often opening to smaller tiled alcove rooms. I'm surprised to see the exact patterns and colors that I saw on floors and walls in Andalucía. Moors and Jews exiled from Spain settled in Fez, bringing back skills and crafts with them. Hafid says, "You should buy a house in Fez medina. Very cheap for Americans."

"How much?" I ask, looking at the graceful

arabesques of verses from the Koran carved above diamond-patterned tile.

"Twenty thousand, thirty thousand at most."

"Then you must restore."

"Yes," he shrugs, "but I am here for that."

His friend Rachid meets us. A man of about forty, Rachid was born in the medina and grew up here. He will be our guide. We drink mint tea on the roof and tell him we'd like to see all the important sites, but also the medina he knows. He would like to discuss William Faulkner and Saul Bellow. He has a degree in literature and loves the modern American writers. We set out on a walk. He has no set speeches, fortunately. We simply walk, taking in the scents and scenes. The crafts practiced are mostly for local use. One souk, or district devoted to a particular function, specializes in marriage thrones, enormous shiny metal-faced chairs of hammered designs for the bride and groom. They look like props from **The Wizard of Oz.** In the carpenter's souk, they're making all kinds of carved tables and also coffins. One is ready for a child. One worker displays washboards. I haven't seen a washboard since I was a child in Georgia and my mother dropped off our laundry at Rosa's in colored town, where she scrubbed our clothes on a washboard, then boiled them in a black iron pot.

We pause at carved cedar arches and doors with hinges shaped like the hand of Fatima to protect the house from the evil eye. Rachid takes us to several **madrasahs**, the elaborate medieval theology schools where students lived in cubicles above the courtyards and studied philosophy and astronomy downstairs. Someone must have studied advanced geometry because the mosaic and tile patterns, the layers of borders, and the tooled cedar ceilings inspire investigation into **how** such a panoply synchronizes into pleasing and harmonious spaces.

Months from now when I think of Fez, I will think of mint. I love seeing the mint sellers. They hold out big bouquets or special baskets packed with mint. Tables are heaped with mint. No little handfuls are available; mint is not a garnish, and mint tea is not served with a sprig, as in a mint julep or southern iced tea. Boiling green tea is poured into a glass stuffed with mint, and you take the hot glass to your mouth with your thumb and forefinger at the top and bottom. Everyone drinks mint tea constantly. Rachid takes us upstairs to a teahouse where men sit on rough stools talking. The owner's equipment consists of a table holding a small hotplate for boiling water, a few metal teapots, a bucket for rinsing the glasses (uh-oh), and a mountain of mint. I am the only woman, and no one acknowledges us at all. Rachid says, "The mint from Meknes is the best in Morocco." I don't even like mint tea, but I am drinking it with pleasure. The quantity of mint gives the tea a robust dimension. It tastes curative, it tastes of summer in a desert tent, it tastes like time.

Rachid says, "There are nine thousand streets in the medina. One thousand have no exit." For lunch he leads us into a mobbed small space presided over by a magical-looking man I wish I could understand. He's fey and strange and light on his feet like a dancer. Rachid says he used to be a storyteller in Marrakech. He still weaves a spell. He grabs Ed and takes him through the kitchen, giving him spoonfuls of spicy ground meat, lamb **tajines**, cauliflower, and a layered cheese and pastry dish just out of the oven. Ed selects too many dishes, and Rachid is perhaps embarrassed. But he eats. The **kefta**, the ground meat, he says, is camel. The joke he tells us involves tourists who refuse to eat camel and are tricked constantly. Regular customers go in and out of the kitchen, serving themselves. The barbecued turkey on skewers may be the best thing that's happened to turkey. We clean the plates, except for the ground mystery meat.

Surely the tannery souk is not long for the world. Every tourist is taken there, followed by detours into leather shops. Before you arrive, the traffic of donkeys loaded with fresh animal skins stiff as cracker bread announces where you are. The hides are soaked in pigeon excrement as part of the curing process. A man stands up to his knees dunking skins. Vats the size of hot tubs contain bright colors. Where is the industrial revolution? We're not exactly rushing toward it here at the vats; this work goes back to roots of industry.

Rachid says, "The yellow is from saffron or mimosa, the red from poppies, the green from mint." I don't believe that; the colors are lurid. His shop-owner friend hands customers a sprig of mint to hold to their noses. I buy a pair of the yellow slippers everyone wears. Rachid says, "Everything goes with yellow." Later I leave them on the roof under the sun to dispel the smell. Couldn't they give the leather a dip in rose water as well? Bins of pink rosebuds are my favorite sight in the food stalls.

Bundles on the street are often incredibly tiny women beggars, their faces the color and texture of walnut shells, their hands like paws.

Rachid says, "A good Muslim gives alms to the poor."

Ed, only a fallen-away Catholic, reaches into his pocket. "How much?"

"One cent."

Late in the day we return to the **masseria** to meet Fatima, a cousin of Hafid, who has come to prepare a home-cooked dinner for us. She sets up a round clay habachi-sized charcoal cooker and wipes off her **tajine**, the conical glazed terra-cotta dish that gives its name to the famous Moroccan one-dish meal of infinite variety. Fatima, who must be sweltering in her heavy pink **djellaba**, is a substantial woman with her hair covered. Her eyes are not downcast, however, and she smiles as she unloads her sack of groceries and starts to prepare vegetables for the **tajine**. She improvises a kitchen on the roof, drawing a bucket of water from the faucet for rinsing, and spreading an oilcloth tablecloth for her work surface.

She minces more parsley than I would have

thought, then cuts up a parsnip, potatoes, zucchini, onions, and tomato. How easily she starts the charcoal going. As soon as the coals glow, she pours oil in the **tajine** and sets it on the fire. Then she lays the beef—I hope it's not from one of the fly-specked piles I've seen for sale—in the oil, then places onions on top of the beef. She makes sure we understand that the vegetables go on the meat, not in the oil. She sprinkles on some salt, lots of black and white pepper, paprika, and cinnamon, then covers the **tajine** and finishes cutting the vegetables. I've never seen anyone hollow carrots before, and Hafid says she always cuts away the center. They don't look woody. After the meat has cooked for about twenty minutes, she layers the other vegetables on top of the onions and adds half a teacup of water and several more pinches of seasoning. The roof is hot, even late in the day, and I'm shocked when Fatima peels off her **djellaba** and continues to cook in her long cotton knit undergarment. Under that I see that she has on another layer of something. I'm warm in a short-sleeved linen shirt. The fire burns slowly now, and the **tajine** cooks on gentle heat for another hour.

We drink mineral water and look out over

the medina at sunset. Ed asks, "Are you going to get on the plane carrying one of those **tajines** on your lap?"

"Yes."

"Why does it have that carnival-hat top?"

"Steam collects on the inside of the cone and drips down on the meat and vegetables, a self-basting process." I make that up, but it might be true.

"Fatima's **tajine** looks like beef stew, only layered."

"Basically, yes—but with a liberal use of spices."

"A stew with attitude. Wish we had some wine."

"We're in the medina. Lightning would strike us. Or a donkey mow us down."

Fatima pulls some jars out of her bag and serves eggplant spread and a tomato and cucumber salad with small round loaves of bread. All over the medina I've seen children running, holding aloft boards covered with cloth. Rachid says everyone still makes their own bread dough, then sends it to the bakery. Peering inside one, I saw the children's boards on tables, stacked with warm bread, ready to be picked up. Every tiny quarter of the vast medina has its own ovens. The face-size flat loaves are perfect for the salads, spreads, and juices of the **tajines**.

We dine under the moon. The **tajine** retains the separate tastes of each vegetable, and the meat is tender. We dip all the bread into the bottom, soaking up every drop of the sauce. The medina turns oddly quiet at night. Considering the density, I find it odd that no TV blares, no one on an adjacent roof plays rap music, and no voices shout, sing, or squabble. The people fold themselves into their houses the way they fold themselves away in their clothing.

Fatima dismantles her makeshift kitchen, dons her **djellaba**, and gives me, not Ed, a big hug. She solemnly shakes Ed's hand, not looking at him, and goes home to her husband and three children.

Three hours later Ed becomes violently ill. I am alarmed at his fever and clammy skin. He spends the night in the bathroom throwing up. His stomach feels ripped and turned inside out. After six hours of this he calms but still feels on fire with pain. He's vacant; his eyes swim; he's so weak he cannot lift his arm. I'm on the phone calling our doctor in Italy, who says this probably is simple food poisoning, not salmonella, since the heaving has stopped after only a few hours. I write names of medicines he recommends, hoping Hafid can help at the pharmacy. I remember the rag Fatima wrung out in the bucket, remember the ground meat at lunch. But I feel fine, in fact unusually energetic. "Did you brush your teeth with the faucet water?" He doesn't answer. Hafid arrives and says Ed ate too much, it often happens when guests come to Fez because the food is so good. Maybe.

By midmorning Hafid has found various pharmaceuticals, and Ed is sleeping as if in a coma. I try not to think of the man who dies in Paul Bowles's **The Sheltering Sky**, leaving his neurotic wife to become a harem prisoner. The lure of the exotic for innocents or rootless people always seems to end badly.

So the gods have conspired again on this trip. For the next three days Ed does not emerge from the **masseria**. I go out for the day with Rachid, and we bring him food he does not eat and bottle after bottle of water, which he forces himself to drink. His state seems beyond the illness, as though he has fallen into a trance. I would like for the ministering angel I was promised at the start of my travels to step forward now.

Without Ed, I find a different dynamic with

the place and with Rachid. I follow behind him, and distracted by a pile of hooves or iron lanterns for sale, I often miss his turns and suddenly stand in the swarm of people where streets cross, having no idea where he is. But he doubles back. I wonder how odd this must be for him—out all day with an infidel woman who constantly pauses to see the man who sells forks, bracelets, and combs fashioned from horn, his ten items spread on a table the size of a platter, and the real estate agent in his cubicle, with twenty iron keys to his listings hanging on nails behind him, and the tomb carvers chiseling epitaphs on marble headstones. "Anyone has to taste death," they write. Rachid says, "A good Muslim visits his dead every Friday."

Brilliantly tiled public fountains for water are everywhere. Surely someone has published a book of photographs of these long basins surrounded by exciting patterns and colors, some of which date from medieval times. They still draw women with buckets and children holding out plastic bottles. Rachid says, "They have water at home, but this way they do not have to pay for it."

He explains the difference between a caftan (no hood) and a **djellaba** (with a hood handy for protection against rain or dust or heat) for men and women. The clothing begins to make sense. At first it seemed that everyone was in their bathrobes. Quickly, when my dust allergy awakened and when the wind felt like a hair dryer aimed at my face, I began to wish for one of those mysterious veils. The sun and dust are formidable. The loose, light robes look elegant, certainly comfortable, while protecting the wearer from the elements. I follow Rashid's tan **djellaba** and almost imagine that I am wearing one myself instead of black pants and black shirt. The women flow in the impossible narrow lanes, a river of color: saffron, burgundy, sage, pistachio, peacock blue threading the crowds, Nile greens and mustard parting, rust, magenta, emerald merging, tomato red, ochre and all the earth colors, the occasional white worn by a woman in mourning. Some are secluded, occluded behind black veils, some wear modest scarves, and some neither. I see them look at me then quickly away.

The concatenation of colors repeats and rings in the food stalls: mulberries, figs, dusty capers, leafy coriander, mint, burlap sacks of golden turmeric, dates, bloody haunches of camels, and stacks of sheep and goats' heads. Rachid says,

"First you singe off the hair, then thoroughly clean out the maggots. Cumin and hot pepper—very good for breakfast when it's hot and spicy." I will be skipping that cooking tip. The whole pale palate of lentils, cumin, couscous, dried fava beans, semolina, coriander, chickpeas, and sesame recalls the colors of the desert. The food stalls reflect the abundance of the table, the love of bold tastes, the agricultural richness of the slopes of the Atlas Mountains. A donkey lumbers by carrying a load of spiny artichokes the size of dates. I stop to photograph the goat cheeses on palm leaves. Rachid says, "Everyone eats camel meat once or twice a week." But Hafid has told me he never has tasted camel. Scrawny cats and new kittens are everywhere. There must be no marauding rats in the medina, I point out, but Rachid says, "The cats in the medina are afraid of the rats."

Rachid shows me a spring where a man is filling a jug and points to where a river used to flow before it was routed underground. We see jacaranda trees outside the Blue Gate. Rachid says, "They send out their musk at night." A few figs protrude from walls, and in the copper and brass souk a large tree startles the eye. Great cauldrons that could hold whole goats and sheep are for sale under the tree. Rachid says, "We rent those for weddings."

"Are weddings in the mosques?"

"No, you ask someone who has a nice house. Mosques are only for prayers."

Not being a Muslim, I am not allowed inside a mosque and only can peer into the courtyards with fountains for the faithful to cleanse themselves. We happen to be outside a huge mosque when Friday services end. A stampede of men feeling holy and righteous thunders out and into the street. We have our backs to a wall to let them pass when a trotting donkey scrapes us and Rachid slips into a pyramid of eggs, knocking several to the ground. No one called **balak, balak**.

On our walks we weave by the house several times a day to check on Ed. Rachid says, "The mailman must be born in the medina, otherwise no one ever would receive mail." Rachid thinks Ed should sit up. I'm giving the doctor in Italy an update. Ed says, "Maybe tomorrow." He has turned a few pages of a book, has showered. He seems cool and peaceful.

I'm not mentioning the slow-roasted lamb with cumin sauce, the **pastilla** (or **bastela**, pigeon in flaky layers of pastry, dusted with confectioner's sugar), or the chicken couscous with melted onions and honey. Rachid and I go by taxi to the new town to buy buns from a French pastry shop and bland cheese and bread for Ed. He takes me to a bookstore with books by Mark Twain and Sherwood Anderson. I find a Moroccan cookbook in English and wish I could make for Ed the chicken stuffed with couscous, cinnamon, and orange flower water, or the lamb with apricots, raisins, and nutmeg. I see much more use of spices than of herbs. And the range of ingredients must be inspiring—quince, pumpkin, **feggous** (a rough, skinny cucumber), Jerusalem artichoke, cardoon, barley semolina. The uses of pomegranate syrup, orange flower oil, almond milk, and rose oil intrigue me. Too bad Ed never wants to eat again. The new town's broad avenue shaded with trees and lined with cafés seems like another world. Many women and young girls here have abandoned the traditional dress altogether, though some still cover their heads even though they're in low jeans. Rachid says, "I like for my wife to dress modestly." And, "I like for my wife to stay at home with our son."

I tease him. "Do you want a second wife?" I know men are allowed to have four.

"One is enough. And who can afford two women?"

"Why would any woman put up with her husband bringing another wife into the house?" The first edged question I have asked him.

"Maybe the first wife cannot have children. There's a law," he says proudly, "that you cannot just throw away the wife."

"What if I wanted two husbands, or four?"

He smiles in Arabic.

On the hottest day so far, I tell Rachid I would like to look at fabric. We visit workshops where men sit on rugs sewing **djellabas** and embroidering the necklines. In the street, they card the thread, extending it and pulling it onto rolls. I resist ordering one of these splendid garments because it would hang in my closet until doomsday. I would like to find silk for table draperies or curtains. But most everything is precut to three meters, enough to make the **djellaba**. I find one square of antique ivory silk embroidered with apricot flowers. Rachid steps back when bargaining begins. Nothing ever seems to have a price, and I'm pressed to offer one. I offer so little that the seller appears to be shocked. Rachid puts his hand to his mouth to hide a smile. "What will you pay, madame?" I offer slightly more, then the seller says he must have at least four hundred euros. That is so far from what I would pay that I thank him, compliment him on the silk, and walk away. He's dumbfounded that the American has escaped, having bought only a small silver hand of Fatima.

I'm not very interested in shopping here. I buy an embroidered black cotton blouse and a blue one for my friend Aurora, and slippers for my daughter. Rachid takes me to the ceramics district, and we watch pots and bowls being thrown from gray clay and painted. The Fez blue decorates most everything. I pick up a couple of small bowls for olives.

We stop into a herb store. Rachid says, "The owner is a special person. You will see." Mon Kade Khalid, a pale man with a slight hunch, introduces himself and shows me his oils, hennas, and barks. He holds to my nose something that looks like yellow erasers—the musk gland of the gazelle. "The animal rubs against a tree, and we then gather the gland. It will scent your drawer for two years." He has jars of colored rocks on a high shelf and explains that they ward off the evil eye. I pick out a packet of the forty-spice seasoning called **rasse el hanoute**, which translates as "heat of the shop."

"How do you feel, madame?" he asks.

"Very good."

"People come to me. If they have problems. I have things to make the baby. I have argan oil against arthritis. I have things also for the cooking. Here, give me your hand." He rubs my hand between his, then holds his hands an inch away from mine, above and below. I feel a definite warmth emanating from his hands. He is staring into my eyes. Oh no, the lure of the exotic. The odd thing is, when he moves his hands away, I feel a sudden shiver. "Now how do you feel?"

"Wonderful," I say. And I do. A fresh push of strength courses down my back, through my legs, like an adrenaline rush. All afternoon I experience a euphoria, a feeling of bodily force I knew in childhood.

We see tombs and museums. I think my feet have covered every inch of the medina. We walk a long way in the heat and stop at what looks like remains of a fortress. Rachid says, "This is Palais Glaoui. Since you are interested in houses." He knocks at a huge wooden door in a block-long wall. A dark, narrow-faced man who looks like a forgotten jazz musician opens the door. They embrace. "Welcome to my family," Abdel Khalek says. "This is my home." We enter a vast tiled courtyard with a fountain surrounded by a grand pool. Weeds grow out of the fountain, and the pool is home to a lone goose standing in mud. The scale of the house triples any house I've seen in the medina. Ballroom-size rooms open on the outer side to overgrown gardens, where I glimpse remains of tiled fountains and scraggly citrus trees. My mind restores the gardens to those I've seen in old Persian paintings. Abdel takes us through corridors to another wing, where his grandfather once kept one hundred women. The hallways overhanging the courtyard sag, but the floral delicacy of the carved plaster still bespeaks the feminine world of the harem.

"Did he say one hundred?"

Rachid says, "His grandfather was a busy man."

Abdel leads us to the palace kitchen, not so

different, except for being run-down and dusty, from a big kitchen in an English manor house—a bank of stoves, copper pots, cavernous space. Then he shows us "the first bathroom in Fez," with English Edwardian fixtures and even a porcelain, not tile, tub. In his room, also a large room with a center door to the courtyard, I see a picture of his grandmother, perhaps age twenty, in a stiff, voluminous white dress, her face young and bright. No veil, no robes—I want to ask who she was in the hierarchy but don't dare. This complex is only one of seventeen adjoining houses, all closed, all verging on ruin. I don't ask, but I imagine that with a hundred women producing children, the inheritances won't ever be sorted out. We sit on long banquettes and are served mint tea and gazelle horns, an almond cookie in a crescent shape. Not a jazz musician, Abdel paints as a vocation and wanders his ancestral home, sometimes showing it to guests the guides bring.

Ed feels like walking out, so we stroll to La Maison Bleue, a fine palace house restored as a hotel. A scattering of French and English tourists are having drinks in the courtyard where two men play crude string instruments. We sit by a fountain, and I drink a glass of champagne while Ed sips water. Then we are shown to colorful banquettes and a low table. I love the Moroccan style of dining. "**Tajine**?" the waiter offers.

Ed sinks back and whispers, "Never."

We order couscous with lamb and all the usual salads. Ed takes a few bites; he's on his way but not there yet. The serene beauty of the place takes me far from the rough and heady medina I have come to know through Rachid.

Ed wants to go out on our last morning. Rachid guides us to a taxi, and we get out in the **mellah**, the old Jewish ghetto. Rachid says, "Give the driver one euro." The low, low prices here continue to startle me. The ghetto, with timbered overhangs, the characteristic windows where women could see out but not be seen, twisted alleys and small shops would seem atmospheric if I had not seen the medina still sunk in its medieval mindset. This ghetto is quite spruced up. We look at a UNESCO-restored synagogue, with a ritual bathing tub underground where the crypt would be in a Christian church. Rachid then leads us through the Jewish cemetery with blinding-white humped graves. Rachid says, "The **mellah** was formalized in 1438, but Jews had lived here for centuries. The wall around it was actually built for their protection from Arabs but later became a confinement. The Jews were kept to their quarter by the ban on wearing their black shoes outside it. Only in the seventeen hundreds were they allowed a woven sandal, which enabled them to leave."

"What does **mellah** mean?" Ed wonders.

Rachid says, "Salt. The place of salt processing. This is the old word for the place. And the legend is that heads of victims killed in battle were salted and preserved here so they could be displayed on the walls." He points toward the king's palace.

"Any Jews left?"

Rachid says, "A few. They live in the new town. Everyone lives together in the new town with no problem."

We stop at the Royal Palace, huge and shut tight. There must be gardens—even trees—inside that the sun-struck populace could enjoy of a Friday evening.

In a side street we meet a boy toddling with his older brother. The small one wears a red fez and a white robe. Rachid says, "He is very important. He has recently been circumcised." He lets us take his picture.

We eat almond pastries and sesame cookies with our late morning tea, then go back to the **masseria** to pack. Rachid talks about Joseph Conrad. Ed is limpid and insubstantial, like an angel. Rachid says, "You are leaving two kilos in Fez." The energy imparted to me by the hunched man still courses. We give Rachid four **Times Literary Supplements** that we brought with us, knowing he will devour every word. We promise to send him books. Perhaps he surprises himself—he gives me a goodbye hug.

Hafid appears with the handcart. Ed is happy that we are not going home with a **tajine.** We're picked up in front of a hotel, and I am presented with a bouquet of flowers by the representative of the company who stranded us on the road into Fez. We are whisked to Casablanca, where we see nothing but a fringe of harbor, palm trees, and the hotel, which we reach in the dark. In bed Ed recounts the whole movie **Casablanca** to me. When he sleeps, I think of my sister Nancy. When she married, her husband had just graduated from the University of Georgia and had become an ensign in the navy. They were assigned to a base near Rabat in Morocco. Our family was stunned by this posting. We took out the atlas to see exactly where that remote outpost on the globe might be. She sailed away, knowing our sick father would die while she was gone. He ranted that she would be among people "only three generations away from cannibalism." We were remote people ourselves. Soon the letters arrived with descriptions of Berbers and hot springs in the desert and the bleak navy base. Her son was born there. I was fourteen. I devoured the letters. They were allowed to travel around the Mediterranean on a navy ship that called for several days in Marseilles, Naples, Athens, and Cyprus, a list of over-the-rainbow names. I followed the trip through the rose, aqua, and yellow colors on the map. My mother cried when pictures of Boo, the baby, arrived. He was held by a dark woman with sparkling eyes, jewelry on her arms and ankles, and henna tattoos on her hands.

Now, late at night in Casablanca, so many eons later, I can follow my sister and her husband around a souk, see them young again, intent on buying a leather hassock. They drive off in their minute Morris Minor, across a plain that looks like an enormous loaf of bread, then through sesame fields, mint fields, the forests of cork oak, back to that dot on the map where they started their life together.

This afternoon we must have passed the left turn they took. The loops, the stops, the intersections, the unrolling, the catching up, the intertwinings, the following, the leading in a life—all more mysterious than the rotations of stars. And my mother, whose radius of travel was short, tied the letters with ribbon and kept them in her desk. "When you get the chance," she said to me, "go."

A Paperweight for Colette

Burgundy

Cherries, quail eggs, sweet potatoes, white asparagus at six euros a kilo, plump, erotic apricots, haricots verts (but they're from Kenya), buckets of peonies and roses, clusters of crimson tomatoes—the middle of the Auxerre covered market buzzes with shoppers loading their cloth bags at fruit and vegetable stands, and groups of farm women visiting over their baskets of eggs. We could be at a market in Italy or Portugal. But around the perimeter we could be nowhere but France. The meat displays are as carefully arranged as the gold jewelry cases on the Ponte Vecchio. We gaze at trussed turkey stuffed with prunes, paupiettes of pork, rosy jellied hams, black-footed chickens, and roasts wrapped in lacy cauls. I count twenty kinds of terrines: fish, various livers, chunky pork, layered vegetables, and chicken. The bakery cases offer puffy **gougères** the size of softballs, rabbit pies, and great craggy loaves of bread. Cheese would be reason enough for a trip to France. A woman shopping next to me discreetly pokes several when the cheese monger looks away. Her shrewd thumb knows the stages of ripeness. She leans close to inspect the rind. She then points to her selection, a buttery-looking mound soft as a baby's cheek. Ed selects several pillowy farm cheeses, several goat ones that look like chalky elf cakes or coat buttons. Two people are taking money. I pay one, and we start to walk away. The other money-taker shouts that we must pay, the one I paid shouts at him, and a big family argument breaks out but no one pays any attention.

Loading the car, we're happy. This is our third day in Burgundy, and we have been turning around as dogs turn before they settle down. We have rented a beautiful, if unkempt, old stone place in the tiny village of Magny on the Yonne River. I wish my friends Susan and Cole could buy the place. They love France and would make the garden into a little Eden. Already the fruit trees are in place. Houses inevitably exude the essential sense of the owners, and so I start to invent narratives about the English owner's Early Ikea bed that smells like someone recently died there, and the news he looked for in his stacks of ten-year-old newspapers. A baronial fireplace and a grand piano, combined with plastic chairs, leave me trying in vain to answer the question **why**? There's a novel here.

The rental agency's photographs showed a romantically set table and a blurry living room with French doors overlooking the river—the owner's dream of the house as it was before the unfortunate action in the novel took place. The idyllic river **is** there—I love the smell of rivers. A rowboat lies half submerged at the shore. The telephone does not work (of course by chapter two he didn't want to hear from anyone), and even the cell phones receive no signal. What if one of us trips over a pile of mouldy jigsaw puzzles and needs an ambulance? When we asked the caretaker how to connect the telephone, she said, "Oh, he probably didn't pay the bill." The plot thickens. The owner is too sad to pay attention to basic details. The kitchen . . . **the well-equipped and spacious kitchen with dining area**. I try to see it as a challenge instead of as a place fit only for boiling cabbage. Two greasy shelves, mildew, a freestanding relic of a stove with doll-size burners, and an oven no bigger than a toaster. We shall dine on melamine. I would not be surprised to see a snake crawl from under the fridge. I met an exotic yard-long green and black one sunning on the kitchen doorstep. When I beat the path with a stick, he languidly slithered away. The caretaker from the village somehow started the stove for us without causing an explosion. But the novelistic potential remains—a Christmas tree from several years ago provides a fire hazard in the garage. This image grounds the novel I never will write—a tragic breakup occurred during the holidays. The dried-up tree symbolizes all that went wrong. Perhaps the wife took up with a mechanic in the village. But we are dreamy fools seduced by river light.

We stop to see Auxerre's Gothic cathedral. The town looks appealing and prosperous. A city situated on a river is fortunate, especially when a cathedral soars against the sky. Shoppers crowd the streets, and people lounge at outdoor cafés. We detour to a gigantic French Wal-Mart–type megacomplex, where we buy sheets, towels, dish towels, a tablecloth, napkins, and a few cooking utensils. I think I'm dreaming of how my friends in their happiness would scrub and paint this house into its full and lovely potential. Yes, even our open windows, fresh flowered sheets, vases of flowers, and some scrubbing could perk up the rooms.

When Colette was a child in nearby Saint-Sauveur-en-Puisaye, her mother, Sido, travelled to Auxerre every three months. The aura of the nineteenth-century market town it must have been lingers still. She set out in the Victoria at two in the morning in her quest for luxuries: a sugarloaf wrapped in indigo paper, ten pounds of chocolate, cinnamon, nutmeg, rum for grog, pepper, vanilla, and soap. Colette perched on the backseat. I can imagine her intense interest, the bumpy ride under the stars, slowing at first light as they entered the waking town. My mother used to take me shopping in Macon, our Auxerre, when I was little. Suddenly there were things to want. I selected a skirt with wide rickrack. I was able to buy books, not available in my small Georgia town. Once my desires overcame me, and I threw a tantrum in Davison's when my mother would not buy me a stuffed animal that played music.

I came to Burgundy to revisit Colette. We drove our own car from Cortona because Ed wants to take back special wines, preferably those paired with dinners here. I'm hoping to find for my Bramasole garden herbs unavailable in Tuscany: sorrel, chervil, tarragon, and new-to-Bramasole varieties of basil. We brought a stack of French cookbooks and a book on cheese. And then there's Burgundy, land of the **Very Rich Hours**, to see.

We meander on country lanes flanked by undulating fields. The villages seem ghostly, empty except for cats. We go through the village of Misery twice, and: "Stop, did you see the name of this place? Go back!" The town of Anus. We stop off "at home" to store the food. An amber light slants across the back garden, once an orchard. I step out onto the balcony to look, but the rusty railings do not seem entirely secure. The sight of the broken, overturned deck chairs reminds me of the owner's saga. Did he consider leaping to the river below? "Let's go somewhere wonderful for dinner," I call to Ed.

After a drive, we walk along the river, then find a small restaurant beside a canal. I look up from the menu. There's our house's caretaker, working as a waiter. She brings us a complimentary aperitif and olives. The slanting light rakes the water. I love the long summer twilights. I'm always happy when I can see blue boats riding on their reflections. A little string of lights comes on, and we feast on simple salads and roast chicken.

When I was studying for my master's degree, I had to select three writers for my oral exam. I chose Keats, the American poet Louise Bogan, and Colette. The department chair called me in to discuss my choices. "Keats is great. Bogan is marginal," he said, "a limited poet but acceptable to the committee. But this Colette? What has she written of value? Wasn't she in the Folies Bergère?"

This was 1975 and hard to imagine from here. I was studying Craft of Fiction with

Wright Morris, a writer I revered for his ingrained sense of place and his careful, revealing images. When he handed out the semester reading list, all the novelists were men. After class I approached him. "Mr. Morris, I was wondering about the list of books. Why aren't there any by women?"

"Oh, hello, my dear. Oh yes, I thought of that myself. I considered Virginia Woolf, but really, she becomes tiresome. I want to give you examples you really can delve into." Maybe he was farsighted, but he appeared to be looking down a rather proud nose at me, so far, far away.

"So." Pause. "Ford Madox Ford is more important than Virginia Woolf?" My tone was infused not with aggression but with protective coloring.

"More to offer the novice writer, Miss Meyer."

"Mayes."

"Yes, of course. Miss Mayes, our southern belle."

No one avoids conflict more than I. But pushed, I can throw a conniption fit, and I will go to any mat if necessary. I was reeling from this second blow. The next week, carrying a stack of Colette's books, I visited each committee member. I admit to reaching for some southern charm. Finally they relented, probably not out of sudden conversion to the literary merit of my author but to avoid having to justify a decision if a troublemaker student, southern charm or no, forced them.

Colette was new to me. I'd read the Claudine books and **Break of Day**, which I thought was a classic. Soon Colette became my close friend. One of this life's pleasures: a writer's books can intersect with your life and lead you to the next largest space you can occupy. Her writing catapulted me forward. Even now, each time I pick up one of her books, her perceptions and images continue to wake up my perceptions. Life drenches her prose. She's astute. I know the members of her family as well as my own. I follow every turn of her story, how she made her way alone, her mistakes, her droll perspective. Her story, compelling as it is, would not be enough to bind me to her. Story is not enough. She peels and sections and bites into experience like an orange. She's wise and self-sufficient, two qualities I stand by. Her passion for roses, dogs, sunrise, and all the felt sensations of life runs through the molten alchemical process of selecting words. Her prose—immediate and spellbinding—lets me touch the hand of the writer herself. I feel most bound to her when I read about her childhood in Burgundy. Those years sustained her throughout her life. Her original house and garden remained a real and metaphorical world of **home**, her stern and passionate mother, the presiding grace.

My abiding friendship with her is only incidentally affected by the fact that she is dead. I know her intimately. In daydreams, I can sit down for a scrumptious lunch in her adored Palais Royale apartment in Paris. What would we eat? A delicious speculation. Oysters served on a bed of seaweed and ice. A champagne of Colette's choice. A little pheasant stuffed with morels and nuts, a salad of field greens that she somehow managed to find at a street market. For dessert, wild strawberries, of course. What would we talk about? Prose style? Publishing? No. I'd tell her about the pink hellebores I planted under the crape myrtles, how my whole California garden revolves around what the deer won't eat. We'd talk about politics, dogs, the boredom of dogma, winter coats, flamenco. The bouquet of red and purple anemones I brought attracts two bees. We're fascinated to watch them roll in the vibrant petals. The warm hummm . . . blends with a few splats of rain beginning to fall in the garden below. We can watch this in silence.

Ed and I light out for the great medieval pilgrimage towns. Autun's cathedral, boxed in by houses and buildings, is hard to see. Mad twisted gargoyles look down at us. One pokes his rear end outward so that roof water drains out of his bottom. The world's first instance of mooning? I light candles for the desperately ill mothers of my friends Robin and Madeline, then look for the relics of Lazarus. The Romanesque stone carving of the Last Judgment compels me to stand awhile in the cold for a good look at the depicted lineup of humans waiting to be sent to heaven or hell. They catch every range of emotion—praying, hand-wringing, eyes cast to heaven, head held in hands. Clearly, they are scared. And graphically, a crab-claw descends to snatch each one up a level to the judging. One capital shows Judas hanging himself, his head drooped between two flowers. I've always pitied Judas, who threw away his big chance. Someone practices on the organ but without much force. The music sounds snuffed, as though organ and organist were locked inside a trunk.

I never find Lazarus. This time he's not going to rise.

Pilgrims always come to Vézelay because the relics of Mary Magdalen reside at the basilica that bears her name. Vézelay—the name suits an exotic woman and is as intriguing as the place. The town serves as a grand entrance to the cathedral. Beneath the half-timbered houses and minute shops lining the street, vaulted basements once used to house the hordes who came at the beginnings of Crusades or out of devotion to the relics. The basilica looks small, with its bell tower and narrow facade, but a walk to the side reveals a long, buttressed structure with many windows. Inside, the soaring space feels open because of the white light falling through clear glass. The psychology of the plan: you are drawn through the long embrace of the nave to the luminous altar. The tympanum, recessed half circles over the front door, fascinates me. A master stone carver portrays an elongated Christ gathering his apostles before the crucifixion. His hands are expressionistic—enlarged and sending forth wavy rays of spiritual energy to his apostles, who must take His word into the world and convert the heathens. The variety of heathens imagined is amusing: dog-headed men, pygmies, people with enormous ears or snout-faces. Ancient cartographers scrawled **there be beasties** when the known terrain ran out. Here those beasties are given form. This enlightens me. How encompassing was medieval Christianity—even the fearful dog faces should be converted. Some of the apostles in the group look distinctly worried. The Romanesque imagination requires study. All those carnival, grotesque, whimsical, fanciful, monstrous figures came out of a fertile intersection of the pagan and the Christian. They manifest the rumblings of the collective unconscious, the worries about where the wild things are. One creature looks like a winged cow holding a suitcase.

The carved capitals of supporting columns are masterful. I especially love the one of grapes being crushed in a press, no doubt a metaphor for the blood of Christ. In one of the tourist shops, I buy a book on the carvings to savor later.

Ed spots a **pâtisserie**. The French pastry

shops—aqua, blue, or pink with gold letters—look like their own confections. The little bell rings, and you're welcomed into a tidy shop with buttery, warm smells wafting from the kitchen. The pastries are about form as well as taste. The rich puffs and ruffles and layers and colors form tasty morsels, but they also reward the eye. Ed chooses two or three delectables a day: delicate lemon or strawberry tarts, napoleons, pleated foil cups of dark chocolate, rustic plum galettes oozing juice. After each he says, **"Viva la France."**

The village houses look private and closed. Lace curtains hang in all the windows. Not traditional handmade ones, these are machine worked with corny designs of gamboling horses, cats with balls of yarn, and windmills. No doubt made in China. Lace curtains exist solely for a hand to part them, for someone to peer secretly at the street. **What's going on there among those others? Especially that Mary Magdalen**.

In the characteristic wine town Beaune, we choose the archetypal sidewalk café and linger under the plane trees. Henry James in **A Little**

Tour of France describes Beaune as "a drowsy little Burgundian town, very old and ripe, with crooked streets, vistas always oblique, and steep, moss-covered roofs." No longer drowsy, the town today perks with energy—inviting shops, the Saturday market, and locals out to visit with friends. I would like to photograph all the weathervanes. We find a heavy copper pot to take back home to Giusi, who cooks with us. We probably should go to the Marché aux Vins, which my notebook reminds me is at 2, rue Nicolas Rolin, named for the man who founded the famous medieval hospital here. There you buy a **taste-vin**, a tasting cup, and then by candlelight sample up to eighteen regional wines. Sounds overwhelming. I could taste three, then my active little buds would shut down.

Ed photographs the glazed orange, green, black, and tan geometrically patterned tile roofs on the hospital, L'Hôtel Dieu des Hospices de Beaune. Half-timbered sections, jacquard-patterned gables, and pitched roofs give a toy-like appeal to the buildings. The colonnaded courtyard sheltered nuns going from wing to wing, carrying, I imagine, vats of **boeuf bourguignon**, and loaves of bread tucked under their arms. We walk through thinking of being sick in one of those red-draped beds. Not bad, as long as the illness were not the plague. Rogier van der Weyden's great painting, **The Last Judgment**, which once hung above the altar in the paupers' section, crowns the hospital's gallery. How sobering from the sickbed to contemplate the damned heading toward an inferno. Fewer in the painting look toward paradise.

The charity hospital was richly endowed, thanks to the fifteenth-century Duc de Bourgogne, who solicited donations to finance the construction and continuance. Sixty hectares of donated prime land proved to be the lasting boon. Thirty-nine vintages are created from these hillsides, and the hospital's benefit auction every November on the third Sunday is one of the most important wine events in France.

In Beaune we're in the heart of Côte d'Or wine country. Pommard is just down the road. In the wine shop the great bottles are lined up like jousting knights: Gevrey-Chambertin, Corton, Meursault, Pouilly-Fuissé, Puligny-Montrachet. A knowledgeable man helps us select a case. I'm already imagining bringing out these wines for our Italian friends.

Colette, with her innate understanding of the natural world, writes about wine in the most elemental way. A great vintage, she maintained, results from "celestial sorcery," not the hand of the vintner. She writes:

> The vine and the wine it produces are two great mysteries. Alone in the vegetable kingdom, the vine makes the true savor of the earth intelligible to man. With what fidelity it makes the translation! It senses, then expresses, in its clusters of fruit the secrets of the soil. The flint, through the vine, tells us that it is living, fusible, a giver of nourishment. Only in wine does the ungrateful chalk pour out its golden tears. A vine, transported across mountains and over seas, will struggle to keep its personality, and sometimes triumphs over the powerful chemistries of the mineral world. Harvested near Algiers, a white wine will still remember . . . the noble Bordeaux graft that gave it exactly the right hint of sweetness, lightened its body, and endowed it with gaiety. And it is far-off Jerez that gives its warmth and color to the dry and cordial wine that ripens at Château Chalon, on the summit of a narrow, rocky plateau.

While Ed indulges in a chocolate walnut tart, I step inside a cheese heaven. Hundreds of artisan cheeses. The women who work here are dressed impeccably in white, like nurses presiding over newborns. One waves a branch of leaves so that no flies land on one of her charges. She looks mythic. Why was there no goddess of cheese?

To surprise Ed, I buy a round wooden box of **epoisse**, buttery, runny, tangy, and local. Its pert orange rind, the nurse/goddess tells me, comes from the **marc** it's bathed in after it ages for a month. I select two little goat's nubbins, too, both the size of my thumbprint. We find bread and return quickly to our shabby manse. Ed empties the rowboat and dries it with the house's scruffy bath towels. We row upriver to a fenny area and spread a cloth on the middle seat. If the cheese is right, the bread is right, and the wine—this a Pouilly-Fuissé—is right, then a floating dinner with the boat resting on a glissade of light eases us happily into darkening twilight. We propose a few toasts. First I raise my glass to Colette.

As we hoist the rowboat out of the water, Ed says, "When are we going to Saint-Sauveur? We're not far away."

He knows that I've saved the trip to Colette's childhood town, savoring the anticipation.

Saint-Sauveur—the crucible. "I'm ready. Let's go tomorrow."

Standing in front of 8, rue de Colette (formerly rue de l'Hospice), with her inspired, passionate descriptions in mind, I confront a tall dun-colored house with white shutters. It looks neglected. A doctor's name is above the doorbell, which I imagine ringing—**would it be possible to see Colette's room**—but don't. She wrote:

> A large solemn house, rather forbidding, with its shrill bell and its carriage entrance with a huge bolt like an ancient dungeon, a house that smiled only on its garden side. The back, invisible to passers-by, was a sun trap, swathed in a mantle of wisteria and bignonia too heavy for the trellis of worn ironwork, which sagged in the middle like a hammock and provided shade for the little flagged terrace and the threshold of the sitting room.

Her perspective: the child hiding while her mother looked for her. "Where are the children?" Sido calls, never looking up into the branches of the walnut where gleamed the "pale, pointed face of a child who lay stretched like a tomcat along a big branch and who never uttered a word." Colette interrupts her description long enough to ask herself, "Is it worthwhile, I wonder, seeking for adequate words to describe the rest?" She then continues in a lyric key:

> I shall never be able to conjure up the splendor that adorns, in my memory, the ruddy festoons of an autumn vine borne down by its own weight and clinging despairingly to some branch of the fir trees. And the massive lilacs, whose compact flowers—blue in the shade and purple in the sunshine—withered so soon, stifled by their own exuberance. The lilacs long since dead will not be revived at my bidding, any more than the terrifying moonlight—silver, quicksilver, leaden-gray, with facets of dazzling amethyst or scintillating points of sapphire—all depending on a certain pane in the blue glass window of the summerhouse at the bottom of the garden.

The flash of memories accompanies her realization that "the secret is lost that opened to me a whole world."

Time, sun-baked time, time that keeps on slipping, slipping, elusive time, time like the stone Romanesque eyes peering from behind a clump of leaves, the startled pagan looking toward a transformed future. Art historians refer to this recurrent motif of the face in the leaves as "the green man."

My childhood was not edenic, far from it, but the concatenation of first experiences remains a vein of gold in memory. Going back, dipping into those impressions, gives me not nostalgia, no, no, no, but private renaissances. Swinging on the wooden supports of my mother's canopied bed, climbing out the window to play in the moonlit garden, painting myself all over with house paint (my mother shrieking **You're going to die**), riding on the back of a sea turtle making its way back to the waves, the sweet reek of pork roasting on a pit fire, my sashes tied in bows, my father whispering **You can have anything you want**, hiding in the hydrangeas, imagining my face as one of the pale blooms—the ten thousand images that compose a childhood, those imprints last forever. Wright Morris, of the Craft of Fiction class and the important novels, told me, "If you've had a childhood, you have enough to write about for the rest of your life."

I wonder if the garden once was larger or if her memory expanded the dimensions, out of love for every petal and twig.

The reality of her home must remain a cipher. The present facade reveals as much of Colette as a tombstone tells about the occupant below. I visited the house twenty years ago. I remember a young couple whizzing up on a Vespa. They paused, he revved the engine, and the girl waved to the upstairs window. "**Bonjour**, Colette," she called as they spun off.

This time I have come to see the recently opened Musée Colette. Too bad they could not buy her family home. The museum, only a stroll away, is in a seventeenth-century château, a grander villa than her mother's house. If Colette had come back to Saint-Sauveur in her later years, she might have bought this house. But I suddenly realize that after she married and moved to Paris, she could have, but never did, return to live here. She loved other parts of France, especially La Treille Muscate (The Musk Vine Arbor), her house in Saint-Tropez. She liked in her early adult life to "move house." Intensely domestic, she was also restless. This oxymoron is one source of my identification with her. "Wherever you are, you're thinking of somewhere else," my first husband accused me. Sadly, he spoke the truth. Only later, when I lived in places I wanted to be, did the restlessness cool.

The house on rue de l'Hospice became the lost paradise, endlessly there in memory for replenishment, for revisiting, and perhaps even for reinventing. But not for actual return. This is one answer that solves the riddle of home. Icons from this house and garden are scattered across her books like handfuls of fairy dust: a copper knob that used to shine on her bedroom door, the drumroll played in the village on New Year's morning, a warming pan she took to school, the nectar inside a flagon swathed in spiderwebs, a broken basket of spindle berries, a bouquet of meadow saffron, her hooded cape that casts her in a heraldic role—thousands of images as fresh as the slushy paths in autumn, where she sought the "yellow chanterelles that go so well with creamy sauces and casserole of veal." Her childhood is almost as real to me as my own: a "skimpy little urchin, brave under my red hood, I would crack boiled chestnuts with my teeth as I slid along on my small pointed sabots." Forty-five years in Paris, she claimed, did nothing to erase the provincial girl in quest of the country home she lost.

Is there a more personal museum in the world? This house **is** Colette. Slides of her eyes are projected on the stair landing wall, her haunting eyes from infancy to old age, flashing as you ascend and descend the steps. You come to a museum to look; in this one, Colette is looking at you. On the stair risers, the names of her books are carved in gold letters. Scattered in the marble floor, her many addresses are engraved. She must have been one of the most photographed people of her time. Photographs of her line one room. The frames' mats are colored, giving the room an air of gaiety. Seeing the early photo of her sitting at the piano with her braid hanging to the floor and her creamy shoulders poised, you almost can hear the music. An alcove is filled with photos of her with animals. She always had pets, usually an ugly dog. I'm thrilled to see handwritten manuscripts with corrections and her address book written in brown ink. Her pot of pens and eyeglass case echo in the photo behind them, where she is reaching into the same pot.

Around the doors the stone is painted with

blue vines, reminding me of her garden in Saint-Tropez. One leads to her writing room and bedroom, copied and furnished from her apartment at the Palais Royale. The designers have managed to make the rooms seem real, not at all house-of-wax. I get to gaze at her library steps, white china dogs made into lamps, feminine slipper chairs with needlepoint panels of flowers, mottled pomegranate and sunflower-yellow walls, and the narrow bed wedged under a window. When she was bedridden with arthritis, this room is where she lived. Under a fur throw, with a neat wheeled desk built over the bed, she wrote, entertained her friends, and regarded her collections of butterflies, framed not in rigid rows but randomly as though in flight. She loved glass objects. Her glass bracelets and horse are saved, along with a rare collection of Cartesian diver bottles in many colors. I can see her lifting one of her paperweights with an imprisoned butterfly or flower as she stops mid-sentence to think. She often wrote on blue paper and even shaded her desk lamp with a sheet of it. Her blue light in the window of the Palais Royale apartment became famous. Those passing below at night would look up and know that Colette was writing. So much of her still lives in the intensely personal rooms lit with the colors of the South.

She would approve of the café downstairs. I wish she could join us for pâté, cheese, baguette, and a glass of wine.

What would make the **musée** a true earthly paradise would be a Colette garden planted from her memories of her mother's, her own, and the garden she imagined when she no longer had one. If a garden is impossible, perhaps a meditative, labyrinthine walk could be constructed. Punctuating the way would be painted signs with quotes so powerful that the real garden could rise in the mind's eye. Instead of leaning to sniff the bountiful roses, one could read:

> The first stir of spring is such a solemn thing that the accession of the rose, coming after it, is celebrated with less fervor. Yet everything is permitted to the rose: splendor, conspiring scents, petals with flesh that tempts the nostrils, the lips, the teeth. But all has been said, everything has been born already in any year when once the rose has entered it; the first rose but heralds all the other roses that must fol-

low . . . Riper than fruit, more sensuous than cheek or breast . . .

And:

> Don't ask me where I shall plant the white rose disheveled by a single gust of wind, the yellow rose which has a scent of fine cigars, the pink rose which has a scent of roses, the red rose which dies unceasingly from the pouring out of its odors and whose dry and weightless corpse still lavishes its balm upon the air. I shall not crucify my red rose against a wall; I shall not bind it to the edge of the water tank. It shall grow, if my good destiny allows it so, just beside the open bedroom, the room that will have only three walls instead of four, and stand open to the rising sun.

Even roses she didn't like can bloom vividly on a sign:

> Roses the color of nasturtiums, with a scent of peaches; starved-looking roses tinged with dirty mauve that smelled of crushed ants; orange roses that smelled of nothing at all; and

> finally a little horror of a rosebush with tiny yellowish flowers covered in hairs, badly set on their stalks, bushing out all over the place, and giving off an odor like a musk-filled menagerie, like a gymnasium frequented exclusively by young red-headed women, like artificial vanilla extract . . .

Back at our musty house on the greeny banks of the Yonne, we reconsider the hapless neglect in the light of Colette's loved and radiant ambiance. No one lavishes care on this lovely house at the end of the village. "Can we just go now? It's only three. We could be in a sweet little inn somewhere by dark. Is the map in the car?"

"I can be ready in fifteen minutes."

We drive to Dijon, feast well, and leave the next day for a country **relais** near Avignon. The heat becomes serious.

Today I buy the herbs I want at a nursery, and some yellow lilies for our room. When we visit the antique market town of Île-sur-la-Sorgue, we are so hot I don't care about looking at fine monogrammed napkins and silver serving pieces. We walk through, drinking bottle after bottle of water, buy nothing, and return to our golden stone **mas** under a massive oak for lunch and a swim.

The room has a fine escritoire, waxed for generations. Ed falls into a late siesta, and I shift the desk closer to the window for the pleasure of opening my notebook, writing a few words that have been floating in my brain, **nidify, pith, efflorescence, tesserae**. I keep glancing outside into the oak's spreading branches. A perfect tree for green-eyed Colette to climb. On the trunk, patches of silvery gray lichen look like squiggly maps. A young waiter on break tips his chair back and raises his face to the sun. His smooth arms the color of butterscotch dapple with shadow. My lilies in a water pitcher look freshly gilded against the soft blue messaline draperies. Colette so loved the shades, contrasts, colors, and sensations of the world. A wasp hovers over two crescents of honeydew melon on a yellow plate.

From Garden to Garden

The British Isles

Lower Swell—we are at home in a stone schoolhouse that has undergone conversion into a comfortable Cotswold home and enclosed garden. The tiny cluster of surrounding houses looks equally mellow and natural in green, green radiant fields where sheep look as if they are posing for "Mary Had a Little Lamb," and the word **chlorophyll** comes to mind.

Our schoolhouse seems especially welcoming—three sofas to sink into, long windows where pink mallow branches sway, a table to seat twelve, if we knew so many to invite, and a fireplace. I could settle in for months. I imagine slanting rain on winter evenings, imagine reading the local writers, from Laurie Lee to Shakespeare. Right now in July we open all the windows, page through garden books, and spread our area maps on the coffee table for the pleasure of saying names aloud: Stow-on-the-Wold, Bourton-on-the-Water, Upper Slaughter, Chipping Campden—all places we will see—and names of places farther afield—Hextable, Wootten-under-Edge, Chorleywood, Plumpton Green, Leigh-on-Sea, Frogmore, Midsomer Norton, Flackwell Heath. These could be settings for novels in which an intended note under the door slides under the rug instead and lies undetected until too late, far too late. The cheerful kitchen makes me want to whip up a batch of buttermilk biscuits. Maybe it's the sunlight pouring through the door, maybe it's the blue-checked curtains at the window and under the sink, maybe it's the yellow bowl of plums on the counter, or that the four burners on the stove are called **hobs** here. I like **hobs**.

We must feel at home because we taught for so many years. I wonder which way the desks faced and where the chalkboard hung. Two staircases branch off, going up to dormer bedrooms. Perhaps two teachers lived here, retiring to their separate quarters at night. From upstairs, the small windows look out at the golden village on one side and onto a walled garden on the other. Beyond, the open countryside lures me to walk in every direction. A road sign cautions to watch for badgers. Travelling in the Cotswolds is the polar opposite to adventure travel. The sheep will part to let us cross their bucolic meadows. Downstairs the garden awaits with drowsy charms. An intimate, informal space about twice the size of the house, the garden blooms haphazardly; the scraggly beds could stand a visit from those patron saints of English gardens, Vita Sackville-West or Gertrude Jekyl, to tidy up and add some flowers and bushes with rhythm and texture. I have planted thyme and basil near the kitchen door. A primitive urge, I think, that instinct to put something with roots into the ground, even though I am transient here. "The garden could be so heavenly—and we could transform it in a week."

"Resist. Just enjoy the spontaneous qualities."

"Actually, it's pretty this way, a jumble, a blur of color."

We have come to visit the great English gardens—to feel, as Edith Wharton said, "the secret vibrations of their beauty"—and my list is long.

We started a week ago in Bath. **Bah-th,** we said, walking down streets where Jane Austen's skirts once grazed the stones. Our hotel outside town was a former priory with a formal but livable garden of small ponds and boxwood knots, and a good kitchen garden, too, that supplied their restaurant. Immediately, I liked living there. This is jolly England, I thought, the English major's England. The England of my great-great-grandfather's people, although I don't know if they lived like serfs or lords. The drawing room, just so, was lined with portraits and paintings and crowded with the classic English-style mix of striped and flowered and velvet furniture and Oriental rugs. We felt like guests at a country house where someone is perhaps poisoned, the inspector droll, and all the weekend guests suspects. The large room opened onto the garden terrace. The staff settled us on a sofa and brought champagne while we ordered dinner. When we were shown to the table, course after course appeared, ending with a trolley of Cheshire and Stilton cheeses. Our bedroom was serene and large, furnished in sage and coral with duvets and down and a view of the knot garden and fountain. I realized that the formal terrace gardens were designed not only for strolling but for the pleasure of viewing them from the house.

That first night after dinner we drove into Bath late and saw it empty except for jammed pubs and a few doorways where not-so-innocent teenagers lurked. We'd thought we were tired after the flight from Italy and after the rental car's flat tire in the rain on a lane where we were turning around, having taken a wrong turn. But the curves of Bath's streets, lighted shop windows, and the looming church kept us walking until midnight.

In the morning we walked to the Royal Crescent, then through dignified streets lined with town houses. What noble spaces for living. In the park I stopped to photograph the small raised circular beds of double pink begonias edged with thyme. Among the begonias a few lavender and dusty millers had been plunked down here and there to good effect—they undid the studied look of a park bed. Wallace Stevens liked to insert one "ugly" word, a rough-textured word, into each poem, seamless beauty being boring. The silk-textured petals and the jaunty little pale-leafed thyme—such a simple and inspired choice.

We shopped with the matrons for those delectable local cheeses we'd been served the night before. If I had a kitchen in Bath, I would try the cockles and samfire, a seaweed offered in bins outside the fishmonger's. We loaded our shopping bag with scones, buns and fresh breads, and bottles of elder flower juice. Walking back to the car, we fell into step with a brisk lady, upswept hair and linen suit, who hoped we liked Bath and pointed out her black varnished door in a circle of gracious houses around a park with one vast tree. "Don't come in town at night. It's shameful what has happened. Hippies and drugs, the girls are devils, tough as boys. They'll take your teeth if they're false."

At an outdoor antique/junk market, Beatles music blared. Humming "Hey, Jude," I found a starch-and-crochet christening dress some baby wore 150 years ago, four ivory-handled cheese knives (forty pence apiece!), and a pair of tiny horn spectacles, also worn by a child whose eyes are long since shut. Ed found an old level and an unfolding wood and brass measurer. I overheard a Scottish woman say, "Their junk is different from our junk." By midmorning, the sidewalks were thronged with tourists and local shoppers. Morris dancers performed in a closed street. A homeless man leaned against a doorway reading **Wild Spain**. The street people are known as **crusties**. They are **cuffy**, meaning "down and out."

We were herded through the Roman baths, then spent an hour in the big parish church, reading the epitaphs on gravestones in the floor and on the walls: Walter Clarke Darby, Mary Henrietta Cotgrave, Marmaduke Peacocke, Cecilia Blake. Maybe Jane Austen perused the stones for her characters' names. Amid the tourists, one of whom was eating from a box of Cracker Jacks, a priest was conducting a religious ceremony for a group of five ancient ladies. As we passed, we heard him boom out, "Lead us not into temptation." Four silver heads were bowed; the fifth lady, looking contemplative, examined her manicure, her hand outstretched. Of the five, perhaps she was the one once led into temptation.

We took care of the split tire and headed for Wales.

We crossed into Wales and drove up to the Isle of Anglesey, Ynys Môn in Welsh, where we had rented a cottage with the beguiling name of Mermaid, right on the water. Taking slow roads through pastureland put us there at nine at night, still the long Welsh summer twilight, with the tide rushing back in to fill the strait, and the slanted rays striking a great castle across the water. We carried our Bath provisions inside, looking forward to a picnic of various meat pies and cheeses on the terrace. On the road in, we'd stopped at an organic vegetable stand and a pick-your-own berries field. The customers chatted in Welsh, oldest of Great Britain's languages. We paused, fingering the beans, just to listen. The sound was at once musical and hard, like a vase of marbles emptied into the sink. We felt ebullient to be in Wales. Nearby was the first garden on my list, Plas Newydd, designed by my distant ancestor, Humphrey Repton. Our garden-to-garden vacation was beginning. As we unloaded the car, the rising moon looked like a big gooseberry, translucent gold in the milky sky. The white-washed cottage, a former stable, had been remodeled recently. When we walked inside, we almost dropped our bags. It was hideous. Someone had furnished it like a cheap trailer. "No. This can't be." I walked through, peering into two cramped bedrooms. "It has a five-teacup rating from the tourist board." I'd thought the Welsh teacup system so cozy.

"Must have been based on quantity, not quality. The number of beds and spoons." Ed pushed the bed, and the mattress sank. The coverlet of pilled polyester was slightly damp, the bath done up like a two-dollar bordello, and the kitchen floor's low-grade plastic wood gave at each step. Only the unattractive living room redeemed it. French doors opened to the water view, and if I concentrated on that, I didn't notice the bad leather furniture "suite" or the plastic flowers atop the TV or the itchy-looking wall-to-wall. "Beware of renting on the Internet. Weren't there photographs?"

"No, they didn't have them yet, and I took a chance. The photo of the outside looked so wonderful, and the agent said the whole place was just redone . . . Let's don't talk about it anymore." I'm guilty.

The luscious twilight lasted until eleven o'clock. We walked along the shore of the Strait of Menai and decided that things would be better in the morning. But in the blank light of day, the place was still tawdry. As if to confirm my impression, a trailer surrounded by various large metal storage containers was parked outside the kitchen window. "Do you want to go? Even though we'll lose the money, I'm not sure we can sleep on that squat little bed. My feet hang off and practically touch the floor. Chalk it up," Ed said. He started looking in the guidebook for a hotel.

"Those synthetic bed linens feel like sandpaper. Let's just stay until we see what's around here." We set off. We found Wales sublime. The saturated-green air looked aquatic, as though someone just pulled the plug, draining away the watery world and leaving swaying meadows, fields, trees, and hills washed and gleaming. "Do we need to **go** to gardens? All Wales seems to be a garden," Ed said. The roads we took were actually lanes, with hedgerows crowding the edges and the green banks profligate with wild foxglove. For three days we left early and stayed out late, eating in pubs and pushing on toward the next interesting town rather than going "home" and cooking, imagining we lived facing that changeable strait, picking fruit down the road, as we'd like to have done.

We spent hours at the garden of Plas Newydd, which also overlooked the Strait of Menai. My distant relative Humphrey Repton, involved in the original planning, created one of his rare design portfolios called a Red Book for the property in 1798–99. We didn't go inside the huge house. I have an allergy to hearing anecdotes about ghosts in the hallway. Dead houses depress me. Unless one looks fascinating, I skip it. In the gardens I'm free to wander among the old guards' legacies that still grow. I can't tell what's left of the Repton design, but the garden has an especially expansive feel, partly because water views open a property as nothing else can. Grand trees and islands of hydrangeas punctuate the greenswards. In Wales hydrangeas bloom prolifically and intensely, that blue of the Madonna's dress in Renaissance painting, and deep pink globes. I've only seen such blue in the hydrangeas on the campus where I used to teach. They bloomed under pine trees, a respite in an urban campus. I always thought the blue came from the Pacific sea air, not from acid levels in the soil; perhaps that's the secret here as well.

Conwy, nearby on the mainland, is an active castle town. I wonder if someday I can take my new grandson Willie to such places in Wales instead of Disneyland. Conwy, like many Welsh towns, centered on a stupendous castle to explore or to climb for the views. We took tea with apple pie on High Street; then while Ed looked for paper supplies, I walked around photographing the window boxes and baskets of flowers that dangled from most shops, the flowers flourishing far above dog level. Riotously blooming, not a dried-up one to be seen, densely planted, these blaring bouquets made the streets gay and cared for. "What kind of fertilizer do you use?" I asked a woman outside a bed and breakfast. I would love to be staying behind her bright blue door.

"Oh, any old thing," she replied. "Can't stop them." Petunias, ivy, impatiens, geraniums, campanula, lobelia, all planted by the armful, even fuchsias mixed with geraniums, shade or sun preference be damned. Breathtaking, a great big yellow and apricot trailing begonia basket hanging against a pale stone wall. This simple addition to the street rescued the whole block from drabness. Mainly for the name, we buy dinky pork pie, along with some Llanboidy cheddar. On the way out of Conwy, we stopped in at the Teapot Museum. After all, we're in England. The eccentric collection consists of more than a thousand teapots, some classic and pretty, some kitschy, and many outlandish, such as Princess Diana with bright yellow hair, a camel, a majolica fish swallowing another fish, Elvis, and a World War II tank. Crammed into one upstairs room, the collections seemed right at home in the castle wall mews.

At night we headed back to Mermaid House with the same lavish view as the great house at Plas Newydd.

Portmeirion—the entire town—is a **folie de grandeur** of Clough Williams-Ellis, who wanted to build the ideal village. His purpose was didactic—he meant to demonstrate that development could be for the good—but his result is peculiar. The village, constructed from 1925 to 1975, never became a real town with cheese monger and dry cleaners, but it did become a magnified toy town with an amalgamated Mediterranean flavor, quite surreal in the Welsh landscape. Now a hotel, with various tea and gift shops, the pretty village on the water feels like a TV set, which it has been. Only the garden, mostly white and blue, anchors Portmeirion in reality. I sketched the iron urns of bountiful snowy white hydrangeas and imagined having a few of their square wrought-iron structures made for Bramasole's roses to climb. As in every Welsh garden, banks of hydrangeas, these a lighter blue, drifted around the park at the town's center. A sublime climbing rose of flat white blooms and pink buds obscured the front of one house. We didn't linger; pretty as Portmeirion was, we found it artificial. I kept thinking of Asolo in the Veneto, a town even lovelier, with real people living and working there, moving easily through layers of time.

Bodnant was also someone's dream, but only of a house and large garden. We glanced at the upright Tudor mansion, perkier than most, with many pointed dormers and crisp white paint between the beams. The sublime first impression of wide terraces above the river Conwy and views of mountains only began the extravagant delights of Bodnant. We thought we were late for roses, but in July they were blooming, especially the pinks. Many were new to me: Octavia Hill's flopping pale clusters; Ann Aberconway, a satin beauty; Rose Gaujard, white with rosy edges; the glorious many-petaled, open-faced Prima Ballerina and, nearby, the similar Picadilly; and the cupped Superstar, exactly the color of watermelon. Another big spender was the splendid yellow rose with the unlikely name of Grandpa Dickson. Boule de Neige, a white miracle with yellow center, changed my opinion of white roses with its delicacy. I've always associated white roses with Mother's Day in the Methodist church of my childhood. Wearing a white rose symbolized that the mother was dead. The rest of us wore red. This particular ball of snow looks distinctly felicitous, not at all sad. Another rose I immediately envisioned planting in my own garden was Glenfiddich, named for the amber Scotch whiskey or the place it's bottled, I suppose, but reminding me of a decadent, burnished yellow-silk slip my mother wore. The veined petals looked bloodshot—like the eyes of someone who drank too much Glenfiddich. I will have to tell my friends Susan and Bernice about City Girl, a saucy little social climber of apricot and pink blooming in bouquets like Sally Holmes.

Although vast, the garden felt totally scaled for enjoyment. Usually gardens are most interesting around the house. When I take outlying paths into woods and dales, my attention is not held. But following Bodnant's woodland paths seems like stepping into a "Sleeping Beauty" landscape. The hydrangeas, lining the banks of the languid little river Hiraethlyn, mimicked the flow of water. Blurry blue reflections doubled the dreaminess. The woods were silent, except for sparkling river sounds. Any minute Peter Pan might have popped out from behind a rock. We might step inside a fairy ring.

"We're in the presence of these trees," I said. Thanks, Henry Duncan. He took over this garden in 1902, continuing the tradition of his grandfather, who began planting trees in 1792. Enchanting, the sun-dappled ferns, the dark-leaved rhododendrons, and the circuitous walk over streams and through glades of straw-colored light.

At the end we came to a long pergola of laburnum. The sun shone through the filigree of leaves, and we dawdled there, imagining the dazzling gold arch in full bloom.

"Isn't that what Rebecca took a fatal dose of—laburnum? In high school I always wondered what it was. Now I know."

"Who? Oh, Daphne du Maurier? I never read **Rebecca**." Ed bought a postcard in the gift shop of the tunnel of bright yellow. "This must be one of the most outstanding accomplishments of any garden in the world. Imagine the bees and butterflies it draws."

"And tourists. Any one of whom could nibble the little black seeds and croak on the spot." We'd enjoyed Bodnant with only a few others that day.

"Let's come back. When the laburnum is blooming, you must feel like you're sleepwalking under here. Or like you're standing in a shower of gold. Are you sure it wasn't laudanum she swallowed?"

Back at the house, we took a last walk along the water. The tide was out. A man out in the mud hauled in the edible seaweed we saw for sale in Bath. The late sunlight seemed liquid, a faded watercolor with pastels smearing the sky into the water already rushing back into the channel from the sea. "Ready to take off?" Ed asked.

"Yes, let's go. Try to exit by eight tomorrow."

• • •

Aiming vaguely for the Cotswolds, we drove through Loughborough, the town where my great-great-grandparents and my great-grandparents were born. My grandfather was born in nearby Leicester. We passed a large cemetery with ancient trees. "Maybe some of the Mayeses are in there. Stop! Let's look." We combed the cemetery but found no family name. We were startled to come upon three men lying in the grass. Were they waiting for burial? But one rose on his elbow and said they were caretakers, having a nap after lunch. I was surprised because the cemetery had a forlorn appearance, with tipped and collapsed graves, caved in so that if you lifted a few stones, you might see a femur or jawbone. Not a posy in the place. I'd never seen such an abandoned graveyard, except in San Miguel de Allende once, where small boys played soccer with a skull, and I picked up one myself, a child's, and have it still. The sleepy one told us he had no record of burials but to call Nelly Callahan at the registry office in town. We finished combing the other half. I half-hoped no ancestor lay there and half-hoped that the next Elizabeth I saw—Elizabeth must have been in the top-ten names in the 1800s—would be my great-grandmother, Elizabeth Repton Mayes. But she lies elsewhere. I wish I'd asked more genealogy questions before my relatives died. Such a small clutch of stories, ending with my grandfather at nine sailing alone to America to join his father and his new wife. Elizabeth Repton, his mother, had died, leaving him and a sister, Lily. I never knew why she stayed behind when the nine-year-old Jack set off with a bag of apples and a small suitcase. Loughborough seems oddly like an American town. Short on charm, it was at least thriving and rather pleasant. I wonder about those Mayeses—what they did, where they lived. When we stopped in a pub, I asked the waitress if I could see a telephone book. I find Mayes at least sixty times. In San Francisco there are five.

Mrs. Callahan called me back after an hour of searching and said no Mayes is buried in a municipal cemetery. She directed me to the Leicester Historical Society and to local parish churches. Ed looked alarmed. The Mayes clan's graves will have to wait for their armfuls of roses.

• • •

By late afternoon we'd checked into a country house in Hambleton, a hamlet with a church and graveyard that could have been a model for Thomas Gray's "Elegy Written in a Country Churchyard," where those whose hearts were "once pregnant with celestial fire" slept in their narrow cells. After the drive from Wales, we walked to unkink. Thatched, calendar-perfect homes with bountiful gardens of yellow hollyhocks and roses lined the road. This was the day for churchyards. Among Hambleton's leaning stones and majestic trees, mourning doves cooed in iambics, and I thought of Gray's "moping owl." The poem seemed dreary and sentimental to me when I read it in college. Later, I saw some of the hard perceptions which his soft decasyllables perhaps glossed. The homiletic inscriptions on the gravestones, he wrote, "teach the rustic moralist to die." At the end of one verse, Gray asks if anything can salvage you:

> **Can storied urn or animated bust**
> **Back to its mansion call the**
> **fleeting breath?**

Can Honour's voice provoke the silent dust,
Or Flatt'ry soothe the dull cold ear of Death?

The answer is a resounding, nihilistic **no**, despite the poem's reputation for romanticism.

Death has a whole different construct here than in Italy, where photo- and flower-bedecked graves keep a continuum with life. The Cortona cemetery, just below the town, replicates the walled town. The graves are lighted at night by votives. You can imagine the dead rising as though from siesta to converse with their friends. These hallowed English stones go solemn immediately and provide no comfort of denial. Even recent burials blend quickly with the most ancient dead.

Like the priory where we spent the first night in England, the hotel where we sought refuge was a manor. We were guests of the lord, paying guests. In the bar, luxuriating in the tempting menu while we had a drink, the owner joined us. He was happy to see Americans. The terrorist scare had kept them at home. "The field is thinning," he said. "There just are not rich

Americans driving up with their chauffeurs anymore." Having driven there in a rented car of the anonymous sort, we simply smiled and nodded. A man and woman at the bar discussed a rally in London in support of fox hunting. "Does four hundred years of tradition mean nothing?" I heard her say. "They're the ones who are barbaric," he scoffed. Scotland recently banned hunting with dogs, and passage of the same law was imminent in England. The House of Commons voted 253–0 in favor of abolishing hunting foxes with dogs—then the bill mired in committee regulations. The foxes feel frisky; soon they'll be free. The woman, middle-aged with fluffy blondish hair, wore a bright flowered dress with big sleeves, belt, and gathered skirt. "Where did she get that dress?" I wondered to Ed. "I haven't seen a dress like that since the one I wore to the junior-senior prom. I loved that dress. I like hers! It's so anti-chic. Mine was white organdy, floor length and strapless, printed with violets."

"She got it out of the same closet where he got that rusty vintage jacket. He looks like the Duke of Windsor. You know they send people out to fill the foxholes the night before a hunt?

That doesn't seem sporting." The waiter refilled our champagne glasses. "What do you think of the fox-hunting law?" Ed asked him.

The waiter smiled. "I'm from Romania. Foxes are vermin there."

Ed raised his glass to me. "Tally-ho." He looked at the couple. "Do you think his jacket reminds him of being 'in the pink'?"

"That dress reminds me of all the gardens here, all splashy and glazed after a rain. Maybe the English just love their gardens so much they want to **wear** them. Ah! Come to think of it, maybe all the flowered chintz sofas and chairs and beds come from the same impulse—to bring the garden inside the house. A counter to the rainy weather."

"I'm happy. I'm happy that we don't have to have an opinion on fox hunting. I'm happy to have, at least, passed over the ground of my ancestors." The waiter brought a plate of delicate morsels—sliced zucchini with a dab of ratatouille on each, a twist of pastry with duck inside, potato puffs, kebabs of chicken and cucumber, and silver spoons filled with tomato mousse.

Soon we moved to the dining room, Ed quoting Oscar Wilde on fox hunting as we walk down the hall: "the unspeakable in full pursuit of the uneatable."

This pastoral landscape and the Rutland Waters, a large man-made reservoir that looks like a piece of the Lake District, turned out to be so lovely that we decided to come back for a week someday. From here I could make the journey to Leicester to check out the family tree.

We explored nearby towns, walked twice a day, and read in our big bedroom decorated with a raj motif. When we found nearby Stamford, we wondered if could live happily ever after there. A dignified, intact town full of its own life, Stamford has kept pure its inheritance of gray stone. Narrow streets, like Italian **vicoli**, cutting between larger streets, add medieval shadows. I liked the tiny shops, where from the middle desk a person could reach almost anything. Right in the center of town we came upon a cemetery, which doubled as a small park right across from the library and the bank. In most places on the globe, that cemetery would have been dozed long ago. A man read his paper on a bench just beside William Hare, who departed this life aged twelve and had been resting there calmly since 1797. We stopped for nut and ginger biscuits with tea, passing up a variety of traybakes—chocolate, tipsy, apricot almond, and sultana. "What is a traybake?" I asked the lady at the cash register.

"Oh, just something baked on a tray. Like that." She had a voice like a bicycle bell. She pointed to the pans in the window. "Trays." Another one of those little differences between English English and American English. She was pointing to what was essentially a small cookie sheet with slightly higher sides. English desserts—all that voluptuous cream and ripe fruit. Even the names imply that you will be comforted and cosseted by a plate of sticky tealoaf, sticky toffee pudding, oatmeal biscuits, or jam roly-poly.

Oakham, too, was a town of character. We bought a sturdy plaid market basket, had lunch, and meandered. In the pharmacy, while Ed bought Band-Aids, I looked at the baby food. Since Willie joined our family, I've liked looking at the foods for infants for sale in different countries, a microview of the country's cuisine. Here I find pea and parsnip, carrot and parsnip, peachy porridge, creamed porridge, oats and prunes, banana, and cream fool. In Italy, it's prosciutto and peas, pasta, pigeon, veal, even minced horsemeat. What cultural message does the baby absorb? Perhaps the English baby is lulled by mild flavors, while the bambino gets the message early on that the world tastes savory and varied. That might change with a little Winston's first taste of bangers and mash or bubble and squeak. Even during his first months, Willie was treated by Ed to aroma training. He held espresso, shrimp, ribs, and toast under Willie's nose. He looked consistently startled and interested.

A speciality of this area, pork pie is baked in a crust made with hot water. Such a sturdy pie won't break if carried in a saddlebag, I read. Local pigs are especially succulent because they're raised on the whey left over from the Stilton-making process. When we bought a fluted pork pie to taste, it was lardy and dense—maybe good to eat after filling in foxholes, but not appealing on a warm July day.

A gardener famous on British TV opened his garden called Barnsdale a few years ago. Early in the morning we had it to ourselves except for a couple of workers who were rendered catatonic by their hoes' rhythmic chopping of weeds. This was a teaching garden, divided into areas such as cottage garden, typical suburban backyard, kitchen garden. We found several ideas for our own plots. In the orchard CDs on strings twinkled from the branches and bamboo poles, keeping birds from eating the fruit. They looked rather magical. Asparagus, planted in an ornamental bed of flowers, looked soft and ferny. Recycled plastic water bottles had been halved, and the top part, with cap off, placed over new plants like the glass cloches in French gardens. This protects them from slugs while keeping in moisture and warmth and allowing them to breathe. I'm going to try this next spring when I plant tomatoes from seed. Crisp white bee boxes were used as focal points in divided gardens, instead of the usual nymph or shepherdess. Ed admired a compost box about five by twelve feet divided into three parts, one side of which had boards that slid up for removal of soil. We watched several voles darting from border to border, adorable and probably the reason for the recycled water bottles. I stood eye to eye with swaying yellow hollyhocks everywhere, sunny and cheerful. I wished I were in my own garden, fertilizing the lemons and training the morning glories up the pergola. I love how the British gardens all have so many places to sit, so many arbors, armillaries, arches—how **furnished** they are. I photographed an urn dripping with lantana, fuchsia, petunias, impatiens—who would think to combine those? Then I realize that in my two climates, you couldn't. Lantana and petunias like sun, while the unprotected fuchsia and impatiens would shrivel in one day in the heat of Italy or California. The cool and rainy English climate seems to encourage strange bedfellows.

At the urging of Mr. Hart, our host, we visited Burghley, a supergrand house in a vast deer park. We went, despite my allergy to such places, which I developed one year after seeing one too many French châteaux. In Burghley's kitchen some strange soul saved all the turtle skulls boiled clean when soup was made and arranged them in a pyramid on one wall. Immense copper pots and long work tables conjured a vision of mincemeat pies and of a pig roasting on a spit. I read that the smallest man in the world once was served in a venison pie as a surprise for the resident earl and his wife. Outside the kitchen we passed through a room with one wall covered in bells, each one labeled with a room designation so the servant would know where to hie himself. A long tour through corridors and wings, under the tutelage of a knowledgeable guide, confirmed my resolve to avoid these tours. Even though the house is filled with lively portraits, the lifeless rooms with impeccably restored bed hangings, porcelain **objets**, and don't-touch atmosphere made me want to run. Surprisingly, at the end we came to an immense horror-house stairway painted with the huge open maw of hell. Skeletons, death holding a mask, winged demons, and a vile eagle eating the liver of Prometheus completed this bit of interior decoration. The guide explained that the populace, seeking audience with the master, was suitably cowed on the way into his august presence. I wondered. We'd seen the opposite, the pious family chapel. Then turtle skulls and a dwarf baked in a pie. I thought the earl was just a real kinky guy. The last room, lofty with a fantastic Elizabethan ceiling, had a silver wine cooler large enough to bathe even a normal-sized man. After the stag hunts, it must have been filled with a thousand bottles of claret.

On the Friday our next rental began, we drove to Chipping Norton on the edge of the Cotswolds. My book pinpointed dozens of gardens I wanted to see in this area. The house would be large for us, but it was a last-minute rental and we thought, looking at the photo of

Old Chalford Manor Beech House, that we would cook a great feast and invite friends from London down for a day in the country. In the photographs the exterior was stately and inviting, while the interior looked gracious, with marbled hallway, and enough bedrooms for a sorority. As we followed the directions out of Chipping Norton, we were not exactly in idyllic countryside. We were zipping down a two-lane major trunk road to Oxford. "I hope we won't be able to hear this traffic," Ed said. "How far off the road is the house?"

"Oh, I think it will be fine. It says take a left off this, then a right."

"Did the agent say it was in the country?"

"Well, I told them I only wanted a quiet place. I explained that we are writers. And that you hate any noise at all."

"Good." Then we found the left turn, then immediately the right. The house was spitting distance from the busy road. We stared at each other.

Inside we could hear the constant **vroom, vroom** of motorcycles and see the tops of trucks whizzing by the wall that separated the house from the onslaught. Fascinating how a house inescapably reflects the owner. At the entrance we were greeted with a sign in boldface: PROPERLY PARKED? REMEMBER TO PARK ONLY WHERE DESIGNATED. In the foyer we faced NO BICYCLES, SCOOTERS, ETC. ARE ALLOWED INSIDE THE HOUSE, OF COURSE. I especially liked that **of course**! There were even "no smoking" signs tucked into the hunting prints that decorated the hall. Inside the cupboards were taped lists: TWENTY EGG CUPS, SIX WOODEN MATS, TWO TOAST RACKS . . . My favorite was PENALTY CHARGES WILL BE LEVIED FOR RUBBISH NOT CLEARED. Ed pointed out PLEASE DO NOT ALTER THE TIME CONTROLS and DO NOT MOVE THE FURNITURE and PLEASE DO NOT STICK ANYTHING ONTO THE WALLS. He opened the fridge and called me. "I'm fascinated by the **mind** that created this instruction: DO NOT PUT SODA CANS IN THE VEGETABLE BINS." Ed thumbed through a notebook full of admonishments and instructions. "If you're a hammer," he said, "all you see is nails."

These oh-so-anal admonishments we could ignore, but the traffic astounded me. I reluctantly walked to the house next door and learned that the owner was away. "In Tuscany," her daughter (no sign of damage from **über**-Mama) said blithely, "and no one ever complained before." Isn't that a well-known psychological strategy? Quickly pull the rug. Who rents a vacation house on a highway?

And so we left. And so we find ourselves comfortable at last in the little schoolhouse, which our U.S. agent arranged, even though the Beech House owners refused to give a refund. How might I have avoided this? The agent was appalled. She had not been told about the road noise in all the owner's elaborate description of the place. Mental note: agent must have physically visited property.

Basta! Onward.

Ed has adapted to driving down a mirror quite easily. I occasionally feel the urge to put on the brake or accelerate from my side of the car because we remember the friend of a friend on her first day in England who looked the wrong way before crossing and was mown down by an oncoming truck. As we drive the lanes of the bucolic countryside, patched with hamlets of butterscotch-colored thatched houses and hollyhock gardens, my vocabulary has shifted poles from the austere words—**essential, stony, stark, elemental, harsh, lonely**—that described Spain. **Cozy, cosseted, charming, adorable, sweet,** I'm saying. As I point to a storybook house with shining mullioned windows and an energetic climbing rose arching over the door, Ed says, "You have to watch that word **cute**."

"Okay," I answer, "but really, wasn't Lower Slaughter the sweetest place on earth? Even the rivers are well behaved, as if they flow through only for ornamentation." Everywhere described as "honey-colored," the stone houses **are** that color, but some are dark like chestnut honey, some pale like acacia or linden honey. Every few miles the geology shifts enough to change the shade of the limestone. Like Tuscan farms, the houses seem to have grown out of the land rather than been built. Because of their serene beauty and their ease in the landscape, the Cotswold houses are among the most pleasing domestic buildings in the world.

"They give awards around here for the 'tidiest' villages. I wonder if it's just too tidy for words." He slows to look at a field of blue lupin with a fold of sheep sleeping under a beech tree. "Even the sheep look clean here. Remember the knotted old herds in Portugal gnawing on dead weeds?" He brakes. Across the road three horses in wavy grass look up at us. "Perfect," Ed says. "Why has no one ever ruined it?"

"I know—that's horrible. We expect ruin?"

"Well, much of the world has been ruined. Not here. I just didn't expect so much beauty. I've slept like someone administered knock-out drops. Maybe it comes from counting all these sheep." He drives on, down the green-tunneled road. A golden light sieves through the trees. "Let's find a tea shop. Time for plum and ginger pie or strawberry and apple crumble."

" 'Gravy and potatoes in a good brown pot. Put them in the oven and eat them while they're hot.' " I'm thinking, not for the first time, about the books my daughter memorized when she was three.

"I can't even guess what that's from."

"I believe you've heard a direct quote from Miss Tiggie Winkle in a Beatrix Potter book. Plum and ginger pie reminded me. That's something Jemima Puddle-Duck might have liked, or Peter Rabbit. Or maybe gooseberry tart with clotted cream."

"The desserts are worth a detour around here."

"Except for spotted dick."

"Should I ask what that is?"

"Raisins in a steamed dough. Raisins are the spots. Dick is the pudding they're in, so—spotted dick."

"Sounds like a disease the British Army picked up in colonial jungles."

"'Dick' relates to dough; dog and duff, too. You've heard of plum duff, haven't you? They're old recipes, some with suet. They're covered in custard sauce—which makes anything good. Actually, a big supermarket chain tried to change spotted dick to spotted Richard because women customers were squeamish about asking for it."

"I'll stick to plum and ginger pie, **mille grazie**, just the same. Custard sauce—blaaa."

"Think crème anglaise, and it'll taste better. Just north in Mickleton the hotel Three Ways House is totally devoted to English puddings—even their bedrooms are named Oriental Ginger Pudding, Summer Pudding, Sticky Toffee and Date Pudding, Lord Randall's Pudding."

"That sounds as if it would promote sweet dreams."

"They have the Pudding Club there, which anyone can join. They meet on the first and third Fridays for dinner, which is served with seven traditional puddings. 'Lashings of custard' are promised."

"Seven? One is enough. So rich."

As we drive to gardens, we listen to radio plays on the BBC. They're addictive. We don't get out of the car when we arrive at the garden. We have to hear the end.

Chipping Campden's houses are the color of toast, of the wheat ripening in the nearby fields, and many are thatched. They are shockingly beautiful and mellow. This area is the ancestral home of the famous Cotswold sheep, known as the Cotswold Lion, whose fleecy wool was sold all over medieval Europe. Even today more sheep make up the census than humans. **Chipping**, from Anglo-Saxon **ceapen**, means "market." Many of the Cotswold towns still have the lively market air they must have had when wool merchants made their fortunes and the farmers herded their flocks down the many Sheep Streets to sell. The fine country churches, indebted to those merchants, are known as "wool churches." Chipping Campden has an excellent bakery, numerous tearooms lavish in their use of clotted cream, and cheerful shops adorned with hanging baskets. Also, one of the most famous gardens in England, Hidcote Manor, lies just outside town, with Kifsgate and numerous others nearby.

Hidcote lavender attracts all the butterflies in Tuscany to my garden. The name comes from here. For the avid gardener, Hidcote deserves several visits. I always think about garden "rooms." This garden abundantly illustrates that concept. Tall hedges outline rooms, with doors cut into them. Within a room a plethora of flowers madly spilling and bolting and climbing creates an intimate space, like a room in a Vuillard painting. Big sweeps of lawn break up the room idea, as does the simple dignity of an aisle of hornbeam trees. These extravagant lawns keep the ten-acre garden from becoming claustrophobic. Hidcote was developed by Lawrence Johnston, who used to winter with Edith Wharton on Hyères. He was influenced by her book **Italian Villas and Their Gardens**. I spot the influence in the architecture of the hedges and the staginess of the lawns, one of which ends with a raised bed where theatricals might have been performed if there had not been a beech tree planted right in the middle.

The hedges sometimes ascend into a topiary cut, a stylized bird that makes you smile when you see it. That, too, is an Italian touch. Starting from farmland, Lawrence Johnston had fun sculpting these walls. Did he begin with foot-high plants? In odd contrast to the classic lawns with busts and yew borders, Hidcote does several flip-flops and also features elements of cottage-style Arts and Crafts gardens. A ginger cat curls under a bamboo teepee of sweetpeas. Every English garden should have a sleeping cat. We suddenly spot a rose similar to our mystery rose at Bramasole. We've searched every book, as well as Cavriglia in Tuscany, the largest private rose garden in the world, and have not found this rose, which survived the thirty years of neglect our house suffered. A peonylike form, our rose blooms only once in early summer, but the flowers are profuse and the scent divine. I step out every morning and press my face against many blossoms, breathing in enough heart-of-rose scent to last all summer. The few renegades thrown out later in the summer lack that ethereal perfume. The one we find at Hidcote is Empress Josephine. Ed thinks the leaf is different. Then we spot another similar rose: Surpasse Tout, also a Gallica. The bud looks more like our rose's ball-shaped bud. I write down the names and will order them for a comparison. Probably neither will be exactly the same. Maybe the **nonna** I always imagine grafted a friend's rose onto one of hers.

Roses have unattractive feet, but often I've been told not to underplant because the rose won't like it—advice I've ignored. At Hidcote short lilies surround the roses. Hurrah! They look spectacular. I, too, have lilies under a few roses. I'll become bold. One hundred yellow lily bulbs; I can already imagine the bees. I love the blue metal benches, the small poles with eye hooks in the beds for the clematis to climb—a moment of height. A pink rose garden is planted with mixed blue and purple flowers clustered beneath. Lovely. Iron arches, around four feet high, give the roses something to lean on without the rigidity of a stake. I have wanted to make a bed of roses, a literal bed. I see that I can simply make the head and foot from two arches and add crossbars. Hidcote has a classic ha-ha, basically a broad ditch that prohibits animals from escaping. The genius of a ha-ha is that it does not break into the view separating the garden from the fields. From a few feet back, they simply merge.

Across the road from the entrance, we drive into the privately owned Kifsgate Garden, which has a more intimate feel than Hidcote. This garden is rare—a project of women plant collectors and guardian angels since 1920. The position, lovelier than Hidcote's, looks toward the poetically named Vale of Evesham. But why compare, just because they're across the way from each other? Both are remarkable gardens. I marvel at the long yellow border spiked with blue and the paths not edged but utterly romantic with profligate lavender and mallow and cotton lavender. The famous Kifsgate rose, reputed to be the largest in the world, must be glorious in early summer. I write in my notebook: **Love the pink valerian mixed with campanula. If deerproof, plant Allium rosenbachianum in California**. These tall fist-sized pink balls are a type of garlic plant. They're fun exclamation points in a flower bed. A smaller, darker version grows wild on our hillsides in Italy, and I've always picked it to mix in bouquets. This taller version would be wonderful in my California garden, which is planted to look like a natural hillside.

• • •

Meandering around several villages and visiting two gardens fills a day. After pub lunches, we have salad and cheese at night back at our schoolhouse, treating ourselves to bowls of prime strawberries with double cream for dessert. The bad luck of renting two wretched houses has been mitigated by the enormous good luck with the weather. Except for a ten-minute shower one morning, we've had sunny days and blessed temperatures in the high seventies. At night we sit out in the garden with a glass of wine planning the next day. We're appreciating the oh-so-British names, pronunciations, and expressions. **To truffle around,** to look for something. **Ke bab**, not **ke bob**. **Past ah**—like **past**—for pasta. This grates, especially since so many English people go to Italy constantly. Ed's favorite is **rumpy-pumpy**, which we heard on a radio play. It took only a moment to realize what it meant. The image **rumpy-pumpy** calls up—a rump the color of a boiled pig pumping away—is rather horrifyingly comic. We passed Cromp Butt Lane and Old Butt Lane along the way. Crinkley Bottom is a town over in Somerset. We like **bolthole** and **clootie dumplings** and **singin' hinney**, a bread with currants. Sometimes in the South I heard **hinney** for donkey, and we wonder if the bread brays, like bubble and squeak squeaks. Or maybe **hinney** is dialect for honey.

The market town nearest our little schoolhouse is Stow-on-the-Wold, also with a Sheep Street. If we were moving to the Cotswolds, this is where we would aspire to live, within a few miles of this friendly, bustling village. I mourn the loss of small bookstores in America. Stow has several. "No, dear, we don't have that, but you're not missing anything," I'm told when I ask for a recent Booker Prize–winner's book. On the way to the cheese shop and the wine shop, I begin to feel at ease here. Maybe it was buying a book by a writer who lives in these parts, Joanna Trollop. Like Anita Brookner, her books often feature women on their own, cast into a domestic or personal crisis. They're well-written Aga Sagas, a term—not derogatory—for women's relationship novels. Aga, of course, is the stove of choice for British households. I've already been devouring Penelope Lively, whose memoir about growing up in Egypt I liked last year. Since Lively knows this area, I read two novels, looking for clues about living here. But I find that her writerly detachment from her adopted landscape keeps the **place** at a distance. In Italy,

I realize, I have not sought such detachment myself, although when I moved part of my life there, I intended to maintain just such a separation between home and Tuscany. Italy would be a place to write, a place to have friends visit, a locus for travel. Against my will, Italy slowly became home. My long internal, secret desire to return to the American South, where I was born and grew up, slowly dissolved. All my adult life I'd felt exiled and I am shocked, but the South of Tuscany became home for me, who had no Italian ancestor, not a drop of Mediterranean blood. By the time that happened, I felt a strange rapture within. Another landscape had taken over, taken me in, shaped me to its own requirements, pleasures, and history. If I lived **here**, I probably would start making cheese and collecting teapots. I have a feeling this place would **take** me. I'd get heather-hued sweaters, a golden retriever, and a large umbrella, take up knitting, and become a strictly no-nonsense, practical village woman who volunteered at the church jumble sale.

Stow has a tall limestone cross in the center of town, an old reminder to be good while sheep trading at the market. This large open center could function as a piazza for the citizens were it not filled with cars. Maybe so much rain makes parking close to the action a necessity, but the town would be drastically altered for the good if pedestrians ruled rather than cars. I collect several cheeses, bottles of damson and peach cordial to take home, and a bottle of elder flower and apple, which I've been drinking in place of the iced tea that is nowhere to be found in this land of purist tea drinkers. In the South where I grew up, our iced tea was mixed with pineapple juice, lemon, and sugar. Egregious, I'm sure, to the English sensibility. My grandmother steeped elder flowers for wine, which my father swore could cause blindness. In the bakery I find Sally Lunn, something my mother used to make. This legendary bread originated in seventeenth-century Bath, either by someone named Sally Lunn or by a Frenchwoman who made buns and hawked them, calling **"sol et lune."** The tea shop remains open on North Parade Passage in Bath. In the basement Roman ruins reveal that the building was used for preparing foods even in Roman times. This Stow version of Sally Lunn is nothing like my mother's. Perhaps her recipe mutated after years in America. Hers was a light, light sweet cake but was served with meals. Southerners like sweet touches with their dinners. This Sally Lunn is a yeast bread, rather lumpy looking, possibly improved with a slathering of raspberry jam.

The butcher, the baker—this way of shopping is my favorite. The scale is right. I meet Ed, coming in from a countryside walk. He takes my packages, and because we are currently garden-mad, he buys a bunch of delphinium, larkspur, and foxglove for the schoolhouse dining room.

In Woodstock we skip Winston Churchill's birthplace, Blenheim Palace, having seen it years ago. In an old, old pub, The Bear, we have lunch in the bar, then walk. Each town's little shops speak for life there. We see a sign, HATS FOR HIRE. The butcher shop is adorned with flowers. I am so happy to see the Winchester Glove Shop and Harriet's Tea Rooms. There's even an Aga store with a purple stove in the window and a teapot shaped like the stove.

From Woodstock we drive to Rousham Gardens, entering near a conservatory path crowded with apricot lilies and lavender. The crenellated house with statues in niches looks Jacobean with Italian overlays. Even from the forecourt, Rousham seems like someone's personal garden, and it is. Since 1635 the property has been in the same family. The garden, first designed by Charles Bridgeman (inventor of the ha-ha), was taken over by William Kent in 1738. He began life as a coachman but somehow got to Rome, where he lived and painted for ten years. He made a living buying paintings and selling them to the English aristocracy, then gradually metamorphosed into an architect and designer. Rousham survives intact and offers a textbook lesson on the fascination of the English for Roman culture.

We walk first through the gardens nearest the house. Walled gardens are the ultimate garden rooms. At eleven I loved **The Secret Garden**, locked and overgrown, a place for transformation. This one we glimpse through a lacy iron gate. Flower beds are backed by ancient apples, formerly espaliered, now just on their own with their leafy arms spread as if they were protecting the winsome carnations, yarrow, Peruvian lilies, and sweetpeas that climb teepees made of twiggy branches. At home in Italy, Beppe, our farmer, makes these same teepees for the beans and peas in the **orto**, our vegetable garden. All the gardens I've seen have variations of this teepee. Some are iron; most are willow. The willow or twig teepees suit the casual grace of the ever-blooming, abundant style of English garden design. Rule of green thumb: plant twice as much. Another rule: forget rules, forget order—blowsy is best. Another: no sharply edged beds—let the flowers creep and flop onto the path or grass border. Some beds are backed with espaliered plum trees, clusters of ripe damsons like great garnets ripening against a stone wall.

So many ideas. The caves and playhouses formed inside thick hedges would be paradise for children to play spooky games. Rousham has a cutting garden within the kitchen garden, where they're growing enough asparagus to feed the Cotswolds. The strawberries grow in a patch of straw, with a screen cover staked at the four sides. Light dawns—that's why they're called strawberries. With each plant separated, you can see exactly how many bowls of luscious berries you have for dinner. I see Ed studying this method, too. "Ours is a mess. The birds get more than we do. What if we move it up a terrace higher and build this kind of frame?"

"I'd love that. I hate putting down my hand in there—I'm always thinking I'm going to touch a snake."

A later Rousham designer loved circles. A small round pond stands at the center of a large circle of roses. Four iron arches at the cardinal points lead in and out. Between the arches the circle is maintained by a few poles, with wire running between. Some roses are trained on the poles, some are free-standing. Quite simple, and a very clever design! This circle garden could transform a plain square backyard. I give wide berth to a peacock strolling through the rose garden dragging his train. He stops by the delphinium because his feathers sport the exact same blue. I was once attacked by a peacock at Warwick Castle, and the memory forms part of my old bird phobia.

A characteristic Cotswold dovecote, like a chopped-off tower topped with a conical roof, anchors one area. Against it grows an espaliered cherry bright with fruit.

Almost three hundred years later Kent's design philosophy, "Nature abhors a straight line," still guides well. Around the house the garden is similar to others, although I find it more vivacious, but away from the house we suddenly see

Kent's mind at work. "This is exciting—early, early landscape design," I say. We pass statues and a folly, a serpentine, stone-lined rill that mysteriously quotes the Arab gardens in the Alhambra. "This is theory in action. He was in love with Roman gardens."

"And England was once all Roman, of course. So it has double roots."

We stop for a pastoral view. "This looks like a painting. The rural distance seems placed there for our benefit." Kent created landscape tableaux: a cold pool for dipping, an "eyecatcher" fake ruin, cunningly placed statues of Venus, Apollo, and Pan, a pond, a small columned temple looking down on the river Cherwell. "I remember that Kent also was a set designer for the theatre. It makes sense."

"Some gardens back then had resident hermits to add to the picturesque."

"Maybe each garden should take a few homeless people."

"We haven't seen a single homeless person in the Cotswolds."

"Is this your favorite? I like it the best."

"After Bodnant, yes. No, maybe I like this one more. Do I have to choose?"

"No, but let's go find a pub. I'm starving."

• • •

After lunch, sleepy and saturated with gardens, we press on regardless to Waddeson, the grandiose house and garden built by Ferdinand de Rothschild, that was picked up from the château country of France, whirled through Renaissance Italy, and miraculously set down in Buckinghamshire. The garden must live up to the fairy-tale architecture. The terrace level just behind the house makes another foray. A flamboyant fountain with horses reminds us of the Piazza Navona. The formal garden surrounding the fountain features built-up, squared-off mounds planted with primary red, with a few dashes of purple. Gray-green foliage tempers the effect somewhat, but it looks harsh and municipal. In fact, they love red here. New Guinea impatiens beds, surrounded by hens-and-chickens, also look quite bad. The weather is threatening, but no rain falls. We wander among the vast, hypnotic trees. Lots of naked boys holding grapes aloft and other classical statues punctuate the park. Friends are picnicking with folding tables and champagne glasses or lounging on the grass. Ed spots the grave of Poupon, a Rothschild dog. I'm not thrilled to come upon a wedding-cake aviary, though I like the confectionary demilune design. Ed visits all the birds, and I stand back. I do respond to one bird. Perhaps fifteen feet high, wittily placed in front of the aviary, the wire bird's plumage is made of clipped lavender, hens-and-chickens, and many other plants that cleverly outline feathers and wings. Two immense crowns in front of the house are also "carpet planted." A nineteenth-century idea, carpet bedding, now called Instaplant, is plotted by computer. The plants in trays slide into a form. Jeff Koons must have designed his giant flower puppy this way. Another playful focal point is an oversize—maybe twelve feet long—woven basket planted with herbs, nasturtiums, artichokes, and asparagus. The humor refreshes.

Scrawling on my garden guide, I note the names of several magnificent roses new to me. Gorgeous apricot Crown Princess Margereta grows in clusters. Mrs. Oakley Fisher reminds me of a flat rose I have in California, only Mrs. F. is creamy apricot. A must-have Crocus Rose radiates that happy icy salmon color.

I lean close to each, for the possibility of heady perfume. Most are what the rose books call "lightly scented," which usually means you can't smell a thing. In the gardens I've seen in England, scent does not figure as a major concern. Maybe you need fecund southern gardens for those hits of perfume that can make your head reel. I've always felt dizzy in the presence of gardenias. Is there some sedative element in the fragrance? The first gardens I knew, my mother's, our neighbor's, and my grandmother's, remain a secret joy. High-as-the-house azaleas to hide under; ruffled pink camellias to float in a bowl until the edges of the petals turn brown; dwarf nasturtiums to gather so the dolls could smell their volatile, spicy fragrance; tough St. Augustine grass lawns to cartwheel across; crape myrtle with bark—pearly gray on one side, russet on the other—to peel; tea olive to inhale in my bedroom when there blew the slightest night breeze on a calm summer night; bridal wreath to tie into crowns; daylilies to shelter my dog, Tish, napping on the cool side of the house; the honeysuckle where every summer the bees built their swarm.

I tell Ed all these memories. Except for red geraniums in urns on the porch, his parents' Winona garden was given over to vegetables—his daddy was a farmer until the age of thirty-five. They grew and pickled beets. Their potatoes and kohlrabi lasted into the cold weather, marrying well with the kielbasa, head cheese, and dill pickles his Polish mother made, along with several big loaves of bread every week. His strongest scent memory is lilac. He times his trips back to Minnesota to coincide with the lilac bloom. In California around Easter he always comes home with armfuls of lilac the minute it appears at the farmer's market. The California lilac's scent is faint but identifiable enough to transport him back to the lilac hedge behind his home in Winona.

We talk as we fall into the ritual of afternoon tea. I've never been a tea drinker, but I'm pouring several cups a day. Maybe the tannin counterbalances the sweet we inevitably order: today, peach crème brûlée with lime sorbet, and a little plate of cookies. Salad tonight.

We go into parish churches when we find them open. St. Kenelm in Minster Lovell may be our favorite. Minster Lovell's long street of thatched houses could win any "tidy" award. "Too much," Ed says. "Damn, can you believe yet another idyllic hamlet?" A fantastic ruined manor house's partial walls stand behind St. Kenelm. A remaining roof section looks precipitous. Two small girls in sundresses climb among the foundation rocks while their mother reads on a picnic blanket in the overgrown grass. I recognize the cover of **The Man Who Mistook His Wife for a Hat**. A small river, the Windrush, now with new ducks and two white swans, must have been a pleasure to those who lived in the house in the fifteenth and sixteenth centuries. A plaque says the house was dismantled in 1747. The stone walls remain over two and a half centuries later.

Inside the church Ed sees a list of vicars since 1184. A shaft of morning light strikes the tomb of a praying knight, turning the cold alabaster waxy and gleaming. Each of the box pews has six needlepoint cushions for kneeling. Some have names and dates worked into the patterns. In winter the worshipers must need them on the stone floors. Near the altar I run my fingers over the carving in a wooden chair. On the back, **The same yesterday**, and down the arms, **Jesus Christ, today and tomorrow**. How perfect for this hallowed place where the vicars go back to 1184 and the precipitous roof of the manor house peaks as it did yesterday, and the day before and before and before.

In nearby Burford, another bustling market town, we have an excellent dinner with an Australian Shiraz. Pubs, many mourn, are disappearing. But good numbers of them are converting to restaurants, like this one, with an emphasis on local products and traditional fare reinterpreted without the instant-cardiac-arrest fat factor. These are bistro or trattoria equivalents—homey atmosphere and honest food. There's nothing wrong at all with good pub food, but often you find microwaved, processed bangers, whipped potatoes from a box, and scary salads. We've seen several signs announcing PUB GRUB. We have come to know what that indicates. But the pub tradition is a hub of community. And the low-ceilinged, dark-wood atmosphere makes you feel that you've paused in a horse-drawn coach and alighted for a rest. Even though I don't often drink beer, I felt the impulse to order the amber foamy ales that Ed did. The pub/restaurant in Burford kept its cozy bar area but only as a place to wait for a table and have a drink. The local mates no longer gather there for a pint. Burford in the dark was deserted except for the warmly lighted Copper

Kettle tearoom. I thought of Christmas Eve, of buying pastry and bells and wrapping paper and socks, then stopping for soup there. The Cotswolds for the holidays—a perfect place.

Our last three gardens all have the highly personal touch. I am glad to get to see the garden of Rosemary Verey. Since her death Barnsley has been sold, fated to become an inn. Already the tennis court is seedy. The front yard, bordering a rather busy road, presents nothing special, but the back is eccentrically off-kilter and appealing. I sense the person who wanted the informality of a rope swing and a small wooden summerhouse on one side of the garden and a columned pavilion and pond on the other. Against the back wall, splayed bamboo trellises fan out for roses to climb. The garden is not large, but she has managed to squeeze in a small **allée**.

Her kitchen garden—such fun. Boxwood outlines beds, as in knot gardens, but she filled each bed with a taggy mix of vegetables and flowers. Simple flowers such as mallow, sweet-pea, larkspur, and cosmos go wild with onions or artichokes or corn. Tangles of parsley, a scarecrow with a bird on top of his head, four-foot-tall gone-to-seed lettuces, mint—a little **paradiso**. We laugh when Ed points to a bed of roses, garlic, and onions. What a sure hand shaped this **potager**. As at Rousham, I like the mind I see behind the composition. What pleasure it must have given her.

In the village of Barnsley we find one of those pubs gone gourmet. No bubble and squeak here. Ed orders seared pigeon breast with grilled pineapple, and I have artichoke, asparagus, and pea salad. I suddenly order a Wadsworth, the first whole beer of my life. Ed has a Hook Norton Bitter, and I like his, too.

Today we return to the schoolhouse to read, write, and sip one of the lightly sparkling organic Belvoir Pressé juices we're loving here. Nonalcoholic and not too sweet, they occupy the heretofore empty space between a soda and a glass of wine. The ginger and lime and the lime and lemongrass are perfect for enjoying the late sun in the garden. The tame northern sun feels like a balm.

• • •

English pronunciations often surprise, beginning with Worcestershire, which was fully pronounced in Georgia, where we used the sauce over steak, in oyster stew, and lord knows where else. **Wooster!** My great-great-grandparents' town of Loughborough is pronounced **Luftsborough**. At the winsome garden and house of Snowshill Manor, the ticket taker pronounces the name **snozzle**. I rather like **snozzle**. Sounds like the activity of garden voles or moles; they snozzle under the plants. We adore this classic cottage garden with foxgloves, ferns, lavender. Ed remarks that Snowshill is totally organic. Many gardens must remain only fantasies, but this two-acre plot, with a few years of diligence, seems within reach for a good gardener. Like an added-on farm, the house has the same haphazard charm as the garden. Did the original owner, Charles Wade, nail a line of horseshoes over a door? I read that he didn't sleep in the house but instead slept in what looks like a shed. The house had to be given over to his various collections. Ah, a proper eccentric. He thought only apricot, creamy yellow, blue, and mauve looked best against stone walls. Orange was banned from his garden. Boxwood balls grow in wine barrels. The garden descends a hill, which always interests me, passing stone steps and little ponds and garden houses and hollow places in walls for birds to nest. Again the room concept, as if the house simply opened to other rooms furnished by arranging nature. And beyond the garden, the vegetable garden. Mr. McGregor, where are you? The hills beckon. Requisite sheep roam about, ignoring all of us trooping up and down the hill.

Kelmscott, the summer home of William Morris, has quite a modest garden, with a three-hole privy in the back—more than you want to know about the leader of the Arts and Crafts movement. The gift shop is quite an ambitious enterprise, selling needlepoint, postcards, tea cozies, dish towels, wrapping paper, and the like, all in Morris's designs. Morris took his inspiration from the past, and to me, his stylized medieval patterns and muted colors become claustrophobic if taken in these large doses. We flee the gift shop and enter the garden, in search of the foliage, strawberries, rabbits, and flowers that inspired him.

Jane Burden, Morris's wife, had been the model for the paintings of Dante Gabriel Rossetti—the pin-up girl for the pre-Raphaelites—

when Morris met her. Rossetti painted her more than a hundred times. Morris fell for her even though he was from the upper class and she was the daughter of a stable groom. Rossetti and Morris leased Kelmscott House together, and despite the presence of William and Jane's two daughters, Jane and Rossetti conducted a flagrant love affair. Morris put up with their liaison for years, running off to Iceland when the heat became too much. Finally Jane tired of Rossetti. The rooms give no indication of extreme natures, but hers must have been. She is **the** beauty of the Arts and Crafts era. When Henry James met her, he found her mysterious, "a wonder," "a figure cut out of a missal," "a tall lean woman in a dress of some dead purple stuff . . . a thin pale face, a pair of strange, sad, deep, dark, Swinburnian eyes, and with great thick black oblique brows." Those five adjectives for her eyes reveal how hard James had to work to approach a description. As La Belle Iseult, she survives as Morris's only painting. When he died, the doctor said the cause was "being William Morris and having done more work than most ten men." But maybe life with Jane wore him out.

Morris was a person who lived on many creative levels at once, from typography to roses to gutters to textiles to stained glass. George Bernard Shaw's eloquent tribute took only two sentences: "You can lose a man like that by your own death, but not by his. And so, until then, let us rejoice in him."

As we walk around and look at the rooms, we think a vicar and his family could have lived here. Odd to think of a ménage à trois in this staid house and village. The gossip must have warmed the whole village on winter nights. Odd to think, too, of the fermenting artistic fervor, with influence on Europe, North America, and the far antipodes.

Ed notices the odd wooden gutters that jut way out from the house and pour into the yard. A stone walk lined with rose topiaries leads to the door, as it does in thousands of gardens where no Jane ever juggled two men. William and Jane must have forged a truce because they're sleeping soundly together on the edge of the churchyard.

On the last night in England, I order bangers and mash at the pub in Stow-on-the-Wold. I walk out feeling as though I'd swallowed a handful of lead sinkers. "I did it! It was great and greasy. A million grams of fat." We take a last walk around the shut village. No sheep are expected at market. Wine store, cheese store, drugstore, antique shops, bookstore, and the place with hats Queen Elizabeth might wear—all asleep, deeply asleep.

Washed by Time's Waters

Islands of Greece

At sea, the first surprise: the horizon becomes a circle. From land, the horizon seems ruler-drawn between ocean and sky. As I walk from stern to bow and back, thinking of intrepid explorers who feared the world was flat and sailed anyway, I watch the steady brushstroke of the horizon line, a curving cobalt mark overstruck with purple. Clearly, we could drop over that edge, our tiny ship falling through space forever. But we are sailing in the center of a blown-glass bowl filled to the brim.

Just yesterday the ship slipped out of the lagoon into the Adriatic. Already I see that something happens to time because I feel that we set sail a full moon ago and must be over to the next latitude.

"Somewhere between Calabria and Corfu," Lawrence Durrell writes, "the blue really begins." A few hours out of Venice the churning green-gray Adriatic shifted to intense blue and the water smoothed. I could walk or roll across this water. Our prow slicing the swells trailed scrolls of white marble. Easy to see how, when Saint Augustine touched something smooth, he began to think of music and God. I saw as far as I could see shimmering blue, out to that finite line navigators through the centuries aimed toward and beyond.

Because we're in high summer, friends in Cortona were astonished that we planned to travel in this direction. "You're going to Greece? Greece is finished," my friend Alain announced at dinner, his perfect French assurance combined with the throat-cutting gesture that years of living in Italy have made natural to his speech.

"Finished?" I said. "That can't be; I've never been."

"And summer—it is impossible," he continues. "Heat and mobs, mobs and heat." He plans to spend the summer at his stone house in the serene hills above Cortona. “Swarms,” he emphasized.

This I knew, but I had been invited to speak on a cruise ship, and of all their trips, only the blue Aegean pulled me. To sail out of La Serenissima! An old dream, to ply these waters: Corfu, Crete, Rhodes, Santorini, Piraeus, Náfplio, Volos, then over to the other side of the Aegean—Bodrum, Kusadasi, up to the fabled Bosporus. Irresistible—to disembark in Istanbul!

At first I refused the offer. My mother used to take cruises in the Carribean. I remember her talking about the constant eating—I’m easily tempted—and duplicate bridge games on the deck, with rum drinks arriving between every rubber. There was one incident in Barbados when her group was pelted with rotten oranges by the locals. Fortunately the stains came out of my mother’s pink linen dress.

But recently two friends took a Mediterranean cruise and came home raving about it. As I looked through their photographs of yellow and purple fish in the limpid waters of the Sinai, the moon-white cubical houses of Mykonos at sunset, and Peter perched on a camel, I started to dream of dropping anchor off Corfu's coast, sailing into the Rhodes harbor where the Colossus once stood, rocking to sleep in the ancient waters where Jason sailed, and of seaside tavernas with silhouettes of Knights Templar castles in the distance.

Finally I said yes because I have been haunted forever by the fateful pentameter lines: **And therefore I have sailed the seas and come/to the holy city of Byzantium**, from W. B. Yeats's "Sailing to Byzantium." When I think of the poem, the images of saffron-colored sails at sunrise and the reflection of a sleek white sailboat skim across the waves of my mind. All of Western history criss-crossed this sea. I too want to follow in the troughs of the Argonauts' wake.

With such lofty aspirations, I did not expect to make my mythic voyage on a ship that is twin to an American convention hotel. This giant floating tub is nautical on its decks, which are polished and furnished with proper teak chairs with proper marine-blue cushions. Inside, crystal chandeliers remain steady, miles of floral teal carpet cushion every step, and guests lounge on curved upholstered sofas designed to absorb sloshed drinks without stains. We are eight hundred on board, which seems like a floating town but is actually a midsize cruise ship.

In our cabin I can also feel that we are on a ship. Through our blurry porthole we see the water not far below. I hear odd sluicing sounds running under our beds. Those old navigators with their sextants, hourglasses, astrolabes, and gimbaled barometers surely slept in more comfortable quarters. We do have a little marble bath with a tub. The water flows clearly for a minute, then turns the hue of tea. Hepatitis? Staph infection? In the tiny room, about twice the size of my closet in California, each bed is narrow as a coffin. When Ed stands, the ceiling almost grazes the top of his head, and when he lies down, his feet hit the desk. My looming Gulliver. Last night he woke from a nightmare that the room was filling with water. Doesn't matter, we tell each other; we'll be on deck most of the time.

We arrived in Venice with more luggage than we've ever hauled on a trip. Having been on month-long book tours with carry-on luggage,

I am the master of light packing, but because the cruise has five formal events, we have brought a tuxedo (sleeves stuffed with tissue) with its starched shirts, my evening bags, dresses, and strappy high heels. All the paraphernalia required a bag of its own. I broke my own rules and also brought a bathrobe and too many linens that wrinkle. And we are a travelling library—guides, histories, and books of poetry stuffed in all the luggage pockets, lining the bottoms of bags and weighing down carry-ons. Ed, ever optimistic that he will have time to study Italian verbs, packed workbooks and texts, as well as the laptop, voice recorder, and earphones. Hannibal over the Alps—we almost sank the water taxi. "The word **portage** comes to mind," Ed said, as the driver lowered a bag into the boat in a controlled fall. He groaned and clutched his shoulder. Disembarking at the **fondamenta**, we fortunately had help hoisting the four bags to the hotel.

Looking for the camera, Ed rummaged to the bottom of one bag and said, "Do you know you have brought **twelve** pairs of shoes." We stashed three bags in the closet and walked out into Venice. We love this city. It is **the** walking city. The Basilica di San Marco could have been transported on a flying carpet from Constantinople/Byzantium and deposited in front of the million pigeons waiting for **biscotti** crumbs. The five domes and the church's rhythmic exterior look strangely squat, with that feeling of low horizontal spread that in mosques invites Muslims to fall to the floor in prayer. With the construction of this holy building beginning in 829, Venice became the first moment of the East. The four bronze horses, cut apart for the journey to Venice then reconnected, could rear and fly home to Constantinople. Many of the church's ornaments and crown jewels are spoils brought home to glorify the city by the Republic of Venice's aggressive conquerors of the Mediterranean. A glance, however, into the San Marco area on a steamy August day made us determined to stay away from the **centro**. Even in summer, that's easy. We visited the Rialto market for the buckets of breathing silver eels, the virtuoso artichoke peelers—thirty seconds and voilà! the clean heart—and the live spider crabs, and to inhale the briny sea smell from rainbow arrays of spiny, rocky, scaly fish and mollusks on ice.

I thought of all the shops for heavenly silks and cut velvet, the luxurious velour robes and pillows, and the artisan shops with vellum-bound books of paper that looks like communion wafers. With our bulging suitcases in mind, I didn't even mention those directions.

We walked to the Basilica di San Pietro, Venice's cathedral before San Marco landed from the skies. St. Peter's bell tower leans slightly, and the grounds are weedy. No one was there except a monk nodding in a chair tipped back against the outside wall. The throne chair inside, fit for Saint Peter, was made from a Muslim funeral stele and is inscribed with lines from the Koran. Look under anything religious in Italy, and you find the previous civilization's religious stones. The holy hot spots remain. **Spoglia**, a word I like, an object incorporated into a new use. The site of this St. Peter's was originally occupied by a shrine to Bacchus. There, we're already linking to our voyage, to myth, and to the desert fathers.

We walked, just walked, anywhere but the infested San Marco area. The Arsenal and San Pietro in the Castello area were curiously deserted. Families disembarked from serviceable blue or red boats, holding their bathing suits and baskets and shuffling in beach shoes, which they wore from a day at the Lido. Everyone dropped away except for a man walking his dog. Late in the afternoon we stopped for a Tintoretto—champagne and pomegranate juice—at a bar and watched a miniature crane mounted on a flat boat dig silt from a small canal. Barriers on two ends blocked the area where the crane worked, and the water had been pumped out. How difficult and specialized, the work of keeping Venice afloat.

At dinnertime we chose a restaurant new to us, Acquapazza, crazy water, what a good name for a restaurant in Venice. The Santo Stefano area is one of my favorite parts of Venice. After zucchini gnocchi and a platter of fried shellfish, we were served a tiny glass of **basilicocello**, like limoncello only made with basil leaves and steeped for two months before being poured into icy, icy glasses. Venice always lures us to walk even late at night, especially a night with a full August moon, but we would board the ship early tomorrow and so went back to our hotel, where we leaned out of the window before we sank into bed, looking at the trillion ribboned reflections of moonlight in the canal. A window opened in an adjacent house, and a man lifted a small dog out onto the tile rooftop. The dog pattered a few feet away. He squatted, peering down into the Grand Canal, while his quivering backside deposited **merde** onto the roof.

Sailing out of Venice would excite the heart of a robot. The watery city of sublime Tiepolo-to-Turner colors and shapes slid away like a good dream upon waking, as the ship met the open sea. Venice, I realized, is a fabulous **idea**. Like nowhere else in the world, it suggests human imagination—how the irrational is sometimes the best idea. Centuries of people have lived their lives on these unlikely earth platforms in the tides. From birth they were saturated with beauty, their first patterning was beauty, their last breath drawn with beauty.

What was known, known well and loved, receded, and what was unknown and alluring beckoned. We left the stern and moved up to the bow, listening to the chuff-chuff of waves against the hull as the ship picked up speed.

At sea, at first light, I look out the porthole and see that we are in the craggy shadow of what must be Albania. And what a grim historical shadow the hills cast. The water seems darker, the coast formidable, but breakfast in the dining room throws me from any dour reflections to a comfortable midwestern motel—waffles, pancakes, French toast. We resolve immediately not to fall into the severe temptation of two-thousand-calorie breakfasts. "Fruit," I tell our Italian waiter. "Every day, fruit, please, coffee, perhaps a little cheese and bread." In the vast dining room we are assigned to a table for two and are relieved. What if you had two weeks of meals with great bores? But we wonder—what if we were at a table of eight potential lifelong friends? Ed signs up for a massage, and I head for the deck chairs with my notebook and several books. In the afternoon we have a swim, lounging on deck while unidentified coasts and islands swim by us. We are moving over ancient wrecks that lie far below, far below the nets of fishermen, a mile, two miles deep, the golden sand bottom littered with barnacled amphorae, anchors, a cooking pot. We're plowing in the watery furrows of old trade routes. Silks, wines, and spices transported to Venice for the pleasure of doges and merchants and courtesans. I begin **The Voyage of Argo** by Apollonius of Rhodes, written three centuries before Christ, in the time of the Ptolemies, the introduction tells me. It has stood on my bookshelf for a decade, unread. Now I am interested in Jason and the Argonauts, brave as astronauts in our time, from the moment the **Argo** was hoisted into the sea until it returned, after epic adventures, from the quest for the Golden Fleece.

We have no such mission on this ship, although individually, I imagine, many have embarked with some private quest. I have. Martin Buber said, "All journeys have secret destinations of which the traveller is unaware." This voyage I'm taking in honor of my youth. At nineteen I dreamed of Greece. If there is another inner destination, I will wait for it to be revealed. All the reasons I dreamed of Greece that year influenced my whole life, though until now I have never travelled east of Slovenia.

It's exhilarating simply to sit on deck looking out at the Homeric sea. I would not be surprised to see a mermaid surface, flip up her fish tail, and disappear. Sunglasses, hat, and the vantage point of my deck chair give me the chance to observe my fellow passengers. I see many miniwomen, eighty or so and weighing about the same. Two of these ladies fascinate me. They are twins and wear identical white lace cover-ups over two-piece suits. Their bluish hair is cut in a cap of curls, and one has painted her eyebrows in an ogival arch; the other paints hers in a horseshoe extending far above a usual eyebrow. One looks demonic, the other as though she is always about to ask a question. They leave a wake of dense floral perfume with a metallic edge cutting the sea air. No beach thongs or deck shoes for them; they walk steadily in high-heeled backless clear plastic, decorated with a puff of pink feathers. They don't seem to speak to each other; perhaps they don't have to.

At earliest dawn we dock at Corfu. I first heard of this island from my Greek professor when I was a sophomore in college. I'd conceived a passion for Greece, a transference of my intense crush on the professor. From him I took a course in Greek and Roman history, followed by Greek tragedies, then Greek and Latin etymology. I was ignoring the mundane requirements in plain old humanities and science courses after seeing the lost expression in Professor Hunter's eyes as he pronounced Byron's line Ζώη μου σάς αγαπώ, my life, I love you. In the summer, babysitting for my two-year-old nephew, I taught him, instead of Mother Goose, Byron's verses about Greece:

The mountains look on Marathon
And Marathon looks on the sea
And dreaming there an hour alone
I thought that Greece might still be free.

All his dissolute life behind him, the poet drowned swimming the straits at Missolonghi while fighting with his life and his fortune for Greece's freedom. A dreamer who plunged into action. That I liked.

The professor had spent time on Corfu, which he pronounced **Corfee**. When I later read Lawrence Durrell, it was the professor's face that I superimposed on the author's. I was someone very young who never had been anywhere, except for a few twirls around the South, once to New York, and once for three days to Pennsylvania to retrace the Confederates' bloody battle at Gettysburg. **Never forget, never**, my mother said. Professor Hunter was something so very special, a **classicist**. The word spun in my mind. I wanted that world in my voice, in my eyes. I wanted his wisdom and a sense of beauty. I fixated too on his big tanned hands and crisp shirts. In the tiny classroom, where the six other students seemed actually interested in the texts, I dreamed of Greek light. I wrote verses from the plays on index cards and kept them with me to memorize. I charged the terra-cotta–bound, boxed edition of the Greek plays, volumes of poetry, and ancient histories to my bookstore account, causing a nasty letter to arrive from my grandfather, which ended, "Get your head out of the clouds. Now." If only he'd known that I wove garlands of laurel and wildflowers and left them at night on the professor's office doorknob. That I waited in the rose garden under the full moon, hoping he'd stroll by. Now I should say how mortifying memory can be, but instead I'm happy to have slipped anonymous poems, the edges of the paper burned, under his door, to have been called "our Maenad." Me, editor of the yearbook at Fitzgerald High School, referred to as a member of the ecstatic Bacchic chorus. **Corfeeeee,** the professor intoned. He remembered the Aegean wind, falling asleep in a small boat. I imagined my sunburned lips on his warm back. But I loved as well the chiseled cadences of Aeschylus (he said **Ice-q-loss**), and the sensuous whimsy of Sappho, and the reverberating phrases **the house of Thebes, the Argive host, on ye Bacchae**. The basement classroom floated in a classical sea. I rocked in that sea as if in the small boat. Exiting was a shock—into the late autumn Virginia day, the ginkgo trees a riot of yellow.

We disembark at Corfeeeee, and the boat crowd moves in a lumpen mass toward town. Hoping to circumvent the group and see something on our own, Ed and I immediately take a taxi to our farthest point, the seventeenth-century monastery of Vlahérna. We need not have bothered because busloads of other tourists are already there. Looking down, we see the monastery, pure and white, on its own tiny island ringed by boats. Pondikoníssi, another small island, greener, lies beyond. According to local legend, the island formed when Poseidon turned Odysseus's ship to stone. The walkway to the monastery might sink under its load of visitors. We jump in another taxi and drive back to the old town. Corfu looks Italian. I knew of the Neapolitan and more profoundly influential Venetian dominations, but did not expect the extent of that heritage. The colors are those of Italy: sun-warmed peach, ripe mango, lemon, darkened apricot, and cream. I feel instantly at home among balconies dripping vines, arcades along a plaza, and tiny piazzas ringed with houses where the inhabitants can smell the lamb the neighbors are roasting. The town feels like a swatch of Venice.

Pulled into a small Orthodox church by the sound of a priest chanting, we are suddenly in a dim crowded space heavy with the smell of wax and incense, moving in a line toward a coffin, where people are leaning down to kiss the body. It is too late to exit. I'm crushed between the large rump of the man in front of me and the copious bosom of the woman behind. "It's a saint," Ed whispers, "not a corpse." Soon we are leaning to kiss a robe, and the priest breathes in my face, "Spyridon." He is dressed in about a hundred pounds of robes himself but does not sweat. He hands Ed a square of blue folded paper. Conveyed outside, we unwrap it and find a tiny scrap of the saint's robe. Everyone coming out buys thin tallow candles like long pencils, lights them, and stands them in a tin box filled with sand. I do the same, saying to Ed, "Make a wish." In an antique shop down the street, the owner tells us that half the men he knows are named for the saint who'd saved the island many times. We were lucky—Spyridon is only brought out four times a year. I had read about the saint in Durrell, never suspecting that someday I would keep a smidgen of his robe in my jewelry drawer.

At lunch I learn my first Greek working words—**mono nero**, only water, and the word for Greek salad, χωριάτικη, which I copy in my notebook. Ed is impressed that I can sound out all the Greek letters, a benefit of having been in a sorority. I learned to draw the chi (X) and omega (Ω) letters at five, when my older sister pledged at the University of Georgia. Being able to read the letters unlocks cognate words. But almost everything remains impenetrable. It's daunting to find the language so foreign, so distant, but also so thrilling. One is absolved of responsibility when the language is incomprehensible. Is this one of the mysteries of travel? One returns to preverbal pointing, smiling, shaping the air with gestures.

This first day off the ship, I see how the trip will be. We may choose one dish from a whole menu, one sip from a great bottle of wine. One monastery, not ten. The sublime Byzantine icon museum, but not the Archaeology Museum. We'll have a glimpse, a taste, a few impressions to memorize, and then we go back on board, flashing our ID cards, and sail on. As the ship pulls away from the dock, Corfu recedes, becoming a smear of gold; then the island is eclipsed by distance and disappears. I explore the rest of the island in my imagination: coves and beaches, a goat tethered to an olive tree, remote overgrown gardens, a dangling ripe tomato splitting in the sun, a decadent villa where an ancient woman writes her memoirs.

At sea, cocktail hour begins early, ends late, and reappears at unexpected times of the day. "Gentlemen hosts," who probably retired from teaching or sales and finally get to go out to see the world, mix with the many single women and ask them to dance to "it's cherry pink and apple blossom white . . . when you're in love" and "Racing with the Moon," and, oh no, the tinkly bars of "tea for two and two for tea." This seems ludicrous at first, then tragic, then ludicrous. But from whose point of view? The women probably were married to men who danced only reluctantly. Now they can dance, rediscovering the tango and jitterbug from college days, and the hosts dance so well, unlike their husbands, who huffed at weddings and followed the box step. Not like the Florida boy I met early in my senior year of college. My roommate Saralynn and I stopped by a table in the student union where a bunch of ΣAEs were playing cards. Only Frank stood up. He and I both felt electricity between us. Later he told me he said to himself the moment we met that I was the girl he would marry. He knew how to dance with such ease and grace that we danced into marriage the summer after graduation, and eons later I have a recurrent dream of dancing with him.

The hosts look so professional, whereas there's a way of dancing that exudes a sense of life. When I try to express this to Ed, he says, "You're taking this a bit seriously. Let's go in the casino and win a million dollars." Ten quarters later we find the deliciously comfortable and empty movie theatre and watch two movies we missed when they first came around.

Crete—I love the word. We board a bus for a land tour and head out of Agios Nikolaos toward Heraklion and Knossos. I am doused in number-fifty sunblock because when I stepped out on deck at seven A.M., the sun felt like a branding iron. "You're well acquainted with A.D., I expect," the guide announces. "Everything you'll see today will all be B.C." We turn into the grounds of the legendary Minoan ruins and pour off the bus into a steaming lot packed with other people streaming out of other heaving buses. Stained backpacks, water bottles, fat rear ends, pale flesh oozing out of tank tops, sweat, exhaust, belching, cameras—we herd into the beginnings of myth, the palace of King Minos.

In protest, the cicadas are shrieking, drowning out the voices of the guides. I've heard cicadas all my life; I never have heard them tune up to this break-the-sound-barrier decibel level. How spooky, as though a mad Greek chorus has been activated. The guide pauses at the snaking queue for the labyrinthine palace, then says that because of the crowds we won't be seeing this, this, and that. She lingers before a row of terracotta pots and explains at length that their use is disputed. I try to focus on the fact that the pots are older than the oldest Etruscans. The wall behind them—painted with soot and bulls' blood? But instead I'm remembering the myth of Talos, who was made of bronze. He heated himself until he glowed and almost turned molten, then stepped up to grab and embrace strangers as they arrived on the island. We are in his arms. The cicadas twang with a primitive, rhythmic cadence. The guide's voice can't reach beyond the third layer of people surrounding her. "Can you speak louder?" I ask. I'm anxious to hear everything about this place.

"Oh, no," she responds, waving her hand toward the cicada-infested trees. "They'll just screech louder." So the latter-day chorus continues its commentary. I may turn molten. Everywhere the dusty caper plants sprawl. I pick a pod to take home to Bramasole. If I blow the seed through a straw into the crevice of a stone wall, it might sprout.

The famous labyrinth never has been found. I am sure it existed and was not simply this intricate palace itself, as one of my books suggests. The labyrinth—one of our oldest stories. That it has been repeated through the centuries means that elements of the story strike lightning in the collective psyche. Theseus: lost in a maze, you are given by your lover a ball of white thread (the **mitos**), and you find your way out, having slain the dark force that pulled you in there. Daedalus: locked inside a labyrinth of your own creation, you therefore must escape by your own wits. The messages are clear enough.

Early in the myth, Poseidon gave a fabulous white bull to Minos, who was supposed to sacrifice it. He did not. He sacrificed a lesser bull. To punish Minos, Poseidon caused Minos's wife, Pasiphaë, to become enamored of the white bull. She coaxed Daedalus to build a wooden cow, where she could hide and sexually encounter the bull. The product of that union was the half-bull, half-man, the Minotaur. This gets murky. Parts of the myth do not yield easy metaphorical meanings.

Instead of all the things we came to see, we see the oldest road in Europe, complete with side channels for drainage. Under the hooves of today's herds, the white stones are getting about a hundred years of wear. I stand off to the side, fanning with a guidebook. This sun is a bull. I could be trampled by heat-incensed tourists. Ed looks stricken. **Alain, you are so right**. Mobs in heat. Lord.

We drive on to the museum in Heraklion, a further exercise in frustration. Here's the fabulous Minoan collection, and I do see it—through the crook of an elbow, over a shoulder, and as someone steps on my feet. I imagine myself wearing blinders in order to see the pitted ivory acrobat at full stretch before executing a somersault off the bull's back. This acrobatic bull leaping recurs in Minoan art and appears to connect with worship of the bull. Although some scholars find the feat an aerodynamic, physical impossibility, the representation makes the leap look quite plausible. One painting shows three figures, fore, on, and aft the bull. Two of the androgynous figures are white, the other is red, also probably painted with bull blood. While some consider color to reveal gender, maybe instead the figure in red, the one flipping over the bull, is transformed for the moment of sympathetic magic with the bull, and becomes white again when back on the ground. The art emits energy, as though these people still were among us.

Oddly, the galleries are hushed, only a faint

hum like a faraway hive. In the afternoon's intense heat we are Minoan zombies moving from room to room.

The bull symbol, heavily potent. This early bull mythology caused the powerful **corno** (horn) symbolism throughout the Mediterranean world—the crescent moon, the forefinger-pinkie sign which, when raised, is used to denote a cuckold, when pushed outward from the body to poke out the eyes of a witch, and when pointed at the ground assures that something will not happen here, to us.

In the back of the bus I'm trying to solve part of the old labyrinthine myth. The cryptic part is Pasiphaë, all fired up, creeping inside Daedalus's wooden bull, positioning herself so she could mate with the bull her husband was supposed to have sacrificed but didn't. The physical logistics are hard to picture. And how to read that myth? If a woman goes for the purely sexual, there's hell to pay? Lust can drive you to far extremes? The oldest stories are usually illustrative, as are frescoes for the illiterate, those visual stories that show within the same frame a span of narrative time—the life of a saint from birth, including his miracles and death. Visual aids, teaching tools. The myth of the mating of Pasiphaë and the white bull stumps me. Surely there's more to it than her scarlet ways or the punishment of Minos.

Much more appealing and understandable that careless exuberance of Icarus, who flew out of Knossos on wings of wax and feathers designed by his father, the ever-inventive Daedalus. A sun like today's would surely melt his wings and send him plunging into the sea.

Myths must have grown out of the lives of actual humans. Some were elevated over time into gods; others, such as Icarus, remained touchingly human. Someone named Icarus once mysteriously disappeared from Knossos without a trace. A visitor trading oil or wine later reported a body washing up near a small island. The small curved scar on his forehead, the hand clutching a carved dowel, the clay pendant of a bull still around his neck—why, it must be that crazy boy, Icarus. He flew. His old man Daedalus was pushy, an entrepreneur whose social climbing almost did him in. He was always involved in some disaster. No wonder the king imprisoned him. The father-son story was told a thousand times, evolving them into myth. Daedalus flew on, after the death of his son, and landed in Sicily. If you're smart enough, you escape.

At sea, the water is lighter than lapis. Endless blue, the bluest blue, forget-me-not blue. If only I could find a word to anneal to the blue, a lucid, gossamer word. The ship's bow raises a V of foam that folds over into the blue. I could stand on deck all day, just looking at this endless shift of patterning on the surface of the sea. Vinca, periwinkle—not quite. A lively blue, a wet enamel shine, a depth of blue. Sapphire—yes, that much play of light. A mystery with all the weight and expanse of land. In summer calm, exuberant.

At the first of the five formal evenings, the twins wear their preferred white lace, this time as strapless, fitted long dresses, time-warped from senior prom in Yonkers, circa 1945. With strands and dangles of rhinestones, they sparkle into the dining room and find their table for two. We enjoy the cold champagne, the resplendent captain graciously welcoming us, and the unruffled sea. How glamorous Ed looks in his

Italian tuxedo, his "smoking" as it's called by Italians who frequently leave off the second word of an imported term: **basket**, instead of **basketball**, **night** instead of **nightclub**. The band advances a few decades and plays "Saturday Night Fever," then lapses back to "Misty."

We board a bus in the port of Piraeus and drive through shady streets into Athens, calm in early morning, plumbago falling over fences. Ed says, "Remember the line in **The Graduate**? The old guy advises Dustin Hoffman that the future is in plastics? Look at this." Only ten million people live in Greece; five million live in Athens. Half of them have unloaded bags of trash along the road. We see startling litter everywhere: tires, barrels, crates, plastic sheeting, conduits, plastic bottles, plastic everything.

Suddenly we're in the country, dusty olive trees, massive, maybe as old as the myth of Oedipus and Jocasta. We pass Thebes. **Thebes**. The cotton fields of Thebes, blue beehives, apartment blocks, Tiresias in the road. We cross plains planted with wheat and tomatoes. Along the edges of the fields, women sit behind blue boxes mounded with San Marzano tomatoes for sale. There—broken towers, a blue tractor, a man in a blue cap, then jumps into view an Austrian chalet selling Asian antiques.

We're en route to Delphi, with perhaps a few questions for the oracle. When Jupiter wanted to find the center of the world, the omphalos, he released two eagles at the far corners. Where they met was Delphi. Would that we had oracles, who gave absolute, if often ambiguous, answers to essential questions for twelve centuries. Our guide for today looks bored. At the front of the bus with her microphone, she lurches with every pothole. Already she has irked me by asking how many of us have heard of Delphi. Then she asks, "Have you seen a map of Greece?"

I want to shout, **I was studying Greece before you were born**.

"Don't say **Del-fie**!" she admonishes someone who has ventured a question. "It's **Del-fee**!" I want to smack her for condescending, even though I did pronounce it **Del-fie**. As soon as we leave the bus, we break off from her strident voice. We have our own books to consult, with the imagined tones of an oracle reading to us, not her sandpaper voice. Proper pilgrims, we have brought a small bottle to collect some water from the holy spring, although we have brought no propitiatory honeypies for the snakes. We are walking on the foundations of literature, up the steep, stony path in the fiery heat. On walls of Delphi were inscribed: Σ, sigma, meaning "energy" and "one's own force." They also carved **Know Thyself** and **Nothing to Excess**, all still valid, though I've always been a fan of excess, siding with Colette, who said, "It's no good having any unless you can have too much." Blake went farther: "The road of excess leads to the palace of wisdom."

The ruins—more extensive than I imagined—look like rocks picked up and made into walls and houses that are returning to their natural positions in the fields.

My grandmother, who died when I was eleven, waits on a rock outside the entrance. I spotted her on the bus, her very body, bosomy but thin and spongy, deer legs, white hair fluffed just right, and her little pointed chin and watery, sad blue eyes. She wore high heels to Delphi and could not climb up to see where the oracle held forth for all those centuries. Instead, she bought a hamburger and sat on a stone feeding it to the birds. The voile print dress is the same, and the bony ankles. I know she will smell of Shalimar, exotic and cloying. As we reboard the bus, she sits in front of me. I see that her hair grows low on her nape, as mine does. I expect her to turn around, recognize me, and say, "Why, **Frances**, my dear, after so many years," but instead she swivels in the bus seat and says, "Darlin', could you unhook my bra? I'm sure as hell not riding all the way back to the ship in the heat with this thing stranglin' me." My wafty grandmother, Frances Smith Mayes, whose mother was so importantly named Sarah America Gray. I oblige. And remember Apollo, god of prophecy, and all the gods who extract revenge if you come too close. Memory is like that, too. The layers unshuffle, about to reveal something, then show you only a wild card.

On the way back to the ship, I catch a glimpse of the Acropolis at sunset, far away, and lines by Kóstos Kariotákis rise in my mind: "And there beyond, the Akropolis like a Queen/wears all the sunset like a crimson robe."

At sea, at night, women's fantasies come alive. The deep rhythms of the sea must retrieve primal longings. By day, they lounge or walk or attend lectures and performances in muted linen pants or shorts and simple shirts. At the dances and candlelight dinners on board, our main delight is not the good food or the music. It is the fabulous sight of a large Dutch woman in blue taffeta with puffed sleeves and a little bustle. A bustle! A straight yellow dress with an Empire waist reminds me of the bridesmaid's dress I wore at my friend Anne's wedding when she fainted from the heat and the priest just kept on with the ceremony until she revived. The twins, with upsweeps and dangling rhinestones, have switched for this gala, to black lace numbers with fake red roses around the scooped necks. Ed and I are in our anonymous Italian black. Others, too, are in this minimalist mode, tasteful, fitted sheaths, the discreet powdery colors and simple cuts. There's the Isabella Rosselini look-alike, with tanned perfect shoulders and arms, riding into the ballroom like Aphrodite on the waves, her cloud of pink chiffon drifting from her ankles. There's the young daughter of hefty, blond South Africans in her sea-foam silk dress with billowing sleeves, who looks like an Annunciation angel except for the dragon tattoo on her shoulder.

Our eyes are drawn to the flamboyant, the ravishing variety of the species on show. Ed likes a three-tiered muu-muu with enough fringe around the hem to bind a five-by-six rug. Following her, on the arm of her handsome husband, a red-haired beauty who looks as though she has somehow been expanded by a bicycle pump wears white Lycra so tight it fits like a plaster cast over her blimp-sized buttocks. The neck is V-ed to the last possible moment, revealing generous slices of Cycladic breasts. Where did she get long white gloves with diamond-shaped cutouts? I'm drawn to the woman with hair piled high, then cascading into curls. She's in voluminous ruffles splotched with red flowers and what might be banana leaves. At around three hundred pounds, she looks like a moving garden. The gentlemen hosts go to work, and the band saws away at tunes the dolphins must dive far under the waves to escape.

In Santorini the paint stores don't have to stock a range of colors. Shelves of Aegean blue and stark white will do. White, white houses, white as bleached bones, with gates, windows, and doors of blue, a vibrating blue when fresh, fading through the seasons to chalky gray. The blue-trimmed domed churches are profoundly appealing, not only for their stark purity and isolation but because at a subconscious level they must remind us of the dome of the skull and the interior life. An occasional iconoclast has painted a door green or a fence lavender. Still, those are sea colors in shallows or at twilight. We are let loose for the day and have rented a car. Here I experience the legendary Greek light in the harsh landscape, which looks unbenevolent but also spaciously opens to the sun. The hills, almost treeless except for the fig, hardly intrude on essential sky and sea, and the lava-scoured land looks as plain as the sea. Few trees escape from the volcanic soil, except the fig. Stubby, but proof that this tree will have its way with rock or mountain or field anywhere in the Mediterranean world. Ed pulls over, and I get out to watch grape-pickers loading baskets with dusky fruit. The vines sprawl on the ground, as though unable to stand up against the hard sun. Even the middle distance shimmers in the heat, warping the lines of grapes. My head feels struck by the sun, the rays warping my skull. The Praxitilean ideals must have come from standing in a field in Greece, from realizing that finding the essentials of beauty is a reductive process. Take away the extras—but leave the hot wind, the hand cutting the grape, the sun filling your bones with arid light.

At sea, I am loving the days. Blue, blue, we're skimming, sliding over blue. At times I see rivers running in the sea, angling across the choppy tides. The color of blue—immortal. Cheery orange and yellow tenders with names like Herakles and Perikles toot out to meet us as we approach an island, then tug or guide us into harbor.

On deck in hard sunlight, the worshipers reveal their quadruple bypass scars (one fresh, puckered red), knees swollen and purple, withered cesarean slashes. On California beaches I'm used to seeing the gorgeous. Here, alongside those at the peak of perfection, the ancient, the obese, the damaged shed their clothes and forget their vein-popped legs, horn-thick toenails, liver-spotted skin. Facing the human's last or ruined or excessive forms contrasts sharply with the archaic statues of human perfection we are seeing in the museums. The man we call Mr.

Good Morning, for his enthusiastic greeting, lets out a long toot every time he stands. His posture makes the letter lambda, Γ. My eyes are riveted by a scarecrow man whose withered penis, so **huge**, hangs from the side of his wide-legged bathing trunks. I suddenly recall my daughter's horse, Chelsea. One crane-legged man raises his drink and says, "Let's party." Yes, let's.

Wanting to lose twelve pounds, I am especially drawn to the grandly obese. The loving mother with two frisky children lowers herself into the pool. **Good for her**, I think. The hell with people like me who feel as though a spotlight shines on them if they carry a bulge on the thigh, if the stomach is not concave. Her ankles merge seamlessly into Colossus of Rhodes thighs, overlapped at the knees as though a meltdown has begun. She has, remarkably, chosen a white suit. Backing down the ladder into the water, she looks like an albino hippopotamus; breasts, stomach, hips converge, hiding even from her the cleft of her sex. How light she becomes in the salt water. She frolics with her blond boy, her skinny girl, tossing them in the air, letting them splash with a shriek, until she hoists herself out with heavy effort. Luxuriating on a chaise longue, she falls asleep. The girl's head rests on her breasts, in this life or the next the softest pillow she ever will feel against her face.

Late at night when I am alone on deck, I see the woman again near the rail in a red caftan, arms spread, dancing alone. A pleasure to the eye. At sea, she is goddess of the waves. Her heart is working overtime. Is she sleeping in the same bunk-width beds everyone else is?

We love Náfplio, named for Náfplios, the son of Poseidon, on the coast of mainland Greece. Long shady esplanade along the sea, a sand-castle-type castle just offshore, pastel houses, and boisterous people. By chance we find the museum of the **komboloi** (worry beads). I've watched men fingering those beads in the cafés. The museum is Aris Evangelinos's lifetime collection, displayed in a small house. He also makes and sells them. He has stories to tell. His fierce black eyebrows shoot up and down. "The beads are nonreligious in Greece," he explains; "they are a friend, they are for the comfort of touch, for the clacking noise they make, for the color." He holds up an antique **komboloi** made of amber. "In Muslim countries, often you find three sets of thirty-three beads for three prayers. The Hindus call them **mala**, meaning 'prayer book.' But in Greece they are companions to life. Friends. Many men are buried holding their **komboloi**. If you wear one around your neck, the evil eye knows to stay away from you."

His collection includes beads made of snakes' backbones, black coral, olive pits, ebony, flower seeds, mother of pearl, thread knots, yak horn, rare green amber, aromatic wood, ivory, and amber powder. Some are incised, limned with secret symbols. I pick out a bracelet-size **komboloi** of pale yellow onyx. I'm a paperclip-bender at my desk. I'll try picking up this instead. We buy his book, and he signs it for us. At lunch I open it and read, "To my friends Frances and Edward with love, Aris." Such moments make travel a deep pleasure.

Náfplio elicits the word **charming**. The major industry seems to be the benign production of gold jewelry. I look in several shops, admiring the hammered Byzantine crosses, rings of many-colored semiprecious stones, and coral pins. You can imagine living here, strolling along the water, sitting in the piazza listening to the wandering minstrels with their open guitar cases spotted with coins, which is what I do until time to dash to the ship, already sounding its bellowing horn for departure. Ed goes off to mail some cards, gets lost, and barely runs across the gangplank in time.

We like getting dressed for dinner as we slip out of a harbor every night. Our mood as we enter the dining room shifts to celebratory. We're having great dates. I begin to remember that I was quite good at flirting. Ed becomes more romantic, swooping out of his jacket pocket a small blue-velvet box. Inside I find gold earrings with round sapphires—the very ones I'd coveted in a jewelry shop. And I thought he was off looking for stamps. They will remind me of the color of the sea. After dinner we walk all around the deck. The stars are enough to break your heart, so intensely present, close enough to reach. They do not seem like the same stars that hang over the rest of the planet.

At sea, in the night, Ed dreams again of water pouring into the cabin. "Remember the old

Paul Newman movie? When he's in a cistern and the water starts to rise and someone covers the top with steel and the water keeps coming up?"

"No. Why was he in a cistern?"

"I don't know. Anyway, the water comes almost to the top where he has only a tiny space to breathe."

"How did he get out?"

"That's not the point. The point is the **feeling**. I can't take this." I too sometimes wake in the night feeling as though I am inside an egg.

Out on deck early, I spot people thrashing in the water. Suicides? Two at once? Crazies on speed? Just then a life preserver is thrown from our boat, and the two swim toward it. Soon two crewmen haul them out of the water into a dinghy. Later I hear that they are two Afghan or Albanian or Kurdish refugees, now recovering in the ship infirmary. Rumors buzz around the decks. A nearby sailboat picked up three men in the night when they were dumped by the person they'd paid to take them to safety. Were there seventeen originally? One refugee said so. If so, twelve have drowned and possibly we have sailed over their bodies.

This rescue is a brutal reminder of the scrappy courage of those caught in the crosshairs of world events not of their making. And also a reminder of privilege and luck. We stared down into the water where two flecks were adrift. How surreal their night, landing in the sharp water and treading until morning. Death was right there in a lungful of salt water, a passing shark, or the failure of the body to keep on moving. Suddenly they are saved. Then we necessarily move on through the day, gnawed at (for years) by the image of the two faces looking up.

My talk is late morning. I see in the daily program that it has not been listed among the day's activities, and at eleven I face an audience of five. Unsettling, because I am on board as a guest in exchange for speaking. We have an intimate little chat, and then everyone is back to sunning and reading on this day at sea. The entertainment director says not to worry, but I feel as though I've slipped into a theatre without a ticket.

All afternoon in the deck chair, I try to describe to my notebook the colors of the water and sky.

How to translate sunlight into words? Beneath my vision of this sea, the green waters of Angel Island wash, weekends at anchor in Alaya cove with my first husband and daughter on our sailboat, **Primavera**. Often we were the only boat. After four, when the last tourist ferry departed, the deer came out, dozens of them, to drink from the sprinklers on the caretaker's lawns. We rowed the dinghy to shore and walked around the island for the sunset views of San Francisco, which looked like a fabled city rising white out of the ocean. The always-improbable span of the Golden Gate seemed like some link between memories rather than a practical bridge that is constantly being repainted. Those **Primavera** evenings were close to sublime. In the tiny galley I made dinner, then we watched for falling stars on clear nights or slipped early into the nifty beds below, where we were rocked all night like newborns in the treetops before the cradle fell.

I kept those evenings to hold against days when my mind felt like a kerosene-soaked rag. Now I'll have these, too. The natural world saves me.

• • •

Everyone heads for the buses bound for the monastery where monks had to lower themselves in baskets from the sheer mountain. I get vertigo and claustrophobia just thinking of that, and Ed refuses to board a bus so soon after the long trek to Delphi. We are docked at Volos, close to where Jason and the Argonauts set sail. Dozens of cafés and fishing boats line the harbor. One taverna displays fifty or so octopuses on a clothesline. Take your pick. At the dusty archaeological museum, we discover the grave stele with faint paintings revealing the faces of those long gone to more dust. And we see necklaces they wore, with wrought charms of inlaid sapphires, rubies, and etched-gold portraits. Back out in the heat, we decide to take a taxi to the village of Μακρινίτσα (Makrynitsa), where thousand-year-old sycamore trees cast their immense shade over the plaza. They're as impressive as California redwoods. We visit the little Byzantine church. I'm used to lighting thin candles in churches by now, standing them up in sand. One for my aunt Mary, sick in Savannah. One, always, for my family. Protect them, please. One for all those I love, and one for the conviction I once had that red and yellow, black and white, Jesus loves all the little children of the world.

I buy a jar of pickled caper leaves, something I've never seen before. I'm tempted by dried foot-long stalks called "tea of the mountain," opaque dark honeys, dried mint, and oregano. Ed nudges me on. Working donkeys with men on sidesaddle plod up the hilly streets.

At a taverna under the trees, we skip the rabbit in sauce and the boiled goat, so heavy in the heat, and order instead spiced feta to spread on delicious rough bread, savory eggplant with tomatoes, and—because the platter at the next table lured us—fried potatoes, golden and light. A man at that table has finished his lunch, and his wife chats with people at adjacent tables. He takes out his **komboloi** and seems to go into another world. The plying of his gold beads sounds soft like water over rocks. He fingers his red "god" stone, then each bead, rubs the red one all around, and starts over, looping the whole circle around in his hand before he starts again.

Leaving—we sail at five—we find no taxi. Oh no, we're told, taxis only **come** here; try the next village, only two miles. We set off in the heat and after-lunch torpor—easy to write, but we're walking down an oven-roasted paved road in August, temperature easily over a hundred degrees, with steam coming up off the asphalt. Hot wind in the aspens sounds like waterfalls, but the stony streams are dry. We're winding slowly downhill, thank Zeus, to another village—where there is no taxi. My sandals rub blisters across all my toes. My heel is bleeding. Finally we get on a bus and slowly inch down to Volos again, getting off near the harbor and walking another mile to the ship.

Here, at sea, I am breathing cooled Hellenic air again. The gossamer breeze makes me want to say the word **aeolian**. The Milky Way strews a path of grated diamonds. Off the port side the coast rises, mysterious in shadowy outlines against the sky, and on the starboard, only swells breaking against the ship, swells that almost break. Out there somewhere a shell rides the foam, bearing Aphrodite covering her breasts with a handful of seaweed. Tonight the sea resembles shiny obsidian, the calm water a mirror, the mirror into which Ed's father looked in his last week on earth and said, **Who is that, and why isn't he saying anything?**

Inside they're always dancing to music that

goes way, way back: "Night and day, you are the one," I sing along. "Listen to that, Eddie. You are the one."

Since distances are not far, the ship zigzags to fill the allotted days. At Rhodes we hit the full tourist impact. Although we skip breakfast and disembark early, the streets are a human avalanche; you could be crushed. We decide to return to the ship and come back someday to Rhodes, perhaps some rainy February. As we retrace our steps, we see one of the gentlemen hosts sitting on the curb drinking a beer and looking dejected.

We cross to the Turkish coast and moor at Kusadasi. Back on a bus, we're en route to Ephesus, zooming past figs along the road, peach and orange orchards, and broken columns and carved blocks scattered along the way as though unremarkable. The messy nests of storks festoon chimney tops and electrical poles. If we were driving, we would stop for a basket of peaches, park under crape myrtles, and let the juices run over our fingers. Instead, I sip bottled water and pray that the sun does not turn us into pools of butter.

We make an unexpected stop at the House of the Virgin Mary. A Jewish friend told me he was unexpectedly moved by the house and the outside wall of Kleenex ex-votos, tied on for memory. I see, also, one knee-high stocking, a few rags, and scrawled notes on paper napkins, as though we are all unprepared when we want to give thanks. Inside the little house—it is almost surely only a wish that Mary lived here—the familiar candles in sand lift the gloom. The idea of Mary in her later life living in a small house near the ruins intrigues me. Maybe she had another child, a girl who climbed the dusty trees and played on the marble streets of Ephesus. As we board the bus, I hear a British tourist say, "That was spot on."

Ephesus—hallowed by Saint Paul and by Heraclitus. At the entrance an impish child sells thirty postcards for one American dollar. As we pass up that bargain, he says, "You break my heart."

"Jingle jangle," the guide says. "These stands are selling jingle jangle."

Then we're walking those marble streets in a

stream of other people. Several guides are lecturing in front of the famous library, after Alexandria and Pergamum the greatest in the ancient world. By now adverse to our guides, I walk around the groups, listening to snatches of their guides' spiels. The statues are protections by Wisdom, Intelligence, Destiny, and Science, although another guide omits Science and says Love.

Medusa's blue eyes protected the Temple of Hadrian. Was this, as the guide claims, the origin of protection against the evil eye? That eye decorates the prows of boats and the doorways of houses. It is to Greece what the household shrine is to Italy. **Protect this house**.

Our guide lets us roam the amphitheatre after telling us in an accusing tone that Sting, in a high-decibel rock concert, cracked the theatre's foundation. "Imagine, after all the centuries, the American causes this." She grimaces and glares. We don't bother to tell her that Sting is English.

Where is Heraclitus' Maeander, the river you cannot step in twice? I can see only stone and tourists. **For the water is already far downstream**. But Heraclitus, it's not the water, it's the **river**, and I always step in the same river twice. The flow of the river is memory, just as the **mitos**, the white ball of thread Ariadne handed to Theseus as he entered the labyrinth, was the thread of memory.

The bus makes a stop at a center for rug making. A concept for tourists, but nevertheless we see that the colors of the wool are the colors of herbs and spices—saffron, bay, cinnamon, paprika, sage, turmeric. I like hearing that one cocoon yields one and a half miles of silk thread. My favorite art springs from folk tradition, and I've always loved the spontaneity of woven rugs—the little animal and human figures that interrupt a design, the abrupt changes of color when the thread runs out and the nomads have moved on to other locales with other colors available for dying the wool. I like the use of what's at hand, walnut shells, rock-rose hips, oak bark, tobacco leaves, medlar. Even these bored women hired by the state to demonstrate weaving techniques must find a little magic emerging on the loom.

In the hour we have to roam in Kusadasi, we go into a couple of rug stores. One dealer says, "I can take your money."

• • •

At sea, tooling along the coast at night, the water looks blue, the darkest blue, a folded uniform at the bottom of a trunk. And the air in the dark—great tides of fresh sea air. The lights of fishing boats blink in the distance, and I imagine the men on board playing cards, looking up at the white apparition of our ship passing across their porthole. At sea, I get up early for the dawn colors reflected in the lovely, lovely water, bluer than thy first love's eyes. I could not have imagined the glancing of light on these waters. All I want to do is lean over and watch the petticoat flounces of white foam and the heaven-sent blue. The impulse to jump feels strong and not destructive but rather a joyous desire to join another element.

Bodrum, the next stop on the Turkish coast, is simply appalling. Not yet totally ruined by development, it soon will be. The streets pulse with holiday people in T-shirts, halters, and short shorts, drinking beer as they go. Ticky-tacky condos spread like a case of shingles on the hills. I wonder why at this late date the town powers would allow such a rape of their sublime coast, the old city of Halicarnassus. Isn't it obvious that development quickly reaches the point of diminishing returns? Those previously drawn to the glorious place will go elsewhere. We trudge through the castle and have lunch in a waterside restaurant where garbage floats just under our table. "Height of summer," Ed says.

"Let's go back to the ship where it's cool. We can have a frozen daiquiri and go to the string quartet concert."

"To hell with Halicarnassus."

As we enter the Dardanelles, the color of the sea changes to green, and the green does not have the happiness of the blue. We're entering the territory of Dardano, our hometown boy. He was born in Cortona, according to legend. In his wanderings he founded Troy; then Aeneas left Troy to found Rome. Because of Dardano's circuitous history, he made Cortona the "mother of Troy, grandmother of Rome."

We wonder if the pillboxes along the shore are "the tumbled towers of Ilium," but no, we are passing a more recent catastrophe in these historic waters, the site of the battle of Gallipoli. All the British passengers move up to the bow and silently watch as we glide by. Their fathers, grandfathers, even great-grandfathers have perhaps breathed the word **Gallipoli**. As the captain recounts the action over the loudspeaker, the Germans stick to their novels and deck chairs and the Americans look puzzled: Gallipoli rings a bell but far away. We were not raised on stories of how the sea turned red with blood in 1915.

We awaken just in time to see the cut-out domes and minarets against the sky as the ship glides into the Istanbul harbor at dawn. This is the bookend to the evening sail out of Venice. The memory of arriving in Istanbul as the opaline colors spread across the sky and the city comes to life will always be worth the mobs of Rhodes and Bodrum. Our bags are by the door of our "stateroom," and we do not bother with breakfast. We disembark without a backward glance.

• • •

The Turkish poet Nazim Hikmet was imprisoned for years in what is now our hotel. We arrive early, but our room is ready. In the dining room I see on the menu "wine leaves," "clothed cream." The gorgeous young woman server offers to read Ed's fortune in his coffee grounds. She looks at him with great solemnity and says, "Your mother has died and she wants you to visit her grave." We are silent. This comes out of nowhere. Since Ed's mother's death, he has not returned to his hometown.

In a magazine I read a recipe for Head Broth. It begins, scrub a sheep's head with salt and spices, rub with onion juice, wrap in parchment and roast. Undaunted, we are ready to taste Turkish food in the capital. On the first dinner menu we find **söylenmez kebap**—kebab that shall not be named. The waiter enlightens us; the kebab is made of ram testicles. I prefer bride's soup: red lentils and rice, with mint, tomatoes, and herbs. For dessert, **güllac**: sheets of pastry flavored with rose water. The waiter takes our credit card and smiles. "I'll see you tomorrow."

We sleep in the luxurious hotel in great comfort. Big bed, soft, and no sound of water sluicing below, threatening to rise and swamp us.

Only the memory of the literary prisoner, who might have written his poems in this very room. I awaken to the call of the muezzin from a minaret. Mournful, innocent, shrill, otherworldly—a call of the wild—it stops my heart. If I were Muslim, I would prostrate myself immediately for prayer. The domes are rising suns, the minarets its rays.

On the way to Topkapi, we pass shops emitting smells of lacquer, spices, leather, straw, lanolin. Topkapi is still a wonder of the world! Those sultans! When they wanted someone executed, they stamped their feet. They sprinkled rose water on their hands. Their spoons were made of mother-of-pearl or horn, with handles inset with rubies and turquoise. The crests for their turbans were huge emeralds with plumes. I stare at the hand and occipital bone of Saint John the Baptist, a dagger with a carved emerald handle, wild dress-up clothes with crests of jewels startlingly large, water pitchers and rose-water sprinklers bedecked with pearl, lapis, and coral. The place itself is leafy and serene, with courtyards and pavilions and cool tiled fountains and delicate wall paintings. The architecture, perhaps inspired by a tent camp in the desert, feels harmonious and inviting and at the same time utterly strange and fascinating. In feeling, it reminds me of its opposite, a fine liberal arts college.

There's a long line waiting to go inside the Harem, which once was home sweet home to a thousand concubine slaves. Hardly anyone stirs in the rooms where the treasures are displayed, and I can imagine the sultan stepping into one of the lavish robes in the Royal Wardrobe and making his way to his prayer room.

This is our two-day tasting menu of Istanbul, a city that requires at least a month. Those mosques! Muslim men prostrate themselves in the courtyards, on the steps, and at the entrances to the mosques on Friday. They spill over into the street, among the parked cars. The Blue Mosque, Hagia Sophia (built as a Christian church, mutated into a Muslim mosque, now a museum), the Tulip Mosque, the dozens of scattered mosques, all punctuated by the minarets, offer their domes to the sky, giving the city a soft aspect. How far back does this city travel across time? In 658 B.C. Byzas, a Greek, consulted the Delphic oracle. Where to go? he wanted to know. She advised him to settle on the banks of the Bosporus. His city became his namesake, Byzantium.

Istanbul! It **is** nobody's business but the Turks'—that is, the mysterious city does not open to the foreigner easily, though anyone will be struck by the architecture, the bazaars, the encounters with merchants and buskers who stroll around trying to lasso tourists into some shop. The old-quarter outdoor cafés look so inviting with low benches and tables covered with kelims. Little wheeled carts are laden with **mesir**, roasted corn. In the cobbled, narrow street behind Hagia Sophia, we find a row of wooden Ottoman houses built against the town walls, a quiet enclave of fountains and birdbaths, a place one could live.

Many women wear ankle-length coats of ugly gabardine over long sleeves, with gray long skirts, leggings. They must be boiling. I'd faint. This must be their choice, since many Turkish girls are in short skirts and sleeveless T-shirts, with bra straps showing. For the covered, only the feet are exposed. Ugly sandals, too. I bet they have on pink silk thongs and push-up lace bras. A few are masked but walk hand in hand with young children in shorts. The young wife of a rug merchant tells us, "I like fashion and alcohol, and I don't want to cover myself. For what? I have Allah inside. That's what matters."

The hawkers are aggressive. "My brother lives in Seattle," they call.

"Honeymoon?"

"Second honeymoon?"

"Do you want to be my first customer today?"

"I've seen you three times. We are already well acquainted." We have to laugh at that and are then followed for blocks.

"You are going the wrong way," one calls. They are lined up outside a shop near our hotel. Much of their banter is for their mutual amusement.

We ask our concierge for a recommendation. "What kind of rug do you want?" he asks.

"Old, faded colors, like the one we're standing on."

"Oh, that is for sale. The rugs we have are from a merchant we know. Go there." And so I fall into the hands of an expert rug merchant.

We meet Guven Demer, speaker of eight languages, young and passionate. We are no match for Istanbul rug dealers. They are performers and shrewd psychologists. They are relentless and should give lessons to international negotiators of foreign affairs. They could prevent wars. Guven, in business with four brothers and several cousins, has practiced his craft for two thousand years around the Mediterranean. After an hour he has the smell of the hunt about him. The rugs are flying through the air, the prices fly, combining with other prices, turning from Turkish billions into dollars and back again. The showroom is windowless, stacked with rugs that go back, in the heat, to the scents of camel. He begins to touch us, a tap on the shoulder, a hand on Ed's knee. Sweet tea is served, boxes of Turkish delight presented. The rugs are too bright for me, too new, and he asks for two hours, during which time he scours his contacts. When we return, the rug I had envisioned lies on the floor, and I nod and say "Guven, it's beautiful." It is a hundred-year-old Herez of faded blue and salmon and biscuit colors.

He turns around and around. He's a dervish. "She likes it, praise to Allah," and he dramatically falls to the floor in the prayer position. By the time we have bought the rug, plus two small ones and the one on the floor of the hotel, he is embracing us, inviting us home, inviting us for two days on the Asian side to see how real Turks live. He is coming to visit us in California. We walk out dazed; he had us in the palm of his hand.

"And therefore I have sailed the seas and come/to the holy city of Byzantium." What a clunky rhyme, **come /-tium**, I suddenly notice. But I, too, finally have come to Byzantium, to the fabled Bosporus, to the Sea of Marmara. The word, **mar, mar**, has the breaking of waves in it, the oldest sound other than that of mama, mama.

Leaving Istanbul, the taxi careens along the Bosporus, hot wind blowing my hair behind my ears. We are not "dewy," as my southern relatives used to say, we are downright sweating. I flash on an image of Alain back on his terrace in Cortona sipping a glass of cold white wine. Then we enter the most state-of-the-art airport in the world, where we are cooled down to morgue temperature until we enter the sleeve of the plane, where it is again one hundred degrees. Everyone is emanating hot odors—oil, the wrung-out stink of lamb, rancid breaths, pungent underwear, a whiff of tea tannin, dirt.

I've been to Greece and have grazed the edge of Turkey. Praise Allah. Praise Professor Hunter who called me a Maenad. Praise the Oracle. In the plane the fans blow away the smells.

Alitalia seems to take off with more confidence than other airlines. The pilot angles up as soon as the tires lift off the runway, accelerates, spirals up, and turns with brio. We are over Romania, Bulgaria. We are served our last tastes of Turkish food—little meat kebabs and fried pastries stuffed with vegetables, baklava. Then down into Fumicino and home to Bramasole, home to our green **paradiso**. Home to no electricity and a broken water line, a printer zapped by lightning. Rampant morning glories have vaulted onto the jasmine and across the terrace wall, the blooms, blue as the Aegean, trumpeting joy.

In a few weeks a package from the merchant in Istanbul arrives. On a small wooden loom we read, woven in a miniature rug of red and tan wool, our names and below:

In Love, Guven.

Bulls, Poets, Archangels

Crete and Mani

You heard your voice saying
thanks
. . . you were certain now:
a large piece of eternity
belonged to you.

—Yannis Ritsos

We have come to Greece for the baptism of Constantine Demetrios Mavromihalis at the Church of the Archangels, Ayion Taxiarchon, in Areopolis, ancestral home of the fierce Mavromihalis clan, deep in the Mani.

First we light in western Crete, near Chaniá. On our cruise through the Greek islands, the stop at Knossos and Heraklion seemed more frustrating than not seeing the places at all. The deadly heat, the crowds, the limited time, and the head 'em up, move 'em out aspects skewed our experience of the island. We vowed to return. Even inside those blighted circumstances, I glimpsed, in a hand flipping a rag at a window, in the rotten sweet scent of fallen apricots that even the bees had left to the ants, in the philosophical goats among the dusty tamarisks, the elemental nature of Crete.

We have rented a house in Chaniá, where watercolored Venetian buildings line the C-shaped harbor, the scene nicely accented by a domed Arab mosque and a lively quay of tavernas with outdoor tables. The town, long swamped by tourism, yields charms at night. Around the bend from the crowds, you can have dinner right beside the water and, looking through your glass of local white wine, imagine the din and activity of the trading port as successive conquerors arrived and took over for a century or two. A sloe-eyed Gypsy girl jangles with bracelets and anklets as she offers her roses for sale. Four old women, who surely would have worn heavy black a few decades ago, sit down next to us, order tall lime daiquiris, and settle in to talk. We dine to the music of their laughter, the occasional clomp of the horse-drawn carriages, and the slap of small waves against the mole.

Our house, on a scruffy hillside overlooking the bay, calms me just to be inside the four rooms. The two bedrooms and kitchen—all small—jog off a large main room, with French doors opening to spacious outside terraces that drop abruptly to citrus trees and shrubs. Night wanderers beware. The utter simplicity of the architecture corresponds to the plain furniture, comfortable enough, with chairs draped in bright cotton cloth. The coolness of white marble floors promotes serenity. A white shoebox of a house, but petals of plumbago and bougainvillea blow in the windows and doors, filling the bottom of the bathtub and gathering in pools in the hall. One covered terrace with chairs around a low table becomes my favorite place to read. Ed takes his notebooks to the second bedroom and closes the shutter. He likes to work in semidarkness.

Because our other trip was go, go, go, this time we are going nowhere for at least a week, except on short drives and down to a family beach nearby. We play in the water of a clear cove, sit in the sand, and throw back the kids' ball when it falls near us. Olive trees grow to the edge of the beach, giving the landscape a timeless appeal. Frothy aqua water, golden sand, a little drink stand under the trees—we stay for hours, floating on rafts out into the horseshoe cove and drifting. The pleasure feels so simple. I can visualize the ventricles of my heart filling with salt and sunlight.

At Irini's in Horifaki, not far from another beach where much of Kazanzakis's book **Zorba the Greek** was filmed, the lamb has been roasted a long time and slakes off the bone in meltingly tender hunks. The waitress takes us back in the kitchen to select what we will eat, and there's Irini, wrapped in a white apron, rosy cheeks, and a big greeting. She's yanking huge pans of moussaka out of the oven. We choose lamb, baked chicory stuffed tomatoes, and the ubiquitous Greek salad, which they serve not with crumbled feta but with a thick slab. First she brings rough bread with olive paste and sesame on top. A menu exists, but everyone is taken to the kitchen. **Lamb** has been translated as "lamp," which she offers as "lamp with fricassee bad," whatever that might mean. Also listed: humburger and fish soap (soup). "Well, her English is better than my Greek," Ed says.

Irini's becomes our favorite. Every visit

there's a new big cheese pie, **pikilia**, seafood tidbits with orange avocado salad, or **ofto**, lamb on skewers grilled upright in the fire and brought to us on pasta mixed with creamy cheese and broth. Platters of crisp roasted potatoes, which benefit from the drippings from chickens, are plunked down on every table.

On our third day we've settled into a routine. Read. Beach. Irini's for lunch. Nap. Walk. Shop for food in town. Cook something utterly simple. The potatoes are wonderful, fresh and earthy. We make dinners of Greek salad and steamed potatoes and bread. At night we lie out on the terrace watching the stars. We see no neighbors, only swaying lights on boats.

We vary on the fourth day and visit the Chaniá museum in the morning. They've rescued a patchy mosaic of Dionysus on a panther with a companion satyr. That's what passed for a floor covering in Chaniá in the third century A.D. Another of Poseidon also shows two roosters trying to peck the same cherry. Such whimsy! Poseidon was worshiped around here not as a sea god but as a fertility deity. The museum displays cases of votive oxen and bulls from a rural sanctuary active from the fourth century B.C. to the second century A.D. The pots look like the first things you'd throw in beginning ceramics, but the jewelry! Exquisite. Gold hair spirals, a rock crystal and gold ring, and the most fabulous earrings from the eighth century B.C. Could I reach in and snatch the necklace inlaid with lapis and medallions with raised heads? The artists were playful, too—a clay censer shaped like a hedgehog from 1800 B.C. makes me smile, as does the drinking cup with eyes on it to protect the drinker from the evil eye. The ancient **pithoi**, terra-cotta storage jars, are taller than I am. Most mysterious are the coins for Charon, made to go in the mouths of the dead. I guess they came from long-gone-to-dust skulls, the fare uncollected. I first thought a clay ship from 1900 to 1650 B.C. was a child's toy, but with the honeycomb inside, this must be another object to speed the dead on their way. Honey, so essential to the Greeks. Glaukos, son of legendary king Minos, fell into a **pitho** of honey and drowned. Some bodies, according to Herodotus, were buried in honey.

At the covered market, a short walk away, piles of lambs' heads, eyes open, regard us as we enter, and bunnies, with white fur only on their feet like little bedroom shoes, line up on ice. Vats of yogurts and fruits and nuts in syrup, and dried fruits, especially figs, give a totally Mediterranean cast to our shopping. The herbs mostly come in packages convenient for tourists to tuck into their bags. But they look stale to me. When I see the cheeses—so fresh—I know that my attempts at home to reproduce the luscious dill-scented pies we're eating everywhere will not be the same. We taste the specialty of the area, **pyktogalo**, a soft, slightly spicy cheese, and **malaka**, also a Chaniá cheese, similar to Gruyère. **Anthotyro**, a cream cheese, and **staka**, a big pale mound in the market case, both go in my notebook, along with **cheirokasi**, and **stakovoutyro**—what is that? How wonderful—everything is so unfamiliar. Ah, **-kasi**—that must mean cheese. Big wreaths of bread for a wedding are decorated with bread roses. An organ grinder pumps away. We walk out with fennel, yogurt, and cheeses—but who knows which is which—and a bunch of dill.

Such activity. We don't get to the beach until late afternoon, when the sun angles across the water and the children are gone. We have twilight to ourselves, splashing like the gods.

• • •

From a crack in the house, two yellow beaks open and the mother sparrow flits over our heads, to and fro from the grove. Her angry chirp warns us that she might dive-bomb our reclining forms. A visiting gray cat stretches on the warm stone terrace, purring at her reflection in the door. She ignores the sparrow. Under my pulled-down hat, I begin to think of old attachments, friends, those I have failed, those who failed me. The elemental nature of Greece, I suppose. Or sometimes travel just unlocks Pandora's box. What I've put off considering in my quotidian life rushes forward when the body and mind achieve a quiet level of receptivity. What has been lost comes looking. Problems overly suppressed can erupt as a full-blown crisis. I start with the drifty thought, **Mother would love this**, followed by the petulant, childish (but true) thought, **She failed me, no?** Then an old friendship I bluntly broke off. My mind jumps to Bill D. **Oh, he let you down, big time**, then the tidal rush of how he would have loved Greece, how funny he was, and what a good poet. Drunk, he lurches over the hors d'oeuvres table, I reach to catch him, but he crashes into the bowls and plates. Hardest to understand, the friends who recede, become vague, their names in the address book but their numbers forgotten. Friends from college stay fixed. I pick up with Anne and Rena immediately, out of such long connections. As an adult, I moved six times, and for the most part the intense friendships of each place gradually faded, replaced by the next set. And yet I still care about Ralph and Mitra and Gabby and Hunter and Alan and, and, and. That conference when I shared a room with Karen and we talked late. In the dark, her voice sounded so familiar, a little sister whispering from the other twin bed, kicking off the quilt. We lost touch. I always mean to **go back**, pick up the dropped stitch, continue the round hem. But the present grounds me—I first wrote **grinds me**—so firmly. A tidal wash of losses, all under the big energy sun. I gather Ed's shirt, dried over a chairback in the sun, the blue cotton warming my hands.

At a little monastery on the sea, the caretaker shakes his head sadly at Ed in shorts. He points to a rack inside the door with various pairs of jogging pants and beach wraps for visitors to cover their shameful bodies. "Am I okay?" I ask. He regards my white linen Capri pants and short-sleeved T-shirt and concedes that I am. Determined to break through his officious manner, I start asking him about the fountain outside the monastery, which looks distinctly Arab to me, but he doesn't know.

"Could be anything," he shrugs. His friend rounds the corner of the building with a handful of sprigs. Ah, the universal language. Ed, now in navy pants, asks what he's picked. He holds up a handful.

"Origano dictamnus." We later recognize this oregano growing in the maquis that covers the coastal hillsides. "This one is very good if you cut yourself, and for the ladies, it helps in birth."

"And for cooking," the caretaker adds. An Italian would launch into recipes right now, but they are more interested in the other herb. They both begin to explain at once that this is a special plant, used to make tea. **"Fascomilo,"** the friend says. He writes the name in Greek on our guidebook and gives us a few branches that perfume our car with a sage and dust scent. "Smells like marijuana. Throw it out." Ed fans his face. But I slip the leaves inside my guidebook to scent the pages with the smell of the countryside.

The deep country monasteries deeply stir me. Triada seems holy, holy, and someone is chanting in one of the monastery rooms. He has a loud and terrible voice, accompanied by the rattle of pots and dishes. Women are cleaning up after a wedding lunch. The priest in stone gray robes sits against a stone wall under the arched entrance, cooling off after his duties. Inside, the floor is scattered with crumbled bay leaves, as in the Middle Ages when santolina was piled on the floors of cathedrals to keep down the stench of the unwashed. At the entrance a man fills an enormous basket with leftover slices of bread. I can't get enough of the Byzantine icons and altars, the heady scents of incense, and the elaborate iconostases. The Orthodox churches feel very close to the bone, as if they tap into those same archetypal openings where myth comes from. So many are smaller than the Italian and French neighborhood churches. The domes are blue and covered with stars, a motif I adore. The top section of the cross-shaped churches always are closed off by a curtain, suggesting mystery.

At the Holy Monastery of Hyperaghia, Lady of Goniá, in Kolymbari, another visitor gives us the φασκομηλο, the **fascomilo** again. Must be the day for gathering—his basket is piled high. This monastery sits above the Chaniá bay. An icon of Mary is completely covered with exvotos—rings, watches, metal eyes, and tiny crosses. The wooden crucifix, with two side panels held by carved gold dragons, looks as though it landed from the Far East. But the three domes of immense blue covered with stars and the incense burning bring us back to Greece. We are not able to see the famed icon collection in a small building across the courtyard. The caretaker must have been out picking **fascomilo**. We take a path to the earlier ruins of the monastery, another outpost of peace.

En route to Rethymnon, we see a wreck. In the driver's seat a young man with black hair, trickles of blood running down his face—his seriously dead face. He sits upright inside his crushed car. How impossible to come upon. The visceral desire rises to rerun the moment, have him swerve from the truck, right himself, and speed on home to the dinner his mother probably is preparing at this moment. The shiny Japanese compact, brand new, now smushed like a stepped-on Coke can. **Get up**, we want to say, but he is gone, someone's love, someone's boy, someone. Just before we left Cortona, two American tourists' car struck a college student's Vespa. He jumped up and went in the bar across the road and had a glass of water. The drivers must have been immensely relieved. But when the ambulance came, he was weak, and he died—punctured lungs filled with blood. Why seek danger? It may be on the loose for you.

As we drive on, we realize no airbag popped out for him. Cheap car, but what a crime. I look down and notice that there's no airbag on my side of this rental car. We will go to the airport tomorrow and trade this compact for a heavier car.

In Rethymnon bakeries make bread in the shapes of swans, dinosaurs, and deer. Street after street in the old section entices us to wander.

Turkish balconies, Venetian fountain, curtained doorways, broken arches, stone-edged Cretan windows, twisting medinalike streets, where an ancient way of life asserts itself in spite of the mobs of tourists a few streets away. An old man plays backgammon with a child, a woman shells beans under a grape arbor, women in black sit in doorways, children play in a street as narrow as a good hallway. I step into the timelessness I expected when I came to Greece.

We linger into the evening, not wanting to drive by the place the boy died. We choose the restaurant for the vine-draped arbors and the sound of music. A sweet-faced mandolin player and his child stroll among the tables. The British couple at the next table will not look at him when he stops to play right at their table. The waiter laughs. "They're afraid." Greece on a summer evening, someone strumming a mandolin just for you, and you ignore him? Ed always tips musicians lavishly, thinking that people who bring music should be crowned with laurel. We're treated to several songs and a shy smile from the little girl.

• • •

Now we're in the car every day, wanting to explore this wild end of Crete. The land is scattered with pink, blue, and green beehives in fields. Wild goats with long black hair chomp away on the sparse hills. Tall hollyhocks punctuate the roadsides, along with the memorials to the dead that you see all too often. I start photographing these small dollhouse structures, which are furnished with photographs and candles and sometimes objects belonging to the deceased. Some are plaster models of a church, some look more like homes. There are just so many of these memorials, so often on straight stretches of road. I doubt that **so** many people have met their fate in these spots. They must also be primitive votives or tributes to gods of the crossroads and the journey.

Up on the hills I see groves of butter-yellow and pink oleander along the dry watercourses. The vibrant double blooms often entwine with profligate pink and blue morning glories. I love these liaisons of two or three plants and vines. The vivid pink bougainvillea cooled by its white partner. The orange trumpet vine twirled with pale blue plumbago, the blue morning glories splendid within masses of fluffy white bougainvillea, woody honeysuckle tangled with the flat pink rose.

We jump out at cemeteries in the countryside and their pure white churches, so white they hurt your eyes. Their blue doors and blue-edged windows seem cut out of heaven. The graves have glass-fronted marble boxes at the heads. Inside, a photo of the person laid to rest, an oil lamp, with perhaps a plastic bottle of extra oil, and some matches. The box may have pictures of a saint, notes, wicks, lace mats, or mementos of the dead person—a teddy bear, a bottle of Johnnie Walker with two shot glasses. Unbearable, a child's grave covered with toy cars, stuffed animals, and his bottle and rattler propped beside his photo, a merry two-year-old with wide-open eyes.

Houses, typically low and white, sometimes have crenellations at the corners of the roofs, a reminder of North Africa, not far away. Many one- and two-story houses are topped with rebar around the edges of the roof, in case they want to build up someday. No one has built a decorative plaster wall around these unsightly metal rods, and it's clear that many of the houses have been there for years and years without the next construction stage. Even prosperous-looking new houses display this odd feature.

The landscape, barren at a sweeping glance, often looks like carefully planted rock gardens. We pass many gorges. "Gorgeous gorge," Ed says.

"You had to, didn't you?" We smell the dry, herbal maquis, the miles of coastal hills blooming with rounded bushes—violet, purple, yellow, sage, mossy green, gray—and the earth ferrous red and sienna with rocks and boulders. A stupendous palette, especially with the blue, blue sea in the distance and the cloudless sky extending the blue as far as the imagination can go.

We come upon war memorials and cemeteries everywhere. At first we'd been puzzled why so many people asked us if we were from Australia or New Zealand. Then we saw the graves of those troops who fought so bitterly hard in this lonely countryside in World War II. Their relatives come here to find their loved ones' graves. As a major gateway to Egypt to the South, and the whole Aegean world to the North, Crete was strategically crucial. Every record attests to the heroism and arduousness of the population here. The Allies did not arm the

Cretans; they fought to the death with whatever they had. In the Souda war cemetery, close to our house, most graves lack names. But there's Archibald Knox Brown. All boys in their early twenties, in peaceful rows, as orderly as war is not. Even in death, they overlook a Greek military base on the harbor and a former NATO site. Red roses grow everywhere, also orderly, and the color of the blood the boys shed so far from home. Many Allied troops evacuated from Souda Bay in 1941; then the Luftwaffe swarmed the area.

Donkeys, few houses, olives everywhere to the sea, shrines, figs—the clarity startles me, and I have the odd thought, **I'd like to rise to this occasion**. From reading the Greek poets I understood intellectually the qualities of this powerful place. Days here move the knowledge into the body. I find in my notebook a few words by Kimon Friar in his preface to **Modern Greek Poetry**:

> Many have felt that in the dazzling sun of Greece the psychological dark labyrinths of the

> mind are penetrated and flooded with light, that in this merciless exposure one is led not to self-exploitation but to self-exploration under the glare of necessity, that to "Know Thyself" is for all Greeks, from ancient into modern times, the only preoccupation worthy of an individual. Beneath the blazing sun of Greece there is a sensuous acceptance of the body without remorse or guilt.

What calls out from the landscape? The purity, essence. Simplicity: a handful of shorn wool. I think only a Greek poet could have written these lines:

> **Here, in this mineral landscape**
> **of rock and sea, sapphire and diamond,**
> **which to the wheel of Time offers nothing**
> **that's perishable;**
>
> **here in the great victorious light**
> **whose only stain is your own shadow,**
> **and where only your body carries**
> **a germ of death;**
>
> **here perhaps for a moment the false idols**
> **will vanish; perhaps once again**

in a dazzling flash you may stare
at your true self.

—Alexander Mátsas

Out early for a swing around the coast, we stop for coffee, good god it's bad, at a terrace taverna overlooking the sea. The young waiter retires to the side to play his lyre, and I can't eat my roll because I am watching the black curls and lithe body of young Orpheus back on earth.

We drive on around where northern Crete curves into western Crete, delicately colored in the morning, but this must be the place for big sunsets. Many plastic greenhouses, that blight so helpful to the farmer, blot the landscape. We stop for walks on deserted beaches and a dip in one irresistible cove of purling turquoise water.

At a taverna at Francocastello's beach, we taste **volvi**, translated on the menu as "wild roots." The waiter's English can't enlighten us, but he brings out a German wildflower book on Crete and points to a purple flowered plant, **Muscari comosum**. Little muscari corms? After we have "stuffed wine leaves," roasted eggplant with an intense taste of roastedness, and tomatoes spiked with mint, we take the person-wide path through bulrushes down to another beach. "What **is** the decibel level of a single Greek cicada?" Ed wonders. The volume approaches that of a rock concert he attended in Perugia. This wide, endless beach, the polar opposite of the hideous holiday villages that ruin much of Crete, invites a long walk. No one at all swims here on a weekday morning. We don't swim but wade—the water stays shallow way out.

When our Chaniá stay ends, we go back to Knossos and the museum at Heraklion. We leave our dream cottage and drive across Crete. We then will stay a couple of days at Elounda on the coast, fly to Athens from Heraklion, and drive to the Mani for the baptism.

We find that we absorbed more than we thought on our first trip, when we were travelling in a group in August. These places probably always are crowded, though much less if you're the first ones there. Getting up early is the key. I have to myself the bull head carved from serpentine, with crystal and jasper eyes and elegantly erect horns, excavated from Knossos. Here's the bull symbol, way back at the beginning. He had holes on top of his head and in his mouth, probably where libations were poured. The double-ax insignia of the Minoans is carved between his eyes. He gazes with distinctly godlike disdain. As evocative, the kinetic ivory carving of a bull leaper and the figure of the snake goddess in her tiered skirt and bodice with her breasts popping out. She holds two snakes at arm's length, and I'm certain something loud and oracular is coming out of her mouth. She's one of many precious artifacts that point to a profoundly symbolic level of Minoan life—the lion, leopard, sea creatures, ax, double spirals, birds, and of course the myriad bulls. I will be studying in detail the famous bull-leaping fresco found in the palace by Sir Arthur Evans, who must have had the most exciting days of any archaeologist. He even named the civilization he was discovering, although Homer says Minos was king for only nine years. We call them Minoans after him, but what they called themselves we do not know. The longer I look, the more mysterious these people become. The fresco's intricate borders prove to be more fascinating than the figures suspended between the spotted bull's long horns, or the leaper on the bull's back, or the standing figure with outstretched arms as if waiting to catch the leaper. An American English professor discovered the hidden meaning of the borders. The tiny stripes and lozenge-shaped overlapping designs represent days of the year and the lunar months. They combine in ways that indicate the magic nine-year cycles that crop up over and over—youths were sacrificed, kings met the goddess. The cycle of nine—and what does this have to do with the leaping acrobat? Interesting as it would be to know, I like being forced to wonder. The art of the Minoans sounds such a dithyrambic call from the ancient world: **We were alive, we feasted and loved beauty and saw the world as an animated, forceful dynamic with our beings. Join us in the dance, the leap over time.**

Minoans were addicted to jewelry—intricate necklaces and earrings, gold hairpins, bracelets and ankle bracelets, gold spirals through which hair was twisted, an artful pendant of two bees, beaded clothing, arm bracelets, tiaras and other hair ornaments made of flat gold leaf—leaves and crowns. Many artifacts reveal how they lived, what they wore. A bit of mosaic shows early houses. They enlivened their rooms with frescoes, as at Pompeii and Herculaneum. An early small cart shows that they had four-wheeled transport. How often women's breasts are displayed. The clothing looks constructed to showcase the breasts. How much and how little we know about these mysterious people who rocked the cradle of civilization. These stones stood at the beginning, and laying a hand on one makes me imagine the hand that placed it.

The site at Knossos again thrums with buses and clumps of people on tours. How good to travel alone and slip in and out at will. Ed seems fascinated by the drains. Flushing toilets were available to the Minoans—something that flashes through my mind when I encounter those hole-in-the-floor toilets with the rippled footprints on either side, apparently to guide a giant to straddle the opening. At one serene and pure monastery perched high above the sea, one of these holes emptied directly into the aqua and violet water below. A fetid barrel of water with a scoop made from a detergent bottle stood by, in case you wanted to flush. I glanced in and backed out, as did two Greek women.

The Minoans guided rainwater from the roof cistern into an open pipe in the floor, located just outside the bathroom, which flowed under the toilet seat. Even when no water flowed from above, by employing the same system as the monastery, you could flush. Even today Cretan houses typically have water tanks on the roof, providing pressure to the system. Knossos is riddled with means for draining or bringing in water to the complex. Little channels run down the sides of staircases; there are stone drains that lead to sediment traps, reminding me of the installation of our elaborate septic system in Italy. A **pozzo**, a little well filled with stones, was constructed every few dozen meters, for settlement and filtration. Ever since, we've been fixated on plumbing.

Ed is wandering. I sit down on a hot stone with my notebook looking down at many terracotta pots, imagining what they held and what people ate. Accounts from Knossos list large quantities of coriander, used both in cooking and perfume making. Pistachios were produced in quantity, too. I can imagine the tables around the bull-leaping ring laden with baklava layered with dried cherries and nuts, plates of **dipla**, those folded pastries with a filling made with sweetened eggs, and others scented with thyme, honey, and nuts. The deeply rustic smoked sausages with cumin, and others with vinegar, and the **omathia**, a sweet sausage stuffed with liver, rice, and raisins—all these must have fed the Minoans, too. Lighter fare might have included the many preparations of snails, and the pilafs—a rice boiled in lamb broth and seasoned. The Mediterranean diet came to fame after a study of long-lived natives. Cretan food does have its spleen with fennel, and "lamp" bowels in various guises, but the strong counterbalance comes from the olive oil, wild greens, cheeses, and salads such as **boureki**, which is made of **dakos**, rusks of barley, topped with tomatoes, cheeses, and oil. We've loved eating here—the rabbit with oranges and olives, meatballs in egg and lemon sauce, but mainly the variety of salads, such as grilled eggplant salad with walnuts, and all the fresh cheeses. I like the invitation to the kitchen in all the tavernas, the olive oil cans planted with begonias, the bright clotheslines strung between massive olive trees. Imagine the table, and the people spring to life.

• • •

Dusty from Knossos, we check into Elounda Mare. The hotel has a basically modern design, but they have recuperated old door surrounds and Cretan stone floors, weavings, and copper trays. Old farm doors are sparingly but effectively used for ornaments, on either side of openings, and for tables. We get lost. The architect must have been inspired by the labyrinth at Knossos. We are luckily upgraded to a room with a private pool, terrace, and small yard with the sea below. We have a couple of days to look around at this part of Crete, but really we just laze about, taking a brief jaunt to see Spinalonga, a tiny island that formerly was a leper colony. Back at the hotel gift shop, I buy glass evil eye protectors for my house in California. The clerk says, "The sun gives us power. If we have two days without sun, we go crazy."

We walk to dinner at the Calypso restaurant. It's under the tutelage of a chef with a two-star restaurant in France. We're seated near a marble pool with fountain jets; below, the sea spreads calmly to infinity. At the next table I'm convinced we have a member of the Russian mafia. The big-muscled, no-neck guy can't put his arms down because of his expanded waist. He's sweating alarmingly. His wife across from him is plump, too, but they have refused to acknowledge girth and are squeezed into clothes from an earlier size. He looks like a bouncer, and she's forced-smiley and crunched into an aqua blue sequined top with tiny straps cutting into her soft meaty shoulders. Square-cut emerald earrings dangle on either side of her puffy little face with darting eyes. She looks trapped. He is silent, she is chattering. He moves to another chair at the table. Didn't want his back to the door? Doubtless my mind is leaping; he made a fortune in cell phones or BMWs. We say good evening to them as they leave, this being a civilized custom practiced all over Europe, but they stare stonily ahead and do not respond.

This is our last night in Crete.

A quick flight to Athens, and we're suddenly in our rental car, heading toward the city. After the solitude of Crete, these roads look chaotic. We're on a bumper-car course, with detours, closed lanes, flares in the road, and **no** signs. I'm gazing at the map, trying to catch a name, a street, a direction. Ed plows forward. We cross the entire city and somehow, miraculously, emerge on the road to Náfplio. The baptism of our friends Steven and Vicki's boy will be in three days.

Just out of the Athens sprawl—oh, please let us find the airport when we return—we pass a building supply company that sells prefabricated chapels, painted yellow, trimmed in white. I want one. I've photographed every one we've passed. They may be memorials to the roadside dead, but I think of them as tributes to the travel gods. Ed keeps driving. "They weigh probably two hundred pounds. Hoist that onto luggage check-in?"

"Look, a Byzantine model, white with blue dome."

"We are not hauling one of those through two airports. Who would be the one to carry it?"

"I could set it in front of our house in California. We could keep a votive lighted and photographs of our own dead inside. Maybe a poem by Ritsos."

"The homeowners' association would be on you in a heartbeat."

• • •

Hotel Byron in Náfplio, not easy to find, hides behind a boarded-up, domed Arab building and across from the church where the Mavromihalis clan assassinated the first president of Greece. I'm looking forward to meeting Steven's Greek family, but the bullet hole in the church wall is disconcerting. We hoist our bags up several flights of stairs to get to the hotel, then hoist again up to the third floor above that. No elevator. Náfplio shows everywhere the inheritance of the Venetian taskmasters. They ruled capriciously and often heartlessly, but wherever their Machiavellian hard hand was felt, the legacy is efficacious—the mellow colors along the water, the genteel houses, the piazzas; the Venetians knew how to set up a city for living pleasantly. We came to Náfplio on the previous trip and now stop by to see George Couveris at his shop Preludio, where Ed bought gold earrings with sapphires to remind me of the Aegean. His is the prettiest jewelry I've seen in Greece. I'm tempted again by a heavy gold cross with other sea-colored stones, but under the influence of Cretan simplicity, I don't even try it on. He remembers us and shows us all the latest designs, then sends us off to eat at Basilis, tables on the street, because they make the spiciest eggplant **imam** in town.

Because Ed likes hardware stores, we stop in to admire those triangular-handled aluminum trays for delivering coffee from the bar to a shop—how Italian **that** is. We buy skewers topped with brass owls, hares, and fish for our neighbor Placido, the master griller. What a throwback—they stock a number of frosted aluminum glasses and pitchers—those redolent of the 1960s colors, fuchsia, magenta, lime, blue, all sheened with the glow of moonlight. I'll take Fiorella a few handmade bells, though she has no sheep or goats.

The road gnarls through the hard mountains of the Peloponnese, and every kilometer subtracts something else from the landscape until only stark rock and determined shrub trees remain. Occasionally a lone monastery, a muscular little donkey, a scrawny mimosa. Finally we arrive in Monemvassía, the poet Yannis Ritsos's hometown, which he called "the rocky ship, my ship of stone, which carries me across the world." I love his poems and quote to Ed, "I've always wanted to tell you about this miracle," and "I am totally inside myself like a person returning home after an exhausting journey." The great heap of a rock island joins the mainland by a causeway. Mostly abandoned, the town carved into the unforgiving rock broods alone, now that the only marauders approaching the islet are tourists. Taken by the Turks, the Venetians, then the Turks again, the history and geography conspire together to emphasize a besieged stance in the world. Ritsos, too, was always in trouble with politics, a resister, exiled to various islands. Monemvassía, built facing sea, turns its back on the mainland. But they had to get their wheat somewhere; perhaps they were vulnerable after all. They had to go to the mainland to farm. A few houses have been restored; most lie empty and often roofless. Everywhere the sea reminds you of its beauty. Every house knew the beauty of the sea at all hours, and now the town's remaining restaurants occupy terraces that offer to visitors the three-hundred-degree views.

After climbing up and down the streets, we walk back to the modern town on the other side of the stone causeway. I sit down with an ice cream cone, while I wait for Ed to have coffee. Practically at my feet a man falls off his bicycle and lies unconscious in the street. People swarm out of their shops, someone slaps him, someone throws a pitcher of cold water in his face. I'm horrified—he's had a heart attack or a brain aneurysm. But no, he rouses, shakes his head, and soon pushes on. They must be used to heat prostration around here. "It happened to my nephew," a waitress tells me. "He fell off the tractor, and the tractor just kept going until it hit a stone wall." We spend a quiet night at a hotel right at the entrance to the secretive town.

Before we leave, I pay a visit to Yannis Ritsos, buried among his townspeople in a simple grave.

By noon we are in Sparta. **Mother, imagine, I went to Sparta!** A clean and modern city that has long since lost its legendary warrior rigor. We drive on in the afternoon to Mystras, another abandoned city, on the precipitous slopes of Mount Taigetos. According to **Nature Guides: Europe/Greece** by Bob Gibbons, there are blooming on this mountain three types of white saxifrage, golden drop, figwort, peacock anemones, giant orchids, spurge, white irises, Judas trees, vetches—blue and yellow—and a scattering of horseshoe, somber, and yellow bee orchids. He lists toadflax, starry clover, and on and on. In the summer heat we don't see anything except dried grasses and a few drifts of something that looks like Queen Anne's lace but isn't. I would like to come back and spot the Nottingham catchfly, asphodel, and cranesbill and, in the air, rock nuthatches, booted eagles, peregrines, and blue rock thrushes. But will we ever come back to Mystras? The places people have abandoned have the rub of loss, the erasure of the particulars of living and the remains of form only. Gibbons's description of wildflowers in the Mani and around Mystras creates images in my mind of olive groves lushly carpeted in spring with spotted orchids, milk thistles, bellflowers, and burnt candytuft. Just the names of the mostly unfamiliar flowers lure me: valerian, grass pea, furry-leaved woundwort, catchfly. Dreaming of wildflowers not in bloom, I scurry over the hills peering into the abandoned houses. In the main church, I see for the first time ex-votos of houses. Why should that be surprising? After the body, what do we want to protect? Our homes.

We're drowsy as bees in the heat. Cicadas rhythmically shake their bags of nails, they're chugging like a train, rattling a thousand tambourines. I want to pour a bottle of water over my head. When we get back to the car, the temperature is 44.5 degrees Celsius. That's a heat-stroke-zone 112 degrees in the other world.

Now we head deep into the Mani. The Peloponnese has three thumbs of land protruding at the bottom of the peninsula. Mani is the middle one, and surely the wildest and most individualistic part of Greece. We are meeting our friends at Limeni on the coast, where there is a new hotel. Exhilarating to travel early in the morning with the car packed with luggage, heading into the roaring sun. How forlorn the landscape. Mountains jut straight up, and any slope is littered with low stone walls—sheep folds—that look like archaeological remains of a village. The pastel scent of oleander flies through the window, and no sign of human life appears for mile after mile after mile. If your car broke down, you would be in limbo. As we go deeper, hour after hour—**niente**, only stone. Nary a posy, only the rare pitiful tree. The ultimate subtracted landscape. I can imagine a pterodactyl setting down a big foot on the windshield of the car with an ear-splitting shriek.

But finally we emerge from a pass and wind down to the village of Limeni on the sea. At the taverna suddenly, we are greeted. We must have arrived for the baptism. The owners are cousins of our friend—everyone must be cousins in the Mani—but for now we are taken into the kitchen, fish are pointed out, and we are seated right by the water where cheery fishing boats ride their reflections. The cousins point out the home of Petrobey Mavromihalis, Steven's ancestor, who led the revolt against the Ottomans, in a classic bite-the-hand maneuver. He'd been appointed **bey**, ruler of the area, a move by the Ottomans to give the illusion of power back to local people. Instead he united the famously warring clans of the area and led an attack against the Ottomans that resulted in the liberation of Kalamata. The Mavromihalis family conducted themselves with the same fearless zeal on many fronts. Elias Mavromihalis is honored every July 20 in Styra for a famous battle at a windmill, in which he and six other Maniots lost their lives in a brave exit from the windmill with swords.

During the years Steven and Vicki have been friends of ours, we've heard stories of this intense family. The bullet that made the hole in the Náfplio church was fired at the new president of Greece by Petrobey's brothers because Petrobey and other relatives had been imprisoned in Náfplio when they opposed this first president of the new independent Greece. All it takes is a day's drive through the mountains to see how conquering the Mani would be impossible. Pirates and slave traders frequently raided this area, and the Maniots were not opposed to those activities from time to time themselves. The terrain speaks of isolation, individualism, privation, and xenophobia. Ferocious defenders of their freedom and dreamers of liberty, way in the Mani, they also must dream of green beans and peas.

Our Mavromihalis clan, most peaceful and charming of humans, we find by the pool at the hotel. Vicki's family lives an hour north, and they've come down from her home place this morning with their four children. Steven and

Vicki live near us in Marin, where they have important lives and careers and hundreds of friends. But they passionately love their Greek heritage, and they are giving their children the great gift of a home in this world. Already the three older children, eight, six, and three, speak Greek fluently. They think it's funny to teach us ένας, δύο, τρείς, **énas, thío, tris,** one, two, three. They talk to baby Constantine in Greek, and probably he already understands. Last year Steven and Vicki bought a grove over the sea and are planning to restore a house. Every year they travel to Greece at least twice. Steven is a car buff, and last year they flew to France, where he bought a classic Deux Chevaux, one of those hump-backed vintage Renaults, and the entire family drove all across Europe to Greece. Some might consider that a journey into hell, but they had fun. They always do. Their family life warms anyone who's around them because all the children enjoy each other. They joke and sing and hold hands when they walk. "How did you do this?" I've asked the parents so often. "Why aren't they whining and fighting?"

"They know the family is a team," Steve says. But really, they know they are cherished and appreciated, and the atmosphere of mutual respect in this family feels palpable. I once heard someone say that the best thing a man can do for his children is to love their mother. In Steven's case that must be easy. Vicki shines with intelligence as brightly as with beauty, a clear open face, black eyes, and a smile that makes you see what she looked like as a nine-year-old. Steven, too, remains the boy who studied fencing and went to the Olympics for Greece. His enthusiasm and simpatico personality will always keep him vibrant. A top real estate agent, he continues to study history and philology, often teaching courses at Stanford and Berkeley. Vicki has put aside her work as an attorney for a while and guards the time she spends with her children, Franco, Nikki, and Georgia, followed by Constantine, who is about to be baptized. Now "this girl's through," according to Vicki. What beauties. From one legend springs the source of the clan's beauty: an early Mavromihalis wed a mermaid. I have an Irish runaway priest and nun in my ancestry, but this pales in comparison to a mermaid in the bloodline.

Steven points over the wall to a few stark marble graves by the sea. "Old Petrobey's buried down there." We tell him we've seen the family home in the village. While the children read and rest, Ed and I drive down the coast road and find a place to scramble over the rocks for a dip in the sea.

We meet for dinner in Areopolis, named for Ares, god of war. Formerly the town was called Tsimova but was renamed to honor Petrobey Mavromihalis. This whole area was fighting mad. A male child was known as a "gun." The town has sunk into a summer torpor, the lanes deserted, a few cats asleep in the **plateia**, the town square. Steven takes us to a family friend's restaurant, and he's given a hero's welcome. We begin to understand how Steven's surname resonates in Mani. Dinner goes on and on. "Nikki, did anyone ever tell you that you look exactly how Jacqueline Kennedy must have looked at six? If they make a movie, we're recommending you for the part," Ed teases. She **has** been told, and it's true. She has a rare presence and elegance, odd words for a child. Franco, the oldest, makes jokes. He has a vulnerability about him, a goodness that shines, and Georgia just exudes some kind of golden-haired girlishness that calls up the Greek word **archetype**. Constantine, a baby still, observes all and somehow looks wise beyond his years. By all rights, this late he should be screaming, but instead paws his bread and looks at his siblings as though to say, **Just wait, I'll join you in a moment.**

We're looking over plans for the new house and trading stories about permits and workers. The waiter begins playing games with the children, who are unfazed by dinner beginning at ten P.M. He finally walks them over to the **plateia** and buys them ice cream. He's obviously having a fine time, and they are too. Are they just enchanted children, or could this happen to anyone? **Kaliníkhta**, good night, they call.

The family is busy with arrangements in the morning, so we drive to Váthia and other villages around Areopolis to look at the characteristic Mani towers. We pass more jutting stone and prickly pear, tiny roads, and villages of stone towers crawling up sheer walls and chopped out of rock. For miles we see no one. No car. Nothing. Ah, a baby donkey—sign of life. In a few places old men are playing the same cards they play all over Europe. Roads narrow to rough paths. May the tires hold up. Nowhere else on earth looks like this, so the mind must adjust to the tower mentality, what the tower meant to them, the duty of the male to build his family a tower, the life inside the tower. The tower reflects who they were—and to some extent still are. Steven says that among the two hundred arriving for the baptism, six or seven Mavromihalis families have not spoken to each other in three hundred years. I hope no vendetta erupts.

As a traveller devouring a place for only a short time, the impossibility of developing a profound view bothers me. But sometimes you find a book, a book that so thrills you by its scope and love that your own disappointment dissolves with each page. Such a book is **Mani** by Patrick Leigh Fermor. Published in 1958, **Mani** records a trip he made on foot, by bus, and by boat all around this area. He and his companion, Joan, camped and depended on the kindness of strangers. He does not hesitate to depart into discursive essays on whatever interested him. I think he would have a hard time publishing this brilliant book in this age of the short attention span. He tells all; he's a cataloguer, an ecstatic, and his prose style makes few compromises with the ignorance of his reader. This is one of my favorite books. I did not get to go inside a Mani tower, but through Fermor's description I know what it's like to have dinner on top, the table hauled up by rope, and to sleep there catching any breeze under the stars.

He describes descending, floor by floor, by ladders, each lower floor cooled more by the one above.

Although I hope Steven someday will write his own book about his family, Fermor conveys vividly the Mavromihalis heritage. They reached the pinnacle of their power, riches, and influence in the eighteenth and nineteenth centuries, and part of the reason for their hold on the Mani was their base at Limeni, a considerable harbor and the feasible gateway into Laconia and the rest of the Mani. He describes Petrobey's fine looks, great dignity, and gracious manners, which were "outward signs of an upright and honorable nature, high intelligence, diplomatic skill, generosity, patriotism, unshakable courage and strength of will: qualities suitably leavened by ambition and family pride and occasionally marred by cruelty." Minus the last, these qualities perfectly describe Steven. Petrobey, Fermor writes, "soars far beyond the rocky limitations of these pages into those of modern European history."

Scattered about the landscape, sometimes with almost perfect camouflage, the Byzantine churches are exciting to come upon. In Nomia, in Kitta, in lanes, and half hidden in the hills, these organic, sublime little Byzantine churches dot the landscape. They're one room in size with a curved apse. Often they're locked. They look made of mud with bricks stuffed in, or they're made of square stones, each one outlined in brick. One has an evil eye on a stone, one a shell; many are decorated around the door with bits of carved leaves and vines from other structures. Through a tiny window or keyhole, we can see sections of frescoes of horses or cool icons of Mary inside. So different from the Italian Mary, she looks remote, as though she is exercising Olympian disdain. Religion must have felt as stony as everything else in the land. The architecture gives me joy. A goat munching grass outside the smallest church in the world just looks at us as if to say, **What did you expect?**

We drive to the bottom of the peninsula, a camel-saddle of land with the sea on either side. A powerful zone—in the ancient world, Cape Taínaron was the entrance to hell. Pirates raged for centuries, not only raiding ships of their goods but taking crews and selling them for slaves all over the Mediterranean. My American education about slave trading was woefully inadequate. I thought there was a one-way route from Africa to the American South. Every southern soul carries memories of the slave ships. They're never bound for Italy or Turkey, always Savannah or Charleston. How naïve. As travel pushes me forward, memory keeps dragging me backward. You would think the tension of that string that connects the two is such that I'd hear a strong snap, perhaps while taking a short nap on some slow Einsteinian bus over the mountains.

We gather at the church in Areopolis. In the courtyard Petrobey and his seven thousand allies had their weapons blessed at the beginning of their expedition to Kalamata. Now an American son has brought back his boy for a baptism in the ancestral font. Before the ceremony the children pass around glass dolphin favors for all the guests. We crowd into the church—my god the temperature, we're going to expire—and the priests in their beards and robes begin to chant. I'm woozy. A fresco above depicts an infant baptism in the same font. Constantine is joining a long line of babies who achieve new life in an ancient place. He looks confident, then perturbed as his neat suit is stripped away and he is lowered naked into a vat of olive oil. I mean lowered, not just dipped. He's submerged, and when lifted aloft flailing and dripping, he screams like one of the Turks his ancestors offed. We're swaying in the powerful incense and the scents of sweat that must arise mostly from the robes of the priests. We have travelled many miles to feel the life of this child surge forward into his heritage.

The feast begins. Tables are laid on the rooftop of the hotel, some glimmer of the experience of family occasions on top of a tower. Constantine, no longer dazed, is passed from arm to arm. He seems to know this is all about him. I have never seen so many black mustaches, woolly beards, rampant eyebrows that run together. The dancing begins, and the music that will play all night serenades the grave below of Petrobey Mavromihalis. The full moon casts a marmoreal light on the sea. Vicki stars. She knows all the dances. I'm reminded of our Italian friends who say, "You're more Italian than we are." She's as lovely as a goddess in her green dress. She dances with Steven, who ends on his knees, leaning backward. He then dances with each of his girls. People perform solo dances such as "The Drunken Man." The departure from tradition comes when a woman performs this heretofore male prerogative. She staggers and lurches as everyone applauds wildly. Apparently the old warring factions are dining together. We jolt out of our seats when gunfire goes off. The relatives are packing heat. They blast off round after round into the sky. Children dance; the son of the former prime minister, more gorgeous than any of the gods he has replaced, dances with his girlfriend, who is dressed in a short beach wrap. We meet Mavromihalises from all over Mani. Few of the dances involve couples. Circles and conga lines form, and everyone, even the ancients, join in. Steven gives a welcome toast and speaks eloquently about his family's love of Greece and the importance in their lives of their Greek families. The band plays mostly Greek music but then launches into "What a Wonderful World," with the magnificent line "bright blessed days and dark sacred nights." Tomorrow we drive back to Athens and fly home to Italy. We always will remember this dark sacred night deep in the Mani.

Among Friends Scotland

My friends are my estate.

—Emily Dickinson

"Looks like the quintessential Scottish house." Ed pulls up to the forecourt of a square-cut gray stone house, two stories, with small-paned windows and wings jutting off to the sides. As we rounded the bend on the bumpy dirt road, I glimpsed a terrace and sloping garden on the other side of the house. A Scottie dog looks placed by central casting beside the great white front door. Gigantic trees shade the grounds. From a stable across the driveway, a tiny donkey comes out to see what's up.

We're last to arrive. Two small cars already are parked. The dog barks, the donkey begins to hee-haw, and Kate opens the door. Robin and

Susan are right behind her. My three oldest friends from my California life.

"Where have you been?"

"We thought you'd run into a firth."

"How was the flight?"

"Down, Trumpet. Isn't he adorable? He's staying with the caretaker." Robin points to a small house down a lane. The Scottie seems to be trying to embrace my leg.

"The house is amazing."

"Amazing **good** or amazing **bad**?" I ask. Having had a few weird house rentals, I'm wary.

"Oh, **good**, but still amazing. You'll see." Kate obviously is relishing some surprise in store for me.

"We landed at noon, so along the way we stopped at a pub," Ed explains. "The food was so-so. In the loo they sold Scotch-flavored condoms."

"What's this 'loo' already?" Robin's husband, John, emerges and helps hoist my bag with its **heavy** tag. "Are you bringing Italian groceries in here?"

"Only olive oil. And of course, coffee."

Susan's husband, Cole, comes to the door. Someone should photograph him on the threshold, his characteristic dark purple silk shirt, silver hair pulled back into a tiny ponytail, the gray stone framing him.

"Have you shopped yet?" I ask. Food first.

"Did you all arrive at the same time?" We're answering questions with questions.

"Want some tea?" Susan, a Londoner who has lived all her adult life in California, slips right back toward her roots.

Wellingtons line the flagged foyer. A flock of umbrellas, some with broken jutting spokes, fill a corner. "Come see the living room. What do you think?" Kate gestures around a generously proportioned room with long windows overlooking the garden. Flowered sofas flank the fireplace on either side of a large hassock table loaded with books. Cole and Robin will be happy: a grand piano fills one corner. Comfortable chairs upholstered in worn velvet, portraits, lamps—some with shades askew—and a venerable Oriental rug all confirm Ed's original word, **quintessential**.

The dining-room table would seat twenty. The owners have left the silver candlesticks and lovely silver trays and coffee service on the sideboard. Such a contrast to our English Scrooge rental.

"You'll love the kitchen," Robin says. "It's

huge—fantastic for all of us to cook together." The high-ceilinged kitchen is anchored by the immense creamy yellow Aga stove.

"It's the size of our rental car."

"And much heavier." Ed opens the door to the simmering oven, then the hotter one. "Those little cars are made out of heavy-duty aluminum foil."

"I'm excited—I've always read about the Aga and never have used one. It's on all the time, isn't it?"

Susan points out which areas on the surface are hot and demonstrates how to make toast with a screened gadget that you put bread in and rest on the heat. "We have to slow-roast something."

"Seven-hour leg of lamb," Ed suggests. "So it just stays hot all the time? This wouldn't do in most climates, but it must be nice in this one."

"The kitchen's always cozy. Even in July the room feels nice and snug but not hot."

"What fuels it, Suze?"

"The old ones used wood. This one is oil-fired, but it looks old. I think it has been retrofitted. You can even get electric ones. I guess the cast iron distributes the heat well."

A grand island with chopping-block top, an

ample kitchen table, and a long counter all invite us to start stirring and mincing. Behind the sink, the wall is capriciously tiled in many colors.

They have given us the master bedroom and will hear no protests. In the adjacent bath Queen Victoria should be standing in the shower. The tall half-circle brass contraption sprays you all over as you bask in a mammoth porcelain tub. I can't wait to bathe.

We get lost among the eight bedrooms, numerous other studies, a TV room, playroom, and larders. With seven of us—Kate's fiancé didn't come—a rambling house feels just right. I begin to see what was behind Kate's enigmatic "good, but still amazing" as we explore.

"These figures of the Madonna are everywhere. Everywhere," I notice. They all know of my collection of ex-voto objects and paintings of Mary, Mary Magdalen, and Jesus.

"Yes—paintings, ceramic figures, etched bottles, drawings—super kitsch."

"Any needlepoint chair-bottoms?"

"I'm going to count the Marys," Kate says.

Then Ed notices the TV screen in the room off the kitchen. "Look at this."

An aquarium has been wedged behind the emptied picture opening.

"This house is seriously idiosyncratic," Cole says.

"Yeah, yeah," the four women call out together. The three men look a bit startled, then laugh. Ed and John open the white wine in the fridge and pour. We drift outside to look at the climbing roses. Robin and Susan identify them all.

"Oh, there's the walled garden." I point down a path.

"How huge. Let's go look."

"It's at least half the size of a football field. How would you like to have built those stone walls? They're—what—eight feet tall?" Ed always notices stonework. Our life in Italy consists of moving stone, looking for stone, hauling stone in trucks, and building with stone.

"Too high for a deer to leap over," John observes.

We pass a rustic **cottage orné** with broken panes, full of rakes and wheelbarrows.

The wooden door to the garden should be opened with a big iron key, but Kate turns the handle and we walk in. We have been told we can pick our vegetables and salads on the land. We did not expect this glorious garden. Inside, grass paths intersect large raised beds. Roses scramble up all the walls. The strawberry, gooseberry, and raspberry patches look mysterious under their net draperies over poles tall enough that you can walk as you gather. They are all banked with straw so the leaves do not touch the ground. I realized in England that the name **strawberry** came from this method. Our beds at Bramasole yielded twice their usual amount when we tried the thick straw this year. We also mowed our plants in March, and that also seemed to spur them to new production.

John has brought along the wine bottle, and we sit down on benches along the wall and try to reconstruct the plot of **The Secret Garden**.

The men head back to shower first—or maybe they're not riveted by **The Secret Garden.** The women drift back to the terrace. We're slightly sloshed from two glasses of wine. Along the low stone wall a group of cows has gathered, and we walk down to see them. "These are Highland cows," Kate says. They have shaggy russet coats and long bangs. They regard us with interest.

We begin to sing "Don't Fence Me In" quite loudly, followed by "Home on the Range." They move closer to us and seem to long for something. We set our wineglasses down and pull up handfuls of the grass they already are eating. They decline. But they do seem to like "Amazing Grace." Robin decides that they have the hungry look of her freshman composition students and begins to lecture them on recognizing comma splices and the correct use of **lie** and **lay**. "Only hens lay," she explains. "Just write this down: **lay** takes a direct object. Eggs would be the object." Suddenly the cows toss their bangs, look alarmed, turn into a herd, and stampede away. We think this is very funny. "It's the **lie-lay** dilemma. Does it every time," Robin says.

John becomes our guide. He brought the books with restaurant listings, all the maps, and has noted the sites and gardens he knows we will want to see. This first night we drive to Falkland, a storybook Scottish town, clean and peaceful, with tea shops and a fountain and a thousand hanging flower baskets. They have won best village awards, flowering Britain awards, and they deserve them. We've reserved at the Greenhouse Restaurant, a place of Quaker simplicity and fresh organic food.

Carrot soup, salad, grilled trout. To avoid check scrambles, we've made a "kitty." John, formerly business manager of the San Francisco Symphony and hence quick with figuring everything, including tips, pays for us.

Back at the house, we settle into the downy sofas. The owners have left us a good bottle of Scotch as a welcome gift. Cole pours little shots, but no one drinks more than a few sips. Too much hit for this California Zen-and-chardonnay crowd. Even at ten, light lingers in the trees and out along the horizon, where the cows must be puzzling out the strange behavior of humans. One by one we slip upstairs. Our feather bed envelops us. I can't see any of Ed except for a shoulder. We roll into a heap in the middle and sleep like the newly dead. And then I wake up at three. Streaks of dawn are beginning to touch the east.

I have been out of touch with these friends. I have missed mothers' deaths, operations, dissolving and reforming marriages, children's weddings. The trice-weekly phone calls to exchange small news have not included me. So powerful a force in friendship is propinquity, and I have not been around to take yoga and walk the dog in the Stanford hills. Since they have given up their jobs, they study piano with Cole and participate in book groups and gourmet groups. Susan teaches gardening to children, Kate has laid a labyrinth in her garden and started a new relationship with someone I barely know, and Robin has become a passionate whitewater rafter. I have been travelling and living over half the year in Italy. When I am in the United States, I'm travelling for my speaking engagements and various business commitments. Our friendship was forged when I lived in Palo Alto. When I divorced my first husband, I moved to San Francisco, only thirty minutes north. But when I started spending longer times in Italy, I saw less of them. They've visited Bramasole, but often when we're not around. Susan and Cole married there. I'll never forget the wedding cake we baked in the small oven I had then. The shape came out lopsided, but smothered in cream and cherries, the basic 1-2-3-4 cake tasted worthy of the occasion.

Four years ago we moved to Marin County, an hour, often longer, away from the Palo Alto area. Italy's siren call lures us more and more. Although we exchange e-mails frequently, I found that when I came home and called, I began to feel an uncomfortable distance. I'd summarize what I'd been doing, they'd summarize, and we'd try to stake out a date for lunch, a walk, or dinner.

So I located this house in Fife and proposed a reunion.

"Sounds like a sneeze."

"Sounds like you're lifting your boot out of muck." They're talking about the nearest village, Auchtermuchty. In Gaelic this means "height of the swineherds." The grocery store where we go to stock the kitchen seems strangely bare. "Is this a time warp from post-war rationing?" I wonder. Sparsely filled shelves hold scattered cans of this and that. The produce is sad, woody carrots and brown-around-the-edges cabbage.

"Probably some gross shopping mall has driven them out of business," Robin says. We buy what we can and decide to go back to Falkland, where we were last night. The supplies are only marginally better, but the town is enchanting. Last night we didn't explore the brownish-gray stone town of turrets, steeples, towers, and seventeenth- and eighteenth-century upright houses.

The Stuart royalty kept a hunting retreat here, rebuilding an earlier castle that we are delighted to see was once owned by the Macduffs. A remnant of the older structure's tower stands within the walls. We're attuned to the area as a setting for **Macbeth**. Robin has brought paperbacks of the play for each of us and is planning to cast us for a performance one night. We roam through the castle gardens, imagining young Mary, Queen of Scots, playing in the park in the few years before events and her own nature brought her calamity. How marvelous for the town to have these grounds right near the center.

Falkland is downright obsessed with flowers. Wooden tubs and farm carts overflow with blooms, window boxes adorn even the humblest house, tumbling baskets hang along iron fences and from iron poles, all prolifically spilling with splendid yellow and orange begonias, trailing ivy, lobelia, and petunias. The baskets are started and nurtured in polytunnels, then in spring everyone rushes to a town plant sale.

Roughly cobbled **wynds**, streets barely wider than sidewalks, are lined with old weavers' cottages. One has the wonderful name Sharp's Close. A plain house named the Reading Room gives a sudden flavor of nineteenth-century winter evenings, when a literate stonemason used to read aloud to the weavers. Here they gathered for stories and news. Around town we spot "marriage lintels" over the doors. These insets, some dating to the early 1600s, are carved with the initials of the couple who lived there and their date of marriage. A violin shop adds a musical note of charm to the center, as does a fountain, called Bruce Fountain, with four eroding lions. In Falkland we find two statues of Bruces, one Professor John Bruce and another with the fabulous name Onesiphorus Tyndall-Bruce. I did not learn how he got the name but did find out that he was married to Margaret, niece of the other Bruce. Margaret's father died out in India, leaving an illegitimate daughter that he fathered with "a native lady." The uncle had Margaret brought back to the family mansion, Nuthill, on the castle grounds. She was called Margaret Stuart Hamilton Bruce. Her uncle raised her from age eight. Later he opposed her desire to marry Onesiphorus, who had a pile of debts and was associated with a bank that traded in slavery. "I wish you would marry a man of business," he told her.

Her reply—"He will become a man of business when he marries me"—reveals a gritty determination. In 1828, when she was thirty-eight and her uncle safely dead, she married the risky Onesiphorus and paid off his debts. She must have quickly whipped him into shape because he became a community pillar and an ardent restorer of the royal palace, which the Bruce family owned. He took her surname onto his own. There's no statue of Margaret, but reading about her, I suspect there should be. I wonder what happened to her mother.

We manage to load the trunks of the two cars with supplies. Kate spots a tearoom that looks properly dowdy. We pause for tea and crumpets doused in thick cream. Susan is in heaven; we're not far behind.

After siestas, in the late afternoon, Kate, Robin, Susan, and I take baskets down to the garden. Lettuces, tiny radishes, zucchini, beets, and new onions shine in their beds. I want to come back alone later. The walled garden seems like the perfect metaphor for the solitude of the mind. I pick out the fruit tree I will sit under. All of us have vegetable gardens (though Kate only grows Cabernet grapes on her land), but none has a poetic garden like this, and we are enchanted. The air is sweet and cool, not hot or cold, just deeply fresh. Underfoot the loamy earth sinks. Robin finds dill, and I pick a handful of parsley and thyme. Last we gather ripe, ripe strawberries.

For dinner Cole grills salmon—Scottish, of course—on the terrace. Susan concocts a prawn sauce with fresh dill, and rice with diced peppers. I roast beets in the slower Aga oven and slice them right into the most heavenly salad imaginable. The crisp greens right out of the garden—incomparable. Susan, by now totally into her English mode, creates her mother's summer pudding. Candlelight, a pitcher full of blue hydrangeas and white roses, the table laid—we're living here.

"This seems like something you read about—house parties where people are tipping down the halls to other rooms in the middle of the night," Ed says.

"Or **Upstairs, Downstairs**—only there's no

downstairs." Kate pushes back the draperies for more of the late light.

"There is Violet. She was here this morning. Didn't you notice all the wineglasses got washed? She's the housekeeper and will come later in the week. John and I were the only ones up."

We retire after dinner into what we're calling the drawing room. Cole and Robin play a Brahms waltz for four hands. Then they launch into Methodist hymns and Scottish ballads from a book Cole brought over, **Seventy Scottish Songs for Low Voices**, printed in 1905. I'm hoping no one takes it upon themselves to read Robert Burns's "best-laid schemes o' mice' an' men gang aft agley," or, God forbid, sing "Auld Lang Syne." Robin, I realize, loves to work with her hands. She gardens, does needlepoint, plays the piano, hand-marbles paper, and sets type from dozens of boxes of minuscule lead letters. She started her own letterpress publishing house when I first met her. I marveled at her patience in setting every little comma and putting all those space bars just so. Her first effort was to publish my first book of poetry, and she since has published several collections of

Ed's poems and a fine edition of another book of mine, as well as **Marbling at the Heyeck Press** and many other books cherished by readers of poetry and collectors. Her books are in many rare book rooms in the great libraries. Right now she's banging out "I Come to the Garden Alone," and since I know all the words, I can't resist singing along.

Cole teaches piano at home and gives private concerts. In the past he used to play in jazz clubs in Paris and Southern California. "How many times have I been asked to play 'Misty,' " he muses, launching into it only for a moment.

"Can you play **our** song?" Ed asks. " 'A Whiter Shade of Pale.' "

"**That's** your song? Procol Harum? I don't know—how does it go?"

"You don't pick your song, you all. It picks you. This was playing in all the romantic moments when we first met," I say.

Susan and I try to sing the melody. The words are hard to remember. What makes the song memorable is the quirky voice of Gary Brooker. I'm astounded as Cole gradually pieces it together from our wavery rendition. He tries chord after chord and then is playing as if he'd always known all the notes. "It's Bach," he says, " 'Air on a G-string' and a bit of one of the cantatas, 'Sleepers Awake.' "

"Well, that redeems us," Ed, my bonny laddie, laughs.

Before we go to bed, I get out my notebook and copy Susan's recipe.

Susan's Mother's Summer Pudding

1 pound raspberries, strawberries
¼ pound red or black currants
(or any mixture of above fruits)
½ cup sugar
day-old white bread, sliced as for sandwiches, crusts removed
2 teaspoons cherry brandy or blackberry ratafia (optional)

Wash fruit and place about one cup of it in a saucepan with the sugar and liqueur, and cook lightly for three minutes. Cool.

Line a pudding basin with the bread, leaving no gaps. Gently spoon in the uncooked fruit interlaced with spoonfuls of the cooked fruit, pressing the fruit down gently with the back of a spoon. Place a "hat" of bread on top when the basin is full, cutting bread to fit inside the surrounding bread.

Puddle remaining juice in center of the hat. Cover entire basin top with a piece of waxed paper or plastic wrap, and place a small plate on top so it fits inside the basin. Place a weight (such as a can of tomatoes) on top to hold it down. Refrigerate for 12 to 24 hours.

To serve: Remove saucer and waxed paper. Place serving platter over basin and invert. Your summer pudding should be quite pink. Use extra berry syrup to cover any white spots. Serve with ice cream.

Note: Ours rested only a few hours and was fine. We served it with good Scottish cream, rather divine.

The green countryside and quick little burns with lush grassy banks invite us to walk in the early morning and evening. The house is surrounded by pastures with paths that lead to oak copses and vistas of lochs. The shaggy cows amble to the fence to greet us. Ed and I are out early. Over a rise we see a wooden cross, about thirty feet tall, with dangling leather straps hanging from the crux. This is not a piece of sculpture.

At breakfast Ed tells everyone about the cross on the hill. Then he discovers that he does not have his cell phone. When Kate comes downstairs, she's holding a pad. "I counted eighty-six Jesuses and Marys. **Also**, just so you know, there are a hundred and twenty-nine paintings and prints on the walls. The downstairs bathroom is separate—ninety items on the walls. Not to mention that fake fish that sings 'Take me to the river, drop me in the water' when you sit down on the toilet."

"I wish we could invite the owners for dinner," I say. "They must be fun." We feel half acquainted with them and their four children through the distinct personality of the house.

Everyone searches each room for the cell phone. It's command central for our restoration-in-progress in Italy. The number of all the technicians and workers involved, and they are legion, are on that phone. We are in daily contact with the work going on. Ed has called so many times that the numbers have worn off the buttons. He goes out and retraces our walk. We call the phone; no response. He searches the car. "I'm sure I had it this morning because I meant to call Fulvio." Lost.

• • •

Today we're driving over to Kinross. We're finding gardens we want to see, fine walks, and plenty to do nearby but nothing compelling, so we linger over coffee, catching up. Cole's music drifts through the rooms. We don't care if we get a late start. We brake for bakeries. We circle towns to look at mossy churches and prim houses enlivened by masses of hollyhocks.

Kinross, a stately, austere Georgian house dating from 1693, stands inside a ten-acre walled garden that slopes down to Loch Leven. The present owners descend from the proprietor who took it over in 1902, after eighty years of neglect, and restored the original garden. They can look out their windows every morning and see that the ruined castle on a tiny island in Loch Leven is not at all the fairy-tale illusion it seems to be. Kinross's main garden axis lies from the front door of the house, down the gradually lowering garden, out the gate, and across the water straight to the castle. Famous for imprisoning Mary, star-crossed queen, the castle always was the focal point and orientation of Kinross and provides a thrilling prospect.

Mary tried several escapes during her ten months of confinement. One plan was to jump from the tower into a boat below. This made no sense until I learned that the water used to lap the castle before the loch was lowered in the nineteenth century. Mary endured, with the help of her cook, doctor, and two ladies-in-waiting. She loved falconry; I wonder if she was allowed out at all. Just before she was taken to Loch Leven Castle, she had given birth to still-born twins and felt extremely weak from loss of blood. Her life rivals Job's, beginning with the death of her father when she was one week old. She finally did escape, when a servant grabbed the keys during a banquet and let her out. The daring episode did little good; she fled south to seek help from Queen Elizabeth, but the two had old issues, and her cousin promptly put her under lock and key again.

The gate, which frames the castle from Kinross, has an arched door. Over it there's a carved stone basket full of the seven types of fish of the lake: salmon, blackhead, pike, perch, speckled trout, char, gray trout. When the loch was lowered, the char died out, and the salmon could no longer reach the loch.

Robin remarks on the variegated sage as a border. The soft gray-green with some leaves edged with pink, some purple, frames the beds delicately. Four stone arches parallel a path in the garden at the side of the house, two with sculptures underneath. The arches are not to walk through; they serve as architectural points in the rectangular garden. Susan identifies a plant I don't know as fleabane. We're all charmed with the informality of the formal rose garden—a big mix of colors, all vying for attention. Clumps of catnip throw off a lavender haze. John is snapping millions of photographs. I take one note: plant variegated sage along the top of a wall at Bramasole.

Lochiehead—head of the lake?—is the name of our house. I wish one of us could buy it so we could come back often. Christmas would be ideal. July is **perfetto** too—no rain, balmy days. Cole goes fishing. Susan reads in the living room, and everyone else goes for a walk. Ed launches into making **ragù** for dinner. The downstairs fills with aromas of sautéeing carrots, celery, and onion. Soon a big pot will be simmering on the Aga. I take a book down to the secret garden. A little bell chime rings in a tree somewhere on the land. There is no wind; who is ringing it? I envision a hidden stone church under immense trees. A robed monk tolling the hours, forgetting the hour and just ringing the bell for the pure tone settling over the countryside. The serene landscape has moved into me, and I feel sleepy all the time. I want to curl up under the potting table in the greenhouse, fall deeply into the sofa cushions, tune out as we hurtle along the wrong side of the road toward a tearoom or a castle where the docent will go on forever with cute anecdotes about the earl. At the castles I want to throw myself onto the earl's bearskin by the fireplace and snooze. I'm walking through the gardens like a somnambulist. The light swaying of the massed delphiniums puts me into a trance. The nearby river walks only make me want to lie down in the shallow water and drift. Can it be that I am finally relaxed?

Kate, our house sleuth, solves the mystery of the cross on the hill. She's read a framed article in the downstairs powder room, the one with ninety separate objects on the walls, and discovered that the house's owners put on a play every year and people come from miles around to see the reenactment of the crucifixion. "Hence the donkey," she says. We all rush to the bathroom. She points out, too, a faded photo of the walled garden. Only ten years ago the space was derelict. We read other articles—a miraculous sighting of the Virgin in now-ex-Yugoslavia, a prize at a dog show. Is that our Trumpet, the Scottie, in the picture? I gaze at the derelict secret garden. The owners have performed their own miracle.

Violet arrives early, bearing a ginger cake with toffee sauce. We fall upon it for breakfast and ask her for the recipe. She has wiry curls and fresh Scottish complexion. She tells us how terrible traffic will be if we go to Glamis Castle. She does not say **Glahmiss**, as we do. She says **Glams**.

Violet's Hot Toffee Sauce for Gingerbread

6 ounces soft brown sugar
4 ounces butter
¼ pint double cream

Heat in a pan until sugar dissolves and butter melts. Bring quickly to a boil, then switch off.

She serves this also on waffles. At home we don't get the same kind of double cream that blesses the British desserts. Heavy cream, perhaps thickened with a little crème fraîche, would substitute.

We do drive to Glamis, a castle fit for Sleeping Beauty. We're Californians—what could Violet know about traffic? Almost no cars are on the roads. Glamis was the childhood home of the late Queen Mother. They must have longed for a cozy apartment in Edinburgh during the winters. Most rooms are small, probably the better to heat them, and chilly even in summer. Nothing opulent, all rather rigorous. The picturesque conical towers are, on the inside, spiral stairways of stone. **Whence camest thou, worthy Thane? From Fife, great King.** We could meet someone carrying a bloodied head but instead meet day-trippers like ourselves. The captivating room is the playroom, furnished with doll beds, small stove, high chairs, and stuffed toys. Odd to imagine a tiny Queen Mother there, rocking her bear.

We don't linger but instead drive over to St. Andrews. We stop first at a shop to buy a cloth-wrapped cheese from the Isle of Mull—nutty and golden—and several local pale cheddars and a blue similar to Roquefort. The produce looks better, though nothing compares with our secret garden's tender lettuces. The day is so warm that we're not attracted to the cashmere shops. The name of the town is most holy—St. Andrew, one of the apostles and the patron saint of Scotland. He, the venerable university, and the long history of golfing are the positive history. Much else seems to center on martyrdoms, sieges, reformations, and burnings at the stake. The notable local invention was the thumbscrew. All feels serene along the leafy streets and in the tidy shops. We walk the length of the bustling town and back, find a tearoom for lunch, then decide to go home.

The slack caused by my long absences from my friends seems taut again. I wonder if they assumed I had changed and now see that I did not, or if I did (and yes, I did), it's okay. When everyone walks the same path and then one veers off in a different direction, balance goes out of kilter. We've all always been independent and ambitious. Our first bond was books. Susan, Kate, and I wrote poetry and Robin published a range of poets in her spare hours outside her college teaching job. Kate and I went to graduate school in creative writing together, commuting up to San Francisco and trading secrets along Highway 280. After I graduated, I began to teach in the same program. Susan and Kate, with their friend Jerry, then opened Printers Inc., a literary bookstore on California Street in Palo Alto. They installed a coffee bar/café, which was revolutionary. No other bookstore in California, or maybe the United States, had done that in 1978. We were sipping cappuccino and reading Merwin at Printers long before Starbucks ever pulled an espresso. The bookstore for its whole life was a fulcrum for the entire community and surroundings. **Meet me at Printers**. Eventually they expanded into an adjacent building for a larger café. The reading series was stellar. They opened a second store. We always were swapping books, talking books, reviewing books, publishing books. Kate began to study Chinese and travelled alone to China several times. Then she left to live in Vermont for a few years, and Susan and Jerry continued to run the stores. When she came back, she started her La Questa Press.

This afternoon we're staying home, the women dozing on the sofas, reading without the need to talk. One of us suddenly giggles. "I just remembered." (Discretion prevents identification of the speakers and person spoken to.)

"What?"

"The Valentine's Day when Philip got to your office early and filled the whole room with balloons and roses and left that note, **If you're free some evening stop by for breakfast.**"

"What a good memory you have."

"Well, that affair with Philip raged for a year."

"That note was the best. We all envied you."

"Yes, more for the note than anything else!"

"He was divine. And so was that English guy **you** went off to St. Croix with."

"We fell out of bed in a heap."

"And that therapist who asked why you divorced your first husband, and you said 'I don't remember'?"

"What about that **student**?"

"Oh, come on, he was twenty-six. And had poetry on his lips."

"That's not all he had on his lips."

"What about that watch left on the bedside table?"

A slew of rowdy memories ensues. If men only knew how women talk.

• • •

We drive too far to a country inn for dinner. The wild salmon and game are delicious and the atmosphere clubby and cozy, a half-timbered room hung with copper, baronial tapestry chairs, and a long table set with crystal. I'm loving Scotland. This is my first time here. I want to go to the Hebrides and to the monks' island of Iona, if they allow women.

On our walk at midmorning Ed experiences a miracle in the shadow of the Golgotha cross. We're crossing the fields and meadows talking about the lost phone. "The charge is probably dead," Ed laments. At that instant we hear a ring in waist-high weeds next to the path. We both shout and begin parting the grasses. "Hey!" Ed shouts and holds up the wet phone. He answers, "**Pronto**." Chiara is calling from Cortona, wanting to know how our trip is going. At the very instant we are passing by. Four ragged cows witness the miracle of the phone.

"Ed! This is fantastic—Santa Chiara is the patron saint of telecommunications."

"Thank you, Jesus." With the remaining flicker of charge, he calls Fulvio.

Our favorite garden, probably because it seems within reach, is House of Pitmuies near Forfar. The felicitous and rambling house overlooks wide, blowsy borders blooming so overabundantly that as you walk between the paths, you're brushed by blue, lavender, and pink flowers. What a glory. Stacked from front to back with ascending blooms, they have a "gay abandon about their dress." Like a rigorously trained ballerina, the garden appears spontaneous, as though the flowers just **happened**, rather than having been carefully planted to bloom in height, sequence, and color shade vis-à-vis all the other plants in the border. The white lilies are not staked, but instead the gardener devised a taut string web for them to grow through. Each one's square opening supports it nicely. In the kitchen garden their berries are netted but not as elaborately as in our secret garden. Small flowerpots top the low posts around the perimeter of the bed, and the net drapes over them without snagging on the posts or tearing. Very clever. We wish the lady of the house would invite us into her sunroom, pour a smoky oolong tea, and tell us her life story.

Violet tells us to go to a field nearby for the Scottish games. We find the immense field, where men and boys are going at tug-of-war, vaulting, races, and wrestling with verve. We watch several bagpipe solo contests and follow a marching band of pipers around the field. Bagpipes make me smile. I can't understand how they ever worked as the music of war. An advancing group of mad pipers should make the enemy jump up and jig rather than shoot or run in terror. Several people ask where we're from and seem amused that we're on vacation where they live. Most of the men wear kilts in their family plaids. They look gorgeous. We're all glued to the Highland Fling and other traditional dance competitions performed by serious little girls in folk costumes. The sets begin with a group of eight or ten, and gradually the judges knock off one after the other until the winner is left performing alone. Only then does she usually break into a smile and miss her steps. The community has come together for this sunny afternoon of play. If we lived here, we'd be right where we are.

Having succumbed to sausage rolls at the games, we're content to stir up a simple **risotto primavera**, using carrots, onion, beets, and celery from the garden. And of course, we gather a magnificent salad, the best salad in the world. Kate quickly assembles Violet's toffee sauce recipe. She and Susan bake gingerbread, pouring the sauce onto the cake. Susan and Robin arrange a sublime bowl of roses for the table. Tonight we are launching into our summer-stock performance of **Macbeth** in the drawing room. **Lay on, Macduff.**

After our morning yoga session, the men propose a hike. Not that they have not enjoyed the endless analysis of herbaceous borders. All of them garden, too. John's guidebook describes a ten-mile coastal walk. Perfect for our last afternoon. Tomorrow we all will be folded into airline seats, except for Robin and John, who are spending another week farther north. We're the only ones on the trail for most of the way. The few we pass greet us heartily. I'm sore from all the yoga contortions. They've taken twice-weekly classes for years, while the most exercise I've had has been on the computer keyboard and running for flights. The long motion of walking makes me breathe deeply. I imagine the sun warming every cell in my body. Everywhere the people have been effusively friendly, not just cordial. They're more like the Australians than the reserved English. We find a ruined tower to explore and shining water to look at all the way. Lord, ten miles is long, and some of the paths cross loose sand. We've been only in this wee bit of Scotland, and yet I think we luckily found a core sample. I never came before because I thought it would not be exotic enough. I feared it would seem too familiar. I didn't know how deeply refreshing the landscape could be. The place **does** seem familiar, perhaps at a genetic level, but in a nourishing way. Or maybe I'm just familiar with these friends, and when one is at home with friends, the surrounding world becomes friendly, too.

Aboard the Cevri Hasan

Turkey's Lycian Coast

I'm inside the advancing light,
my hands are hungry, the world
beautiful.

—Nazim Hikmet

Is the one I love **everywhere**?

—Rumi

Bramasole exerts a magnetic force, never stronger than now—the gazebo covered in celestial-blue morning glories, dahlias finally adorning themselves with gay pink pompoms, the Rose Walk making a late August comeback, the fountain repaired and splashing a concerto to the night, dew-soaked grass at dawn, the variegated sage tall enough to brush my legs with scent, thousands of butterflies hovering around the lavender, the basil brought from Naples burgeoning onto the paths, wigwams of weighty ruby-dark tomatoes, and Beppe's rows of lettuces that soon will bolt, the last of the sunflowers drooping their dry faces in shame on the upper terrace, the zucchini flowers blowing their loud yellow party horns. Why leave the last, deliciously heady days of summer?

We're going. Already banging our duffels and carry-on bags down the steps and across the lawn, smearing them with grass stains.

Our friend Giorgio drops us at the Rome airport, where we meet Fulvio, Aurora, and their princely eleven-year-old son, Edoardo. We've seen each other only a few days ago but greet in the Turkish Air queue as though it has been months. We've been friends with the Di Rosa family, who live across the valley in Lucignano, for four years, but we have travelled together only once, when we rented an apartment on the Grand Canal in Venice to celebrate Ed's fiftieth birthday. We experienced then Fulvio's extraordinary energy as he showed us around the Biennale art exhibitions for hours, then led us in a walk all over Venice before we launched into cooking every crustacean we could find at the Rialto market and feasting in our apartment where the floors sloped precipitously toward the canal and dour family portraits looked down on us with remote and foreign gazes. Recently Fulvio has masterminded our restoration of a second property, a ruined twelfth-century hermitage in the mountains above Cortona. Because the house was built by followers of Saint Francis of Assisi, who roamed our hills, we constructed a shrine and had the artist paint Francis with his arms held out to welcome all creatures. The saint, however, has Fulvio's face, since he was saintly himself during three years of restoration. Aurora, his elegant wife, always dresses in the **bella figura** Italian style. She has large blue eyes and the figure of a twenty-year-old girl. She likes jewelry. She's impeccably put together. Her clothes make you wish you paid more attention when you shop. She is also thoughtful of the other person and a bit fierce when her own family's interests are involved. Edoardo, their marvelous child, actually likes adults and, without losing any of his own childhood, relates to them in a natural way. He has his mother's great azure gaze and thick ashen blond hair, his father's wit and searing focus. Slender as a broom, he pokes Ed in the stomach, quite taut really, and says, "You'd better watch that." We love them individually and as a family.

The five of us are embarking on a sailing and hiking expedition to the Mediterranean coast of southern Turkey, from Antalya up to Kusadasi, on a traditional Turkish **gulet** (the **t** is pronounced) with two other people I know and four strangers. This will be our first guided group trip, but the Di Rosas had a fine experience on a small tour in Morocco. First we will stop in Istanbul for two nights.

From Rome, I barely settle into my Turkish novel, **Mehed, My Hawk**, before the descent begins into mythic Constantinople. The other time I came here, the approach was by sea. From the deck I watched as rounded silhouettes of mosque domes appeared against the dawn sky, imprinting forever. From the perspective above, a giant has strewn cubical houses like a sack of dice. How vast the city, and how fortunately it cradles among the waters. Within three hours of leaving Fumicino, we're checking into the Arena, a small hotel owned by a family in the historic quarter.

Walking to a restaurant the hotel recommended for Aurora's birthday, we pass an outdoor café where two whirling dervishes are spinning on a platform under the trees, their white gowns forming storted pyramids that break and re-form. Although I know these must not be the ecstatic mystical dancers of the Mevlana Sufis, they still astonish. Like figures in dreams they reel, right palm up to receive divine energy, left palm down to convey it into the ground, turning on their own axes with irrational control, a feat, a dancing trance on the threshold of Allah's heaven. **Open your hands, / if you want to be held**, I remember from the poet Rumi. The lines always reminded me of the Beatles' aphoristic lyric about the love you take being equal to the love you make. Born in 1207 in what is now Afghanistan, Rumi inspired the whirling dervish order. During his visit to the goldsmiths' quarter, the dainty sounds of all the hammers falling hit him as music, and he began to dance. He danced and danced until he reached a mystical state. My students loved him, as translated by Coleman Barks.

How long can they continue this angelic swirling? I feel holy myself, just standing in the street across from the bazaar's hawkers. At ballets, audiences break into applause when the dancer executes a few perfect spins. In comparison to these twirlers, that is no feat. The dervishes move like water toward the drain; beyond the motion, something magnetic pulls the psyche.

Our table is set right in the street. To extend the garden, the restaurant has simply blocked off an area, strung some lights, and let loose their accordion player. Of course, we ask him to play "Happy Birthday," and the other diners join in singing, as they often do in Italy, as well as raising their glasses. There's no menu and we don't know a word of Turkish, so we just give ourselves over to the waiter. The wine list does exist, and I wish I could have one because the illustrated bottles pop up, as in a child's book. Again, we point and ask with our eyes, and he selects a fragrant little white, suitable for more toasts. Soon we're served various mezes—

shrimp with arugula and lemon, grated and roasted zucchini with yogurt, several kinds of eggplant, fried calamari. **Meze**, which means "a good taste," is quite inadequately translated as "hors d'oeuvre." Meze, instead, can be hors d'oeuvres or can be like tapas.

Then he brings monkfish with tomatoes and peppers and more shrimp, these batter fried. We're all high with excitement. We stroll back in the exotic night through the heart of the old city, looking in windows of rug stores, skirting the great corms of the Blue Mosque, the ellipse of the ancient Hippodrome, where chariots used to race and the condemned lost their heads, then by the outdoor cafés where people talk the evening away while sipping tea from glasses.

At first light the call of the muezzin jerks me awake. The hotel is across the street from an intimately scaled mosque, whose loudspeakers must be aimed at room 306. The caller tunes up a moment, **e-ya eee ya ya**; like a cicada, before he launches into his wailing appeal to prayer. This call equals the church bells in Italy, marking time, sending out a summons that seems to unzip all the way down the spinal cord. I'm thrilled every time it happens. Ed rolls over and says, "Someone hit the wah-wah pedal." We start laughing, and I look out the window at the small boats and silvery water. We have a whole day to play in Istanbul before we fly south tomorrow to board the boat.

First to the Grand Bazaar, where Fulvio reveals a talent for bargaining and Aurora and I acquire sage, apricot, black, taupe, and beige pashmina scarves for a fraction of their cost at home. Usually I hate bargaining and ask at the Arezzo antique market for a **prezzo buono** only because I know the dealers think you're stupid if you don't. Fulvio starts having fun, and I realize that the scarf man does, too. For the first time, I can see the process as a game rather than an annoyance.

We quickly want to leave the touristy shops and the pushy rug merchants. It must be said: the Grand Bazaar, all cleaned up, lacks atmosphere. We exit quickly into the light rain, walking downhill toward the Spice Bazaar, where we hope for more medina ambiance. That happens, I see quickly, actually **between** the two bazaars in the muddle of streets where most of the women are covered except for their eyes. Everything imaginable is for sale. We pass shop windows displaying those impossible gray and sand clothes the women wear, white circumcision outfits for boys, with fake (metaphoric?) swords at the waist, school uniforms, and whole clumps of closet-sized shops selling just collars or thread or buttons. Belly dancer costumes with fringed and spangled gold and silver trim—polar opposite to the gray and sand—zipper shops, plastic kitchenware, toilet seats, laundry baskets. Ah! No rugs! No tourists, either. A former mosque, stripped down, holds racks of cheap children's clothing under its dome. This is what I imagined, a souk, a cramped labyrinth of tiny businesses with street food to sample—**köfte** (little spicy grilled meatballs), roasted corn, a cheese and phyllo pastry, kebabs, and dried figs stuffed with nuts. In the Spice Bazaar we buy garam masala and strawberry tea. Bins are heaped with dill, mint, pistachios, curry, hot paprika, black chili, turmeric, hot peppers—all the colors in the rugs. I don't see fresh herbs at all and have a distrust of dried ones in open bins. The prized item seems to be Iranian saffron, but since it is a seasoning I don't like, I am not tempted. We see mounds of various nuts, honeycombs dripping, heaps of dried apples, apricots, and figs—some look rather dusty. **Lokum**, Turkish delight, appears in many sugary pastels.

We decide to visit the New Mosque we glimpsed on the way here. One merchant calls out to Ed as we leave, "You, my friend, are very handsome."

The five of us don't fit into a single taxi and so rendezvous at each juncture. We communicate by phone that we are lost, found, abandoned by the driver, or heading in the wrong direction. While we wait for the Di Rosas at the Galata tower, we duck out of the rain into a café where everyone is playing **okey**, tile rummy, and drinking tea. More tea must be consumed here than in England. Both teenagers and men are playing, the square chips clacking pleasantly and the wooden racks scraping the chips into piles around the table. When the Di Rosas arrive, we run across the little plaza to the tower. From the catwalk around the top, strangely accessed through a nightclub, we get a rainy 360-degree view of the city. The tower was built in the fourteenth century by the Genoese, who lined many a coast with towers. The area surrounding the tower thrived as a tight Italian enclave—is that why the five of us were drawn here? Noted especially for Florentine banks, the rich neighborhood also had Italian-style stone houses and piazzas. The Ottoman sultans feared the Venetians but valued the rest of the Italians. The Galata area represents so well the mix of cultures that was intermittently encouraged by the Ottomans. Jews, Greeks, Croatians—so many came together in the city and lived, more than in most, in mutual respect and harmony. The level of tolerance is inspiring, but sometimes the sultan simply stamped his foot, a signal to execute the bore.

I am devouring Philip Mansel's **Constantinople: City of the World's Desire, 1453–1924**. How talented you have to be to write the cramped and twisted history of Istanbul as a page-turner. This book captivates me night after night, building, subject by subject, a world like no other. Istanbul—the most multinational city, the quintessential crossroads of east and west, violent, poetic, melancholy, raucous, fleshy, austere, rapacious, sublime—this seems to me the most fascinating city on earth.

The city's saga through time not only crowds the brain with contradictory information, it challenges chronological development with disruptive acts and with backward and forward movements in time.

"The city is all about water," Ed says. Yes, that's true. We inch all the way around the tower, and Istanbul appears as a low abstracted gathering of domes with minarets piercing the sky. Only muted colors—no hint of harem wives killing off their innocent sons who might seek to rule over the other sons. No cast-off concubines stuffed into barrels and thrown into the Bosporus. A city the color of tinsel in the rain, the mysterious waters holding it aloft for our speculation.

The highlight of our day is the Suleyman Mosque and its cemetery, where the gravestones are tall slabs of curvaceous marble carved with floral and vegetal designs. No living figures were allowed. Fulvio interacts with those usually avoided so we have a long visit with a shoe shiner—Istanbul is full of fabulous shoe shiners with brass stands—who even manage to polish tennis shoes. Isn't it a bit odd to have your shoes shined in a cemetery? Old trees shelter and cool the paths among the stones. The dead are the same everywhere, commanding an aura of peace and tranquillity. The mosque, too, seems especially peaceful. Outside, stools along the wall provide places to sit in front of a font and perform ritual cleansing if you are going inside to worship. Mosques are carpeted, often in the repeating pattern of a small prayer rug, which gives each worshiper his own space. Your shoes are left at the door, although at some mosques you are given a plastic bag so you can carry them. Just inside, a partitioned section behind a carved wooden screen designates where you pray if you are a woman. You may see, through a scrim, but not be seen. I find these erasures, even before Allah, hard to fathom. I suppose that women would, if free to prostrate themselves like the men, distract attention from worship. As tourists, Aurora and I cover our heads to enter mosques with the new scarves from the Grand Bazaar. The late afternoon call to prayer begins while we are on the mosque grounds and electrifies us as we comb the neighborhood of wooden Ottoman houses in search of a taxi. Soon we run out of pavement and find ourselves in a squalid neighborhood with many collapsed houses. I have never been in a city with so many houses that have simply fallen onto themselves. Near the hotel, near the Hippodrome in prime tourist territory, you see these Ottoman houses in piles. Our street is dwindling when finally we see downhill to the right a busy road.

At dusk we meet Bernice and Armand from Baltimore, who have just arrived. Ed and I met Bernice on another sailing trip around the boot of Italy two years ago, and we have seen each other since in Reston, during the Washington sniper days, when I was giving a talk and Bernice and Armand bravely came to see me. Armand, tall and scholarly, looks as though he should be a senator. I love the way Bernice pays attention to everything. She doesn't talk a lot but you wait to hear what she will say when she does. We had such fun exploring the boot of Italy on the other sailing voyage that I e-mailed Bernice immediately when we decided to go on this trip, "Are you ready for Turkey? Almost every day we will moor and hike to a different archaeological site." She responded within the hour saying that they would love to join us. They have a farm in Virginia where they garden and raise exotic chickens. She and I have corresponded over the past two years about roses. We meet in the lobby just as the hotel waiter wheels in a cart with a birthday cake for Aurora, somehow forgotten yesterday, and fruit drinks in goblets.

After an endless taxi ride, our increased band of merry pranksters arrives at Marina Restaurant, perched over the waters of the Bosporus, miles from everywhere. We choose fish from a tilted marble slab as we go inside. Large open windows, varnished as on a boat, let in the scent of the night and the water. Soon we are ravished by sole on skewers threaded with lemon and bay leaves, and by grilled scorpion fish steamed in broth with potatoes and tomatoes and sprinkled with oregano and red pepper. En route home in the taxi, I glimpse along a wall photographs of Atatürk. The taxi driver says we are passing the palace where he died. You see this great reformer in Istanbul the way you see the Virgin Mary in Italy, a prevalent presiding presence in banks, restaurants, hotels, everywhere. I wish we had an Atatürk in America now. He had force and vision and a deeply familial love of his country. He's most known for banning the fez and discouraging women from the veils, but his most sweeping change was the adaptation of Latin characters for the alphabet. Imagine our president decreeing that henceforth we will use Cyrillic or Greek letters. I've found it hard to take kilometers and the metric system. But Turkey did forsake Arabic, and that change brought them into the western European neighborhood, enabling him to create a secular Turkish nation. I like his jaw and his eyes that look as though they see what you don't see.

Our flower-filled room must be the bridal suite. Although they are fake, I like the impulse. The bed draped with curtains looks romantic, and the cloth petals scattered across the floor stick to my feet. From the entrance you pass into the bedroom through filmy gauze curtains. Bedside lamps with the lowest wattage possible do not encourage me to read my guidebooks, and since we are too exhausted for a honeymoon night, I lie awake. The phrase **when Mother married Atatürk** keeps floating across my mind, as though a memory would be uncovered. But he was married in 1923 and divorced by 1925, too early for my mother. His true wife and family were Turkey. Rare for a strong-arm president, he had the interests of the people at heart.

• • •

We depart at six for a short flight south to the sprawling city of Antalya along the sharply delineated blue Mediterranean. We're met by our guide, Enver Lucas, a Turkish American who strides up to us in T-shirt and shorts, a backpack slung over his shoulder. He's forthright and friendly. He looks like someone you want to hug. His legs, I notice, are muscular enough to hike to any location. We meet Cheryl and Karl, a couple from San Francisco, and Ian and Sara, a Canadian who recamped to New Orleans and his fifteen-year-old granddaughter. Ian took this same trip with Enver years ago and wants his granddaughter to experience his memories. Enver escorts us out of the airport, into humidity and heat and onto a bus in minutes. "There is a lot to do today, folks," he announces, and somehow I have a feeling we will be hearing this every day. He wastes no time in heading to Perge.

I'm unprepared for the first ruins. I expected a piece of amphitheatre, a few fallen columns, and some stone foundations. But Perge extends as far as I can see. The city axis, a long colonnaded street with cuts from chariot wheels, ends at a fountain, where the water source from the hill above poured over a statue of a river god, then entered the city. No water now, only weeds. I lean to pinch leaves for their scents of thyme, oregano, and mint. The heat bears down harder than history. We stand in clumps of shadow while Enver tells us of the Greeks who settled here in the aftermath of the Trojan War. The baths must have been Las Vegas–spectacular. Walking the ledge around a deep pool, I see traces of the green marble that once faced the surfaces. The raised floor of the columned **caldarium**, the hot bath, still exists enough to see how they channeled steam to heat the floor, and how part of the heat was shunted to the **tepidarium**. We are the only visitors at first; then we see three others. The smell of crushed herbs and dust must be somehow the smell of time. I have the sense that I am actually **discovering** the site. No ropes, no signs, we're free to amble, scramble over blocks of carved stone to see the others behind them—portions of friezes and porticos, bases of columns, keystones. Some are carved with nine, ten layers of egg and dart, acanthus, **denti** (tooth pattern), and vegetal motifs. One, lying in the dirt, is exquisite: a border of Etruscan wave design with clusters of grapes between. When I push aside weeds with my foot, a Medusa face stares back at me. How many standing columns are there? I lose count.

We then drive to the huge theatre at Aspendos, still used for performances. I start to learn the names of some of the features of these ancient theatres:

diazoma: horizontal aisle in the **cavea**
cavea: the auditorium, from the act of digging it out like a cave
parodos: the area between the **cavea** and the stage

And a **vomitorium** is not what I'd always heard but a covered exit from a theatre. How little stadiums have changed really, except to close the oval: the same seats with someone's knees in your back, the same narrow access aisle at a steep pitch. Of course, everyone claps to hear how fine the acoustics are.

Half a day, and we've already seen two stupendous remnants of history. I hope that the scrapes and battles of the Persians, Lycians, Greeks, Romans, and various others who set sail toward this coast will at last reach some kind of coherence during our travels. Alexander swept by and had an enormous impact, killing and conquering, but I'm not too clear on his itinerary. Right now I'm content to slip into a state of awe.

In the late afternoon the curator of the Antalya Museum shows us the statues archaeologists found at Perge. Such finds usually get carted off to the capital, but the museum has managed to keep them. The beauty of the statues makes me wander away from the group, double back, and visit them alone. How eloquent those early people were. Perge was a wonder of a city, with extensive carved facades and fountains. What happened to town planning in the modern era?

We park the bus one more time at the outdoor market. At the strictly local scene I get to see hundreds of Turks shopping for dinner and visiting with friends. One gnarly man with a single tooth has picked all the apples from one tree and sits cross-legged behind a mound. We smell, then see a whole area where fishmongers display the catch of the day. The local women all wear "harem" pants in dark prints, capacious to permit bending or squatting. Barkers sound as if they're about to commit murder but only are extolling the virtues of their garlic braids, peppers, fantastic melons, and tomatoes that we call heirloom at home but are simply tomatoes here.

All these stops are a long buildup to boarding the boat, our home for eleven days. And at last we meander out to the marina where the **Cevri Hasan** is docked. Enver decided to use a marina outside the hubbub of town, and he does not say but I imagine he was influenced by last week's bomb in the Antalya marina. A small incident, but to wary travellers four hundred miles from the raging Iraq war, possibly a source of worry. Mustapha, the captain, welcomes us along with Ali, the chef, and two shy young men who will crew. The **gulet**, about ninety feet long, is spacious, with a long dining table and inviting tangerine-colored cushioned lounging areas on deck both fore and aft. The galley kitchen has marble counters. Under the window Ali grows pots of basil and oregano. What a fun place to cook. A bookcase of paperbacks abandoned by previous voyagers tempts me immediately. For bad weather, a comfortable salon/dining area adjoins the kitchen. The cabins below are small, each with a minute bathroom. If you were obese, you would get stuck.

We have twin bunks, hard as pavement, probably like beds in jails. Not that I expected a stateroom—but this is challenging. There's nowhere to put anything, except for a small shelf and a foot-wide closet. We stuff everything in, and I resign myself to mingled heaps of mine and Ed's clean and dirty clothes. I am the sort of person who has my drawers arranged by color—all light T-shirts in one drawer, medium and dark colors in the next two, all sweaters in plastic bags, socks paired, my underwear folded a particular way, my nightgowns very, very tidy. I will not be spending leisure time in our cabin. Also it is hot as the hinges of hell down below. We stow everything we can and burst back upstairs for air. Soon Ali is passing champagne, and we're on deck in the slight breeze; then we have our first dinner on board with Turkish white wine flowing and Ali presenting a variety of mezes and roast chicken. Enver barely gets to eat because everyone has questions for him.

Tomorrow I will start my ship's log. I loved reading Colombus's account of his voyages. The idea of a captain writing at his desk each day, gimbaled lantern overhead and a draught of rum near the inkwell, appeals to me. Although this trip is a bit minor in comparison to those crossings of unknown seas, all trips are voyages within as well as without. A log: "the record of a ship's speed, progress, and shipboard events of navigational importance," according to the dictionary. I will keep one, although I won't know speed and navigational information. I will simply record what becomes important to me as we progress along the edge of the Mediterranean.

We motor along the quiet coast for a while after dinner. See, I am not an accurate logger—that "a while" is quite imprecise. But after the long dinner that will have to do.

The Log

MONDAY, AUGUST 30: TERMESSOS

A stony trail, up, up Rose Mountain for almost two hours, harder than climbing the Empire State Building several times. The original inhabitants spoke a language all their own—easy to understand why. Once up, you'd stay put. The not-easily-thwarted Alexander gave up his attack here, saying, "Let's move on. I have a long way to go and cannot waste my army in front of an eagle's nest." We're scrambling over fallen stone columns and cornerstones and arches, looking up at spooky tombs cut into the rock face of the mountain. They're smaller than one-car garages, with bas-relief columned doors and simple trims. Some have faces carved on the sides. Wild roses cover the carved stones, along with carnations and oak-holly. This is not just a stony path; the stones littering the way actually are part of the ruined fortress city of Termessos. The theatre rivals Machu Picchu for dramatic setting. But this is more impressive because we are alone on this perch, and Machu Picchu's crowds dilute some of its majesty. This aerie overlooks backdrops of distant mountains through arches of the ruins, the vast landscape dropping behind the theatre's walls. As Enver lectures in the top rungs of the stone seats, I imagine a spectacle performed below. What did they see? Music and poetry? Surely no wild animal fights and gladiator events in this sublime place so close to heaven. Huge tumbles of stones lie in piles where they fell when the earth shook.

We continue climbing over columns, immense sarcophagus lids and building blocks, up higher to the **odeum**, the covered theatre, and to a necropolis of enormous tombs cut from single stones. Someone chiseled each one for months. We come upon a carved Medusa head and a pair of wrestlers worked into the flat end of one sarcophagus. Most have circles incised, where I imagine some metal or wooden disk was attached. These monumental tombs—any museum would covet one—litter the hillside. This is one of the most impressive places I've ever seen. We are all elated at discovering tombs, arches, houses, temples. The sensation of newness seems ironic on such ancient ground.

Enver describes this as a "Pisidian" city. Now who might they be? Simply the tight little wad of people who lived in this area even earlier than the eighth century B.C. Enver sketches out Alexander's path along the coast in 334 B.C., the Lycian war in 200 B.C., then moves onward hundreds of years later, when under Imperial Rome the city flourished. No one knows exactly when or why it was abandoned. Dreary, dreary history—so many wars. And why do we make no progress? I pick up bits of marble and terra-cotta shards. An impressive stone gate for Hadrian survives the loss of the rest of the structure. Piles of stones make me wish for Superman strength; I'd like to lift them like pick-up-sticks and see the carvings no one has seen in centuries. Enver once found a marble foot and hid it in the bushes. I kick up pieces that are clearly rims and handles of ancient pots. We've been cautioned to take nothing, and fearing **Midnight Express** scenes, I leave all my finds in a pile near the gymnasium, the school complex.

The most frequent word on the hike is "Look!" I remember the end of the Rilke poem "Archaic Torso of Apollo": **You must change your life.** His surprising reaction, after looking at and contemplating the beauty of the marble fragment, was that it must prompt you toward change. This impulse begins to seed in my mind. This place alters the currents in my brain waves.

Termessos, a place of myth, casts a mysterious spell. Pegasus, the winged horse, flew Bellerophon over this spot, lifting him high enough to be unreachable by the swords and arrows of the belligerent tribe living on the mountain. Bellerophon, legend goes, defeated them by hurling down rocks. How they carried enough rocks goes unrecorded. I guess if you can have a winged horse, you can have enough rocks, too.

After our first real hike, we're all exuberant at lunch. We're seated under trees in the garden of a roadside restaurant, and a stream running by adds to the coolness. We feast on mezes—fava purée, eggplant, a dip that looks like melted bricks, tiny okra with tomatoes (I love this), grilled sea bass and puffed bread, then slices of watermelon and yellow figs. No matter how many plates arrive, we clear them immediately.

We sail out of the harbor in late afternoon, the water changing from pewter to obsidian. The coast, backed by craggy mountains, resembles a Chinese painting on scrolls. I almost expect a calligraphic poem to appear in the sky:

Above shadow-dark waters
Of this ancient port, where Alexander
Launched war, the hills reign
In mist, always peaceful.

The two young Turkish boys who crew for our captain, Mustapha, drop anchor in a small cove. We swim in the dark water around the boat. Late, late, Ali serves a roasted lamb in the warm night air. We attack the plate of various goat and cow's milk cheeses. The food is a great good surprise. I should start a list of mezes. One I like is yogurt with watercress—the peppery, sharp tastes accent each other. Instead, I write words I learned today:

ashlar—large stones square cut
heroon—shrine to a mortal hero or a demigod
ostothek—urn for bones
kline—funeral bier

The Di Rosas and we lie on the bow watching the full moon appear to rock in the sky as the boat sways. More stars than I've seen in years rock along with the moon. We're cradled, we're lulled. Way in the distance we see fireworks celebrating the anniversary of Atatürk's defeat of someone. I hope it was not the Armenians. What was it like to put out the last lights of the Ottomans and to catapult the country into the twentieth century?

Ah, Atatürk, I have a longing to know you. I imagine my mother at eighteen, invited to the embassy in Istanbul. She's wearing burgundy silk, and her dark hair fans over the side of her translucent face. She is twirling a long loop of pearls, thinking of escape, thinking of a sail with the English boy on the Bosporus tomorrow, when **he** walks in. The music sinks briefly, then quickens. His white silk handkerchief arranged like a flower in his lapel pocket catches her attention. Then his jaw like the back edge of an ax. Then his moody Turkish black eyes pin her. She pauses midlaugh. His eyes, the color of charcoal. He motions to an aide, then suddenly stands at her side. She smiles. Those all-American teeth. He kisses her hand. She meets his gaze with her eyes as blue as these sapphire seas. He's accustomed to deference that he does not want and she does not provide.

Peaceful evening, much laughter. If they knew I am dreaming of Atatürk . . .

Cheryl, Karl, and Ian have abandoned their cabins and sleep on deck.

TUESDAY, AUGUST 31: PHASELIS

Edoardo, just eleven last month, is the most charming child. He never whines or complains. His good nature will carry him throughout his life. He loves to try new foods. He listens like an adult to long historical background information about ruins. He has the quality that will make his time on earth enjoyable—curiosity. He seems interested to know everyone on the trip. I am surprised when he curls next to me to read what I am writing in my log. "I want to see what you see," he tells me. He also is keeping a log. He's reading a novel and working in a puzzle book and learning sailing knots from Mustapha.

Midmorning, after swims, we take the dinghy to shore. From the crescent beach we walk into the pine woods of Phaselis, a seventh century B.C. town with a processional street ending on another beach at the other side of this small peninsula. This was a trading outpost for wood and purple dye from murex shells. Like Manhattan, Phaselis originally was sold for nothing. The colonizer Lakios offered a shepherd some dried fish in exchange for his land; a "Phaselis offer" still means a cheap one. The oldest coins are Persian, dating to 466 B.C. They're stamped with a boat prow on one side and the stern on the reverse. Coming and going. Along the broad way in, still recognizable as a street with sidewalks, I run my finger over Greek inscriptions engraved with calligraphic flourishes on stone columns, the β (beta) and Ω (omega) with extra curves and the A (alpha) with a little arrow in the crossbar. The many potsherds are sea-washed smooth. I pick up handfuls, marveling that after all this time they're still underfoot. Decorative indentations, painted designs, ridges, what a thrill. I leave them in a magic hexagon pattern on a stone.

The baths are more intimate than at Perge and less grand, but the underfloor in the **caldarium** still has round terra-cotta pillars that held up the warmed floor and the arches for the flow of water into the **tepidarium**, then the **frigidarium**. Fulvio and I are fascinated that the terra-cotta stacks rest on twenty-five-centimeters-square **cotto** tiles with wavy designs that could have been made in Italy today. Terra-cotta is eternal, like the stones. We are walking everywhere on mosaics. Kick away a few inches of dirt, and underfoot are white tesserae in the running heart-shaped leaf design that we've seen in the other ruins.

Behind this excavated street lie the agora (the piazza) and the remainder of this town, still unexcavated.

We sail along a wild and wilder coast, after passing a clump of hotels. Fulvio says, "We're lucky to see this. It will be ruined in ten years." Every day Edoardo holds out a fishing line, trawling through the water, but nothing bites. Ed suns. Aurora looks out at the water. Cheryl listens to music with her earphones. The others read. I'm happy propped on the orange cushions with my log.

Lycia. This is the Lycian coast, formerly a league of twenty-three cities stretching from outside present-day Antalya west to Dalaman. Sorting out the history makes me pity Turkish schoolchildren who must be examined on the waves of sieges that beset this area. Along this coast lived early Anatolians. They were up and running in time to fight the Egyptians with the Hittites, and to take the side of Troy in the Trojan war. All the mighty ancient-world warlords had their way with Lycia. By the time Alexander appeared here, most towns considered him their deliverer from a long struggle with the Persians and the Carians. At this pivot the Lycian language morphed into

Greek. Some Lycian letters survive on tombs; a few inscriptions are even bilingual Greek and Lycian. Ptolemy, king of Egypt, had his fling here, and later Syria took over. The convoluted history, packed into paragraphs in texts, actually was spread over many centuries, but it's difficult not to be overwhelmed by the preponderance of war. Too bad no one recorded more about sculpture, architecture, love, celebration, food, sex, birth, poetry. When Lycia later became a Roman province in A.D. 46, the area prospered and Christianity developed alongside the pagan religions. Given as a prize to Rhodes by the Romans, the Lycian coast finally appealed to Rome and won its freedom. At that late date the Lycian League was formed along democratic principles, and the long-suffering twenty-three cities joined together. The cities fell in the eighth century to Arab warriors. Writing this in my log gives me a solid context in which to plug Enver's lectures.

About four we anchor in a cove and take the dinghy to a pebble beach at Çirali, where

Enver's in-laws have a house. Through orange and pomegranate orchards, we walk to their octagonal house, set on a larger porch of the same shape. Inside, I have the impression of being in a tent; perhaps their inspiration was nomadic. Six beams radiate from the center. Each side of the octagon has a double door opening to the surrounding grove. I would like to fall asleep to the scent of orange blossoms. The inside walls are irregular white stones lying flat like a jigsaw. His father-in-law, a famous sponge-diver, also did archaeological diving at Gallipoli. There's a photograph of him in the depths among World War I torpedos at rest with the fish. The in-laws are off on their boat, but we eat their olives and drink their tea and beer.

A neighbor, a reed-slender Turk who looks quite amused, comes around with his tractor pulling an open trailer spread with a Turkish rug and a long cushion. We climb in, sitting back to back, and he takes off down a dirt road, going full out. Who knew a tractor could fly? The air smells of pine and figs. We pass rude, ramshackle houses where children on the porch wave enthusiastically, laughing at crazy foreigners bouncing in the trailer. The houses look as though they were thrown together over a weekend and could as easily be dismantled tomorrow.

At dusk we again embark on a vertical climb. This time other people are walking, too. Hiking at the low-biorhythm time of day doubles the trouble. I lag behind and fall into step with a very pregnant Turkish woman and her husband. We pass a clump of scraggly bushes with limbs and twigs tied with tissue paper, tickets, and receipts. At this ancient place you make a wish on the way to the home of the Chimaera, the mythical fire-breathing monster. Women formerly tied their hair to the branches if they wished for health or a child. The pregnant woman ties nothing and does not pause at the magic bush.

Finally we arrive at a rock slope where eight or so fires blaze out of small openings. My group already is seated around the largest, listening to Enver tell the legend of the Chimaera who terrorized Lycia. Bellerophon, astride Pegasus, slayed the monster Chimaera by shooting arrows of lead that melted in her fiery throat, suffocating her. Around here, however, they say the monster was driven underground forever, and her breath flares out in eternal, inextinguishable fires on the mountain. The rational explanation for the flames is that gases leaking from the magma of the earth spontaneously ignite. If you put out one fire with dirt, gases escape from other crevices and combust. The oldest seafarers knew these natural lighthouses and looked for them as they sailed by far below. Who can explain this phenomenon? Surely gas leaks elsewhere, but nothing like the Chimaera fires exist, except on this rough slope. The legend of the raging female goat/lion/serpent driven underground may be as good an explanation as any. Some myths seem to answer the question **why**: Why does winter come? Why did the war begin? And why does the mountainside stay on fire?

The mythical beast is an old friend of ours. A fabulous bronze statue of the Chimaera made during Etruscan times was found by men digging trenches outside Arezzo's Porta San Laurentino in 1553 and now can be visited at the Archaeological Museum in Florence. Arezzo has two reproductions at one entrance to the city. They're positioned inside fountains, which cools the idea of fire-breathing. The legend is complex, and no one fully understands the monster, whose father was a giant and mother a half-serpent. Those two had some powerful recessive genes working. The other children were Orthrus, a dog with several heads; Hydra, a water snake with nine heads; and Cerberus, the hound of hell. The Chimaera was **not** from a nice family.

Twilight lasts long; the fires look even more mythic. This home of the Chimaera in Lycia, this hot spot, draws young couples who gather around the flames. Is there an erotic element to the myth? Or maybe it's just the young who can make the climb.

We descend to the dark beach, and the first group of five jumps into the dinghy. I wait—for the pleasure of sitting on the still-warm beach pebbles with my feet in the silky water. I find a white rock, smoothed by the waters, like a miniature moon. Or maybe it's like a round of pita dough left to rest for half an hour, or the egg of some secret sea creature. I will steady my desk papers at Bramasole with its nice heft.

As we near the boat, Ali's flavorsome shish kebabs send out their scent to lure us. Mustapha and Ali have suspended a grill over the side of the boat. We motor down a few coves to a quieter spot, passing Leek Island with, Enver tells us, ancient ship anchors and amphorae scattered on the bottom. Everyone has a swim in the dark before we sit down to red cabbage shredded with yogurt, roasted peppers with garlic, a variety of grilled meats, and fried potatoes.

The thematic current that draws our little ship of fools together proves to be an interest in buildings. Ian, formerly a racetrack owner, has restored forty-four historic buildings in New Orleans. Fulvio, of course, is the master builder of Tuscany, well known for his impeccable use of materials and his sensibility for the vernacular architecture. Karl is a builder in San Francisco who has worked on small houses as well as mega-estates in Atherton. Bernice and Armand have restored not only a Baltimore firehouse but also a farm in Virginia. Ed and I have our own restoration passions that have involved us for fifteen years. After dinner we trade stories of various projects. There's a lingo, a bond, a mutual sympathy.

WEDNESDAY, SEPTEMBER 1: PORTO GENOESE

Those men of Genoa covered the globe. What a strange landscape. We've gone from rugged and sheer multicolored stone mountains plunging into the sea, grottoes and clear water, goat trails, scrubby trees, and maquis to what looks like the Okefenokee Swamp. Instead of alligators and water moccasins, we find scattered ruins tangled in vines. At the start of the path, we pass two grand stone tombs. On one I find a carved boat and a poem that ends:

After the light carried by the dawn had left, Captain Eudemos
There buried the ship with a life as short as a day, like a broken wave.

The dense oily incense of bay trees saturates the humid air. We pass a Turk chewing on myrtle leaves. Seeing our curiosity, he strips a branch and offers us some. It tastes astringent and bitter—no thanks. Meandering in the jungle, we cross several streams. Ed and I have the impractical shoes; everyone else bought the kind of sandal you can wear in water, rejected by us as too ugly when we shopped for our gear. We're **bella figura** trained but are taking to this kind of travel with a passion. Ed has a two-day beard. This morning I slipped on a T-shirt I'd worn twice.

We come upon two young archaeologists surveying an area for possible excavation. They look rather befuddled in all the vegetation. Where to begin? At least there are no mosquitoes.

Stone columns lie everywhere in the mud. Enver knows where delicate mosaics lie secluded in the broken buildings. He points out Byzantine overlays that came long after the Roman temple and theatre. A bit of low aqueduct remains. We're crawling through arches under a canopy of trees and vines. One doorway has a flat keystone.

12:30. Sailing along the uninhabited coast. Ali is making stuffed eggplant. I'm reading **The Lycian Shore** by one of my favorite travel writers, Freya Stark, who made this journey with a friend in a small boat in the 1950s. I turn to my word list, which begins with short strong nouns: **ada**, island, **dağ**, mountain, **dere**, river, **göl**, lake, **köy**, village, **su**, water, **yol**, road.

Late in the day we are driven to Arycanda, a Lycian city from the fifth century, built dramatically like Delphi on a steep incline, with an even more dramatic setting. The site has a feeling of peace because, spread along the hill, it fans open to the view. The pines give their blue tint to the air. Splendid, splendid. These places knock the breath out of you. Empty, lonely, remote, beautiful, more than beautiful, a tantalizing atavism that displaces all my assumptions, all my prosaic everyday expectations. And in each ruin unforgettable designs or carvings. One floor has a clever mosaic floor in a fish scale pattern.

Here's the pure stony evidence of layer upon layer of nationalities, each imprinting itself in a unique form on the site. Each recycling the previous stones, using them casually and for their own purposes. In Greece and the South of Italy and here, that moves me most. Without regard for the Greek language, a Roman builder might incorporate an engraved stone in a wall and place it upside down. Who cares what it says—it holds up the column. We're scrambling like goats all over this stupendous site—three high baths with windows framing the view, an enormous cistern (water was always precious in these sere Mediterranean lands), then the theatre like a poem in a tight Ω (omega) shape. I scuff through piles of terra-cotta shards.

Oops, I dropped the snorkel mask. Mustapha, formerly a sponge diver, goes down and down, but waving algae cover the floor of the sea here. He looks as natural as a seal as he breaks the surface of the water. How does he hold his breath for so long?

I am loving the water as I did when I was a child. The freedom Mustapha must feel in his strong body comes back to me. At some embryonic state the fetus has gill slits, a reminder of when we were finny and water flowed through us. I can **relax** in these old Mediterranean waters, feel at one. The resistance I usually carry, the reluctance to **get wet**, fears of being held under in baptism, the tension against water going into my lungs, all that has vanished. Play returns. To swim—a joy, as when the mothers, lined up (smoking) in hard candy-colored enamel chairs, watched while the children swam. I remember the poised attention at the edge of the high dive in my woolly suit, slender as a fish, my disdain at the boys' cannonballing. Then the release of swanning in the air and the cut into the water, scissors through silk, down to the rough concrete bottom of Bowen's Mill Pool. Touch the drain (you must), then flutter kick, breaking out of the cold spring water, a little otter. Then the mothers through the screen in their summer sundresses. Is my mother watching?

THURSDAY, SEPTEMBER 2: KEKOVA

Günaydin, good morning in Turkish: phonetically **gun eye'den**. It means "bright day," and these days are. The fresh sea invites me as soon as I'm awake. The salty water makes us buoyant. Floating is effortless. On a Styrofoam "noodle" I can really drift and dream. Fulvio, always more purposeful, splashes in with his snorkel every possible moment. He's rewarded with a crusty pot found at about ten meters, just offshore. He shows it to me briefly—a small pumpkin shape—and takes it to his cabin without telling anyone else. Surely he does not intend to take it home to Italy.

Yes, Enver says, this is the typical Turkish breakfast—breads, honey, yogurt, olives, eggs, fruit, cheeses. Ed and I usually don't eat breakfast, but now even the Italians rush to the table. I'm taking a scoop of scrambled eggs, bread spread with fig jam, a luscious peach. What a great word for bread: **ekmek**.

At Myra we see the high lavish Lycian tombs carved in the rocks. Heatstroke time—it must be 110 degrees. We look straight up at the columned houselike tombs. A cat in the shade of a carob tree has a good idea. I am thankful that visitors are prohibited to climb the rocks. Enver would be on his way up. Instead, we investigate the low tombs with rare Lycian script—Greek with the addition of several letters and embellishments.

In the town of Myra we dutifully visit the Church of St. Nicolas, packed with Turkish tourists. His life story doesn't sound much like the jolly old Saint Nick we know at all. His church is stripped, but the choir feels very early Christian, and the remaining mosaics have been polished to a shine by feet. Feathery colors of fresco remain. I feel that I've been here before. In a dream? In an art history class slide lecture?

Joy, the joy we were born with, is the sea in serene twilight, the encircling coves scented with pine. The water is Coca-Cola-bottle green or limpid turquoise, clear to the bottom where fissured light ripples across the sand. No one can wait to get back to the boat, don the masks, plunge in. I've read that the broken patterns of light reflected on the sea bottom are the same as the designs on a giraffe's back, the same as cracks in dried mud. Nature limits her design possibilities. Sun glances off the water, reflecting the gray and white rock as lavender, the lichen-spotted, rain-streaked darker rock as wine-dark.

We moor late at Kekova, island of submerged harbors, tombs, and buildings. Some of us go by dinghy into the village of Kale. We're besieged by girls, aged four to twenty-four, who sell scarves and beads along the paths and among the ruins of the Crusader castle crowning the hill above their village. No road leads into the village; hence, no cars. The poor, improvised houses all face the water. Blue morning glories scramble over fences and roofs. The harbor's open-air restaurants (one advertises "fresh sea frood") are festooned with impatiens, four o'clocks, and geraniums planted in big olive oil cans. Enameled blue wooden tables with red-checked cloths are arranged on docks right along the water. Flags hanging from the rafters add more primary color. A lone sarcophagus rises from the water. Ed remarks that the etymology of **sarcophagus** goes back to roots meaning "flesh-eater." Off to the side of each structure is a makeshift covered porch with Turkish rugs and pillows around a crude table, often holding a water pipe. All news comes by boat. The girls wear the traditional loose, dark-flowered pants, but most of them top those with T-shirts printed with American university names (Boport University?) or English phrases. Each carries a basket filled with thin cotton scarves their mothers have trimmed with beads against the evil eye, or with pearls or shells. "What's your name? You're mine," says one of the older girls, who starts to walk with me. Gülgün, with light green eyes and an earthy aroma, announces loudly, "She's mine." Other girls claim each member of our group, and I see that Ed has been chosen by a tiny girl, Nazika, with the brown eyes of a colt. He will be buying scarves. Fatima, latched onto Fulvio, says, "Americans love to shop."

"But I'm Italian," he says. Nonetheless he buys several for Aurora, who has stayed on board. We zigzag up the village path to the castle with its 360-degree view. Ed falls into conversation with a young Turkish doctor and his gorgeous wife. We exchange addresses, and it is nice to think we might sometime meet again. I love these moments of connection in travel. **We might be good friends**. They go with us down the back way into a field scattered with stone sarcophagi and twisted olive trees that must be a thousand years old. There the village girls await us for final reckoning. We sit down with them among the tombs and look through scarves we don't need but buy anyway because we don't want to disappoint them. Several mothers and grandmothers are sewing as the girls unfold their aqua, pink, and salmon scarves. Ed throws me a **help** look; he's having an impossible time resisting little Nazika. Gülgün ties a white, pearl-edged scarf around my head in a turban, and I suddenly feel quite exotic. The girls are persistent but genuinely friendly and fun, too, like the rug merchants.

The **Cevri Hasan** sleeps at anchor in the harbor. The village, by ten, is almost totally dark, and the Milky Way, like one of the pearl-edged white scarves flung, offers once more the sacrament of beauty. I lie on deck, letting the shooting stars fall through my mind. How small the village, how big the night. All winter Gülgün must look out at the wide sea and wider sky, and her green, green eyes have taken some of the mystery of both.

Hot, hot, not a slap of wave against the bow. I won't sleep tonight. But finally I dream and am awakened before light by aggressive roosters on shore heralding the day. They seem to be calling, **Atatürk, Atatürk**.

FRIDAY, SEPTEMBER 3: KAS

Seher—"dawn" in Turkish. The **seher**-sea. I need a Turkish word because the sea light I swim through before breakfast transcends my

English. The light unto itself. Green eyes of my first love, iridescent green of a Roman vial, green of the emerald in the sultan's turban. To part the radiant green waters with my own body, green moving deeper to malachite, only clear. In other coves the water is liquefied sapphire. The water—where I so easily flip and kick, scurry down with the side-to-side motion of a dolphin, and burst back into air.

Kas. A little seaside village with pierced wooden balconies hidden by mixed pink and white bougainvillea. A large sarcophagus remains at a street juncture where a street musician leans, playing his guitar. I stop in a rug shop, how fatal for me, and exit with seven rugs—six small for bedside or bath, one about four feet square in stripes. All tribal, which I've slowly collected since my twenties for the humane, earthy soft colors and the spontaneity of design. These, so inexpensive I couldn't **not**. Fulvio also found a striped tribal rug and two saddlebags. One skill of the rug merchants is folding rugs so that they take no more space than a towel.

Ali serves a fish soup with mint and lemon, the bream and grouper Enver bought in Kekova yesterday. And as always, we're into the water, fishes ourselves.

SATURDAY, SEPTEMBER 4: KALKAN

Another village seemingly given over to tourism but pleasant and low key, flowery, with many more sleeping cats than tourists. We looked for rugs again! Irresistible. Fulvio found a Kurdish weaving that reminded me of a Paul Klee painting gone wild—dramatic, a live piece of art woven, the Kurdish dealer said, for a wedding bed. The two panels were joined together when the marriage took place. The weaving can be major art on a large wall, always exciting to look at. I love the "folk" tradition. When I held up a garment covered with shells, bells, metal flowers, and beads, Fulvio insisted on buying it for me. Enver complimented us and identified it as a circumcision garment, a Yürük piece about eighty or so years old. Bernice and Armand found a bright rug for their farm, and Cheryl and Karl picked out a runner. Fifteen-year-old

Sara bought armfuls of bracelets. All our cabins are even more crowded.

Late in the morning we wind our way into the mountains to our van driver Mehmet's home. He's also the school bus driver, a postman, and formerly a tailor, but his village had too many. We come to no town, in terms of shops, but are let off on a dirt road with scattered houses. The buildings all seem improvised—slapped together and abandoned as easily. The fences are constructed of whatever boards and sticks could be found. Shaded by grapevine pergolas, the outdoor living areas are covered with rugs (sometimes a rug-stamped design on woven plastic) and multipatterned cotton cushions. The abundant grapes dangle so low you could take a bite. At a cleared area under spreading sycamores, a dozen men play cards and tile rummy. There's a new mosque with stools around a fountain for washing away a layer or two before entering the mosque.

Mehmet's house reminds me of the black people's houses I knew back in the stone age in Georgia. Dishes, few, they store in an unpainted wooden open cabinet. On the walls six photographs, an embroidered cloth hanging from the mantel—so little, but what they have seems iconographic. His wife, Fatoş, sweet round face and intelligence sparkling in her eyes, and his mother, Ayşe, a soft walking rag doll, invite us to sit around the fireplace. With long thin rolling pins, they're making **gözleme**, a flatbread to fill, fold over, and cook quickly on the griddle. They're quick and skillful! They use a low round board (it doubles as a table) expressly made for the purpose. From a wooden bowl of dough, they take handfuls and form little flattened balls about the size of a tennis ball. The younger woman rolls, makes a quick one-eighth or so turn, rolls again. In an aluminum pan she's mixed beet leaves, parsley, mint, and scallions. She sprinkles this over half of the big white circle of dough, then sprinkles on some feta and red pepper, folds it over, and crimps down the edges. With her rolling pin she scoops it up and unrolls it on a metal disk in the fire. Again, just the right size. Her mother-in-law brushes on olive oil and tends to the grilling. She rolls some slightly thicker, spreads the dough with tahini and a little sugar, pulls a hole in the center out to four edges, bunches up a section, and begins to turn the dough, as in a cinnamon roll. When it's wound around, she rolls it again. This—crisp and hot—we dip into a mixture of boiled-to-syrup grape juice mixed with tahini.

These two are delicious. The vegetable one crackly and very fresh, the slightly sweet one scrumptious!

We move out onto the covered porch and all sit on cushions around three low tables—tin trays on stands—and the family serves us cucumbers and tomato salad, little finger-sized dolmas of vine leaves stuffed with vegetables, peppers stuffed with rice, fried potatoes, pasta—very tender. Thick yogurt, of course.

For dessert, watermelon and melon from the garden, more of the tahini pastry, and rice pudding with nutmeg. At one end of the porch is a sink with no faucets and a rearview mirror from a car attached to the wall. The grandmother takes me by the hand into their new room. Like the porch, it's full of pillows, each one made or bought on its own merits, a wild mélange, lively to look at. With so many patterns and colors, they come together in a new way. A blue eye ornament to counteract evil hangs from the ceiling. She shows me a photo of her grandson on his circumcision day, his big rite of passage at seven. She touches my bracelets, then slips one off and onto her own wrist. Also an evil eye protection amulet, which I bought in Greece; it is unlike the local ones. Since she does not give it back, I'm glad it was not emeralds. She and her daughter-in-law are dressed in the semifolkloric "harem" pants and scarf. Shirt checked, scarf flowered, pants another flower. The clean and tidy house has almost no furniture except for a plastic-protected sofa and several sorts of banquettes or daybeds where they can sit or sleep. Riotous pattern reigns. The wife says, "When we eat at a table, we are never full." The driver, wearing totally Western clothes, nevertheless has an impressive black mustache. They all seem very pleased that we came. The grandmother holds my hand and sits touching me.

Careening through the hills, bumpy road, no air-conditioning, we press on in the sweltering afternoon to mythic Xanthus, where I am simply too hot to go on. I walk far enough to see the big pillar with Lycian script on four sides, then with Aurora retreat to the shade and guzzle two bottles of water. When I've cooled, I rejoin the others and walk to the remains of a Byzantine church. I'm happy to see the familiar borders of leaves, as well as geometric and entwined Carolingian-looking designs, on pieces of white-tesserae floor. Enver pours water onto one section and shows us palm trees, then clears a threshold of dust with his foot to show us a large mosaic rabbit.

We stop for a swim at long, sandy Patara Beach, then rest with drinks under **palapa**. Cool at last. Apollo is supposed to have wintered here, which must be to say the coast stays warm all year. This was an ancient-world site of oracular predictions, second only to Delphi, but no one ever has located either the shrine or the oracle to Apollo. Just his sun chariot charging across the sky every day. The boat will meet us at another cove, so we hike across flatland (the silted harbor) and grasses incredibly scattered with ruins that hark back to Alexander and before. My map notes Patara as the only Lycian site continuously occupied since the Bronze Age. Silky long-haired goats graze among the foundations. Three brown-bearded ones pause and look up, as if to say, **What brings you here?** Mustapha sees us coming and sends the dinghy. We board in the same spot where Saint Luke and Saint Paul, that most peripatetic traveller, having landed here from Cos then Rhodes, found a ship to take them on to Phoenicia. There must have been a Christian settlement here by then. I'm awash in histories, stories.

And we swim again, off the boat. Dinner on board—grilled chicken and lamb, various mezes, and a bulgur salad similar to tabouli. We are anchored off Gemile Adasi. **Adasi**, my second word for "island." Almost everyone sleeps on deck tonight. Our souls are rocked.

SUNDAY, SEPTEMBER 5: GEMILE ADASI

Easy day off this sacred island covered with Byzantine monastery stones. We hike to the top of the island. My hiking shoes hold on slippery terrain. That hour with the good hiking adviser at REI in Corte Madera was wise time. The astronaut-size shoes give me confidence to leap from rock to rock. Of the lives of the monks who lived on this austere island, five churches and several cisterns remain. They tried to catch every drop of rain, since there are no wells. We come upon a most curious structure, a covered walkway or narrow street with gaps in the roof as the building descends the hill. Arches open on the east and west sides. The functional effect is to cool the "street." The gaps in the arched roof slightly overlap to the next layer down so no rain gets in but air circulates. Besides being a corridor from the church at the top of the hill, it must have been a place to linger. I've never seen anything like this. The views all around from the top of the island are blue, blue, blue. We find a small necropolis and nearby a domed kiln large enough to bake bread for all the monks. Some graves are carved directly out of stone. We're alone on a mythic Mediterranean island with sage and myrtle-scented scrubby hillsides littered with sacred stone. We all photograph the views of coves. Going back, we follow the snags of goat hair in the bushes. They know the best ways down.

A swim, a peaceful afternoon on deck. Bernice and I stayed behind this afternoon while everyone else hiked to the large Greek ghost town, Kayaköy, only empty since 1922, when Atatürk arranged an exchange program that brought Turks from Greece and sent Greeks back to their original homes.

We lounge, talk books, and nap. I admit my weakness for the Aga Saga, the English tempest-in-a-teapot novel of domestic life, often written with Austen influences of skill and restraint. I pass one on to Bernice. She falls into it immediately and doesn't look up again. Cumulatively the hot days and little sleep make me want a few hours to read my hero, Freya Stark. She mentions finding myrtle tied to tombstones.

Hiking in the full sun this morning, we heard a loud boom. When we got back on board, Mustapha said we had had an earthquake.

MONDAY, SEPTEMBER 6:
FETHIYE/LYDAE/CLEOPATRA'S BATHS

Into the small resort of Fethiye for a stroll among trellised houses with vines shading the street and pleasant small squares with fountains. The people are everywhere warm. Big smiles, and they touch you. They're eager to shake hands. A hand on my shoulder surprises me in a Muslim country. I buy several alabaster soap dishes and a T-shirt with a Medusa head on it. The Di Rosas help us select good snorkeling masks. Now we are really equipped. At the market Enver buys fish, and we find enormous loaves of rustic bread.

Mustapha takes us up the coast to the spot where Anthony and Cleopatra are rumored to have cavorted in the baths of a small harbor. No perfumed sails and poop of beaten gold here. Their little ruin sank long ago in an earthquake. A squalid settlement remains, where a beached rowboat has been strangely fitted out as a bread oven and various nasty chickens and dogs roam, peck, and snuffle in the bare dirt. A black pot sits in coals near a sign for Amigo Restaurant, now defunct, which is fortunate for the health of all concerned. We see no one, but a terrier comes wagging and follows us into the hills.

Up, up as usual from sea level to a peak, along a stony path, with Bernice saying, "I am not a goat." We enter a forest of Aleppo pines, heavily scented, cross more rocky terrain, and meet a Yürük (nomad) family with their daughters, ages one and two, tied onto donkeys. They're moving a herd of goats with assistance from two dogs. One girl has on an evil eye necklace. Enver has met them before, and they graciously allow us to photograph them. The girls are shy, but the mother smiles confidently. Her husband follows the ridge, calling to the goats. Soon we pass their dark tents. Following a high path, we arrive at an empty green valley, where we find a domed cistern, then another, quite intact. Channels trap the rain, which collects below. Several partial structures loom against the sunset sky. I step on a marble torso, the navel and drapery easily identifiable, and other marble pieces broken and lying around. Enver calls to another nomad, asking him if he has found any coins lately, but he has not. The man stares as we pass. We look weird to him. Possibly zoological.

On through woods scattered with rocks and ruins, so many that I can't tell them apart. A few stone tombs and views of Robinson Crusoe coves of emerald water.

Back for a golden light swim.

TUESDAY, SEPTEMBER 7: DALYAN CAUNUS

Boarded a riverboat piloted by a sinewy young man and his eight-year-old boy, who can't keep his eyes off us. These glimpses of how pale-faced and odd we must look amuse both of us.

We travel a few miles up the Dalyan River, around the bend from where we moored. Slow old river—Moses in the bulrushes! Big turtles, kingfishers flashing blue, rock-carved temple tombs on the hills high above. Because one was left unfinished during the Persian War, I can see the method of construction. First smooth the rock face, then carve the house-shaped tomb into it so that it's freestanding except at the bottom, where it's anchored in rock. These rock tombs are eerie and also fascinating because they mimic the temples or domestic architecture of the ruling class of that time. Peaked roofs, columned entrances, friezes, and carvings over the doors reveal a sophisticated aesthetic for the living and the dead.

Marshes on either side line the milky jade waters. Marshes are my favorite landscape. Not water. Not land. Childhood summers along the Georgia coast with its vast Marshes of Glynn imprinted the serene watery beauty in my psyche. I loved the subtle shifts of color in the grasses and the sudden flop of an alligator from a log into the water. In this area the preservation of the loggerhead turtle is important. We see several sunning on mud banks, oblivious to the fuss made about where they lay their eggs. We tie up, and Enver leads us to a hot sulfur pool—very stinky—where we soak among warm rocks, then slather each other with green mud. Rheumatism and gynecological abnormalities will be cured, and male potency enhanced. So tonight the boat may rock with a power over and beyond the tides. Many photographs ensue, since we all look like the night of the living dead. Soon the mud dries to silver, and we each emit a big rotten egg smell. Karl, who is handsome and partially bald, looks the scariest.

We dry as we motor to the large lake of Köyceğiz. I wonder but don't ask if this is the Lake of Leeches I read about. I don't fancy jumping off the boat into the murky water, but I do. When I climb back up the ladder, I still have a sheen of mud on my back and legs. I jump in again. We're all soothed and smoothed by the healing properties of the mud. Still, we look bedraggled in the garden restaurant, with our snaky hair and scoured faces. We don't care and enjoy a long lunch of grilled shrimp, lamb kebabs with spicy yogurt, tomato salad, and fresh humus on sesame pita that we picked up in the village of Dalyan.

Enver keeps us moving. In the afternoon we hike to Caunus, a site where extensive roads have been uncovered. I'm attracted by a round "measuring platform" in stone, about thirty feet in diameter with concentric markings. The practical explanation may be right, but to me it looks like an astronomical layout. I've heard nothing about astronomy in any of the ruins, but surely these brilliant builders of cities wondered about the skies. More goats graze. They think they're in an astronomical zone.

The low landscape and reedy water look like Asia. Small fishing boats with awnings could be in the Mekong Delta. From one we buy a box of blue crabs.

I'm shocked to realize this is our last night on board. Life on the water, never familiar to me, has come to seem divine. Wouldn't my ex-husband be surprised? A sailboat figured largely in the breakup of our marriage. All Frank wanted to do was sail, every weekend. As a child he'd built his own sailboat in Pensacola, and I remember well the picture of him at six sitting in it, a sheet for a sail, his determined, intelligent little face. His father had a large sailboat, the **Mignon**, with its own china, and the loss of that in some financial fiasco involving a gas well reverberated still. Sailing was in his genes. But he was the captain, and I was the one running all over the boat hoisting the jib, trimming the main, throwing the anchor, plus cooking down below on the stove with two saucer-size burners. Some days were sublime. But San Francisco Bay is cold, rough, and often shallow. Sometimes we ran aground when the sonar malfunctioned, and one New Year's Eve when we were stuck and had to wait for the tide to rise, I had a little epiphany: I would sail no more.

The privacy and freedom to maneuver this squiggly coast has been a great gift—the small coves where we slept to the calls of five kinds of owls and awoke to a visitation of bees at breakfast. Warm waters, the moon's paths of wavering light, the boat's billowing sails and little creaks—I've adored the life on board. I even find myself nodding agreement when Fulvio talks about buying a boat. We could sail for six months. Have I gone mad?

Tonight the crab feast, a huge mound in the middle of the table, with couscous enlivened by parsley, raisins, and nuts, and the "priest fainted" eggplant, **imam bayildi**, rich with concentrated tomatoes and onions. Ali concocts a flaming tower made of fruits for a finale.

WEDNESDAY, SEPTEMBER 8: KUSADASI

Cast out of Eden, we disembark at Marmaris, what a lovely name, and drive forever (three hours is forever in a bus) to Aphrodisias, one of the earliest settlements of Asia Minor. We pass sesame fields just harvested, the shocks gathered into upright pyramids for drying.

The layers of shards found at the site start in 5800 B.C. Overwhelming. This is where I am hit with Stendhal's syndrome. So much of the ancient world has been given to our eyes. The difference between this and all the other ruins is that Aphrodisias was a sculpture center, because of a white marble quarry nearby, where artists from all over the Roman provinces came to study. The site abounds with carved surfaces and soaring fluted columns, an astonishing number of them. This approaches a paradisiacal city with a pleasure garden—the most ancient garden I've ever known about. A circle of marble seats surrounds a decorative pond, where one could sit with baby and friends. My dear symbol, the bull, was important—a whole pediment of bull heads lies along a colonnade, and a "changing room" in the theatre is full of others. Is the site more simpatico because it lay in a fertile land where they worshiped the great mother—who later became Aphrodite? Even the theatre seats are marble, many with drawings and Greek writing on them. The upturned stones are carved with the familiar figures of Pan, Medusa, Pegasus, and putti. We've seen so many theatres, but here the personal touches of the writing and symbolic figures bring the reality closer. There's more—much. The stadium—astounding. University of Florida could play Georgia there tonight. The huge ellipse of stone seats is undamaged by the centuries. Very easily I visualize a chariot race. We could not pull ourselves away from all the wonders and so lost the opportunity to see the museum, which closed at five.

Again we board the bus for two hours to the port city Kusadasi, where we check into a

1970s hotel. Our suite is shades of turquoise and blue, all of which have seen brighter days. The place is truly dreary, after the freedom of the boat with always the exquisite water and fresh coastal view. We have dinner outside, the only bad meal we've had in Turkey. **Buffet** is a bad word anyway, and here, partly because we are eating late, everything oversimmered in the stainless-steel bain-marie has toughened and saddened. The only consolation is that the hotel garden faces the harbor in front, with the lights of the town stretching beyond.

FRIDAY, SEPTEMBER 10: KUSADASI AND EPHESUS

But we sleep. A real bed. And wake at ten. Out the window the leafy tropical garden and the sea resemble a Matisse painting. To Ephesus this afternoon!

The site we'd seen before on a sizzling August day with mobs. Spoiled we are now by hiking to remote ruins. Even with few tourists at Ephesus this time, the experience is so vastly different. Of course, this is one of the most interesting and arresting of the ancient sites, but the sense of discovery feels missing. All has been laid out, pointed out, explicated. The effect of "main street," a marble street lined with astonishing houses and temples, even a public toilet room, cannot be overstated. The grandeur of the ancient world lies beneath our feet. Still, no shard to turn over with your toe, no torso in the weeds. And the end of the trip.

SATURDAY, SEPTEMBER 11: KUSADASI/ISTANBUL

Seeing that we are rug mad, Enver takes us to the workshop of his friend, Dr. Ögül Orhan. We're given tea and a show of antique kelims, as well as the process of making silk thread from cocoons. Women are weaving under an open-walled room. This is a school that preserves the traditional dying techniques and provides training for village women. The owner is also a motorcycle collector, and Armand would like to take off on a vintage Moto Guzzi. We find a few primitive weavings and have them shipped to California. "World very small. The rugs will be home before you will," Dr. Orhan tells us.

We have lunch outside a Greek village,

which looks as if it landed from some Aegean island. We have a stewed seaweed, and hot crispy spinach filo with feta, and a wheat gruel with onions, something you have to have acquired a taste for in early childhood. My favorite bread of the trip is their sesame pan bread made with garbanzo flour.

From Izmir, old Smyrna, we fly back to our little hotel in Istanbul. After much confabulation about the best kebab restaurant, we take an insufferably long taxi through traffic to a strictly local but enormous restaurant. It is mediocre, after all the trouble.

SUNDAY, SEPTEMBER 12: ISTANBUL

Enver goes off to see friends, and a young guide takes us to the Blue Mosque, the Byzantine Cistern, and Hagia Sophia. We did not see the cistern when we were here before. How dangerous, our assumptions. I'd thought, **Oh, a cistern; we have one at Bramasole**. This cistern is up there with the wonders of the world—a columned temple of water underground, formerly the city's drinking water. There are fish and low lights and a feeling of being in the afterlife. Many of the

336 columns were recycled from other places. Some are Doric, some Corinthian. One is based on an enormous head placed sideways for the right column height. "This must be the ultimate in improvisation," Bernice remarks. I see Greek writing all over one, and a teardrop design on another.

Topkapi is half the size of Monaco, six kilometers around the walls. As I child I collected postcards and Viewmasters. Although I'd been nowhere farther than Atlanta, I was a traveller in training. The first book I remember reading on my own was **Sally Goes Travelling Alone**. The moral of the story was, **Don't forget your belongings**. Sally had four items and compulsively counted them. The lesson did not take; I frequently leave voice recorders, underwear, even jewelry behind. One of my Viewmasters—you inserted a disk of tiny slides in a viewer and clicked from scene to scene—was of Topkapi. I wonder now where I acquired such exotic sights in my shoebox full of treasures. I would like to whisper to the child way down in rural Georgia, **Someday you will see Topkapi**.

Sometimes you get a new glimpse of a friend just from a throwaway remark. Aurora walking in the garden at Topkapi says, "In my neighborhood in Torino I walked to school down a street lined with sycamores." And suddenly I have a vision of her, a small blond girl with long legs, shy and beautiful, the drying scent of the leaves, and the gold light of a Torino autumn. The day to day of childhood, how long it lasts, then how it turns to a few memories that stay. How we wish we could reclaim memory. And now so many years later she's a lovely mother chasing her boy around the big trees on this first autumn day at Topkapi. I see hundreds of faces in the white hydrangea.

If I could choose one gift from the Topkapi trove, it would not be a big emerald that the sultans were so fond of, or the mirror of twisted gold wire, or even the blackamoor the size of a votive with his pearl pantaloons, turban and jacket of rubies, anklets of diamonds, and his foot on a diamond pillow. I wouldn't take a rose-water sprinkler—my goodness, they are divine—or the little trees of pearl, or even the eighty-six-carat diamond found in a rubbish dump and sold for three spoons. But I would take one of the gold writing boxes all bejeweled. Hidden inside, there must be precious indigo and bloodroot inks and sheets of vellum large enough for a love letter or a poem. To open it and write—what would be the words? Maybe only the essential ones, **salt, star, stone.**

While we were on the boat, the season changed in Istanbul: mid-September. Today a light rain falls off and on. We have lunch in the greenhouse of a historic Ottoman-style hotel. This is my third visit to the city, and a sense of being in place begins. Sitting here in the watery light with friends, through the glass roof I can see minarets against the gray sky. The music piped in takes me back to high school, "Stranger in Paradise," augmented by a trickling fountain. **Take my hand, I'm a stranger in paradise**. True. The waiters are touchingly attentive as they serve pasta stuffed with veal and a cream sauce of dill and pepper oil. A kitten pounces around and sweeps her body around my legs. A place, and a place like no other.

Briefly I get to see Guven, whom we met on our first visit here. He has been to California twice since then. He's handsome in an Armani-style suit, his black curls long over the collar. He takes us and our friends to look at some rugs, but we are rugged out. With true Turkish fierceness, he has adopted us as friends. When he came to California, Guven hid something in the house to protect us. He worried about us in violent America and asked if he should send an uncle to guard us.

As a farewell, Enver arranges for a boat to take us up the Bosporus to a restaurant. After all the hikes in T-shirts and big shoes, we look fresh in nice clothes. I take pictures of houses along the shore. Like everything in Turkey, they are a mix of charm, interest, decay, and improvisation. Some dark wooden restored houses look as if they could be on a lake in the Adirondacks. Some look as if Tolstoy or Chekhov is inside writing something immortal, a distinctly eastern, dacha cast. Others have a gingerbread Victorian trim, but one frame off, the way nineteenth-century houses look in New Zealand. Others are simply on the verge of collapse. This must be one of the most fabulous places to live in the world. The architecture reflects what a crossroads these waters always have been. They face the choppy Bosporus always hacking at the shore, and the long history of those who have passed this way.

We pull up to a seafood restaurant and are all surprisingly subdued for our gala goodbye. We want to arrange to meet later with Guven, to sip a little tea somewhere, but our phone does not connect with his. We all give Enver notes of thanks and books and little gifts. He is an inspired guide and gave us great joy by revealing his country to us.

Back in the bridal chamber, I dream of walking down steps in ruined Greek theatres, and then before the early call of the muezzin, which I am awaiting, there are other dreams of watery colors and patterns—hooks, snakes, scorpions, ram's horns, and **göz**, the eye, a rug motif based on the belief that the human eye is the best protection against the evil eye. Especially if the eye is blue. I think of Willie's clear, clear gaze and hope it always protects him against evil. He has the lucky darker ring around the iris. When I said to him, "You have my mother Frankye's eyes," he looked surprised and said, "Why?" And I whispered to him, "Because she told me to pass them on to you." At two he understands. If my mother and Atatürk had married, I still would have inherited blue eyes. Her gene for them was stronger than his black eyes. I wish my mother had sailed in the afternoon on his caïque, admiring the lacy Crimean houses over his shoulder. That they had laughed when she told him her grandmother's name, Sarah America Gray. No, impossible. Sarah America Gray was my father's grandmother, and my father has not yet entered this picture. For now, it's only Frankye in shorts and a white sailor top, and Mustafa Kemal who whispers to her, "America, America." He smells of the carnations of Iznik, his lips are wet with salt water, and the sun rains down a silver sheen over the mosques . . .

Then the dreams are just images, no narrative, the tribal symbols of birds and stars rise up, and they must mean holiness, hope, and luck. The dreams give me again glimpses of carved stones. The thousand patterns that I saw, I see again, as though I am walking over them, which, I suppose, I am and always will. The muezzin cry splits the sky.

An Armful of Bougainvillea
Capri

But is it really we who are
approaching the island,
or is the island, having broken
loose from its granite
moorings, moving toward us?

—Alberto Savinio

"The kingdom of Capri," I say to Ed. He's leaning on the ferry rail, taking in the first close glimpses of the mythic island's sheer cliffs.

"I'm listening for the Sirens' song."

"You **have** to be a poet to imagine that," I answer, looking around at the crude churning bucket we're on, with its load of fellow travellers. I point to white villas with domed roofs and bright boats along the coast.

"Water is probably scarce. The domes channel it to a cistern."

With the others, we thunder off the ferry from Ischia, where we have spent three sybaritic days soaking in the volcanic thermal pools and eating grilled fish with lemon. I approach Capri with some apprehension. The island's reputation does not entice—posing glitterati flashing megawatt smiles as flashbulbs pop, international lounge lizards sipping prosecco in the piazza, and yacht owners parading their nubile companions through shops that sell only about ten items, size zero, all priced to impress. Then, worse, the disturbing sequence of northern European pederasts who preyed on local boys. Some of these decadents' actions are affectionately recorded in local writing, which just illustrates the Italian ability to isolate and ignore the elephant in the living room, preferring to focus on the view and what's served at the table. Maybe this talent contributes to their quality of being the most flexible people on earth.

The early history, too, is blotted by the sway of Tiberius, one of the ugliest of the Romans, who built a splendid villa. Some say the whole island was his villa. He often flung those who displeased him from the cliffs. And of course, the Sirens. Easy to see how a ship could crack up on the rocks, song or no song. "I wish I didn't know anything about that pedophiliac revel that went on for years. I wish I could approach Capri as an earthly paradise."

"Paradise will always be full of fools, my love."

"But that's my most unfavorite kind of kinky. And Norman Douglas—one of the grossest—was a superb travel writer. Remember I took his **Old Calabria** when we went there? He looked for the heart of a place. Civilized, erudite, curious . . ."

"Just think of him as an old pagan. The gods always sported with anything that took their fancy."

I am offered a paper cone of green grapes at the marina. As always in Italy, the disconcerting touch of the personal, even in unlikely moments. The waiting taxis set a mood—white convertibles, low and slinky, ready to whisk you off to the upper echelon of the island, the tiny village of Anacapri. "They're Fiat Mareas," Ed says, "built especially for Capri. So nice! **Marea** means 'tide.' "

We are staying in the village below, where no cars are allowed. A man with a handcart takes away our luggage and sets off at a canter toward the hotel. We walk behind our porter and see no Jackie O, no Gina L., no latter-day sirens at all in the piazza. Soon we're following him along the swerves of a winding flowery path with glimpses of the divine sea. No wonder we all swarm off the ferries. No wonder the most glamorous seek this place. No wonder Shirley Hazzard and Graham Greene and Arshile Gorky secluded themselves here for years. For working on a creative project, to be **buoyed** by the blissful climate must impart a godlike joy. Waking to the scent of orange blossoms on the air and the temperature that says, **You're mine, don't worry, I always will caress you like this**—the book or the painting must thrive. The air alone immediately makes me feel rocked in the cradle. I have come to explore this little kingdom, to escape the intricacies of house restoration, and to seek as many shades of blue as the sky and sea can offer. Ed wants to reread Homer, continue his eternal study of the past remote tense in Italian, and write poems. What a luxury. Capri, a place to hide.

We have spent, not enough, but a lot of time in the South of Italy in recent years. The constant presence of the sea, the Greek profiles and eyes, the robust cuisine, and the brink-of-chaos atmosphere appeal to me deeply. Even the refined and educated people have time to give you, not just those you encounter on daily rounds. Days in the South seem long. Nights seem longer. In the South I begin to feel that eternity takes place in one lifetime.

Last May we sailed from Naples to Sicily, then around the boot and up to Venice, with stops in Sorrento, Taromina, Gallipoli, Lecce, Brindisi, Pescara, and Ravenna, disembarking in Venice during a high-water siege. Naples has become a spiritual home. Our first trip south was in the company of our friend from Cortona, Ann Cornelisen, whose **Torregreca** and **Women of the Shadows** I consider classics. What better person to introduce her loved Tricarico (the town she called Torregreca in her writing), the conical houses of Puglia, the castles of Frederick I, and the austere, time-broken villages of the countryside? During her years of living in the South, Ann absorbed the austerity, or more likely, she took that trait with her when she settled there and found herself profoundly at home. Her move north was a mistake. She thought she wanted a comfortable place to write, but she never identified with the more gentrified Tuscan country life. One side of her austerity was a scrupulous splitting of expenses, down to cups of coffee. She also refused to cotton to the heat. Her car was not air-conditioned, and the summer days were brutal. In awe of her self-denial, I didn't murmur a single complaint. Ed drove; Ann navigated. I was wedged into the backseat with the hot wind from the front seat's windows blasting into my face. For days. Still, the nights were cool and the stories were good.

If I were young, I'd probably up and move to the less-charted, more raucous South. As I am, though, I keep the place as a dream and drop into the reality as often as I can. In less than an hour I already am thinking: Capri may be where dream and reality anneal.

As soon as we check in and leave the bags, we're out in the early October morning. It's seventy-five degrees and cloudless. The shining dome of sky over us resembles an inverted glazed, cobalt, china teacup. On the island's maze of cunning paths, soon we're on not a walk but a hike, down, down, down. We reach a precipice—I can see that **precipice** is a word I am going to be saying over and over—overlooking a cove that lures you to take a big dive. On a sailboat anchored near rocks, people are clinking glasses and propping up their tanned legs. The striated blues bring my loyalty for blue back to Italy from Greece. The colors of the water remind me of some of my favorite flowers—lobelia, delphinium, and a particular pansy the color of the sky on a starry night.

The upward return completely takes my breath—over and over I have to pause. My Achilles tendons feel like the beef jerky bones that dogs love to chew. I may wheeze. "We're climbing Mont Blanc ten times." My lungs are little hot-air balloons about to burst against my ribs. Going down did not seem so vertical; going up I am suddenly a hundred years old. Ed's long-ago summers spent hiking and camping in the Rockies give him stamina I never had. He ascends like a mountain goat.

On Capri they actually serve **caprese**, that simple marvel of basil, mozzarella, and tomatoes. And the three textures set the bar because the basil is pungent, the mozzarella fresh from Naples, and the tomatoes grow in the magic soil on the volcanic slope of Vesuvius, which gives them a voluptuous taste. We have lunch by the hotel pool: good bread, **caprese**, a plate of prosciutto and melon. **Basta!** Our room at the Scalinatella opens to a terrace overlooking the sea. The room is cool with marble floors, icy colors, glass tables, and a grand sense of space. I remember a hotel room in New York where I stayed on a book tour. The bed barely fit within the four walls, and I left with a scraped shin from scuttling crab-style around it and my luggage. Here we could dance. I should be wearing silver lamé to dinner. Instead, I am soaking my poor feet in the bidet with a vial of bath gel.

Ed has opened a sweetly sharp white wine and pours a taste of the crags and minerals of this **terra** into a glass. We're wrapped in the hotel robes, for a little chill has come in with the evening. A seagull lands on the terrace, eyeing our wine and maybe us. I read that the sea is seriously overfished and gulls get vicious when they come up empty from their dives. For one with a bird phobia—me, for example—a vicious gull is equivalent to a normal person's mugger. Ed waves his arms and says, "Shoo," but the bird only glares and flaps his—my god—considerable wings. **Don't mess with me**, it croaks. "Weren't the Sirens half birds?" I ask with a shudder.

"Yes, bottom half."

The sunset tunes high notes of tangerine and rose, followed by throaty bass notes of indigo and grapey purple. Where shall we dine? My favorite question. We unpack completely in order to more easily pretend that we are living here. Two bathrooms, I like that. I paint my toenails a color called Your Villa or Mine and let them dry while I have another splash of the wine and the sea turns the splotched purple of a fresh bruise. My pomegranate silk pants and shirt are not too wrinkled. We go off in search of pasta with clams.

Early morning, out the door. How simple life is. Houses offering views of the ideal life—long walks with silence, with mesmerizing scents of flowers, swims in a transparent sea layered with emerald, lapis, turquoise water. A house with a terrace over this sea must be the ideal dwelling. Axel Munthe, a Swedish doctor whose villa and garden are open to visitors, wrote about coming to Capri:

> What daring dream had made my heart beat so violently a moment ago when Mastro Vincenzo had told me that he was getting old and tired, and that his son wanted him to sell his house? What wild thoughts had flashed through my boisterous brain when he had said that the chapel belonged to nobody? Why not to me? Why should I not buy Mastro Vincenzo's house and join the chapel and the house with garlands of vines and cypresses and columns supporting white loggias.

I recognize the impulse. Why not, indeed.

Capri must be the most captivating, stupendously beautiful, felicitous place on the planet—but also the most haunted. The plumb-line cliffs inspire vertigo in the happiest person; for the disturbed or depressed, they must lure with a promise of oblivion into beauty. And the history of locals and visitors who simply disappear one day adds to the mysterious magnetic pull of the edge. Of the many, many edges. I am surprised to feel that Capri retains some whiff of ancient mythological origins. Hidden coves, grottoes, dramatic landscape, ruins—all these **suggest** primal spirits, gods, omens. At the Grotta delle Felci, locals swear they hear the breath of a buried prehistoric creature, ghosts of Saracens who raided the coast for centuries, or perhaps souls still tormented by suicide or execution. In **Capri and No Longer Capri**, Raffaele La Capria describes groups going at night to listen to an anguished sigh emanating from the earth. From his terrace nearby, he senses "the bewitched atmosphere that at times the nights of Capri exhale . . . and I await the arrival of the great sigh that the people call **il fiatone**, the big breath."

Other places have secret grottoes and ravines and tormentors in their pasts, but only here have I actually **felt** a strange presence of forces. Any sense of place, sense of home on Capri, must have a taproot reaching back to the Sirens' song. But pushing farther, why were the Sirens singing on these rocks? Why **here**?

Lentisk, prickly pear, pine, asphodel, myrtle. Perhaps they were planted by the gods. On Capri, by fortunate fluke, you're out in the Tyrrhenian Sea, riding a rocky fortress, away, lost, in a chosen **paradiso** but one that—surprise!—gives you the melancholy perspective of the outsider. Islands do that. With the mainland in view—Naples and the Sorrento peninsula—you see daily the fact of isolation. I think six months here would change me completely. I might emerge, finally, as a disciplined writer. I would certainly emerge with iron calf muscles. The outsider's solitude and loneliness breed fantasy. Could not a sea monster arise from the waves, the ghosts of all those women abducted by pirates not cry out from the rocks? Maybe I would finish my abandoned long poem.

With the designer shops—**che bella** that cashmere blanket—and the luxuries of the Quisisana (Here One Heals) Hotel, the twilight Campari in the piazza, you can drift right through. A glass of limoncello at midnight and off to dreamland. But if you stay away from the **centro** and walk all over the island, the complexity and deeper beauty reveal themselves.

Mornings settle into a pattern—an early walk followed by a **cornetto** and cappuccino in the piazza. I'm surprised at how few tourists are here. I know that in summer this piazza pulsates with the northern nationalities. Americans don't come as much anymore, scared off by the island's reputation for being spoiled by the likes of us. When the first ferry empties a group of bare-chested men, women in shorts that cannot cover the subject, and a bewildered group of ancients in identical baseball caps, we flee before they reach the piazza. If they are American, I do not want to know it. I think of an English friend's remark, "The human on holiday is a sad affair."

We walk. Of all the books and articles I've read, not one has said that Capri is stupendous for those who like to see on foot. We're walking all over the island. The tiny lanes must be former donkey paths. Palm, mimosa, olive, dried fennel stalks, laurel. We meet few others, and of course no cars. Like Venice, Capri is jammed only in the center; strike out, and the place offers solitude. We spend hours in the library at the Certosa di San Giacomo, the Carthusian monastery. The young man who works there brings out ancient books bound in vellum and first editions of Norman Douglas's **Siren Land**, long out of print. He shows us watercolors by artists who've visited the island.

In the bookstore in town, we talk to a woman who has lived all her life on Capri. She says Tiberius has been refurbished; he had good traits after all, and that Krupp—of the bomb and coffeepot family—definitely was misjudged. There is no proof at all that he diddled little boys, not her words, and his suicide over the accusations was a tragedy because he loved the local people. We'd noticed a **vicolo** with his name. But Fersen, the Frenchman—well, that is another story; yes, he lived with a fifteen-year-old Roman boy. The opium parlor at his house . . . She moves on to the Scottish writer Compton MacKenzie, also ahead of his time in kiddie porn, and I tune out. Ed switches the subject by asking, "What are your favorite restaurants?" Since I've been here, I have come to realize that the decadence of these men had more to do with who they were in the repressive countries they were escaping than with Capri itself. The tragic slant, to me, is that island families sometimes encouraged their boys to make liaisons with the sugar daddies. And that speaks more to the poverty of their expectations for their sons than to their approval of sex with old roosters. The writer I admire, Norman Douglas, at eighty, with his **thirteen-year-old boyfriend**. How titillating. The knowledge taints, when really these perverts are no more than small gargoyles on the rocky cathedral Capri.

I reread instead **Greene on Capri**, less for

what Shirley Hazzard has to say about her friend Graham Greene than to learn what kind of writer **she** is, and how she quietly goes about crafting her fine novels. Her intense sense of Capri, the enchanting place, comes clearly through.

Afternoons, we retreat to our serene chamber above the sea. Ed reads about the flora of the island and the small blue lizards found only on the Faraglioni, the prominent offshore rocks where the surf perpetually fizzes.

Another walk, out to the ruins of the mean Tiberius's villa, scattered over a vast area of **primo** real estate. How can the paths be so endless, when the island measures only four miles long and two miles wide? One of Capri's primordial appeals must be the scale. In a lifetime you could know the island as well as you know the loved one's body. Know each carob, every stone wall with dangling capers, all outbreaks of yellow broom, all caves and coves.

The Italian custom of naming their homes has a mysterious aspect. A house named becomes more of an entity. The name becomes its fate and charm. All over the island owners have designed individual name tiles for the gates of their houses. I take photos of the tiles of Casa Mandorla (Almond House), La Veronica with a spray of flowers, Casa Amore e Musica (House of Love and Music), La Falconetta (The Little Falcon Roost), L'Aranceto (The Little Orange Grove), La Raffica (The Squall) with its boat, La Primavera with birds, L'Agrumeto di Gigi (Gigi's Citrus Grove), Casa Serena with facing dolphins, La Melagrana surrounded by pomegranates, and Casa Solatia (Sunny House). We glimpse columned pergolas tangled with roses and wisteria, kitchen gardens, and shady terraces where cats sleep among geranium pots. Simplicity shines from these essential island homes. Move in, and soon you would be painting the walls blue, setting a pot of basil by the door to keep out the bugs, and napping away the hot hours under a grape arbor.

Along the walk we meet a group of six women holding paper plates piled with red rose petals. A bride is expected soon, and they are out to strew her path. They joke that we are the bride and groom. They have vibrant faces. I would like to stay with them all day.

• • •

Something ugly becomes apparent at this divine hotel. On the stairs to our room, I look and look again at a bronze bust. "Is that, it can't be, Mussolini?" We look more closely. Benito, why yes. Then when we're asking at the desk about the boats to the Blue Grotto, we spot a large print of his potato face again on the wall. In the peaceful garden we find a marble monument to Il Duce. What arrogance and gall. The hotel may be splendid, but this offends me. I would never again stay here or at the Quisisana, owned by the same people. If they love the fascist, fine—but please don't subject me to his mug.

The Blue Grotto. I am glad to go, just to see that particular shade of blue water. The experience requires that you suspend expectation of fresh experience because you are piled into a boat, then near the small opening into the grotto you are handed onto a smaller rowboat. Going becomes real only when you must duck, and flatten yourself across others in order to squeeze inside. We waited three days because of high seas, and this morning was still choppy. You easily could scrape your back. Caves give me the creeps. It's too late when I decide I don't want to go. We're all scrunched down in the boat, then suddenly we emerge inside, floating in the legendary water. And blue it is, the color of the blue band at the bottom of my computer screen. No, the blue of a damask chair at my sister's house. Or the brilliant tropical fish in my dentist's aquarium. An explanation is given: because of the angle of the small opening, the red part of the color spectrum is kept out and only blue is refracted from outside.

You must imagine, because it will not happen now, that you can row yourself into the grotto, slip over the side, and swim like a mermaid in the excited blue water with your mercurial body sending off a silvery sheen. Instead, you are uncomfortable and jammed with others, wishing they would be quiet at least, but they won't and you're in and out of there quicker than you can say "ten euros."

At last we take one of the glamorous taxis up to Anacapri. Next time I will find a hotel here. Axel Munthe's garden views stop the heart. The tunneled green paths seem familiar. We walk by a grand hotel where my sister once stayed when she was in her twenties and travelling in the Mediterranean. I would like to see her walk out the gate, her fresh laughing face, heading toward the shop where sandals will be made to measure just for her foot. For a moment I try to conjure that image into my mind. The ceramic scenes in the church beguile with their strangely mixed religious and pagan images. A big golden sun on the church floor jolts all my expectations of what I will see in a church. The walks are even more rigorous, with views across the known world, and sheer knife-pleated cliffs dropping into the sea. The mind goes plunging, happily, scarily, vertiginously. I step inside an armoire-size shop where a woman is sewing baby clothes. Soon we are talking about our families. I buy a yellow playsuit for my friend Robin's new grandchild. The woman shows me the French seams, all hand sewn with crocheted edges, like the mice's stitches in **The Tailor of Gloucester**. She opens a cupboard and brings out christening gowns and smocked dresses. Then I notice the clippings on the wall. She has been photographed and written about in American magazines, as has everything commercial on Capri. Ed waits outside in the Piazza della Vittoria on a tile bench. He has found a **gelateria** and holds out his cone of pistachio, lemon, and melon. I have not seen him so relaxed in weeks.

Odd, so much said about Capri in the books I've read, and the essence missed. What comprises the essence of this place? The guidebooks don't tell me; I had to come here. The waves on the rocks tell me, the fisherman's blue shirt shouts it out, the delicate shadow of an almond tree on a white wall scrawls three reasons in black. Capri—combing the island, inhaling the sun-baked scents of wild mint and the sea, making love in a mother-of-pearl light, joking with the woman chopping weeds along her fence, memorizing a tumble of pink and apricot bougainvillea intertwining on a white wall, picnicking on a pebble beach and leaning to catch a hot grape Ed tosses toward my open mouth.

For Example
Mantova

Rain and fog alternate with snow and wind all the way to Mantova. Driving from Cortona, we are shocked to see, so soon, piles of snow north of Florence, and then a Christmas-card landscape. "Freakish for mid-November," Ed observes. We pass farmhouses with roofs that look frosted with boiled icing. Not-yet-picked olive trees stand in prickled white fields.

As soon as we cross into Lombardia, the land flattens and the eponymous poplars appear in long windbreaks. They rise in plumes from the land where large barns catch my eye because of their brick **salto di gatto**, cat exit, ventilation windows. I could spend a happy week roaming the countryside photographing these patterned barn windows. The ghostly trees are mesmerizing, flashing by the window. I sink into a kind of daze thinking of Mantova, made famous by the ruling Gonzaga family's love of art. While they held sway from 1328 until 1707, they kept a coterie of artists on ladders in every room of their palaces. They left their little city to the world. Suddenly I remember Romeo. Hot for Juliet, he thundered out of Mantua (the English name) toward Verona, only twenty miles away, and with such immortal results.

Three lakes surround the city. In the 1930s, someone planted lotus along the edges, and I've read that in summer the blooms add a touch of the exotic. Pleasure boats ply the waters in warm weather, but today they are huddled at the shore, pelted by rain. We find our hotel easily. The lobby, all pale marble and Bauhaus leather, zings with contemporary art, but the spirit runs out on the floors above. Our room is ordinary. A salesman of machines for the vast agribusiness in the Po valley might sink onto the bed and surf the TV channels. The large painting reminds me of a blown-up Rorschach card, a smashed, magnified spider in a pool of blood. We drop our bags, take umbrellas, and walk out into the early afternoon.

That quality a homing pigeon possesses, Ed has for **his** bar. As soon as we land somewhere, he navigates toward what will be our destination several times a day for the duration. We always try others, but his first instinct proves right. And so we turn in to La Ducale, with their excellent coffee and pastry and an owner who pronounces each word with the enunciation of a speech teacher. She tells us about their special chocolates flavored with black pepper, cardamom, and cinnamon, then offers a piece flavored with **peperoncini**, little red peppers. This, she says, stimulates amorous activities. Espresso purist that he is, Ed is lured into having his coffee with one layer of zabaglione and another of cream. Other coffees come with liqueurs or rich concoctions of orange, almond, and lemon. The owner recommends a spiced pumpkin tart. We have that and a layered chocolate meringue tart, also with zabaglione that is violently gold because of the very fresh eggs. All this before we've walked two blocks.

The compact historic center is lined with colonnaded arcaded sidewalks. The marble columns are of different orders, as though brought from various sites for new use here. The shops are small and chic, one after another, with no chain stores, no junk. The people on the street look as though they have stepped just now out of these stylish shops. We pass several made-to-measure shirt makers' windows, herbal cosmetics shops, displays of slippers of natural wool and fine linen nightgowns and comforters, many baby shops, luxurious lingerie and hosiery boutiques, and bookstores. Cooks must be happy. **Gastronomie** glisten with an array of **salume**, marmalades, vats and jars of **mostarde**, varieties of local rices, and chocolates from Lombardia and Piemonte. **Torrefazioni** send layers of roasted-coffee-bean aromas to the sidewalk, bread stores are abundant, and one has loaves like works of art. We pass several wine bars. **Che elegante questa città!**

As in many Italian towns, the human scale of the buildings and the lack of cars in the **centro** make wandering a joy. We linger in front of the pastry shops, where we spot the treats we want to try next. An **anello di monaco**, monk's ring, a big cake that looks like a frosted chef's hat, looks appealing, as does the **sbrisolona**, a polenta and almond crumb cake usually served with a strawberry, fig, or cherry confiture. Paved with round stones, the streets and piazzas would be ankle breakers in Prada heels. In the rain they are shiny and gleaming. Little neon-green plugs of grass poke up from cracks.

Around the Piazza Broletto, presided over by Virgil who was born nearby, you can see contrasting medieval and Renaissance structures, even the revision of the former for the latter: square windows have been superimposed over arched ones, leaving the original idea in place. A little dolphin fountain may be too small for the space but gurgles happily anyway. The thirteenth-century town hall and the surrounding buildings each have something to offer the eye: the dome of Sant'Andrea over one, wonderful chimneys that look like houses, a tower, oculus windows, **denti** trim, lanterns, even a subtle McDonald's, barely distinguishable from other facades and fortunately not emanating its usual noxious odor.

Shakespeare chose well Romeo's departure point. Mantova is a storybook setting. It looks constructed by a child with a great set of blocks; at the end of the day the castles and arches go back in a box under the bed. If circumstances had turned out better, perhaps Romeo would have brought Juliet back for a visit, because surely he would have been impressed with this small elegant city almost surrounded by water, with spacious piazzas, castles, and substantial churches, all filled with art. The poet Politziano, born in our area of Tuscany, left the Medici patronage for a while to live under Gonzaga patronage. Verdi's **Rigoletto** is set here, and also a novel by D'Annunzio. All these artists are eclipsed by Pisanello, then by Mantegna, who wielded many brushes for the Gonzaga households and made Mantova a crucible of Renaissance art.

A passageway links to the market Piazza Erbe, with a clock tower and the charming round church dedicated to San Lorenzo, which looks like a big cupcake with a small cupcake on top. From there we walk over to the grand Piazza Sordello, which feels way back in time with its stand of trees, the duomo anchoring one end and the entire side flanked by the old Gonzaga palace. We cut back through the piazzas, admiring facades with ornate windows and wrought-iron balconies still trailing a few summer geraniums. Slipping through small streets, stopping to look at churches, and pausing for yet another espresso, we while away the afternoon, ending at the **rio**, a little river that cuts across town from one lake to another. Houses along the water make me reach for my camera—jutting balconies, reflections, trees dipping their branches, a small boat tied to mossy steps.

What is up with the Mantova restaurants? Something contagious happened with the naming. One translates as the Black Eagle, others as the White Griffon, the Swan, Two Ponies, White Goose. We choose L'Aquila Nigra, on a cobbled **vicolo** off the Piazza Sordella. All the guidebooks agree that it's the best in town, and the desk clerk at the hotel concurs. We do, too. A few tables of diners are scattered about a spacious room with a lofty ceiling and walls of ochre Venetian plaster with remnants of frescoes. The room could welcome the bon vivants of the nineteenth century just as it is, except for the lighting, downfall of many Italian restaurants. I can't forgive them for the spotlights in the four corners and the ugly black modern lights jutting out into this otherwise splendidly traditional room. At our neighboring table a woman in her thirties is dining with a man in his late seventies. They do not seem like father and daughter, but they both order poached eggs with truffles to go with their merlot in oversize glasses. Eggs seem like a familial thing to order together. Every few minutes she swishes out in her short skirt to smoke at the wine bar in the foyer. He looks sad and dejected the instant she leaves. Does he begin to brood about the family he left behind for this chain-smoker with great legs? Still, eggs with white truffles—a sublimely sophisticated dish. They eat with relish and drain their glasses of wine.

We're wild about the food. When I go home, I will be re-creating the **insalata di fagianella al melograno e arancia candita**, slices of pheasant with pomegranate and bits of candied orange. Ed gives me bites of his local **culatello**, house-cured rump of pork, and local **salume** with **mostarda** of apples. Nearby Cremona is most famous for its **mostarda**, but actually it first appeared at the Gonzaga tables in Mantova. Various fruits and vegetables are put up in jars of sugar syrup and that hit that makes the difference, ground mustard seeds. Since the Romans, and even earlier back to the Greeks, Mediterranean people have enjoyed sweet/sour tastes.

Ed orders the quintessential Mantovana pasta, **tortelli di zucca**. Pumpkins, big green ones as well as the usual orange, star in the cuisine around here. The little **tortelli** are stuffed with spicy **mostarda** of pumpkin, ground almond cookies, and walnuts. The taste seems quite medieval. **Mostarda** seems deeply familiar to me because in the South I grew up with spicy chutneys, peach pickles under vinegar, something called chow-chow, and watermelon rind pickles. The **mostarda** provides a light touch—a taste here, a taste there—to complement a texture or taste with a gossamer sweetness and a kickball punch.

Then our **secondi** arrive—**guancia di vitello**, meltingly tender veal cheeks with thyme and artichokes, and for me **lombatina di vitello con tartufi bianchi**, ah, white truffles smothering a piece of delectable veal roast. We thrill to the sips of Nino Negri Cinque Stelle Sfursat—tops on Ed's lists of Lombardia reds. We contemplate the menu, discussing the dinners we did not order: a snail strudel, little pig feet with fennel seeds, pike in anchovy sauce with parsley, capers, and green peppers, wild boar with prunes. The chef, Vera Bin, is ambitious. Her restaurant introduces the food of Mantova with imagination and panache. After our cheese extravaganza we congratulate her on her fine kitchen. The evening is winding down so she has time to chat for a while.

A pleasure of a small city: you can walk. I love to walk at night. In Italy usually one can, even a woman alone. The blind beggar we saw earlier under the sidewalk arcade in the Piazza Erbe still sits there with his accordion. Ed gives him five euros and wishes him a **buona notte**. As we walk away in the fog, he begins to play and we pause in the piazza. Then he sings, breaks out a big romantic voice that totally belies his circumstance. Several books describe Mantova as melancholy, and we have not felt that emotion here until now.

Back in our room we're talking about Shakespeare because I'm still thinking of Romeo. "Shakespeare never set foot in Italy, and Italy was a major locus of his imagination," I begin.

"What plays are set here besides **Romeo and Juliet**? Wonder why he didn't use the Italian, **Giulietta**."

"Let's see. **Othello**, **Two Gentlemen of Verona**. What else? What was the movie with Gwyneth Paltrow set at a villa?"

"That wasn't Gwyneth Paltrow; it was Emma

Thompson in **The Taming of the Shrew**. And there's **The Merchant of Venice**. I really prefer the Italian pronunciation of **Romeo**."

"As in Alfa Romeo."

"Yes, and one of the great Alfas was the Giula. There was a Giulietta, too. I miss my first Alfa." Long an **alfista**—there's actually a word for an Alfa lover in Italy—he's mourning the silver 1972 GTV that he drove throughout the 1980s.

I veer back to the subject. "When Juliet took her sleeping draught, the nurse told her that when she woke, 'that very night/Shall Romeo bear thee hence to Mantua.' "

"Star-crossed."

The room feels stuffy. When I open the window, the main street into town three floors down is empty with a light mist falling around the lights. No stars at all.

A night of insomnia. When I have one, I try to think of new projects or good things that have happened instead of swirling down some drain of regret. Often the thoughts tumble like coins in a dryer, circling, banging, going nowhere. So now I think of Mantova, walk again all the streets, focusing on details I liked such as the enormous magnolia in the middle of a piazza, or surprises such as coming upon the remaining house of the ghetto and the sign over a trattoria saying **Lo Scrittore** Charles Dickens stayed there in 1844. Mantova has two fabulous wedding-cake theatres with tiers of gilded boxes. I count five other theatres for plays. The season for opera and music runs long. Italian towns offer astonishing cultural activities. Consider what an American town of fifty thousand offers culturally, then glance at the brochures from similar-size towns in Italy. Art and music, plays, even poetry still resonate in everyday lives.

Take, for example, a city I love down in Puglia. Like Mantova, Lecce is a small proud city unique unto itself: flamboyant baroque architecture, loaves of bread the size of two shoeboxes, the antique craft of papier-mâché angels and crèche figures—a dignity. Mantova has the close attractions of Verona, Ferrara, and Modena. Lecce, way down on the heel of the boot, has the Puglian beaches and the charming town of Gallipoli nearby. Another small city where I could set up household is Ascoli Piceno in the Marche, inland from the Adriatic beaches. Self-contained and cared for, Ascoli Piceno, set in sweet countryside, has one of the most glorious piazzas in Italy. Città di Castello, a Renaissance jewel cask over the hills from us into Umbria, is another town not overtaken by tourists, where one's child could roam free and grow up in a place full of beauty. These are cities for lovers. Lovers of good life. Imagine the clean days behind one of those ornate facades, a little view into a **piazzetta**. The butcher can deliver a pheasant or woodcock the next day. The wine comes from the valley below the town. With your ten best friends you go to the opera all winter and feast afterward until late, late. Your child remains a child for the normal period and doesn't nag for **things**. The priest comes to bless the house in spring, just after cleaning, even if you are a pagan.

When I asked my friend Fulvio where he thought the ideal place to live might be, he said, "Nowhere, close to somewhere." A wonderful answer. But these magnetic small Italian cities may be even better because they offer a grounded sense of community, which seems to me more and more desirable in a tilting world. I would prefer to have several lives.

Ed stirs in his sleep. "**Much Ado about Nothing**," he says, "and **All's Well That Ends**

Well. I think there's one more. He should have come here."

"Right. Good. I can't sleep. He should have written one called **Buona Notte**."

Washed by the rain, Mantova looks splendid in the morning sun. No wonder the Gonzaga boys loved the sun so much in this place of winter mists and summer humidity. In earlier centuries a rain cloak was called a mantua. The city has been misty since the first Gonzaga rode into town. This morning the air sparkles like the local Franciacorta wine. We will devote the day to the Gonzaga, but first a chocolate **cornetto** at our bar, at our table by the lace-curtained window. I see the waiter from last night ride by on a bicycle. Grabbing the moment, cafés all over town are setting up outdoor tables and washing the sidewalks under the arcades. Mantova has the most good-looking men I have ever seen in one place. Fine features, alluring eyes, slight and tall, black, black hair.

I wish we did not have to see the Palazzo Ducale in a group. What a thrill it would be to roam at will through the five hundred rooms, the dusty unrestored ones as well as the famous ones. We are lucky that our group numbers only six, plus the guide who simply announces where we are, as we go, and offers a few remarks. The major art here, Mantegna's **La Camera degli Sposi,** the Married Couple's Room, dominates the attention of art historians. If it were not here, the sequence of other utterly stupendous rooms would be joy enough. The apartments of the Gonzaga family, spanning several generations, attest to their exuberant love of art and to their own personal lives. The frieze of children and dogs playing, the faces in the portrait room, the hand holding a letter and another reaching down to pet a dog while something auspicious is happening in the rest of the painting, the painted frames at child height of rabbits and birds, the many, many horses so loved by the Gonzaga, the dog resting under a chair, the child holding an apple—so many of these details bring the cold fortress rooms close and say to the viewer, **We were here**. There are dogs everywhere; even their rear ends with dangling balls are rendered precisely.

Pisanello worked here prior to Mantegna. His large sinopie—the artist's design under a fresco—remain. Seeing his terra-cotta and black underpinning is like glimpsing someone in their underwear—possibly shocking and very revealing. When the Gonzaga fell on hard times, most of the incredible collection of art was sold. What paintings—not frescoes—remain have migrated back there over the years. One painting of the family adoring the trinity by Raphael was cut into bits by marauding soldiers and has been patched together again.

We pass through long galleries of dark paintings. We both stop to examine Karl Santner's **Annunciation**, with a companion painting of the angel from 1630. The Virgin's basket of sewing and scissors sits at her feet. The angel carries a big lily you almost can smell. Santner was probably a Bavarian monk, one of many artists invited to create this city.

I lag behind in the music room, where Apollo pulls the chariot of dawn across the ceiling. This room feels different, with long windows on one side, mirrors on the other. The guide says it started as a lodge. Eventually the Austrians remodeled it; hence the gilt. What attracts me are the painted allegories of eloquence, kindness, immortality, intellect, magnanimity, affability, and generosity. In another space: harmony, humility, magnificence. On the southern side: innocence, happiness, philosophy. Where is my group? Which way to go? Lost in Gonzagaland.

What life among all these riotous walls and ceilings! I wish I could photograph the painted borders around doors, one after another, lovely foliage and flower designs, fake marble, grotesques. One room has eight panels of decoration around the doors, each six or so inches to a foot wide, like the borders in an intricate rug. The vast painting of the Judith legend must have scared the tunics off the Gonzaga tots. Seen through heavy brown tents, the ugly scene plays out, brooding across the wall to the head of Holofernes on a stick. One of the best rooms has a lapis-blue ceiling painted with the fabled zodiac figures connecting the stars.

The family loved labyrinths, possibly because they lived in one. The boxed coffers of a remarkable green and gold boxed ceiling form a labyrinth. It makes me want to lie on the floor and trace the route to the center. The words **forse che sì, forse che no**, perhaps yes, perhaps no, repeat along all the paths. In another room we see a startling painting of Mount Olympus rising from a water labyrinth, with boats in the circular lanes of the water. Fantasy all over the place. Startling—what will ambush you in the next **sala**?

When we finally reach **La Camera degli Sposi**, the room is full of children on portable seats, listening to the teacher. I hear a skinny boy say **che bella**, how beautiful. I'd expected the room to be bigger. Instead, the intimate scale intensifies Mantegna's experiment with reality and illusion. The children fold their seats and move on. The celebrated Gonzaga family group, arranged above the mantel, causes the odd effect of making the mantel appear to be painted, too. The Oriental rug under them drapes down the wall beside the fireplace, a fantastic touch that stabilizes the vision of them on another tier of the room. Though the sections suggest narrative, no one knows whether the painting commemorates an occasion or was just an ambitious, extended portrait of the family and court life. After the completion of the work, the Gonzaga children were brought into the room and shown to visitors so Mantegna's skill could be appreciated. The wonderful faces **are** realistic, but more goes on than depiction. Rich draperies appear to be flung aside so that we can view the Gonzagas. I imagine Mantegna decided that he was going to have some fun as long as he was spending over ten years closed up in that tiny room. The background landscapes, classical ruins, intricate details of farming and daily life, luscious fabrics, borders (where the artist included a small self-portrait), putti with butterfly wings, and most of all the oculus in the center of the ceiling give him room to dream and play. The oculus seems to be his big joke. He pulls out all the stops with perspective and foreshortening as he allows women, roly-poly putti, and a peacock to stare down into the room from the seemingly open dome. A wooden bar painted across an edge of the dome supports a pot of lemons—a fantastic trompe l'oeil detail. One of the women is Moorish in a striped turban; the three looking down on the Gonzaga spectacle below have enigmatic expressions on their faces.

We are allowed to linger. The sign says groups are limited to five minutes, which is absurd. A pleasure of late November travel.

Let out into the light of day, we are dazed. What rambunctious art—pagan and secular! Strenuous gods galloping their chariots and feasting among satyrs and buxom mortal nudes.

Not a moment of piety, no cycle of a saint's miracles and tribulations, nary a Madonna.

We seek refuge at an **osteria** off the old piazza of Matilde Canossa, who ruled before the Gonzaga group. The iron kiosk for newspapers and the intimate chapel for the Madonna of the Earthquake are situated in the piazza, not far from movie posters for my friend Audrey Wells's new film. We take a picture to send her of the magnified face of Richard Gere looking out toward the rusticated stone palazzo of the warring Matilde.

I order shrimp with carrot velouté, which I don't like, and Ed has a selection of **salume** served on a piece of butcher's paper, with dabs of chestnut honey and apple **mostarda**. Then we choose tagliatelle with quail, the boned stuffed rabbit, and a glass of merlot from Lake Garda. We split a piece of the local **sbrisolona** served with a dish of cherry preserves. In Turkey we loved all the "spoon" tastes like this, fruit condiments served with tea and desserts. As with many cherished Italian desserts, the famous cake does not enchant me. The dryness seems deeply **wrong** to one raised on coconut cake, pecan pie, and chocolate icebox cake. Ed likes it. He likes most desserts. The man we pay, who walks us to the door, is stop-traffic gorgeous. He's more handsome than any Gonzaga face Mantegna captured. He smiles like a flood of sunlight, and if I were twenty-five and single, I would be coming back tonight for dinner. As it is, I say to Ed, "His mother must be so proud of him." All the beautiful men of Mantova are reincarnations of Romeo sent to grace the city. Longing for him, Juliet said:

> **Come, gentle night, come, loving, black-brow'd night**
> **Give me my Romeo; and when he shall die**
> **Take him and cut him out in little stars,**
> **And he will make the face of heaven so fine**
> **That all the world will be in love with night,**
> **And pay no worship to the garish sun.**

In high school I memorized many parts of the play and have them with me this afternoon in Mantova.

We make it back to the hotel for a long pause with the books we've accumulated since we've been here. So frequently when I travel, I have to rest to absorb all I've seen before I can go on. The local books help, providing context, facts, and places not found in guidebooks, and always maps, which we both pore over, imagining how the city works.

One of those books, **A tavola con gli Dei**, contains antique recipes of the Gonzaga court with illustrations from psalters and manuscripts: a pig about to be slaughtered, a boar among flowers, a woman gathering honey from hives under a charming pergola, a sheet of music decorated with an artichoke, a bird, and a moth. I read about almond confiture, **offelle**, little cakes made of two disks and filled with marmalade or marzipan. This is how the nuns make biscotti: cook them in a slow oven, and halfway through, sprinkle them with sugar. Still good advice. For **Pesce in Agrodolce**, sweet and sour fish, you're told to mix strong vinegar with sugar and boil it with good olive oil to dissolve the sugar, then to add sweet spices (unspecified), laurel leaves, and pepper. This and the fish go into a little barrel for pickling. Since **polpettoni**, meatballs, are one of my favorite Tuscan dishes, I'm interested to read a 1714 recipe that calls for adding eggs "conforming to the quantity of the meat" and seasonings of cheese, pepper, cinnamon, and nutmeg, all well incorporated. If you cook this slowly in broth, you will have a dinner **"stupendissimo."** Other recipes call for saffron, vanilla, ginger, cloves (a quite rare spice at that time), **caxo**, which I take to mean ground chocolate, and—what's this—**nitro**, also listed as **salnitro**, nitrate salt. Olive oil is recommended in **buona quantità**, a given throughout Italy forever. In 1519 Isabelle d'Este wrote from Mantova to her brother the Duke of Ferrara her recipe for cabbage, and suddenly I imagine the smell drifting through the palace's zodiac room, the garden room of the river gods, and into the quarters of the court dwarf. (If only her memoirs would surface in some remote **armadio**.) The aromas and imagined tastes of food reach across centuries. The duke opens the letter. He instructs the cook. But isn't his sister's recipe rather plain, cabbage just boiled until tender and dressed with oil and vinegar? "Add some garlic," he tells the cook, "and some of the little raisins soaked in wine, and a few sliced eggs on top."

We emerge for a late dinner on the Piazza Erbe and eat only pasta with white truffles, 'tis the season, and salad. Tonight I sleep and have one of those single-image dreams that happen often when I travel: in a large glass of water, a pink flower is submerged. The dream seems heraldic. Is it Mantova in the world?

The other Gonzaga residence, Palazzo Te, is in every way the flip side of the Palazzo Ducale. Built by Federico II right where town now turns to country, the palazzo sings an ode to pleasure and light; the fortress mentality was left on the doorstep of the Palazzo Ducale. Palazzo Te, no longer surrounded by water as it once was, still invokes a sense of leisure and plein air. Here Federico cavorted with his mistress and enjoyed the life-size portraits of his best horses that ring a large entrance hall. Mixed with friezes and niches of putti and pagan gods, the horses are plain outrageous. You can't help but laugh. I imagine the place was thought to be in quite bad taste back in the sixteenth century; the patina of time allows a suspension of judgment. In a room with salamanders depicted on panels, we read Federico's lament: **ciò che a lui manca, tormenta me**. The cold-blooded salamander lacks passion: "what he lacks torments me." Perhaps Federico identified most with the room of Cupid and Psyche and the banquet celebrated with the gods. In one scene a naked, semi-reclining woman with her left leg hiked about a robust man might have personified his sexual torment. The man, who unfortunately tapers into a merman with a seahorse-type tail, has an erection that puts to shame the poor pornographic paintings of Pompeii or Mapplethorpe photographs of black studs. He is aiming straight between her legs. Perhaps this was a very private chamber.

We cross a grand external loggia between garden and courtyard. The palazzo's endless rooms, each with its theme—eagles, falcons, zodiac, emperors—somehow still form a contained villa. We leave with a sense of lived life and a bit of sympathy for the hot-blooded Federico.

The walk back to town takes us past the house of Mantegna, which looks something like a shoe factory. Just a square brick building with plain windows. The inside opens to a round courtyard. The ambience suggests Mantegna's sense of privacy. From the street, nothing is given away, nothing is suggested. We stop at a **gastronomia** with open crocks of **mostarde**—

orange, fig, pear, vegetables, cherry, **cedro** (those oversize strange citruses), apricots, so many. Ed buys several to take home—pumpkin and apple, the pear, the plain apple, and the grape.

On our last day we tour the churches. They all are different, and without fail you discover something of interest in each. The duomo on the Piazza Sordello sustained drastic remodeling along the way, so that the facade and the sides have little to do with each other. Still, its lovely sage-green doors lead in to a dim interior with a squared-off feel and gray marble arches. In side chapels, wonderful blue wooden-faced tombs are trimmed with gold. We find their prize objects—sarcophagi from the fourth and fifth century. The dome! Layers, orders of angels, archangels, with God in the center, eight layers, getting smaller as they near the center, all painted in colors of blue, peach, grayish indigo. I sit for a moment on the old worn leather seat in the priest's confessional, thankful that I have not had to listen to recitals of endless sins. Several people are praying, and we slip out, across the floor paved in big squares of apricot and sand marble, with decorative intarsia panels to interrupt the geometry.

On a brick tower a black iron **gabbia**, a cage usually for domestic animals, is suspended halfway up. Criminals used to be hoisted up the tower and displayed, as part of their punishment. Only pigeons reside there now. If you lived here, the streets would be as familiar as the lines in the palm of your hand. Mantova, a city to explore on foot, makes me wish for a yellow bicycle. Everyone zips and careens around town, ringing their little bells. A side passage from Sant'Andrea leads to Piazza Alberti, where a wing of a Benedictine monastery remains on one side of the cobbled piazza. I turn to look at a yellow house, a ruined house, a pink one, which is the restored right end of the ruined house, a little wine bar, and a trattoria with outdoor tables. Others are ochre and cream, a sweet palette. A little water fountain perpetually runs—they must have a lot of water.

Near San Francesco's church, we enter an area obviously bombed. The Palazzo d'Arco looms over the piazza. You enter a circular courtyard backed by a columned semicircle, with a statue under the trees. Alight from the carriage in your icy blue silk and muff of ermine. The persimmon ices and all the cakes decorated with candied violets are waiting by the fire. These Italian aristocrats had their own worlds.

"I wonder if it was the Allies," Ed says. We always hope in towns where the abrupt postwar concrete rears before us that we are not responsible. The church was not spared and lost much wall art. Something strange happens here. We are alone in the vasty church with stripped round brick columns, plain and raw, formerly frescoed. The walls have only fragments. These bits are somehow even more moving for their small survivals. The largest remaining fresco represents the death of Mary or some female saint. First she's seated, then lying on the deathbed, while off to the right three men already are opening a crypt. The compressed narrative reads eloquently.

And then as we walk out, the strange thing: Ed says, "I want to be Catholic again."

"What! I'm the one always going to churches. My altar boy is going home?"

"Just a flash. But the first one since high school."

• • •

This trip lasts only a long weekend. Paradisaical, to travel three hours and find all the synapses of the mind engaged with the new. Much as I enjoy California weekend breaks at Carmel, La Jolla, or the wine country, I slide through them without anything more really happening to me than a fine dinner, a new wine. Pleasures, yes, but here a vitalizing current ticks through the bloodstream. And the joy lingers. I will take home recipes, books for my bedside table, a new interest in preserved fruits, a desire to reread Kate Simon's book on the Gonzaga history, and I'll look forward to winter mornings with coffee, poring over my two giant fresco books, devouring Mantegna's smallest details, and of course, I will preserve a hundred images of the place to savor on insomniac nights.

The transparent winter sky remains clear. We are leaving Mantova, driving to a few places in the Po valley—to a Gonzaga hunting lodge, then an abbey near the river, and before heading back to Bramasole, to Sabbioneta, a Renaissance town. Like Pienza in Tuscany, which was created as an ideal town by a pope born there, Sabbioneta was a dream of Vespasiano Gonzaga. The fortress town's plan is hexagonal, with star-shaped projections, and a main street that makes two sharp turns to slow the onslaught of invaders. The Gonzaga with their labyrinthine ways. The buildings of luminous local stone pictured in my guidebook look harmonious and graceful. Nothing to do with warmongering.

I had never heard of Sabbioneta until yesterday. Now we are going. The open road in Italy—**andiamo**.

Envoi

The Riddle of Home

When I finish my travels, I will open the Yellow Café.

For now, I'm enthralled by the blue rowboat pushing off from Delos, the arrow-straight cypress-lined road into an Italian hilltown set up on its perch like a five-carat Tiffany diamond, the spine-tingling muezzin call to prayer from a minaret in Antalya, way south in Turkey.

Unforgettable the evening light on the Bay of Naples as the boat churns away from the dock. When I can't sleep, I visit Taormina's flowering vines—purple, ghastly magenta, hot pink. A woman in a housedress steps out and shakes a rug over the street below, oblivious of me gaping at her balcony. I run from the dust. Then I taste the sharp cheese in Scotland, where we picked our salads and beets in a walled garden that reminded me of a book I loved as a child. I think of my friends' baby dipped in a vat of olive oil, the Greek church packed and sweat trickling off the priest's beard. Constantine emerges screaming, and everyone smiles as he is held aloft, dripping in a shaft of sunlight. Later, at the baptism party men shoot off guns at the stars far down in the Mani.

When I'm driving or ironing, slide shows flash through my brain. A waiter balancing six plates of tapas along his arm; the painted acrobat vaulting over the head of a bull; Ed shouting **Whoa** and laughing as we careen along the Amalfi coast road; Willie, my grandchild, at two, referring to the piazza in Cortona as a party; slits of gray light angling into a castle bedroom in Portugal; cooking with Carlos and shivering as he pulls off an eel's skin like a glove; sharing chocolate cake with a taxi driver; singing "Happy Birthday" in Istanbul as the hotel manager wheels in the surprise cake. He'd placed paper umbrellas in big fruit drinks. The ten thousand things.

Unpacking the oldest bags, I remember the empty beach in Nicaragua, when two men with machine guns guarded our swim on the deserted beach; I see a flash of my mother driving my sisters and me to St. Simons, me causing maximum pain by singing "Ninety-nine Bottles of Beer on the Wall," exulting that we were escaping my father for a month. And way, way back, the trips to Macon for shopping, when I was allowed to select a rabbit fur muff and my mother squeezed my hand in the unaccustomed traffic, making a red indentation where my bloodstone birthstone ring cut into my fingers. **Daddy, I saw a blind man. He was selling pencils**.

"Packing and Unpacking," my father frequently said. **That's the motto of this family**. Our forays were only to Atlanta or the Georgia coast, sometimes to Highlands and Fernandina—a small radius—but we did **go**. Always, I liked the infinitive **to go**. Let's go, let's go, let's **really** go. **Andare** was the first verb I learned to conjugate in Italian. **Andiamo**, let's go, the sound comes out at a gallop.

I was twenty-six the first time I went to Italy. I went for the art, but I liked the risotto and the shoes, I liked the slicked-back hair and the perfume of the men I passed in the street, I liked the waiter who put his hand on my shoulder when I ordered the osso buco, which I had never heard of. I was drawn to the Bologna arcades, where everyone was downing espresso in quick nips and visiting with their friends. "These people are having more fun than we are," I said to my husband. Cultural analysis had begun. What makes them the way they are? That question is at the taproot of my travel quests. How do place and character intertwine? Could I feel at home here? What is home to those around me? Who are they in their homes, those mysterious others?

To find out, I rented houses. Although I love hotels, the experience of living in a house offers a chance to shop at the Saturday market, venture to the butcher, the flower shop, the mom-and-pop bodega, and the **frutta e verdure**. Suddenly we're in a different relationship with the place, and when I stayed a few weeks, I became known by the neighbors and began to learn the rhythms of their lives. When you're storing your onions, washing leeks, and turning the pages of a local cookbook, the aromas from your kitchen become a territorial marker. **I live here.** If only for a while. When the time to leave comes, often I am disoriented. The thyme I planted by the front door is flourishing. My own tender roots have invaded the foreign soil. The anguish of moving goes down into the bone marrow. Even when I **want** to move, the actual uprooting is traumatic.

Ever since my first trip to Europe—I chose Italy as the first country I wanted to see—my profound desire for home, for the profoundly beautiful nest, the kitchen garden, the friends gathered at my table, for the candlelit baths, and the objects arranged and the books in order, and most of all the sense of **this is my place**—all that has been at the mercy of an equal force, the desire to shut the door, turn the key, and go. Go. The domestic and the opposite. At the beginning of these travels I saw that as a conflict. Now I think the oxymoron is not a double bind but a way forward. Does the way forward imply the way back?

• • •

The Yellow Café already has a location, just outside the town of ten thousand where I grew up in south Georgia. A sandy road turns off the two-lane highway into town and runs along a stand of moss oaks. You cross a low wooden bridge. In the black swampy water fed by a lively creek, I will get my crayfish. There's the house, big, square, with gnarly wisteria raddled around the pillars on either side of the steps. The house is not yellow today but will be when I transform it. I already have the paint chip in my handbag, stuck between the pages of my passport.

From the broad open porch, which seems to float on a raft of daylilies, you enter a wide hall opening to two gracious dining rooms with tall, many-paned windows. The ample kitchen runs all across the back of the house. I will outfit it with the best brass-trimmed blue stoves and expanses of white marble counters for making pasta and pastry. My collection of antique painted tiles will be embedded randomly in the walls. The former living room becomes a wine library, where guests can sip an elixir from my cellar—the raspberry ratafia invented by two women in a village in Abruzzo, or a sparkling wine I will make from local scuppernong grapes—while their table is laid with antique linens I've acquired at Arezzo's monthly antique market, and bowls of smoky blue irises with vinic scents. Gardenias and Casablanca lilies will be allowed only in the library, lest the guests succumb to their narcotizing perfume and forget to eat.

The rear screen porch extends the kitchen. Cooks can sit there and strip sugarcane or shuck corn or mix the spices they have brought from their countries. In the bottomless pond fed by a fresh creek, we'll catch catfish and blind rockfish with rusty hooks dangling from their mouths. I will build a salt pool for shrimp, crab, and lobster, as in the old Tuscan villas.

My rooms are upstairs, and they feel like other manifestations of my body. Bookcases, stuffed with poetry and travel narratives, line the walls. The windows let in the blue light that filters through Spanish moss. Kelims from my travels cover heart pine floors, and on the beds I am torn between using luxurious Venetian silks and the country quilts I have stored for years in a trunk. In the wide upstairs hall my collection of ex-votos, amulets against the evil eye, and folk art gives me joy every time I walk by.

The other eight or nine bedrooms are for visitors and for the cooks who spend six months here, bringing their mothers' recipes and their own culinary inventions. One room always is reserved for a poet who needs nourishment and the scent of gardenias rising from the old mother bush outside the kitchen.

Sunday-night dinners at the Yellow Café commence with a reading of poems in the library. Guests will bring their own favorites. Sunday night calls for a light dinner. It's the beginning and end of the week. Also the copious noon meal on Sunday has driven everyone to their beds. But because all the food was so delicious, we rise and walk on the country roads, picking violets. After the poems perhaps **tortellini in brodo,** tender knots of pasta stuffed with chicken and herbs and floating in the broth made from an old hen. That's a righteous dish in Tuscany. The salad garden yields all year in the benign climate, and several local women bring us field greens they gather. My hometown neighbors are avid to start a Faulkner reading club, and at the end of the table there's talk of performing **A Midsummer Night's Dream** out under the oaks on the solstice. One of the Methodist deacons rises and toasts, "If music be the food of love, play on, give me excess of it . . ." So let's leave it at that for this evening among friends: a fine plate of country Spanish cheeses, and a sliver of lemon tart that will invade everyone's dreams in the form of a citrus grove in full frisson outside Granada.

One night a month is the concert dinner. My old friends from the Cortona Tuscan Sun Festival arrive, speaking Russian and French. They kiss hands and slightly bow; then they fill the twilight with Fauré and Shostakovich. Everyone shouts **bravi, bravi**. We dine late, and the good citizens of my hometown are shocked to drive home at two in the morning, sated with the cello rubbing against their oldest memories, my roasted vegetables, quail with juniper berries, mulled pears, and a little dessert wine that brought them a gust of wind from Pantelleria. In the mornings my neighbors will swing by for brioche and cappuccino, though some insist on the **churros** and **migas** I first savored in Spain. Such will be the enchantment of **paradiso**. They'll start the day hearing a rousing piece by my friend Bobby McFerrin. The McDonald's sausage breakfast and bladder-bursting cup of coffee will cease to be offered in the land. On holidays the cooks will turn out baskets of cheese straws, **pannetone**, pound cakes, caramel cakes, and tiny lemon tarts that I used to devour in a Provençal bistro with a gaslight outside. If you'd like a dessert to take home, you must order the day before.

"Why south Georgia?" my daughter asks. "Why not in Cortona, where you have spent the happiest times of your entire life? Why not California, where you raised me and worked and have all those friends?"

"I don't know. California doesn't need the Yellow Café. California only needs itself. Cortona—certainly not. They already have many places with a heartbeat instead of a marketing concept." I'm not satisfied with my smart-mouth answer. I always try not to alarm my daughter with what I really feel. If I answered, "Because I am looking for the square root of light," I might be alarmed myself. And the question burrows deep into the psyche. The real answer is **home**, the real answer is **beauty**. Living and travelling in Europe, especially Italy, I've lived in places where art and beauty buoy everyday life. And there I have felt the most at home. Home, where everything connects.

At the end of "Four Quartets," T. S. Eliot proposed the idea that at the end of our voyages out, we return to our origins and understand the place for the first time. This idea is so often quoted that it must not be true. The easy and comforting sentiment feels like an old pair of cashmere slippers. I prefer to think of the end of exploring as an invitation to return to my origins and **transform** them. The prodigal, the wanderer, the minstrel, the one who took the first thing smoking on the runway at nineteen—they already **know** the place. Those who stayed know less, caught as they are inside the crystal globe. Shake it, and the snow falls. I, a runaway, return in my coat of many colors to sweep off the family graves and create my café. The spices of Portugal, the music of Angel Barrios, the Venetian vellum book, the bells of Cortona: **offerings**. Why? Because I learned to stir the marrow into the risotto. Because of the place where my mind never comes to rest. Offerings to whom? To anyone who wants a handful of spring rain.

Think of Nietzsche's concept of eternal return. Everything that happened, on some mystic plane, still happens. The first events in your life slap you into the shape you take. The baby child knows within six weeks whether he can trust the parents. The temperature at the window signals bliss, boredom, or alarm. Going back in time is impossible because memory only has a line of front burners. But literally to go back to a place—of course you can go home again, only a blowhard sentimentalist like Thomas Wolfe thinks you can't. I always will be stepping into the same river. Fate decrees that I still love the high school boyfriend. I remember Nancy Lane wet her pants on the first day of kindergarten, and I felt her hot humiliation, the first blush of empathy in my life.

Of course, all roads lead to Rome—or maybe its rhyme, home. This is the third angel I was promised at the beginning of my travels. The transforming angel: you go out, far out, and when you return, you have the power to transform your life. Roads always lead to Rome/home. They always have. In the far countryside of Tuscany, the big truck driver shouted out his window, **"Dov'é Roma?"** and I pointed south. It was only a general direction he was after. He could take it from there.

Bees navigate by a magnet in their heads. I have one, too, just under the pineal gland that looks so much like **broccolo romano**. Instead of true north, the magnitudes of attraction are multidirectional. During any airport delay, I study all the departures. What if I just chose one? Cairo, Mozambique, Catania, Dublin—but I'm in Frankfurt with a ticket to Florence. Someday I will drop that ticket in the wastebasket, step up to the desk, and say, "One way to Zagreb, please."

The lyrics of a torch song, a line in a book, a friend's postcard, a glimpse out the window on the overnight train to Paris, a just-shucked oyster that recalls the briny air at Tomales Bay—even an overheard word can trigger the magnet's force, sending me to check my airline mileage account, propelling me to the computer to scout ticket prices, into the garage to see which suitcase has wheels ready to roll.

When I finish my travels, I will solve the riddle of home. When I finish my travels, I will know the answer. Then I will open the Yellow Café.

Cortona, Italy
San Rafael, California
2005

Bibliography

Burns, John Horne. **The Gallery**. New York: Arbor House, 1985.

Capria, Raffaele La. **Capri and No Longer Capri**, translated by Elizabeth A. Petraff and Richard J. Pioli. New York: Thunder's Mouth Press, 2001.

Carr, Raymond, ed. **Spain: A History**. London: Oxford University Press, 2000.

Colette. **Earthly Paradise: An Autobiography**, translated by Robert Phelps. New York: Farrar, Straus and Giroux, 1966.

Danby, Miles. **Moorish Style**. London: Phaidon Press, 1999.

Durrell, Lawrence. **The Lawrence Durrell Travel Reader**, edited by Clint Willis. New York: Carroll and Graf, 2004.

Fermor, Patrick Leigh. **Mani**. London: Penguin Books, 1958.

Friar, Kimon, ed. and trans. **Modern Greek Poetry**. Greece: Efstathiadis Group S.A. Attikis, 1995.

García Lorca, Federico. **A Season in Granada**, translated by Christopher Maurer. London: Anvil Press Poetry, 1998.

———**Collected Poems**, edited by Christopher Maurer. New York: Farrar, Straus and Giroux, 2002.

———**In Search of Duende**, translated by Christopher Maurer. New York: A New Directions Bibelot, 1998.

Gibson, Ian. **Federico García Lorca: A Life**. New York: Pantheon, 1989.

Hillenbrand, Robert. **Islamic Art and Architecture**. London: Thames and Hudson, 1999.

Hintzen-Bohlen, Brigitte. **Art and Architecture Andalusía**, translated by Helen Atkins. Cologne: Könemann Verlagsgesellschaft mbH, 1999.

Keeley, Edmund, trans. **Yannis Ritsos: Repetitions, Testimonies, Parentheses**. Princeton, N.J.: Princeton University Press, 1991.

Lampedusa, Giuseppe di. **The Leopard**, translated by Archibald Colquhoun. New York: Pantheon Books, 1988.

Machado, Antonio. **Selected Poems**, translated by Alan S. Trueblood. Boston: Harvard University Press, 1999.

Menocal, María Rosa. **The Ornament of the World**. Boston: Little Brown, 2002.

Modesto, Maria de Lourdes. **Traditional Portuguese Cooking**, translated by Fernanda Naylor. Lisbon: Verbo, 2001.

Pessoa, Fernando. **The Book of Disquiet**, translated by Richard Zenith. London: Penguin Books, 2001.

Sand, George. **Winter in Majorca,** translated by Robert Graves. Chicago: Academy Press, 1978.

Sciascia, Leonardo. **Sicilian Uncles**, translated by N. S. Thompson. London: Paladin Grafton Books, 1986.

———**The Wine-Dark Sea**, translated by Avril Bardoni. New York: Carcanet, 1988.

Simeti, Mary Taylor. **On Persephone's Island: A Sicilian Journal.** New York: Alfred A. Knopf, 1986.

Simon, Kate. **A Renaissance Tapestry: The Gonzaga of Mantua**. New York: Harper and Row, 1988.

Stainton, Leslie. **Lorca: A Dream of Life**. New York: Farrar, Straus and Giroux, 1999.

Stark, Freya. **The Lycian Shore**. London: John Murray, 2002.

Wright, Clifford A. **A Mediterranean Feast**. New York: William Morrow and Co., 1999.

Permissions Acknowledgments

Pages 1, 51: Reprinted by permission of Farrar, Straus, and Giroux, LLC 9 lines from "Ballad of the Three Rivers" and "Acacia" from "Garden in Umber" from **Collected Poems Revised Bilingual Edition** by Federico Garcia Lorca, translated by Christopher Maurer. Translations copyright © 1988, 1989, 1990, 1991, 1998, and 2002 by Herederos de Federico García Lorca, and various translators.

Pages 53, 66: By Federico García Lorca, translated by Christopher Maurer, from **In Search of Duende,** copyright © 1955, 1998 by New Directions Publishing Corp., copyright © Herederos de Federico García Lorca, translation copyright © Christopher Maurer and Herederos de Federico García Lorca. Reprinted by permission of New Directions Publishing Corp.

Page 61: Reprinted by permission of the publisher from **Antonio Machado: Selected Poems,** translated by Alan S. Trueblood, p. 265, Cambridge, Mass: Harvard University Press, copyright © 1982 by the President and Fellows of Harvard College.

Pages 145, 147, 148, 149: From **The Leopard** by Giuseppe di Lampedusa, translated by Archibald Colquhoun, copyright © 1960 and renewed 1988 by Wm. Collins Sons & Co. Inc. and Pantheon Books Inc. Used by permission of Pantheon Books, a division of Random House, Inc.

Pages 204, 206, 210, 211: Reprinted by permission of Farrar, Straus, and Giroux, LLC. Excerpts from **Earthly Paradise: An Autobiography** by Colette, edited by Robert Phelps. Translation copyright © 1966, renewed 1994 by Farrar, Straus, and Giroux, Inc.

Page 297: Alexander Matsas, "Landscape," translated by Kimon Friar, **Modern Greek Poetry,** reprinted by permission of Efstathiadis Group S.A.

About the Author

Frances Mayes is the author of four books about Tuscany. The now-classic **Under the Tuscan Sun** remained on the **New York Times** best-seller list for more than two and a half years and became a Touchstone movie starring Diane Lane. It was followed by **Bella Tuscany** and two illustrated books, **In Tuscany** and **Bringing Tuscany Home**. She is also the author of the novel **Swan**, six books of poetry, and **The Discovery of Poetry**. Her books have been translated into more than twenty languages.